LETTERS ON YOGA

Volume III

Sri Aurobindo

Letters on Yoga

Volume III

Sri Aurobindo Ashram
Pondicherry

First edition 1958
Fourth edition (revised and enlarged) 2014
Third impression 2021

Rs 290
ISBN 978-93-5210-061-3

© Sri Aurobindo Ashram Trust 1958, 2014
Published by Sri Aurobindo Ashram Publication Department
Pondicherry 605 002
Web https://www.sabda.in

Printed at Sri Aurobindo Ashram Press, Pondicherry
PRINTED IN INDIA

Publisher's Note

Letters on Yoga — III comprises letters written by Sri Aurobindo on the experiences and realisations that may occur in the practice of the Integral Yoga. It is the third of four volumes of *Letters on Yoga*, arranged by the editors as follows:

    I.   Foundations of the Integral Yoga
    II. Practice of the Integral Yoga
    III. Experiences and Realisations in the Integral Yoga
    IV. Transformation of Human Nature in the Integral Yoga

The letters in these volumes have been selected from the large body of letters that Sri Aurobindo wrote to disciples and others between 1927 and 1950. Other letters from this period are published in *Letters on Poetry and Art*, *The Mother with Letters on the Mother* and *Letters on Himself and the Ashram*, volumes 27, 32 and 35 of THE COMPLETE WORKS OF SRI AUROBINDO. Letters written before 1927 are reproduced in *Autobiographical Notes and Other Writings of Historical Interest*, volume 36 of THE COMPLETE WORKS.

    During Sri Aurobindo's lifetime, relatively few of his letters were published. Three small books of letters on Yoga were brought out in the 1930s. A more substantial collection came out between 1947 and 1951 in a four-volume series entitled *Letters of Sri Aurobindo* (including one volume of letters on poetry and literature). In 1958, many more letters were included in the two large tomes of *On Yoga — II*. A further expanded collection in three volumes entitled *Letters on Yoga* was published in 1970 as part of the Sri Aurobindo Birth Centenary Library. The present collection, also entitled *Letters on Yoga*, constitutes volumes 28–31 of THE COMPLETE WORKS. These volumes incorporate previously published letters and contain many new ones as well.

About one-third of the letters in the present volume were not published in the Centenary Library.

The present volume is arranged by subject in four parts:

1. The Place of Experiences in the Practice of Yoga
2. The Opening of the Inner Senses
3. Experiences of the Inner Consciousness and the Cosmic Consciousness
4. The Fundamental Realisations of the Integral Yoga

The texts of all the letters have been checked against the available manuscripts, typescripts and printed versions.

CONTENTS

PART ONE
THE PLACE OF EXPERIENCES IN THE PRACTICE OF YOGA

Section One
The Nature and Value of Experiences

Experiences and Realisations
    The Difference between Experience and Realisation   5
    The Yogi and the Sadhak   6
    Subordinate and Great Experiences   6
    Feelings as Experiences   7
    Love, Joy and Experience   8
    Imagined Experiences   9
    Mental Knowledge and Spiritual Experience   9
    Mental Realisation and Spiritual Realisation   11
    Spiritual Experience as Substantial Experience   12

The Value of Experiences
    Experience and Development of Consciousness   13
    The Importance of Small Beginnings   14

Inner Experience and Outer Life
    Subjective Experience and the Objective Existence   21
    Experience and the Change of One's Nature   23
    Inner Attitude and Outward Things   26
    The Power of Creative Formation   26

The Danger of the Ego and the Need of Purification
    Spiritual Experiences and the Ego   29
    Purification and Preparation of the Nature   32
    Mixed and Confused Experiences   35
    Purification and Positive Experience   39
    Purification and Consecration   41
    Purification and Transformation   43
    Conditions for the Coming of Experience   44

CONTENTS

Suggestions for Dealing with Experiences
- Letting the Experiences Develop Naturally ... 47
- Thinking about Experiences ... 47
- Observing Experiences without Attachment ... 48
- Observing Experiences without Fear or Alarm ... 49
- Speaking about Experiences ... 50
- The Difficulty of Keeping Experiences ... 52

Section Two
Vicissitudes on the Way to Realisation

Variations in the Intensity of Experience
- The Up and Down Movement in Yoga ... 57
- Alternations, Oscillations, Fluctuations of Consciousness ... 59
- Fluctuations in the Working of the Force ... 62
- Lulls, Pauses, Interim Periods ... 63
- Drops or Falls of Consciousness ... 65
- Fatigue, Inertia and Lowering of the Consciousness ... 66
- Variations during the Day ... 68
- The Need for Periods of Assimilation ... 70

Emptiness, Voidness, Blankness and Silence
- Periods of Emptiness ... 72
- Emptiness — A Transitional State ... 74
- Voidness ... 77
- Blankness ... 78
- Emptiness, Blankness and Silence ... 79
- Emptiness, Voidness and the Self ... 81

PART TWO
THE OPENING OF THE INNER SENSES

Section One
Visions, Sounds, Smells and Tastes

The Value of Visions
- Vision, Experience and Realisation ... 87

CONTENTS

Sensing Supraphysical Things	89
The Importance of Visions	91
Visions Not the Most Important Thing	95
No Reason to Fear Visions	97
Wrong Visions and Voices	97

Kinds of Vision

The Inner Vision	98
Stages in the Development of the Inner Vision	99
The Diverse Nature and Significance of Visions	100
Representative and Dynamic Visions	102
Seeing Forms of the Divine and Other Beings	103
Cosmic, Inner and Psychic Vision	105
Mental Visions	106
Vital Visions	107
Subtle Physical Visions	108

Subtle Sights, Sounds, Smells and Tastes

Sights and Sounds of Other Planes	111
Subtle Sounds	111
Subtle Smells and Tastes	113

Section Two
Lights and Colours

Light

Seeing Light	117
Light and the Illumination of the Consciousness	118
Different Forms of Light	119
Two Visions Explained	120

Colours

The Symbolism of Colours	122
White Light	124
White Light with Light of Other Colours	125
Whitish Blue Light	126
Blue Light	127
Violet Light	128

CONTENTS

Golden Light	129
Gold-Green Light	130
Golden Red or Red Gold Light	130
Orange Light	131
Yellow Light	131
Pink or Rose Light	132
Green Light	132
Purple and Crimson Light	132
Red Light	133
Red and Black	134

Section Three
Symbols

Symbols and Symbolic Visions

Different Kinds of Symbols	137
The Effect of Symbolic Visions	138
Some Symbolic Visions and Dreams Interpreted	139

Sun, Moon, Star, Fire

Sun	142
Moon	144
Star	146
Fire and Burning	147

Sky, Weather, Night and Dawn

Sky	148
Rain, Snow, Clouds, Lightning, Rainbow	149
Night and Dawn	149

Water and Bodies of Water

Water	150
Sea or Ocean	150
Pond, Lake, River	151

Earth

Mountain	152
Earth and Patala	153

CONTENTS

Gods, Goddesses and Semi-Divine Beings
- Agni — 155
- Shiva — 155
- Parvati-Shankara — 155
- Narayana, Vishnu, Brahma, Lakshmi, Saraswati, Ananta — 155
- Krishna — 156
- Hanuman — 157
- Narada — 158
- Mahakali and Kali — 158
- Durga on a Lion — 158
- Ganesh — 158
- Kartikeya — 159
- Sanatkumar — 159
- Buddha — 159
- Apsaras — 159

The Human World
- Child — 160
- Parents and Relatives — 161
- Robbers — 162
- Journeying — 162
- Running Away — 163
- Flying — 163
- Ears — 163
- Teeth — 163
- Flesh — 164
- Being Dead — 164

The Animal World
- Cow — 165
- Bull — 166
- Horse — 166
- Lion — 167
- Tiger — 167
- Elephant — 167
- Giraffe — 168

CONTENTS

Camel	168
Deer and Antelope	168
Boar	168
Buffalo	168
Goat	169
Monkey	169
Dog	169
Black Cat	170
Snake or Serpent	170
Crocodile	173
Frog	173
Fish	173
Bird	173
Swan or Hansa	174
Duck	175
Crane	175
Peacock	175
Dove or Pigeon	175
Crow, Eagle, Kite	176
Ostrich	176
Spider	176
White Ants	176
Flies	176

The Plant World

Aswattha or Peepul Tree	177
Jungle	177
Leaves	177
Fruits	177
Flowers	177
Lotus	178
Other Flowers	180

Constructions

Building	181
Workshop	181
Temple	181

CONTENTS

    Pyramid and Sphinx   181

Objects
    Cross and Shield   183
    Crown   183
    Diamond   183
    Pearl   184
    Flute   184
    Conch   184
    Bells   185
    Vina   185
    Wheel, Disc or Chakra   185
    Bow and Arrow   186
    Key   186
    Book   186
    Mirror, Square and Triangle   186
    Incense Stick and Tobacco   186
    Gramophone   187

Numbers and Letters
    Numbers   188
    Letters (Writing)   188
    OM   188

PART THREE
EXPERIENCES OF THE INNER CONSCIOUSNESS AND THE COSMIC CONSCIOUSNESS

Section One
Experiences on the Inner Planes

Experiences on the Subtle Physical, Vital and Mental Planes
    Subtle Physical Experiences   193
    Vital Experiences   194
    Influence or Possession by Beings of Other Planes   198
    An Experience on the Mental Plane   203

CONTENTS

Exteriorisation or Going Out of the Body
The Experience of Exteriorisation	205
Going Out in the Vital Body	206

Section Two
Experiences of the Inner Being and the Inner Consciousness

The Inward Movement
The Importance of Inner Experiences	211
Becoming Aware of the Inner Being	213
The Piercing of the Veil	214
The Movement Inward	219
The Inner Consciousness and the Body	222
A Transitional State of Inwardness	223
The Growth of the Inner Being and the Inner Consciousness	223
Living Within	225
Living Within and the External Being	228
Acting from Within on the Outer Being	230
The Double Consciousness	231
The Inner Being and Calmness, Silence, Peace	232
The Inner Being and the Inmost or Psychic Being	236

Inner Detachment and the Witness Attitude
Inner Detachment	238
The Witness Attitude	241
The Witness Purusha or Witness Consciousness	244
The Purusha and Change of the Prakriti	246

Inner Experiences in the State of Samadhi
Samadhi or Trance	248
Trance Not Essential	250
Kinds of Samadhi	251
Samadhi and the Waking State	252
Samadhi and Sleep	253
The Trance of Mediums	256

CONTENTS

Three Experiences of the Inner Being
- Opening into the Inner Mental Self — 257
- The Awakening of the Inner Being in Sleep — 259
- A Touch of the Inner Self — 262

Section Three
Experiences of the Cosmic Consciousness

The Universal or Cosmic Consciousness
- The Terms "Universal" and "Cosmic" — 267
- The Nature of the Cosmic Consciousness — 267
- The Cosmic Consciousness and the Overmind — 269
- The Cosmic Consciousness and the Transcendent — 269
- Spiritual, Cosmic and Ordinary Consciousness — 271
- The Widening of the Consciousness — 273
- The Cosmic Consciousness and the Cosmic Self — 277
- The Cosmic Consciousness and Self-Realisation — 279

Aspects of the Cosmic Consciousness
- The Cosmic Ignorance and the Cosmic Truth — 281
- The Cosmic Harmony and Discords — 282
- The Cosmic Will — 283
- Opening to the Cosmic Mind — 284
- Opening to the Cosmic Life — 284
- The Cosmic Consciousness and the Physical — 285

The Universal or Cosmic Forces
- The Nature of the Universal or Cosmic Forces — 287
- The Universal Energies and the Divine Force — 288
- The Cosmic Force and the Overmind — 289
- The Entry of the Universal Forces — 290
- The Universal Forces and the Individual — 290
- Time Vision and the Cosmic Movement — 290

Section Four
The Dangers of Inner and Cosmic Experiences

The Intermediate Zone
- The Nature of the Intermediate Zone — 295

CONTENTS

The Dangers of the Intermediate Zone	303
Avoiding the Dangers of the Intermediate Zone	306

Inner Voices and Indications

The Nature of Voices	308
The Danger of Following Inner Voices	309

PART FOUR
THE FUNDAMENTAL REALISATIONS OF
   THE INTEGRAL YOGA

Section One
Three Stages of Transformation: Psychic, Spiritual, Supramental

The Psychic and Spiritual Realisations

The Fundamental Realisations	319
Four Bases of Realisation	319
Three Realisations for the Soul	319
Foundations of the Sadhana	320
The Central Process of the Yoga	323

Conditions of Transformation

Realisation and Transformation	331
The Three Transformations	331
Preparation for the Supramental Change	333

Section Two
The Psychic Opening, Emergence and Transformation

The Psychic Being and Its Role in Sadhana

The Importance of the Psychic Change	337
The Role of the Psychic in Sadhana	339
The Psychic Deep Within	340
The Psychic and the Mental, Vital and Physical Nature	342
The Psychic Awakening	344
Living in the Psychic	344

CONTENTS

The Psychic Opening
The Meaning of Psychic Opening	347
Conditions for the Psychic Opening	348
An Experience of Psychic Opening	349
The Psychic Opening and the Inner Centres	351
"Opening" and "Coming in Front"	352

The Emergence or Coming Forward of the Psychic
The Meaning of "Coming to the Front"	354
Signs of the Psychic's Coming Forward	355
The Psychic and the Relation with the Divine	359
Means of Bringing Forward the Psychic	360
Obstacles to the Psychic's Emergence	362

Experiences Associated with the Psychic
The Psychic Touch or Influence	367
The Psychic Condition	367
The Psychic Fire	368
The Psychic Fire and Some Inner Visions	369
Agni	371
Agni and the Psychic Fire	373
Psychic Joy	374
Psychic Sorrow	374
Psychic Tears or Weeping	375
Psychic Yearning	376
Psychic Intensity	377
The Psychic and Uneasiness	378

The Psychic and Spiritual Transformations
Psychisation and Spiritualisation	380
The Psychic and the Higher Consciousness	381
The Psychic and Spiritual Movements	383
The Psychic Consciousness and the Descent from Above	385
The Psychic and the Supermind	387

CONTENTS

Section Three
Spiritual Experiences and Realisations

Experiences of the Self, the One and the Infinite

Peace, Calm, Silence and the Self	391
The True Self Within	393
The Self and the Sense of Individuality	394
The Disappearance of the "I" Sense	395
The Self and the Cosmic Consciousness	396
A Vision of the Universal Self	396
The Self Experienced on Various Planes	397
The Self and Time	397
The Self and Life	398
Experiences of Infinity, Oneness, Unity	398
Living in the Divine	399

Experiences on the Higher Planes

The Higher or Spiritual Consciousness	401
Breaking into the Spiritual Consciousness	401
Wideness and the Higher Consciousness	402
Degrees in the Higher Consciousness	403
The Higher Planes and the Supermind	405
Levels of the Higher Mind	406
An Illumined Mind Experience	406
Overmind Experiences	407
Overmind Experiences and the Supermind	408
Reflected Experience of the Higher Planes	410
Trance and the Higher Planes	411
Living in a Higher Plane	411

Section Four
The Spiritual Transformation

Ascent and Descent

The Meaning of Spiritual Transformation	415
A Double Movement in the Sadhana	415
Both Ascent and Descent Necessary	417
The Order of Ascent and Descent	419

CONTENTS

Ascent and Descent of the Kundalini Shakti — 420
Ascent and Descent and Problems of the
   Lower Nature — 422
Experiences of Ascent and Descent — 425

Ascent to the Higher Planes
Contact with the Above — 428
Ascension or Rising above the Head — 429
Ascent and Return to the Ordinary Consciousness — 431
Ascent and Dissolution — 432
Ascent and the Psychic Being — 433
Ascent and the Body — 434
Ascent and Going out of the Body — 434
Fixing the Consciousness Above — 437
Ascent and Change of the Lower Nature — 439

The Descent of the Higher Consciousness and Force
The Purpose of the Descent — 441
Calling in the Higher Consciousness — 441
Preparatory Experiences and Descent — 442
The Order of Descent into the Being — 445
The Effect of Descent into the Lower Planes — 447

The Descent of the Higher Powers
The Descent of Peace, Force, Light, Ananda — 449
Peace, Calm, Quiet as a Basis for the Descent — 450
The Descent of Peace — 452
The Descent of Silence — 453
The Descent of Force or Power — 455
The Descent of Fire — 459
The Descent of Light — 459
The Descent of Knowledge — 461
The Descent of Wideness — 461
The Descent of Ananda — 461
The Flow of Amrita — 462

Descent and Other Kinds of Experience
Descent and Experiences of the Inner Being — 463

CONTENTS

Descent and Psychic Experiences — 464
Descent and Other Experiences — 466

Feelings and Sensations in the Process of Descent
Sensations in the Inner Centres — 469
Pressure — 469
Perforation — 473
Vibration — 473
Electricity — 474
Waves — 475
Flow or Stream — 475
Drizzle or Shower — 475
Coolness — 476
Stoniness — 477
Sound — 477

Difficulties Experienced in the Process of Descent
Alternations in the Intensity of the Force — 479
The Need of Assimilation — 479
Pulling Down the Force — 480
Shaking or Swaying of the Body — 481
Headaches Due to Resistance — 482
Talking Loudly — 483
Fear of the Descending Force — 484
Desires and Descent — 484
Tiredness, Inertia and Sleep — 485
Mixing with the World — 485

Descent and the Lower Nature
The Resistance of the Lower Nature — 487
Descent into the Mind and Vital — 490
Descent into the Physical Consciousness and Body — 493
Experiences in the Subtle Body and the Physical Body — 496
Descent into the Subconscient and Inconscient — 497

NOTE ON THE TEXTS — 499

Part One

The Place of Experiences in the Practice of Yoga

Section One

The Nature and Value of Experiences

Chapter One

Experiences and Realisations

The Difference between Experience and Realisation

Experience is a word that covers almost all the happenings in Yoga; only when something gets settled, then it is no longer an experience but part of the siddhi. E.g. peace when it comes and goes is an experience — when it is settled and goes no more it is a siddhi. Realisation is different — it is when something for which you are aspiring becomes real to you. E.g. you have the idea of the Divine in all, but it is only an idea, a belief; when you feel or see the Divine in all, it becomes a realisation.

*

Experience of Truth is an isolated or repeated descent of the Truth into the consciousness or ascent of the consciousness into it. Realisation is when the Truth becomes a settled part of the consciousness.

*

An experience of a truth in the substance of mind, in the vital or the physical, wherever it may be, is the beginning of realisation. When I experience peace, I begin to realise what it is. Repetition of the experience leads to a fuller and more permanent realisation. When it is settled anywhere, that is the full realisation of it in that plane or in that part of the being.

*

Your going up to a higher plane is an experience — the descent of the higher plane into you, if temporary, is an experience.
 If you become fully aware of the nature of the higher plane and if that becomes part of your consciousness, it is a realisation.
 These are the two words usually used, realisation and experience.

*

There is a fundamental realisation in which one can say, "I have now realised the Divine" and there is no longer any anxiety or straining after something unachieved. But after that even there is a development of this consciousness of realisation into which more and more of the Divine Truth comes into the fundamental experience.

The Yogi and the Sadhak

The Yogi is one who is already established in realisation — the sadhak is one who is getting or still trying to get realisation.

*

A sadhaka is one who is doing sadhana to attain union with the divine consciousness. A Yogi is one who is already living in some kind of oneness with the Divine, not in the ordinary consciousness.

Subordinate and Great Experiences

One who lives in the spiritual consciousness is a spiritual man, just as one who lives in thinking mind is an intellectual man. The spiritual consciousness is that in which you realise the Divine, the Self, the cosmic oneness as the constant living contact with these things. I do not know what you mean by abnormal experiences. There are many abnormal experiences that are not spiritual. There are two kinds of experiences: (1) subordinate things (like visions etc.) that help to open or build up or furnish a new (Yogic) consciousness; (2) the great experiences of Self, Peace, Light, Ananda, etc., also the perception of a deeper knowledge which shows us the truths of Soul and Nature and of the aspects of the Divine. This class of experiences are the beginning of realisation and it is when they settle and become part of the consciousness that realisation is complete.

*

One develops by spiritual knowledge and experience which

comes from above the mind or one develops by psychic perception and experience which comes from within — these are the two main things. But it is also necessary to grow by inner mental and vital experiences and visions and dream experiences play a large part here. One thing may predominate in one sadhak, others in another; each develops according to his nature.

Feelings as Experiences

There is no law that a feeling cannot be an experience; experiences are of all kinds and take all forms in the consciousness. When the consciousness undergoes, sees or feels anything spiritual or psychic or even occult, that is an experience — in the technical Yogic sense, for there are of course all sorts of experiences that are not of that character. Feelings themselves are of many kinds. The word feeling is often used for an emotion, and there can be psychic or spiritual emotions which are numbered among Yogic experiences, such as a wave of shuddha bhakti or the rising of love towards the Divine. A feeling also means a perception of something felt — a perception in the vital or psychic or in the essential substance of the consciousness. I find even often a mental perception when it is very vivid described as a feeling. If you exclude all these feelings and kindred ones and say that they are feelings, not experiences, then there is very little room left for experiences at all. Feeling and vision are the main forms of spiritual experience. One sees and feels the Brahman everywhere; one feels a force enter or go out from one; one feels or sees the presence of the Divine within or around one; one feels or sees the descent of light; one feels the descent of peace or Ananda. Kick all that out on the ground that it is only a feeling and you make a clean sweep of most of the things that we call experience. Again we feel a change in the substance of the consciousness or the state of consciousness. We feel ourselves spreading in wideness and the body only as a small thing in the wideness (this can be seen also); we feel the heart-consciousness becoming wide instead of narrow, soft instead of hard, illumined instead of obscure, the head-consciousness also, the vital, even the physical; we feel thousands of things of all kinds and why are we not to call them experiences? Of course it is an inner sight, an inner feeling, subtle feeling, not material like the feeling of a cold wind or a stone or any other object, but as the inner consciousness deepens it is not less vivid or concrete, it is even more so.

In this case what you felt was not an emotion, though something emotional came with it. You felt a condition in the very substance or consciousness — a softness, a plasticity, even a velvety softness, an ineffable plasticity. Any fellow who knows anything about Yoga would immediately say, "What a fine experience", — a very clear psychic and spiritual experience.

Love, Joy and Experience

Your supposition [*that one cannot love the Divine until one experiences him*] conflicts with the experience of many sadhaks. I think Ramakrishna indicated somewhere that the love and joy and ardour of seeking was much more intense than that of fulfilment. I don't agree, but that shows at least that intense love is possible before realisation.

*

My point is that there have been hundreds of Bhaktas who have the love and seeking without any concrete experience, with only a mental conception or emotional belief in the Divine to support them. The whole point is that it is untrue to say that one must have a decisive or concrete experience before one can have love for the Divine. It is contrary to the facts and the quite ordinary facts of the spiritual experience.

*

The ordinary Bhakta is not a lion heart. The lion hearts get experiences comparatively soon but the ordinary Bhakta has often to feed on his own love or yearning for years and years — and he does it.

*

I really do not know what kind of joy you want. All experiences are not accompanied by joy. Interest is another matter.

Imagined Experiences

When one is living in the physical mind, the only way to escape from it is by imagination. Incidentally, that is why poetry and art etc. have so strong a hold. But these imaginations are often really shadows of supraphysical experience and once the barrier of the physical mind is broken or even swung a little open, there come the experiences themselves if the temperament is favourable. Hence are born visions and other such phenomena — all those that are miscalled psychic phenomena.

*

Even imagined experiences (honestly imagined) can help to mental realisation and mental realisation can be a step to total realisation.

Mental Knowledge and Spiritual Experience

These disadvantages of mental knowledge no doubt exist.[1] But I doubt whether anybody could mentally simulate to himself the experience of the One everywhere or the downflow of peace. He might mistake a first mental realisation for the deeper spiritual one or think the descent was in his physical when it was in his mental influencing the body through the mental sheath of the subtle body — but those who have no mental knowledge can also make these mistakes. The disadvantage of the one who does not know mentally is that he gets the experience without understanding it and this may be a hindrance or at least retardatory to development while he would not get so easily out of a

---

[1] *The correspondent suggested that a mere mental knowledge of spiritual experience might lead one to concoct an experience through imagination or to exaggerate an experience by adding something to it mentally or to doubt an experience, thinking it might be a mental formation. — Ed.*

mistake as one more mentally enlightened.

*

Usually they [*persons without mental knowledge of the Self*] feel first through the psychic centre by union with the Mother and do not call it the Self — or else they simply feel a wideness and peace in the head or in the heart. Previous mental knowledge is not indispensable. I have seen in more cases than one sadhaks getting the Brahman realisation and asking "what is this?" — describing it with great vividness and exactness but without any of the known terms.

Just after writing this I read a letter from a sadhika in which she writes, "I see that my head is becoming very quiet, pure, luminous, universal, *viśvamaya*." Well, that is the beginning of the realisation of the universal Brahman-Self in the mind, but if I put it to her in that language she would understand nothing.

*

Mental realisation is useful at the beginning and prepares spiritual experience.

It [*book-knowledge*] can help too at the beginning — but also it can hinder. It depends on the sadhak.

*

You have to learn by experience. Mental information (badly understood, as it always is without experience) might rather hamper than help. In fact there is no fixed mental knowledge for these things, which vary infinitely. You must learn to go beyond the hankering for mental information and open to the true way of knowledge.

*

All the experiences [*of the Theosophists*] are mental except with a very few. Wordsworth's experience also was mental. Mental experiences are of course a good preparation, but to stop there leaves one far away from the real thing.

*

Yes, if one has thought much of one kind of realisation and absorbed the idea deeply — then it is quite natural that the spiritual experience of it should be one of the first to come.

Mental Realisation and Spiritual Realisation

It [*mental realisation of the Divine*] is a certain kind of living cognition — of which there are two parts — the living perception in thought rising as far as intuition or revelation, the vivid mental feeling and reproduction of what is thus known in the substance of mind. Thus the One in all is felt, seen, realised by the mind by a sort of inner mental sense. The spiritual realisation is more concrete than that — one has the Knowledge by a kind of identity in one's very substance.

*

A mental or vital sense of oneness has not the same essentiality or the same effect as a spiritual realisation of oneness — just as the mental perception of the Divine is not the same thing as the spiritual realisation. The consciousness of one plane is different from the consciousness of another. Spiritual and psychic love are different from mental, vital or physical love — so with everything else. So too with the perception of oneness and its effects. That is why the different planes have their importance; otherwise their existence would have no meaning.

*

You have to know by experience. The mental perception and mental realisation are different from each other — the first is only an idea, in the second the mind in its very substance reflects or reproduces the truth. The spiritual experience is more than the mental — it is in the very substance of the being that the experience takes place.

*

But if you have that [*peace, calm, silence, wideness*] when you concentrate, it is a true spiritual realisation — that which accompanies or prepares the experience of the Atman. It is not merely a mental realisation.

Spiritual Experience as Substantial Experience

Your feeling [*of spiritual experience as a "substance"*] is quite correct. All spiritual experience is a substantial experience — consciousness, Ananda even are felt as something substantial. It is also true that it is felt so by something deeper than mind; it is the mind that turns concrete realities into abstractions.

*

Yes, so long as the attitude is mental it is insecure because it is something imposed on the nature — a mental direction and control. But with the spiritual experience what begins is a change in the stuff of the consciousness itself and by that, as it proceeds to settle and confirm itself, begins naturally what we call the transformation of the nature.

*

The phrase [*"stuff of consciousness"*] simply means "substance of consciousness", the consciousness in itself.

As the Yogic experience develops, consciousness is felt as something quite concrete in which there are movements and formations which are what we call thoughts, feelings etc.

Chapter Two
The Value of Experiences

Experience and Development of Consciousness

It is only by persistent experience and development of consciousness that the veil of Ignorance can be entirely dispelled.

*

An experience is an unmistakable thing and must be given its proper value. The mind may exaggerate in thinking about it, but that does not deprive it of its value.

*

Trances and experiences have their value. There is no question of less or more important — each thing has its place.

*

It is not a question of giving an equal value to everything you do, but of recognising the value of all the different elements of the sadhana. No such rule can be made as that trances are of little value or that experiences are of inferior importance any more than it can be said that work is of no or inferior importance.

*

Your experience is the beginning of the fundamental and decisive realisation which carries the consciousness out of the limited mental into the true spiritual vision and experience in which all is one and all is the Divine. It is this constant and living experience that is the true foundation of spiritual life. There can be no doubt about its truth and value, for it is evidently something living and dynamic and goes beyond a mental realisation. It may add to itself in future different aspects, but the essential fundamental realisation you now have. When this is permanent, one can be said to have passed out of the twilight of the mind into the light of the Spirit.

What you have now to do is to allow the realisation to grow and develop. The necessary movements will probably come of themselves as these have come — provided you keep your will single and faithful towards this Light and Truth. Already it has brought you the guidance towards the next step, cessation of the flow of thought, the inner mind's silence. Once that is won, there is likely to come a settled peace, liberation, wideness. The sense of the need of simplicity and transparency is also a true movement and comes from the same inner guidance. That is necessary for the deepest inmost divine element within behind the mind, life and body to come forward fully in you — when it does you will be able to become aware of the inner guide within you and of a Force working for the full spiritual change. This simplicity comes by a separation from the manifold devious mental and vital movements which lead one in all directions — a quiet, a detachment in the heart which turns one singly towards the one Truth and the one Light till it takes up the whole being and the whole life.

Put your trust in the grace of the One and Divine which has already touched you and opened its door and rely on it for all that is to come.

The Importance of Small Beginnings

What I meant about the experiences was simply this that you have erected your own ideas about what you want from the Yoga and have always been measuring what began to come by that standard and because it was not according to expectation or up to that standard telling yourself after a moment, "It is nothing, it is nothing." That dissatisfaction laid you open at every step to a reaction or recoil which prevented any continuous development. The Yogin who has experience knows that the small beginnings are of the greatest importance and have to be cherished and allowed with great patience to develop. He knows for instance that the neutral quiet so dissatisfying to the vital eagerness of the sadhak is the first step towards the peace that passeth all understanding, the small current or thrill of inner delight the first trickling in of the ocean of Ananda, the play of lights or colours the key of the doors of the inner vision and experience, the descents that stiffen the body into a concentrated stillness the first touch of something at the end of which is the presence of the Divine. He is not impatient; he is rather careful not to disturb the evolution that is beginning. Certainly, some sadhaks have strong and decisive experiences at the beginning, but these are followed by a long labour in which there are many empty periods and many periods of struggle.

*

If you truly decide in all your consciousness to offer your being to the Divine to mould it as He wills, then most of your personal difficulty will disappear — I mean that which still remains, and there will be only the lesser difficulties of the transformation of the ordinary into the Yogic consciousness, normal to all sadhana. Your mental difficulty has been all along that you wanted to mould the sadhana and the reception of experience and the response of the Divine according to your own preconceived mental ideas and left no freedom to the Divine to act or manifest according to His own truth and reality and the need not of your mind and vital but of your soul and spirit. It is as if your vital were to present a coloured glass to the Divine and tell Him, "Now pour yourself into that and I will shut you up there and look at you through the colours", or, from the mental point of view, as if you were to offer a test-tube in a similar way and say, "Get in there and I will test you and see what you are." But the Divine is shy about such processes and His objections are not altogether unintelligible.

At any rate I am glad the experience has come back again — it has come as the result of your effort and mine for the last days and is practically a reminder that the door of entry into Yogic experience is still there and can open at the right touch. You taxed me the other day with making a mistake about your experience of breathing with the name in it and reproached me for drawing a big inference from a very small phenomenon — a thing, by the way, which the scientists are doing daily without the least objection from your reason. You had the same idea, I believe, about my acceptance of your former experiences, this current and the descent of stillness in the body, as signs of the Yogi in you. But these ideas spring from an ignorance of the spiritual realm and its phenomena and only show the incapacity of the outer intellectual reason to play the role you want it to play, that of a supreme judge of spiritual truth and inner experience — a quite natural incapacity because it does not know even the A.B.C. of these things and it passes my comprehension how one can be a judge about a thing of which one knows nothing. I know that the "scientists" are continually doing it with supraphysical phenomena outside their province — those who never had a spiritual or occult experience laying down the law about occult phenomena and Yoga; but that does not make it any more reasonable or excusable. Any Yogi who knows something about pranayama or japa can tell you that the running of the name in the breath is not a small phenomenon but of great importance in these practices and, if it comes naturally, a sign that something in the inner being has done that kind of sadhana in the past. As for the current it is the familiar sign of a first touch of the higher consciousness flowing down in the form of a stream — like the "wave" of light of the scientist — to prepare its possession of mind, vital and physical in the body. So is the stillness and rigidity of the body in your former experience a sign of the same descent of the higher consciousness in its form or tendency of stillness and silence. It is a perfectly sound conclusion that one who gets these experiences at the beginning has the capacity of Yoga in him and can open, even if the opening is delayed by other movements belonging to his ordinary nature. These things are part of the science of Yoga, as familiar as the crucial experiences of physical Science are to the scientific seeker.

As for the impression of swooning, it is simply because you were not in sleep, as you imagined, but in a first condition of what is usually called *svapna samādhi*, dream trance. What you felt like swooning was only the tendency to go deeper in, into a more profound *svapna samādhi* or else into a *suṣupta* trance —

The Value of Experiences

the latter being what the word trance usually means in English, but it can be extended to the *svapna* kind also. To the outer mind this deep loss of the surface consciousness seems like a swoon, though it is really nothing of the kind — hence the impression. Many sadhaks here get at times or sometimes for a long period this deeper *svapna samādhi* in what began as sleep — with the result that a conscious sadhana goes on in their sleeping as in their waking hours. This is different from the dream experiences that one has on the vital or mental plane which are themselves not ordinary dreams but actual experiences on the mental, vital, psychic or subtle physical planes. You have had several dreams which were vital dream experiences, those in which you met the Mother, and recently you had one such contact on the mental plane which, for those who understand these things, means that the inner consciousness is preparing in the mind as well as in the vital, which is a great advance.

You will ask why these things take place either in sleep or in an indrawn meditation and not in the waking state. There is a twofold reason. First, that usually in Yoga these things begin in an indrawn state and not in the waking condition, — it is only if or when the waking mind is ready that they come as readily in the waking state. Again in you the waking mind has been too active in its insistence on the ideas and operations of the outer consciousness to give the inner mind a chance to project itself into the waking state. But it is through the inner consciousness and primarily through the inner mind that these things come; so, if there is not a clear passage from the inner to the outer, it must be in the inner states that they first appear. If the waking mind is subject or surrendered to the inner consciousness and willing to become its instrument, then even from the beginning these openings can come through the waking consciousness. That again is a familiar law of the Yoga.

I may add that when you complain of the want of response, you are probably expecting immediately some kind of direct manifestation of the Divine which, as a rule though there are exceptions, comes only when previous experiences have prepared the consciousness so that it may feel, understand, recognise the response. Ordinarily the spiritual or divine consciousness comes first — what I have called the higher consciousness — the presence or manifestation comes afterwards. But this descent of the higher consciousness is really the touch or influx of the Divine itself, though not at first recognised by the lower nature.

*

"I will try again" is not sufficient; what is needed is to try always — steadily, with a heart free from despondency, as the Gita says, *anirviṇṇacetasā*. You speak of five and a half years as if it were a tremendous time for such an object, but a Yogi who is able in that time to change radically his nature and get the concrete decisive experience of the Divine would have to be considered as one of the rare gallopers of the spiritual Way. Nobody has ever said that the spiritual change was an easy thing; all spiritual seekers will say that it is difficult but supremely worth doing. If one's desire for the Divine has become the master desire, then surely one can give one's whole life to it without repining and not grudge the time, difficulty or labour.

Again you speak of your experiences as vague and dreamlike. In the first place the scorn of small experiences in the inner life is no part of wisdom, reason or common sense. It is in the beginning of the sadhana and for a long time the small experiences that come on each other and, if given their full value, prepare the field, build up a preparatory consciousness and one day break open the walls to big experiences. But if you despise them with the ambitious idea that you must have either the big experiences or nothing, it is not surprising that they come once in a blue moon and cannot do their work. Moreover, all your experiences were not small. There were some like the stilling descent of a Power in the body — what you used to call numbness — which anyone with spiritual knowledge would have recognised as a first strong step towards the opening of the consciousness to the higher Peace and Light. But it was not in the line of your expectations and you gave it no special value. As for vague and dreamlike, you feel it so because you are looking at them and at everything that happens in you from the standpoint of the outward physical mind and intellect which can take only physical things as real and important and vivid and to it inward phenomena are something unreal, vague and truthless. The spiritual experience does not even despise dreams and visions; it is known to it that many of these things are not dreams at all but experiences on an inner plane and if the experiences of the inner planes which lead to the opening of the inner self into the outer so as to influence and change it are not accepted, the experiences of the subtle consciousness and the trance consciousness, how is the waking consciousness to expand out of the narrow prison of the body and the body-mind and the senses? For, to the physical mind untouched by the inner awakened consciousness, even the experience of the cosmic consciousness or the Eternal Self might very well seem merely subjective and unconvincing. It would think, "Curious, no doubt, rather interesting, but very subjective, don't you think? Hallucinations, yes?" The first business of the spiritual seeker is to get away from the outward mind's outlook and to look at inward phenomena with an inward mind to which they soon become powerful and stimulating realities. If one does that, then one begins to see that there is here a wide field of truth and knowledge, in which one can move from discovery to discovery to reach the supreme discovery of all. But the outer physical mind, if it has any ideas about the Divine and spirituality at all, has only hasty *a priori* ideas miles away from the solid ground of inner truth and experience.

I have not left myself time to deal with other matters at any length. You speak of the Divine's stern demands and hard conditions — but what severe demands and iron conditions you are laying on the Divine! You practically say to Him, "I will doubt and deny you at every step, but you must fill me with your unmistakable Presence; I will be full of gloom and despair whenever I think of you or the Yoga, but you must flood my gloom with your rapturous irresistible Ananda; I will meet you only with my outer physical mind and consciousness, but you must give me in that the Power that will transform rapidly my whole nature." Well, I don't say that the Divine won't or can't do it, but if such a miracle is to be worked, you must give Him some time and just a millionth part of a chance.

*

There is no reason certainly for despair. The bliss always comes in drops at first, or a broken trickle. You have to go on cheerfully and in full confidence, till there is the cascade.

Chapter Three
Inner Experience and Outer Life

Subjective Experience and the Objective Existence

Experiences on the mental and vital and subtle physical planes or thought formations and vital formations are often represented as if they were concrete external happenings; true experiences are in the same way distorted by mental and vital accretions and additions. One of the first needs in our Yoga is a discrimination and a psychic tact distinguishing the false from the true, putting each thing in its place and giving it its true value or absence of value, not carried away by the excitement of the mind or the vital being.

*

What do you mean by true? You have a subjective experience belonging to a higher plane of consciousness; when you descend you come down with it into the material and the whole of existence is seen by you in the terms of that consciousness — just as when a man sees the vision of the Divine everywhere, he sees all down to the material world as the Divine.

*

It happens so in the sadhak's own subjective consciousness [*that the Divine is seen everywhere and there is no sorrow or suffering in the world*]. Of course it does not mean that the whole world becomes like that in everybody's consciousness.

If your experience were objective, then that would mean that the whole world had changed, everybody became conscious, no sorrow or suffering anywhere. Needless to say, the material world has not changed objectively in that way. Only in your own consciousness, subjectively, you see the Divine everywhere, all disharmony disappears, sorrow and suffering become impossible for the time at least — that is a subjective experience.

*

It depends on what you mean by subjective and objective. Knowledge and Ignorance are in their nature subjective. But from the personal point of view, the Force of Ignorance may manifest as something objective, outside oneself so that even when one has knowledge for oneself one cannot remove the environing Ignorance. If that is so, Ignorance is not merely a subjective force in oneself, it is there in the world.

*

It seems to have been a series of experiences of the different bhavas of bhakti and it came for experience only — or for a manifold development of the bhakti. These of course are purely subjective experiences meant to educate the consciousness and have no definitive value for the actual manifestation. It is merely for subjective experience and knowledge.

*

Subjective does not mean false. It only means that the Truth is experienced within but it has not yet taken hold of the dynamic relations with the outside existence. It is an inner experience of the cosmic consciousness and the overmind knowledge that you have.

*

The cosmic consciousness, the overmind knowledge and experience is an inner knowledge — but its effect is subjective. As long as one lives in it, one can be free in soul, but to transform the external nature more is needed.

*

I have told you once before that your experiences are subjective — and in the subjective sphere they are correct in substance so far as they go. But to enter the Supermind subjective experience is not sufficient. Some sufficient application of intuition and overmind to life must first be done.

*

The difficulty of the Yoga is not in getting experiences or a subjective realisation of the Truth; it is in objectivising the Truth, that is, in making the outer consciousness down to the material an expression of the inner Truth. So long as that is not done, the attacks of the lower Nature can always continue.

Experience and the Change of One's Nature

Merely to have experiences of the higher consciousness will not change the nature. Either the higher consciousness has to make a dynamic descent into the whole being and change it — or it must establish itself in the inner being down to the inner physical so that the latter feels itself separate from the outer and is able to act freely upon it — or the psychic must come forward and change the nature — or the inner will must awake and force the nature to change. These are the four ways in which change can be brought about.

*

When you are in connection with the higher worlds above the mental, with the mental and the psychic or even with some of the higher vital planes, then there is the peace and Ananda — but connection with the lower vital worlds can easily bring disturbance and unrest, so long as your vital itself is not changed and made full of peace and strength and quiet.

*

You forget that for a long time she was often keeping much more to herself, to X's great anger. During that time she built up an inner life and made some attempt to change certain things in her outer — not in the outward appearance but in the movements governing it. There is still an enormous amount to be done before the inward change can be outwardly visible, but still she is not insincere in her resolution. As for her not having any depression it is because she has established a fundamental calm which is only upset by clashes with X; all the rest passes on the surface ruffling it perhaps, but not breaking the calm. She has also a day or two ago had the experience of the ascent above and of the wideness of peace and joy of the Infinite (free from the bodily sense and limitation) as also the descent down to the Muladhara. She does not know the names or technicalities of these things but her description which was minute and full of details was unmistakable. There are three or four others who have had this experience recently so that we may suppose the working of the Force is not altogether in vain, as this experience is a very big affair and is supposed to be, if stabilised, the summit of the old Yogas. For us it is only a beginning of spiritual transformation. I have said this though it is personal so that you may understand that outside defects and obstacles in the nature or the appearance of unyogicness does not necessarily mean that a person can do or is doing no sadhana.

*

To change the nature is not easy and always takes time, but if there is no inner experience, no gradual emergence of the other purer consciousness that is concealed by all these things you now see, it would be almost impossible even for the strongest will. You say that first you must get rid of all these things, then have the inner experiences. But how is that to be done? These things, anger, jealousy, desire, are the very stuff of the ordinary human vital consciousness. They could not be changed if there were not a deeper consciousness within which is of quite another character. There is within you a psychic being which is divine, directly a part of the Mother, pure of all these defects. It is covered and concealed by the ordinary consciousness and nature, but when it is unveiled and able to come forward and govern the being, then it changes the ordinary consciousness, throws all these undivine things out and changes the outer nature altogether. That is why we want the sadhaks to concentrate, to open this concealed consciousness — it is by concentration of whatever kind and the experiences it brings that one opens and becomes aware within and the new consciousness and nature begin to grow and come out. Of course we want them also to use their will and reject the desires and wrong movements of the vital, for by doing that the emergence of the true consciousness becomes possible. But rejection alone cannot succeed; it is by rejection and by inner experience and growth that it is done.

You say that all these things were hidden within you. No; they were not deep within, they were in the outer or surface nature, only you were not sufficiently conscious of them because the other true consciousness had not opened and grown within you. Now by the experiences you have had the psychic has been growing and it is because of this new psychic consciousness that you are able to see clearly all that has to go. It does not go at once because the vital had so much the habit of them in the past, but they will now have to go because your soul wants to get rid of them and your soul is growing stronger in you. So you must both use your will aided by the Mother's force to get rid of these things, and go on with your inner psychic experiences — it is by the two together that all will be done.

*

The persistence or the obstinate return of the old Adam is a common experience: it is only when there is a sufficient mass of experience and a certain progression of consciousness in the higher parts of the being that the lower can be really transmuted. It is that that one must allow to develop. It is the pressure of the Yoga shakti and the increase of the experiences that is wanted in your case, not this preoccupation with an external "grim" tapasya.

*

Once these experiences [*of peace and the descent of force*] begin, they repeat themselves usually, whether the general condition is good or not. But naturally they cannot make a radical change until they settle themselves and become normal in the whole being or at least in the inner part of it. In the latter case the old movements can still come, but they are felt as something quite superficial and the sadhana increases in spite of them. There is no question of good or wicked. If some part of the being even has been opened the experiences come.

*

The action of the higher consciousness does not usually begin by changing the outer nature — it works on the inner being, prepares that and then goes outward. Before that, whatever change is done in the outer nature has to be done by the psychic.

*

All experiences can be brought into the smallest constituents of the being.

Inner Attitude and Outward Things

You have had some experiences which are signs of a future possibility. To have more within the first one and a half years it would be necessary to have the complete attitude of the sadhak and give up that of the man of the world. It is only then that progress can be rapid from the beginning.

*

All these [*outward restraints such as moderation in eating food and drinking tea*] are external things that have their use, but what I mean [*by "the complete attitude of the sadhak"*] is something more inward. I mean not to be interested in outward things for their own sake, following after them with desire, but at all times to be intent on one's soul, living centrally in the inner being and its progress, taking outward things and action only as a means for the inner progress.

The Power of Creative Formation

It [*feeling that the Mother and Sri Aurobindo are looking at one*] simply means you have a subjective sense of our Presence. But must a subjective sense of things be necessarily a vain imagination? If so, no Yoga is possible. One has to take it as an axiom that subjective things can be as real as objective things. No doubt there may be and are such things as mental formations — but, to begin with, mental formations are or can be very powerful things, producing concrete results; secondly whether what one sees or hears is a mental formation or a real subjective object can only be determined when one has sufficient experience in these inward things.

*

You have a strong power of (subjective) creative formation, mostly, I think, on the mental but partly too on the vital plane. This kind of formative faculty can be used for objective results if accompanied by a sound knowledge of the occult forces and their workings; but by itself it results more often in one's building up an inner world of one's own in which you can live very well satisfied, so long as you live in yourself, apart from any close contact with external physical life; but it does not stand the test of objective experience.

*

In each plane there is an objective as well as a subjective side. It is not the physical plane and life alone that are objective.

When you have the power of formation of which I spoke, whatever is suggested to the mind, the mind constructs and establishes a form of it in itself. But this power can cut two ways; it may tempt the mind to construct mere images of the reality and mistake them for the reality itself. It is one of the many dangers of a too active mind.

You make a formation in your mind or on the vital plane in yourself — it is a kind of creation, but subjective only; it affects only your own mental or vital being. You can create by ideas, thought-forms, images a whole world in yourself or for yourself; but it stops there.

Some have the power of making consciously formations that

go out and affect the minds, actions, vital movements, external lives of others. These formations may be destructive as well as creative.

Finally, there is the power to make formations that become effective realities in the earth-consciousness here, in its mind, life, physical existence. That is what we usually mean by creation.

Chapter Four

The Danger of the Ego and the Need of Purification

Spiritual Experiences and the Ego

A certain exaltation of the being comes naturally with the stronger experiences and the sense of marvel or miracle may go with it, but there should be no egoistic feeling in the exaltation.

*

What you have to be careful about is, when the feeling of power and strength comes into you or when you have experiences, not to allow it to be seized on by any kind of egoistic or vital desire, pride, ambition, wish to dominate others — even if it takes the garb of doing the Mother's work, — for this is your great weakness which always gets in and spoils your progress. Also when you have experiences, do not allow yourself to get exalted and excited by them so as to lose discrimination; for, if you do, then even though the experiences when they begin may be of the right kind, the vital forces take advantage of the excitation and rush in with their own deformations. Remain always calm, collected, quiet within, vigilant — discriminate always. The progress so made may be more slow or seem so; but it is more sure.

*

A true spiritual experience must be free from the claim of the ego. What the ego can do however is to get proud of having the experience and think, "What a great one am I." Or it may think, "I am the Self, the Divine, so let me go and do what I will, for it is the Divine who wills in me." It is only if the experience of Self imposes silence on the other parts and frees the psychic that the ego disappears. Even if not ego itself, numerous fragments and survivals of ego-habit can remain and have to be eliminated.

*

Yes, if there is the solid experience, the ego habit is much diminished, but it does not go altogether. It takes refuge in the sense of being an instrument and — if there is not the psychic turn — it may easily prefer to be the instrument of some Force that feeds the satisfaction of the ego. In such cases the ego may still remain strong although it feels itself instrumental and not the primary actor.

*

Although there is no ego in the spiritual planes, yet by the spiritual experience the ego on the lower planes may get aggrandised through pride and wrong reception of the experience. Also by entering into the larger mental and vital planes one may aggrandise the ego. These things are always possible so long as the higher consciousness and the lower are not harmonised in the being and the lower transformed into the nature of the higher.

*

The first result of the downflow of the overmind forces is very often to exaggerate the ego, which feels itself strong, almost irresistible (though it is not really so), divinised, luminous. The first thing to do, after some experience of the thing, is to get rid of this magnified ego. For that you have to stand back, not allow yourself to be swept in by the movement, but to watch, understand, reject all mixture, aspire for a purer and yet purer light and action. This can only be done perfectly if the psychic comes forward. The mind and vital, especially the vital, receiving these forces, can with difficulty resist the tendency to seize on and use them for the ego's objects or, which comes practically to the same thing, they mix the demands of the ego with the service of a higher object.

*

The Danger of the Ego and the Need of Purification 31

There is [*when one receives forces without a basis of peace, light and love*] more a sense of having power than real power. There are some mixed and quite relative powers — sometimes a little effective, sometimes ineffective — which could be developed into something real if put under the control of the Divine, surrendered. But the ego comes in, exaggerates these small things and represents them as something huge and unique and refuses to surrender. Then the sadhak makes no progress — he wanders about in the jungle of his own imaginations without any discrimination or critical sense or among a play of confused forces he is unable to understand or master.

Forces can come anywhere. The Asuras have their forces, but without peace, light or love — only they are forces of darkness.

*

The man there [*in the correspondent's dream*] symbolises that ego-tendency in the human nature which makes a man, when some realisation comes, to think how great a realisation is this and how great a sadhak am I and to call others to see and admire — perhaps he thinks like the man in the dream, "I have seen the Divine, indeed I feel I am one with the Divine, — I will call everybody to see that." This is a tendency which has injured the sadhana of many and sometimes ruined the sadhana altogether. In the thoughts you describe you came to see something in yourself which is there more or less in all human beings, the desire to be thought well of by others, to occupy a high place in their esteem or their affection, to have honour, position, admiration. When anybody joins this feeling to the idea of sadhana, then the disposition to do the sadhana for that and not purely and simply for the sake of the Divine comes in and there must be disturbance or else an obstruction in the sadhana itself or if in spite of it spiritual experience comes, then there is the danger of his misusing the experience to magnify his ego like the man in the dream. All these dreams are coming to you to give you a vivid and concrete knowledge and experience of what these human defects are so that you may find it easier to throw them out, to recognise them when they come in the waking state and refuse them entrance. These things are not in yourself only but in all human nature; they are the things one has to get rid of or else to guard against so that one's consecration to the Divine may be complete, selfless, true and pure.

Purification and Preparation of the Nature

I don't think there is any cause for dissatisfaction with the progress made by you. Experiences come to many before the nature is ready to make full profit from them; to others a more or less prolonged period of purification and preparation of the stuff of the nature or the instruments comes first while experiences are held up till this process is largely or wholly over. The latter method which seems to be adopted in your case is the safer and sounder of the two. In this respect we think it is evident that you have made considerable progress, for instance in control over the violence and impatience and heat natural to the volcanic energy of your temperament, in sincerity also curbing the devious and errant impulses of an enormously active mind and temperament, in a greater quiet and harmony in the being as a whole. No doubt the process has to be completed, but something very fundamental seems to have been done. It is more important to look at the thing from the positive rather than the negative side. The things that have to be established are — *brahmacaryaṁ śamaḥ satyaṁ praśāntir ātmasaṁyamaḥ*: *brahmacaryam*, a complete sex-purity; *śamaḥ*, quiet and harmony in the being, its forces maintained but controlled, harmonised, disciplined; *satyam*, truth and sincerity in the whole nature; *praśāntiḥ*, a general state of peace and calm; *ātmasaṁyamaḥ*, the power and habit to control whatever needs control in the movements of the nature. When these are fairly established one has laid a foundation on which one can develop the Yogic consciousness and with the Yogic consciousness there comes an easy opening to realisation and experience.

*

The Danger of the Ego and the Need of Purification

The progress does not always come in the way that people expect. There is first a preparation within even for many years before such experiences come as people usually associate with the word progress. There has been this preparation and progress in you, but because struggle is still there you cannot recognise it.

You must put your trust in the Mother and let her Force work in you — keep the attitude of confidence and self-offering and the result will appear as soon as the consciousness is ready.

*

According to the affirmation of people acquainted with the subject, the preliminary purification before getting any Yogic experiences worth the name may extend to 12 years. After that one may legitimately expect something. You are far from the limit yet — so no reason to despair.

*

Do not be over-eager for experience, — for experiences you can always get, having once broken the barrier between the physical mind and the subtle planes. What you have to aspire for most is the improved quality of the recipient consciousness in you — discrimination in the mind, the unattached impersonal Witness look on all that goes on in you and around you, purity in the vital, calm equanimity, enduring patience, absence of pride and the sense of greatness — and more especially, the development of the psychic being in you — surrender, self-giving, psychic humility, devotion. It is a consciousness made up of these things, cast in this mould that can bear without breaking, stumbling or deviation into error the rush of lights, powers and experiences from the supraphysical planes. An entire perfection in these respects is hardly possible until the whole nature from the highest mind to the subconscient physical is made one in the light that is greater than Mind; but a sufficient foundation and a consciousness always self-observant, vigilant and growing in these things is indispensable — for perfect purification is the basis of the perfect siddhi.

*

You must not try to get experiences; you are not yet ready for them; instead of the right experience something abnormal comes. You must get your vital purified and calm so that these movements may not come. Nothing abnormal like not sleeping, not eating — all that is the vital trying to do extraordinary things so as to imagine it is going fast and doing high sadhana. A pure, simple, quiet, well-balanced vital is necessary for this Yoga.

*

The automatic tendency is a good sign as it shows that it is the inner being opening to the Truth which is pressing forward the necessary changes.

As you say, it is the failure of the right attitude that comes in the way of passing through ordeals to a change of nature. The pressure is becoming greater now for this change of character even more than for decisive Yoga experience — for if the experience comes it fails to be decisive because of the want of the requisite change of nature. The mind for instance gets the experience of the One in all, but the vital cannot follow because it is dominated by ego-reaction and ego-motive or the habits of the outer nature keep up a way of thinking, feeling, acting, living which is quite out of harmony with the experience. Or the psychic and part of the mind and emotional being feel frequently the closeness of the Mother, but the rest of the nature is unoffered and goes its own way prolonging division from her nearness, creating distance. It is because the sadhaks have never even tried to have the Yogic attitude in all things — they have been contented with the common ideas, common view of things, common motives of life, — only varied by inner experiences and transferred to the framework of the Asram instead of that of the world outside. It is not enough — and there is great need that this should change.

*

Quite correct. Unless the adhar is made pure, neither the higher truth (intuitive, illumined spiritual) nor the overmental nor the supramental can manifest; whatever forces come down from them get mixed with the inferior consciousness and a half-truth takes the place of the Truth or even sometimes a dangerous error.

*

As for experiences, anybody with an occult bent can have experiences. The thing is to know what to do with them.

Mixed and Confused Experiences

I do not question at all the personal intensity or concreteness of your internal experiences, but experiences can be intense and yet be very mixed in their truth and their character. In your experience your own subjectivity, sometimes your ego-pushes interfere very much and give them their form and the impression they create on you. It is only if there is a pure psychic response that the form given to the experience is likely to be the right one and the mental and vital movements will then present themselves in their true nature. Otherwise the mind, the vital, the ego give their own colour to what happens, their own turn, very usually their own deformation. *Intensity* is not a guarantee of entire truth and correctness in an experience; it is only *purity* of the consciousness that can give an entire truth and correctness.

The Mother's presence is always there; but if you decide to act on your own — your own idea, your own notion of things, your own will and demand upon things, then it is quite likely that her presence will get veiled; it is not she who withdraws from you, but you who draw back from her. But your mind and vital don't want to admit that, because it is always their preoccupation to justify their own movements. If the psychic were allowed its full predominance, this would not happen; it would have felt the veiling, but it would at once have said, "There must have been some mistake in me, a mist has arisen in me," and it would have looked and found the cause.

It is perfectly true that so long as there is not an unreserved self-giving in both the internal and external, there will always be veilings, dark periods and difficulties. But if there is unreserved self-giving in the internal, the unreserved self-giving in the external would naturally follow; if it does not, it means that the internal is not unreservedly surrendered; there are reservations in some part of the mind insisting on its own ideas and notions; reservations in some part of the vital insisting on its own demands, impulses, movements, ego-ideas, formations; reservations in the internal physical insisting on its own old habits of many kinds, and all claiming consciously, half-consciously or subconsciously that these should be upheld, respected, satisfied, taken as an important element in the work, the "creation" or the Yoga.

*

All this is absolutely idiotic confusion. It has come because you have persisted in disobeying and disregarding everything I wrote for you.

I told you you were not to try to decide by your mind. You persistently go on repeating, "*I* must decide. *I* must decide. *I* must take a decision. *I* must take a resolution." You are always repeating this " *I*, *I*, *I* must decide" as if you knew better than myself and the Mother! "*I* must understand, *I* must decide." And always you find that your mind can decide nothing and understand nothing. And yet you go on repeating the same falsehood.

I tell you plainly once again that all your so-called experiences are worth nothing, mere vital ignorance and confusion. The only experience you need is the experience of the presence of the Mother, the Mother's light, the Mother's force, and the change they bring in you.

You have to throw away all other influences and open yourself only to the Mother's influence.

You have to think and talk no longer about energies flowing out and your energies and others' energies. The only energy you have to feel is the descent and inflow and action of the Mother's force.

These were my instructions and so long as you carried them out, you were progressing rapidly.

Throw all these incoherent false experiences away. Go back to the single rule I gave you. Open to the Mother's presence, influence, light, force — reject everything else. Only so will you get back clearness (instead of this confusion), peace, psychic perception and progress in the sadhana.

*

But why be overwhelmed by any wealth of any kind of experiences? What does it amount to after all? The quality of a sadhak does not depend on that; one great spiritual realisation direct and at the centre will often make a great sadhak or Yogi, an army of intermediate Yogic experiences will not, that has been amply proved by a host of instances. You need not therefore compare that wealth to your poverty. To open yourself to the descent of the higher consciousness (the true being) is the one thing needed and that, even if that comes after long effort and many failures, is better than a hectic gallop leading nowhere.

*

You have missed my rather veiled hint about wealth of "any kind of experiences" and the reference to the intermediate zone which, I think at least, I made. I was referring to the wealth of *that* kind of experience. I do not say that these experiences are always of no value, but they are so mixed and confused that if one runs after them without any discrimination at all they end either by leading astray, sometimes tragically astray, or by bringing one into a confused nowhere. That does not mean that all such experiences are useless or without value. There are those that are sound as well as those that are unsound; those that are helpful, in the true line, sometimes signposts, sometimes stages on the way to realisation, sometimes stuff and material of the realisation. These naturally and rightly one seeks for, calls, strives after, or at least one opens oneself in the confident expectation that they will sooner or later arrive. Your own main experiences may have been few or not continuous, but I cannot recollect any that were not sound or were unhelpful. I would say that it is better to have a few of these than a multitude of the others. My only meaning in what I wrote was not to be impressed by mere wealth of experiences or to think that that is sufficient to constitute a great sadhak or that not to have this wealth is necessarily an inferiority, a lamentable deprivation or a poverty of the one thing desirable.

There are two classes of things that happen in Yoga — realisations and experiences. Realisations are the reception in the consciousness and the establishment there of the fundamental truths of the Divine, of the Higher or Divine Nature, of the world-consciousness and the play of its forces, of one's own self and real nature and the inner nature of things, the power of these things growing in one till they are a part of one's inner life and existence, — as for instance, the realisation of the Divine Presence, the descent and settling of the higher Peace, Light, Force, Ananda in the consciousness, their workings there, the realisation of the divine or spiritual love, the perception of one's own psychic being, the discovery of one's own true mental being, true vital being, true physical being, the realisation of the overmind or the supramental consciousness, the clear perception of the relation of all these things to our present inferior nature and their action on it to change that lower nature. The list of course might be infinitely longer. These things also are often called experiences when they only come in flashes, snatches or rare visitations; they are spoken of as full realisations only when they become very positive or frequent or continuous or normal.

Then there are the experiences that help or lead towards the realisation of things spiritual or divine or bring openings or progressions in the sadhana or are supports on the way — experiences of a symbolic character, visions, contacts of one kind or another with the Divine or with the workings of the higher Truth, things like the waking of the Kundalini, the opening of the chakras, messages, intuitions, openings of the inner powers, etc. The one thing that one has to be careful about is to see that they are genuine and sincere and that depends on one's own sincerity, for if one is not sincere, if one is more concerned with the ego or being a big Yogi or becoming a superman than with meeting the Divine or getting the Divine Consciousness which enables one to live in or with the Divine, then a flood of pseudos or mixtures comes in, one is led into the mazes of the intermediate zone or spins in the grooves of one's own formations. There is the truth of the whole matter.

Then why does Krishnaprem say that one should not hunt after experiences but only love and seek the Divine? It simply means that you have not to make experiences your main aim, but the Divine only your aim; and if you do that, you are more likely to get the true helpful experiences and avoid the wrong ones. If one seeks mainly after experiences, his Yoga may become a mere self-indulgence in the lesser things of the mental, vital and subtle physical worlds or in spiritual secondaries, or it may bring down a turmoil or maelstrom of the mixed and the whole or half-pseudo and stand between the soul and the Divine. That is a very sound rule of sadhana. But all these rules and statements must be taken with a sense of measure and in their proper limits, — it does not mean that one should not welcome helpful experiences or that they have no value. Also when a sound line of experience opens, it is perfectly permissible to follow it out, keeping always the central aim in view. All helpful or supporting contacts in dream or vision, such as those you speak of, are to be welcomed and accepted. I had no intention of discouraging such things at all. Experiences of the right kind are a support and help towards the realisation; they are in every way acceptable.

Purification and Positive Experience

It is a mistake to dwell too much on the lower nature and its obstacles, which is the negative side of the sadhana. They have to be seen and purified, but preoccupation with them as the one important thing is not helpful. The positive side of experience of the descent is the more important thing. If one waits for the lower nature to be purified entirely and for all time before calling down the positive experience, one might have to wait for ever. It is true that the more the lower nature is purified, the easier is the descent of the higher Nature, but it is also and more true that the more the higher Nature descends, the more the lower is purified.

Neither the complete purification nor the permanent and perfect manifestation can come all at once, it is a matter of time and patient progress. The two (purification and manifestation) go on progressing side by side and become more and more strong to play into each other's hands — that is the usual course of the sadhana.

*

I do not know what Krishnaprem said or in which article, I do not have it with me. But if the statement is that nobody can have a successful meditation or realise anything till he is pure and perfect, I fail to follow it; it contradicts my own experience. I have always had realisation by meditation first and the purification started afterwards as a result. I have seen many get important, even fundamental realisations by meditation who could not be said to have a great inner development. Are all Yogis who have meditated with effect and had great realisations in their inner consciousness perfect in their nature? It does not look like it to me. I am unable to believe in absolute generalisations in this field, because the development of spiritual consciousness is an exceedingly vast and complex affair in which all sorts of things can happen and one might almost say that for each man it is different according to his nature and that the one thing that is essential is the inner call and aspiration and the perseverance to follow always after it no matter how long it takes or what are the difficulties or impediments — because nothing else will satisfy the soul within us.

It is quite true that a certain amount of purification is indispensable for going on, that the more complete the purification the better because then when the realisations begin they can continue without big difficulties or relapses and without any possibility of fall or failure. It is also true that with many purification is the first need, — certain things have to be got out of the way before one can begin any consecutive inner experience. But the main need is a certain preparation of the consciousness so that it may be able to respond more and more freely to the higher Force. In this preparation many things are useful — the poetry and music you are doing can help, for it acts as a sort of *śravaṇa* and *manana*, even, if the feeling roused is intense, a sort of natural *nididhyāsana*. Psychic preparation, clearing out of the grosser forms of mental and vital ego, opening mind and heart to the Guru and many other things help greatly — it is not perfection or a complete freedom from the dualities or ego that is the indispensable preliminary, but preparedness, a fineness of the inner being which makes spiritual responses and receiving possible.

There is no reason therefore to take as gospel truth these demands which may have been right for Krishnaprem on the way he has trod, but cannot be imposed on all. There is no ground for despondency on that ground — the law of the spirit is not so exacting and inexorable.

Purification and Consecration

What Krishnaprem writes (I have not read it yet) is perfectly true that purification of the heart is necessary before there can be the spiritual attainment. All ways of spiritual seeking are agreed on that. Purification and consecration are two great necessities of sadhana. It is not a fact that one must be pure in heart before one can have *any* Yogic experience at all, but those who have experiences before purification is done run a great risk. It is much better to have the heart pure first, for then the way becomes safe. Nor can the Divine dwell in one's consciousness, if that consciousness is obscure with impurity. It is for the same reason that I advocate the psychic change of the nature first — for that means the purification of the heart, the turning of it wholly to the Divine, the subjection of the mind, of the vital passions, desires, demands, of the physical instincts to the control of the inner being, the soul. What Krishnaprem calls intuitions I would describe as psychic intimations or, as some experience it, the voice of the soul showing the outer members what is the true thing to be done. Always when the soul is in front, one gets the right guidance from within what is to be done, what avoided, what is the wrong thing or the true thing in thought, feeling, action. But this inner intimation emerges in proportion as the consciousness grows more and more pure.

I never intended that X should stay here; he came for darshan and sat down here without a "by your leave". I allowed him to remain for a while to see if he got any profit out of it; afterwards came his repeated illness and he somehow stuck on till now. What I meant by some concrete method was things like repetition of a mantra, pranayama, asana etc. He has been doing these things even here or some of them at least; it is the only thing he really understands (or misunderstands?); but purification of the heart he has not been capable of doing. What I mean by subtle methods is psychological, non-mechanical processes — e.g. concentration in the heart, surrender, self-purification, working out by inner means the change of the consciousness. This does not mean that there is no outer change, — the outer change is necessary but as a part of the inner change. If there is impurity and insincerity within, the outer change will not be effective; but if there is a sincere inner working, the outer change will help it and accelerate the process. What use is X's eating less except for his body's health? But if a man seeks to restrain and get rid of his greed for food or attachment, (not by starvation, though), then he is doing something useful to his sadhana.

Y's case is different. His main stumbling block was ambition, pride, vanity, the desire to be a big Yogi with occult powers. To try to bring down occult powers into an unpurified mind, heart and body — well, you can do it if you want to dance on the edge of a precipice. Or you can do it if your aim is not to be spiritual but to be an occultist, for then you can follow the necessary methods and get the help of the occult powers. But the occult spiritual forces and masteries can be called down or come down without calling only if that is quite secondary to the true thing, the seeking for the Divine, and if it is part of the Divine plan in you. Occult powers can only be for the spiritual man an instrumentation of the Divine Power that uses him, they cannot be the aim or an aim of his sadhana. I don't know who started Y on this false path or whether he hit on it himself; many people here have a habit of doing Yoga according to their own ideas without caring for the guidance of the Guru — from whom however they expect an entire protection and success in sadhana even if they prance or gambol into the wrongest paths possible.

Of course, renunciation of sex is indispensable for the purification you seek, — the heart must be pure and consecrated to the Divine. There must be no turn left that side. As for food, well, that is not so much a purification of the heart as of the vital in the physical, but it is of course very helpful to get control there. The purification of the heart is the central necessity, but a purification of the mind, vital and physical is also called for. But the most important thing for purification of the heart is an absolute sincerity. No pretence with oneself, no concealment from the Divine or oneself or the Guru, a straight look at one's nature and one's movements, a straight will to make them straight. It does not so much matter if it takes time; one must be prepared to make it one's whole life-task to seek the Divine. Purifying the heart means after all a pretty considerable achievement and it is no use getting despondent, despairful etc. because one finds things in oneself that still need to be changed. If one keeps the true will and true attitude, then the intuitions or intimations from within will begin to grow, become clear, precise, unmistakable and the strength to follow them will grow also. And then before even you are satisfied with yourself, the Divine will be satisfied with you and begin to withdraw the veil by which he protects himself and his seeker against a premature and perilous grasping of the greatest thing to which humanity can aspire.

Purification and Transformation

Transformation is made possible by purification.

*

If you remain in a fully conscious state, the clearing of the outer nature ought not to be difficult — afterwards the positive work of its transformation into a perfect instrument can be undertaken.

Conditions for the Coming of Experience

If you make your mind quiet, the experience will come. If you cannot make your mind quiet, work and pray and wait. Those who are able to open to the Divine receive him — but also to those who can wait for the Divine, the Divine comes.

*

If one feels [*the Mother's Force working while in a state of quietness*] it is all right — but it does not always happen. The quietness, silence or peace is a basis for the extension of consciousness, the coming of higher experiences or realisations etc. In what way or order they come differs according to the individual nature.

*

Visions and experiences will come; but the most important thing is to get in the peace, Ananda, confidence and establish it. When that is fixed, afterwards the consciousness can open to the working of the Mother's Force — its coming down into the body and its working will bring all the experience and change that is needed.

*

To fix the calm and strength is the main thing now — more important than fresh experiences; these will come fast enough if the calm and strength become durable, are made the habit and stuff of the consciousness.

*

As for sadhana what is necessary is to arrive at a certain quiet of the inner mind which makes meditation fruitful or a quietude of the heart which creates the psychic opening. It is only by regular concentration, constant aspiration and a will to purify the mind and heart of the things that disquiet and agitate them that this can be done. When a certain basis has been established in these two centres the experiences come of themselves. Many,

The Danger of the Ego and the Need of Purification 45

no doubt, get some kind of experiences such as visions etc. before the basis is well laid by a sort of mental or vital aptitude for these things, but such experiences do not of themselves lead to transformation or realisation — it is by the quietude of the mind and the psychic opening that these greater things can come.

*

Experience in the sadhana is bound to begin with the mental plane, — all that is necessary is that the experience should be sound and genuine. The pressure of understanding and will in the mind and the Godward emotional urge in the heart are the two first agents of Yoga, and peace, purity and calm (with a lulling of the lower unrest) are precisely the first basis that has to be laid; to get that is much more important in the beginning than to get a glimpse of the supraphysical worlds or to have visions, voices and powers. Purification and calm are the first needs in the Yoga. One may have a great wealth of experiences of that kind (worlds, visions, voices etc.) without them, but these experiences occurring in an unpurified and troubled consciousness are usually full of disorder and mixture.

At first the peace and calm are not continuous, they come and go, and it usually takes a long time to get them settled in the nature. It is better therefore to avoid impatience and to go on steadily with what is being done. If you wish to have something beyond the peace and calm, let it be the full opening of the inner being and the consciousness of the Divine Power working in you. Aspire for that sincerely and with a great intensity but without impatience and it will come.

*

It is necessary to lay stress on three things — (1) an entire quietness and calm of the mind and the whole being, (2) a continuance of the movement of purification so that the psychic being (the soul) may govern the whole nature, (3) the maintenance in all conditions and through all experiences of the attitude of adoration and bhakti for the Mother. These are the conditions in which one can grow through all experiences with security and have the right development of the complete realisation without disturbance to the system or being carried away by the intensity of the experiences. Calm, psychic purity, bhakti and spiritual humility before the Divine are the three conditions.

*

The special experiences you are having are glimpses of what is to be and what is growing and preparing and are helping to make the consciousness ready for it. It is not therefore surprising that they change and are replaced by others — that is what usually happens; for it is not these forms that are to be perpetuated, but the essence of the thing which they are bringing. Thus the one thing that has to grow most now is the silence, the quietude, the peace, the free emptiness into which experiences can come, the sense of coolness and release. When that is in possession of the consciousness fully, then something else will come into it which is also essential to the true consciousness and fix itself — it proceeds usually like that. There is nothing strange therefore in the special forms of experience ceasing and being followed by others after you have written about or brought them to the Mother. When the more permanent forms of realisation begin to come, it will no longer be like that.

Chapter Five
Suggestions for Dealing with Experiences

Letting the Experiences Develop Naturally

It is better to let the experiences develop naturally. It is not necessary, when they come freely, to determine with the mind which is to be remembered or sought after.

*

An experience should be allowed its full time to develop or have its full effect. It should not be interrupted except in case of necessity or, of course, if it is not a good experience.

*

You have to watch and see how they [*experiences*] develop. For the most part they carry their own meaning and if you go on observing them with a silent and vigilant mind you will understand more than if you were in a constant turmoil of thought about them.

*

When an experience begins, you should not interfere with it by either questioning or by disturbing movements.

Thinking about Experiences

To think and question about an experience when it is happening is the wrong thing to do; it stops it or diminishes it. Let the experience have its full play — if it is something like this "new life force" or peace or Force or anything else helpful. When it is over, you can think about it — not while it is proceeding. For these experiences are spiritual and not mental and the mind has to be quiet and not interfere.

*

During the experience the mind should be quiet. After the experience is over it can be active. If it is active while it is there, the experience may stop altogether.

*

It was not an imagination, but an experience. When such an experience occurs, the attempt to take hold of it mentally and continue it may on the contrary interrupt it. It is best to let it continue of itself; if it ceases, it is likely to recur.

*

There are two centres or parts of the consciousness — one is a witness, *sākṣī*, and observes, the other consciousness is active and it is this active consciousness that you felt going down deep into the vital being. If your mind had not become active, you would have known where it went and what it went there to experience or do. When there is an experience, you should not begin to think about it, for that is of no use at all and it only stops the experience — you should remain silent, observe and let it go on to its end.

*

There is something in you that does want to stick to the habit of mentalising about everything. So long as you were not having real experiences, it did not matter. But once real experiences begin you have to learn to approach them in the right way.

Observing Experiences without Attachment

At a certain stage of the sadhana, in the beginning (or near it) of the more intense experiences, it sometimes happens that there is the intense realisation of some aspect of the Divine, a sort of communion with it, and that is seen everywhere and all as that. It is a transitory phase and afterwards one gets the larger experience of the Divine in all its aspects and beyond all aspects. Throughout the experience there should be one part of the being that observes and understands — for sometimes ignorant sadhaks are carried away by their experience and stop short there or fall into extravagance. It must be taken as an experience through which you are passing.

Observing Experiences without Fear or Alarm

It is always dangerous to allow fear to come in like that and associate itself with experiences in the sadhana. There is nothing in the experiences themselves as you describe them that are at all alarming. A burning in the head or a creeping or ticklish sensation or a sense of something moving and working in the head has often been felt by many when there was an opening and the Force was working there. The other things also are in themselves usual enough, the sense of something separate from oneself and the opening and connection made between the head and the centre above. But where the anomaly comes in is that with the connection comes the fear and nervous physical upsetting. So long as there is fear it is no use going on with these experiences — you have to stop and get back to the normal consciousness. Besides that, as I have already said, you must realise what it is in you that has come across and created this upsetting. It is not the descent and the experiences, for many have had them or similar things without being any the worse. It is something in you, probably in your lower vital and physical, that does not want the Higher Consciousness because it will have to change and it has no intention of changing. When this pressure acts, it gets at once a fear and shakes the physical mind and system by its fear. You will have then to get rid of this — till then it will not be safe for you to go farther.

*

These experiences are symbolic in their character, so there is no reason to be horrified by the green waters even if you did drown in a well in the last life. All such experiences should be observed quietly without alarm or depression or other such feelings. One can look at them and try to see or feel their meaning, but too active a speculation in the mind rather hinders than helps the seeing.

If you sink down into an unopened part and open it to the light or empty and clear it, that is a quite salutary and necessary operation and there is no reason for alarm. As for self-preservation, one does not drown in these inner wells — it is only a bath or a plunge. And if it happens to be the well of the psychic, nothing more salutary than to plunge into it.

Speaking about Experiences

The usual rule given by Yogis is that one should not speak of one's experience to others except of course the Guru while the sadhana is going on because it wastes the experience, there is what they call *kṣaya* of the tapasya. It is only long past experiences that they speak of and even that not too freely.

*

The Light left you because you spoke of it to someone who was not an *adhikārī*. It is safest not to speak of these experiences except to a guru or to one who can help you. The passing away of an experience as soon as it is spoken of is a frequent happening and for that reason many Yogis make it a rule never to speak of what happens within them unless it is a thing of the past or a settled realisation that nothing can take away. A settled permanent realisation abides, but these were rather things that come to make possible an opening in the consciousness to something more complete — to prepare it for realisation.

*

I thought it was understood that what I wrote to you about persons was private. Experiences one's own or others' if one comes to know of them, should not be talked about or made a matter of gossip. It is only if there can be some spiritual profit to others and even then if they are experiences of the past that one can speak of them. Otherwise it becomes like news of Abyssinia or Spain, something common and trivial for the vital mass-mind to chew or gobble.

*

To show what is written about experiences or to speak about one's experiences to others is always risky. They are much better kept to oneself.

*

I rather doubt whether it should be done.[1] There is a privacy about experiences which stands in the way of their being dealt with like that, at least until the sadhak has got into siddhi. They can be spoken of to a few, if one wishes, but to make public like that in a general way, even without names, is a little difficult. People besides might begin to speculate on these experiences, gossip and ask questions. What might be useful is some experiences with explanation, if the answer gives one, which would make clear certain sides of the sadhana. But they would have to be carefully chosen.

*

General knowledge is another matter, it is intellectual and the intellect gains by the intellectual activity of teaching. Also if in Yoga it were only a matter of imparting intellectually one's mental knowledge of the subject, that rule[2] would perhaps hold; but this mental aspect is only a small part of Yoga. There is something more complex which forms the bigger part of it. In teaching Yoga to another one becomes to some extent a master with disciples. The Yogis have always said that one who takes disciples, takes upon himself the difficulties of his disciples as well as one's own — that is why it is recommended not to take

---

[1] *The correspondent wished to compile a "Journal of Experiences" containing the letters of sadhaks who had written about their experiences to Sri Aurobindo and he had commented on them. This collection of letters would be kept in the Ashram library for sadhaks to read. — Ed.*
[2] *The rule that one understands something better by teaching it. — Ed.*

disciples unless and until one is siddha and even then only if one receives the Divine authority to do it — what Ramakrishna called getting the *cāprās*. Secondly, there is the danger of egoism — when one is free from that, then the objection no longer holds. There is a separate question and that is the telling of one's own experiences to others. That too is very much discouraged by most Yogis — they say it is harmful to the sadhana. I have certainly seen and heard of any number of instances in which people were having a flow of experiences and, when they told it, the flow was lost — so there must be something in this objection. I suppose however it ceases to apply after one has reached a certain long-established stability in the experience, that is to say, when the experience amounts to a definite and permanent realisation, something finally and irrevocably added to the consciousness. I notice that those who keep their experiences to themselves and do not put themselves out on others seem to have a more steady sadhana than others, but I don't know whether it is an invariable rule. It would probably not apply any longer after a certain stage of realisation.

*

It is true that experiences often disappear when spoken or written about to others. But that does not always happen, nor does it happen to everybody.

*

It is not good to talk too much to others about the sadhana and its experiences. There can be exceptions to the rule, but that depends on the person and circumstances.

*

If you want to keep the joy, it will be wise not to speak of it to others. Things spoken about get wings and try to escape.

The Difficulty of Keeping Experiences

The rush of the experience at the beginning is often very powerful, so powerful that the resisting elements remain quiescent —

afterwards they rise up. The experience has then to be brought down and settled in these parts also.

*

Yes, that is the truth of the working. At first what has to be established comes with difficulty and is felt as if abnormal, an experience that one loses easily — afterwards it comes of itself, but does not yet stay; finally it becomes a frequent and intimate state of the being and makes itself constant and normal. On the other hand all the confusions and errors once habitual to the nature are pushed out; at first they return frequently, but afterwards they in their turn become abnormal and foreign to the nature and lose frequency and finally disappear.

*

One can speak of a condition as coming freely and spontaneously when it comes of itself or as soon as it is remembered after an interruption. One can speak of it as coming at will, when it comes back at a slight pressure of the will and nothing more is necessary. Yours comes by an effort of the will which has to be sustained and is kept at the price of a constant vigilance. But this effort and vigilance are quite the right thing and must be done until the condition either becomes stable or comes automatically or at will, as described above. This is not pulling, so you need not hesitate to go on with it fully. It is the necessary tapasya.

What prevents it from remaining is the natural lapse to a lower consciousness which comes either from the mind's or vital's inclination to indulge in accustomed occupations or by sleep or by losing oneself in some outer action such as talking — because these things are associated with the ordinary mental consciousness and still need it to be done. At a later stage it will be possible to do these things with the surface mind only while the new consciousness remains intact and is either found there immediately as soon as the surface occupation ceases or else remains even during the occupation upholding the surface action or enveloping it as a small movement in itself.

*

All that you have written is quite correct; but the smallness is a general characteristic of the human instrument before it has the spiritual change. When the quietude comes, then the wideness also begins to come. The state you feel in which things go right, is the psychic and spiritual condition of the being; it is true that at first it is there only at times, but that is usual in the sadhana. All new states and realisations come like that at first; they are there for a short time, then seem to cease and other things come up from below and cover and hide the new condition. This is because of the habit of the past nature. But the true condition goes on returning till it and not the old things establishes itself as the habit and rule of a new nature.

The inward condition and its new outlook on things without the eagerness of the old consciousness in work is simply a passage through which you are going towards the new nature in which you will remain unmoved and undisturbed by things, but with a new and freer power of action which comes from within and from above.

*

It is more difficult at this stage for the experiences of Ananda (this felicity seems from your description to be an intense psychic Ananda) to be kept permanently than for peace to remain abidingly. The difficulty of keeping up these states in work or reading is more a matter of habit than anything else, because the mind is accustomed to absorb in the reading or work and forget all else for the time being. But once one gets the right poise and can keep in the inner being during work, that difficulty disappears.

Section Two

Vicissitudes on the Way to Realisation

Chapter One

Variations in the Intensity of Experience

The Up and Down Movement in Yoga

The up and down movement which you speak of is common to all ways of Yoga. It is there in the path of bhakti, but there are equally alternations of states of light and states of darkness, sometimes sheer and prolonged darkness, when one follows the path of knowledge. Those who have occult experiences come to periods when all experiences cease and even seem finished for ever. Even when there have been many and permanent realisations, these seem to go behind the veil and leave nothing in front except a dull blank, filled, if at all, only with recurrent attacks and difficulties. These alternations are the result of the nature of human consciousness and are not a proof of unfitness or of predestined failure. One has to be prepared for them and pass through. They are the "day and night" of the Vedic mystics.

As for surrender, everyone has his own first way of approach towards it; but if it is due to fear, "form" or sense of duty, then certainly that is not surrender at all; these things have nothing to do with surrender. Also, complete and total surrender is not so easy as some seem to imagine. There are always many and large reservations; even if one is not conscious of them, they are there. Complete surrender can best come by a complete love and bhakti. Bhakti on the other hand can begin without surrender, but it naturally leads, as it forms itself, to surrender.

You are surely mistaken in thinking that the difficulty of giving up intellectual convictions is a special stumbling-block in you more than in others. The attachment to one's own ideas and convictions, the insistence on them is a common characteristic and here it seems to manifest itself with an especial vehemence. It can be removed by a light of knowledge from above which gives one the direct touch of Truth or the luminous experience of it and takes away all value from mere intellectual opinion, ideas or conviction and removes the necessity for it, or by a right consciousness which brings with it right ideas, right feeling, right action and right everything else. Or else it must come by a spiritual and mental humility which is rare in human nature — especially the mental, for the mind is always apt to think its own ideas, true or false, are the right ideas. Eventually it is the psychic growth that makes this surrender too possible and that again comes most easily by bhakti. In any case, the existence of this difficulty is not in itself a good cause for forecasting failure in Yoga.

*

The rhythm of up and down is fairly general — it is only a few who keep an even course and even these have slight though comparatively rare drops of the consciousness. But the times vary — although it is true that it comes upon a few at the same time, and occasionally there is a massed general attack and shaking. It seems difficult as yet to eliminate these vicissitudes of the sadhana.

*

Everything once gained is there and can be regained. Yoga is not a thing that goes by one decisive rush one way or the other — it is a building up of a new consciousness and is full of ups and downs. But if one keeps to it the ups have a habit of resulting by accumulation in a decisive change — therefore the one thing to do is to keep at it. After a fall don't wail and say, "I'm done for," but get up, dust yourself and proceed farther on the right path.

*

After one has got to a certain stage the things gained are never lost — they may be covered over but they return — they have only gone inside and come back to the surface.

Alternations, Oscillations, Fluctuations of Consciousness

It is always like that — some days of experience, some days of no experience (or only experience of peace and quietude) alternating. It is only later on that the consciousness becomes capable of continuous experience and even then there are alternations of the level.

*

The reason why there are these alternations of which you complain is that the nature of the consciousness is like that; after a little spell of wakefulness it feels the need of a little sleep. Very often in the beginning the wakings are brief, the sleeps long; afterwards it becomes more equal and later on the sleep periods are shorter and shorter. Another cause of these alternations, when one is receiving, is the nature's need of closing up to assimilate. It can take perhaps a great deal, but while the experience is going on it cannot absorb properly what it brings, so it closes down for assimilation. A third cause comes in in the period of transformation, — one part of the nature changes and one feels for a time as if there had been a complete and permanent change. But one is disappointed to find it cease and a period of barrenness or lowered consciousness follows. This is because another part of the consciousness comes up for change and a period of preparation and veiled working follows which seems to be one of unenlightenment or worse. These things alarm, disappoint or perplex the eagerness and impatience of the sadhak; but if one takes them quietly and knows how to use them or adopt the right attitude, one can make these unenlightened periods also a part of the conscious sadhana. So the Vedic Rishis speak of the alternation of "Day and Night both suckling the divine Child".

*

Everyone has these alternations because the total consciousness is not able to remain always in the above experience [*of the higher force working powerfully*]. The point is that in the intervals there should be quietude, at least in the inner being, no restlessness, dissatisfaction or struggle. If that point is attained, then the sadhana can go on smoothly — not that there will be no difficulties, but there will be no disquietude or dissatisfaction etc. etc.

*

The impermanence of the better condition is a fairly general phenomenon. There is an oscillation always, a coming and going till the change that is trying to take place is strong enough to fix itself. This is due to two reasons, first the inability of the vital and physical to give up their old movements at once and accommodate themselves to the new and secondly to the habit of things hiding in the nature somewhere under the pressure from above and turning up as soon as they get an opportunity.

*

These slight oscillations always happen until everything is open. They are due to one of two causes, — either

(1) Some small part or movement of the being comes up which is not quite open and needs to have the Influence brought into it, or

(2) A shadow is thrown by the outside force, bringing back, not the old disturbance, but some temporary obscuration or appearance of obscuration.

Do not be disturbed, but immediately become quite quiet and open yourself.

The important thing is not to allow the old strong disturbance and confusion to come back and, secondly, not to allow a long obscuration, even if the obscuration be without a serious disturbance. To keep hold on quiet persistently will prevent the serious disturbance; to keep quiet and steadily open yourself will prevent any long obscuration.

*

These oscillations [*of consciousness*] always come. The universal lower Nature tries to come back and resume its hold — the lower vital or the physical consciousness responds, not always because

Variations in the Intensity of Experience   61

it wants or likes to do so but because the old habit of response is still so strong that it cannot help it.

The first necessity is to detach yourself, not to regard it as your own, to learn to feel it as something foreign and refuse to be touched or upset. Then it will become easier for the lower vital or physical itself to reject and refuse to admit it.

*

These fluctuations in the force of the aspiration and the power of the sadhana are unavoidable and common to all sadhaks until the whole being has been made ready for the transformation. When the psychic is in front or active and the mind and vital consent, then there is the intensity. When the psychic is less prominent and the lower vital has its ordinary movements or the mind its ignorant action, then the opposing forces can come in unless the sadhak is very vigilant. Inertia comes usually from the ordinary physical consciousness, especially when the vital is not actively supporting the sadhana. These things can only be cured by a persistent bringing down of the higher spiritual consciousness into all the parts of the being.

*

These fluctuations always take place. By insistence and practice it becomes finally possible to keep the aspiration and the open consciousness above continuously, but even then periods of active progress and periods of assimilation alternate.

*

Fluctuations of this kind cannot but come and when they come, one has to remain very quiet and detach oneself from the surface condition and wait for it to pass while calling the Mother's Force. A neutral condition of this kind serves a certain purpose in the economy of the purification and change — it brings up things that have to be transformed or rejected, lifts up some part of the being in order to expose it to the transforming force. If one can understand, remain quiet and detached from the surface movements, not identified, then it goes sooner, the Force can quickly clear out what rises and afterwards it is found that something has been gained and a progress made.

*

Yes, indeed, to keep the fixed consciousness of the soul, even when there are fluctuations in the outer nature, is a great victory. If one can do that, it means that the capacity to arrive is there fixed in the being and only the firm will is needed for the entire certitude.

Fluctuations in the Working of the Force

There are no fixed rules [*about fluctuations in the working of the Force*]. There are simply a mass of tendencies and forces with which one has to become familiar. It is not a fixed machinery which one can manage by devices or by pulling this or that button. It is only by the inner Will, the constant aspiration, by detachment and rejection, by bringing down the true consciousness, force etc. that it can be done.

*

I can only say as before, that there is no specific reason [*for fluctuations in the working of the Force*] which the mind can determine. It depends on the total condition and interaction of the forces. One has to hold on to the aspiration and look steadily towards the goal without being disturbed by these inequalities and fluctuations.

*

I don't know.[1] Times and seasons vary according to the poise and flux and reflux of the forces in the consciousness. It is not a thing to which you can affix a rationalised and systematised explanation. One can feel it and understand in the essence of the consciousness, but not formulate precise cause and effect.

---

[1] *The correspondent asked why he felt an emptiness in the morning, a suspension of sadhana. — Ed.*

Lulls, Pauses, Interim Periods

There are always lulls of this kind. One must not get upset — otherwise they are prolonged and disturbances come in. One must remain quiet, aspire steadily but without vehemence or, if one presses for a change, then too with a quiet steady pressure.

*

There are always periods when all one can do is to remain quiet and aspire. A continuous activity of the light and power is only possible when the whole being has been prepared and the psychic is constantly in front.

*

Everyone has periods when the consciousness is covered up. One has to go on in spite of that, and if you persist in aspiration and keep turned to the Mother, then these periods will diminish and the consciousness more and more open to her.

At such periods instead of allowing these things to hold you, you should separate yourself from them and regard them as something foreign which you have to reject.

*

There are always long periods of this kind at the beginning when the first openings of experience are covered up by the restless mind and vital; but with perseverance they diminish — the experience always returns and takes up more and more of the consciousness till it becomes its normal state.

*

There are always pauses of preparation and assimilation between two movements. You must not regard these with fretfulness or impatience as if they were untoward gaps in the sadhana. Besides, the Force rises up lifting part of the nature on a higher level and then comes down to a lower layer to raise it; this motion of ascent and descent is often extremely trying because the mind partial to an ascent in a straight line and the vital eager for rapid fulfilment cannot understand or follow this intricate movement and are apt to be distressed by it or resent it. But the transformation of the whole nature is not an easy thing to accomplish and the Force that does it knows better than our mental ignorance or our vital impatience.

*

There is nothing wrong in having intervals of passive peace without anything happening — they come naturally in the sadhana as a basis for fresh action when the nature is ready for it. It is only the vital attitude that turns it into a disharmony, because somewhere in its being there is not the assent to or participation in the peace and passivity. To be able often to rest, repose in all the being outspread in the silent Brahman is an indispensable thing for the Yogi. But the vital wants always fuss, action, to feel that it is somebody doing something, getting on, having progress, on the move. The counterpart to this rajasic fuss is inertia. If the whole being can widen itself out, rest satisfied in the silence, then progressively inertia fades out and gives place to *śama*.

*

In the interim periods, if any come, to maintain the calm observing consciousness is the one great necessity.

    The dynamic activity of the higher consciousness may be suspended but once manifested its presence is always there.

*

They [*certain experiences*] are first indications of an opening — but the opening has to be stabilised and enlarged. Also so long as the external mind is very much on the top they come at intervals only. Continuous experience is only possible when one gets inside and stays there.

*

There are always variations in the intensity of experience, due to the necessity of assimilation in the consciousness. It is only at a much later stage that the consciousness remains always at its highest level.

*

These variations are inevitable. They go on until three things are sufficiently and unfluctuatingly established: (1) A fixed peace and gladness. (2) A clear light and understanding. (3) A complete selfless love and surrender.

Drops or Falls of Consciousness

These drops [*of consciousness*] happen to all sadhaks; their causes are various; sometimes it is a pull from below, sometimes an invasion from outside, sometimes a less ascertainable cause. When it happens, one must always remain as quiet as possible behind and call back the better condition.

*

A drop of consciousness need not be so serious or take as long a time to repair. A few hours or, if there is much disturbance or mental obstruction, a few days should be sufficient to recover. Sometimes it takes longer if the sadhak continues to be too troubled or agitated or otherwise stands in his own way by dwelling too much on the obstacle. But years are taken only when there is, not a mere dropping of the consciousness, but a strong fall of the whole nature from the path or other very serious accident etc. There is nothing of this kind here or anything that could cause it.

*

You must have allowed the consciousness to fall — there may have been some tamasic movement or it may merely be the habit of oscillation between the two conditions [*obscure and luminous*] that still persists.

The speedy removal of the difficulties depends on the continuance of the experiences. Otherwise the consciousness oscillates between the higher and the lower condition — which does not prevent the ultimate liberation, but does cause delay.

*

Yes — if the peace is established, then the falls [*of consciousness*] are only on the surface and do not affect the inner consciousness.

*

Fall of the concentration happens to everybody — it has not to be taken as if it were something tragic or allowed to be the cause of depression.

Fatigue, Inertia and Lowering of the Consciousness

The falling down [*of the consciousness*] comes usually by some inertia coming in the consciousness through fatigue or through mere habit of relaxation or it comes through some vital reaction which one may or may not notice or it comes through a wrong movement of the mind. These are the positive lowering causes, but at the back of them is the fact that these alternations are almost inevitable so long as the consciousness is in any way subject to the old nature. The intervals of non-sadhana may however be long or short according to inner circumstances (mainly the power of the will or the psychic or the higher being to restore quickly the true poise).

*

An occasional sinking of the consciousness happens to everybody. The causes are various, some touch from outside, something not yet changed or not sufficiently changed in the vital, especially the lower vital, some inertia or obscurity rising up from the physical parts of nature. When it comes, remain quiet, open yourself to the Mother and call back the true condition, and aspire for a clear and undisturbed discrimination showing you from within yourself the cause or the thing that needs to be set right.

*

Yes, the ordinary physical consciousness is not able to hold the contact and it does get tired — also it cannot assimilate much at a time. But it is not always the Divine who takes away the pressure; the lower consciousness itself loses it or gives it up.

*

An always intense aspiration, an unswerving and unwavering will turned to the one thing only, help to get through the difficulties without discouragement or falling into depression — they give an impetus for a rapid development. But the difficulties come all the same because they are inherent in human nature. Even the best sadhaks have these periods of suspension of the sadhana, of nothing happening, of the absence of the urge of the inner being. It is when some difficulty arises in the physical nature that has to be dealt with or when a pause has to be made for a veiled preparation, or for some similar reason. Even when the working of the sadhana is in the mind or vital which are more plastic such periods are frequent — when the physical is concerned they must necessarily come and are usually marked not so much by any apparent struggle but by an immobility and an inertia of the energies that were at work before. This is very troublesome to the mind because it suggests entire cessation, incapacity to progess or unfitness. But it is not really so. One must be quiet and go on opening oneself to the working or keeping the will to do so — afterwards there will be a greater progress. Many sadhaks indulge in such a period a spirit of despondency and loss of faith in the future which delays the renewal, but this should be avoided.

*

It is difficult to say [*why the veiling of consciousness persists*] — usually it is when something in the mind and vital accepts and indulges the lower forces that this inability to re-enter the true consciousness remains so obstinate. Physical tamas can produce long interregnums of obscure consciousness, but not usually with such a violent obstruction — usually only dull and obstinate.

*

The depression is not the only cause of suspension of experiences. There are others such as inertia etc. If one can have experiences continuously in spite of these things, that means that a part of the consciousness has definitely separated from the rest and is able to go on in spite of the outer resistance.

*

Even if there is physical fatigue sometimes it is not inevitable that it should interfere with the sadhana. The inner movement can always go on.

*

When the physical consciousness prevails, often one does not feel any sign or effect [*of inner or higher experiences*] even if they are there.

*

How do you expect anything so obtuse and forgetful as the physical consciousness to have the effect if the experiences are not repeated? It is as when you learn a lesson, you have to repeat it till the physical mind gets hold of it — otherwise it does not become a part of consciousness.

Variations during the Day

It happens to most sadhaks that in particular parts of the day they feel concentrated and get results, and in others that condition is not there. This is especially in the earlier stages of the progress. It is only after the higher consciousness, peace etc. have settled in the being that one can usually be at all times in the active condition of sadhana.

*

It is often like that — the period of intense activity is limited to a particular part of the day and then the rest of the time there is a lull.

*

It is quite usual to have such periods in the day. The consciousness needs time for rest and assimilation, it cannot be at the same pitch of intensity at all times. During the assimilation a calm quietude is the proper condition.

*

These variations in the consciousness during the day are a thing that is common to almost everybody in the sadhana. The principle of constant oscillation, relaxation, relapse to a normal or a past lower condition from a higher state that is experienced but not yet fixed in realisation or else realised but not yet perfectly stable, becomes very strong and marked when the working of the sadhana is in the physical consciousness. For there is an inertia in the physical nature that does not easily allow the intensity natural to the higher consciousness to remain constant, — the physical is always sinking back to something more ordinary; the higher consciousness and its force have to work long and come again and again before they can become constant and normal in the physical nature. Do not be disturbed or discouraged by these variations or this delay, however long and tedious; remain careful only to be quiet always with an inner quietude and as open as possible to the higher Power, not allowing any really adverse condition to get hold of you. If there is no adverse wave, then the rest is only a persistence of imperfections which all have in abundance; that imperfection and persistence the Force must work out and eliminate, but for the elimination time is needed.

*

There is no mentally definite and rigidly effective reason for the thing [*a fall into inertia*] coming in the evening rather than at 2 p.m. or in the midnight or in the morning. For some people the fall comes in the evening, for some in the morning, for some at other times, and so too with the rise. But the alternations happen to most people in one kind of rhythm or another. The times vary with people and even can vary with the same men. There is no definable reason for it being at a particular time except that it has made itself habitual at that time. The rest is a question of the play of forces which is observable but the reasons of which escape mental definition.

*

That is a frequent experience (though I suppose it is not general) — not only with peace, but other things; there is a tendency towards a lowering of the consciousness in the evening. On the other hand with some it is the opposite. I don't know that it actually depends on work and mixing, though these may have a wearing effect — I find more often that it is a sort of rhythm of rise and fall in the consciousness during the day. Even when peace is perfectly established, there may be this rhythm for other things that are being developed.

The Need for Periods of Assimilation

Intensities like that do not remain so long as the consciousness is not transformed — there has to be a period of assimilation. When the being is unconscious, the assimilation goes on behind the veil or below the surface and meanwhile the surface consciousness sees only dullness and loss of what it had got; but when one is conscious, then one can see the assimilation going on and one sees that nothing is lost, it is only a quiet settling in of what has come down.

*

Yes — the system has to take rest so as to assimilate and renew its receptive power.

*

When one is assimilating, one is not receiving.

*

The periods of assimilation continue really till all that has to be done is fundamentally done. Only they have a different character in the later stages of sadhana. If they cease altogether at an early stage (you are still in a very early stage), it is because all the nature was capable of has been done and that would mean it was not capable of much.

*

What I have written is perfectly clear. The periods of assimilation continue till all that has to be done is fundamentally done. If they stop early, it means that all has been done that could be done and nothing more is possible, the later and more advanced developments of the sadhana are not possible, — if they were, the assimilation periods would continue until all was developed and not cease. The only reason for such a premature end of the sadhana would be that the sadhaka is not capable of going farther.

*

The only change in the assimilation periods afterwards is that certain things remain settled while the assimilation applies to others that are not yet settled in the system. E.g. one feels always a constant peace in the inner being, but disturbances go on on the surface, till the surface also has assimilated peace. Or perhaps peace is settled everywhere and always there but knowledge comes and goes or strength comes and goes. Or all these are there but Ananda comes and goes etc. etc.

*

There is always a gain or progress at some point after these periods of assimilation if one takes them rightly — however dull or troublesome they may be.

*

If your faith is getting firmer day by day, you are certainly progressing in your sadhana and there can have been no fall. An interruption of definite experiences may be only a period of assimilation in which one prepares for a new range of experience. Keep yourself open and aspire.

Chapter Two
Emptiness, Voidness, Blankness and Silence

Periods of Emptiness

If it is only emptiness, there is nothing wrong. Alternations of emptiness and fullness are a quite normal feature of experience in sadhana.

*

Emptiness usually comes as a clearance of the consciousness or some part of it. The consciousness or part becomes like an empty cup into which something new can be poured. The highest emptiness is the pure existence of the Self in which all manifestation can take place.

*

To be an empty vessel is a very good thing if one knows how to make use of the emptiness.

*

Keep the quiet and do not mind if it is for a time empty; the consciousness at times is like a vessel which has to be emptied of its mixed and undesirable contents; it has to be kept vacant for a while till it can be filled with the right contents. The one thing to be avoided is the refilling of the cup with the old contents. Meanwhile wait, open yourself upwards, call very quietly and steadily, not with a too restless eagerness for the peace to come into the silence and, once the peace is there, for the joy and the presence.

*

You have written of the Force coming down [*during a period of emptiness*] — even sometimes of its filling all parts — so what is this "never"? I did not at all mean that there is a mechanical process by which every time there is emptiness afterwards there comes an entire filling up. It depends on the stage of the sadhana. The emptiness may come often or stay long before there is any descent — what fills may be silence and peace or Force or Knowledge and they may fill only the mind or mind and heart or mind and heart and vital or all. But there is nothing fixed and mechanically regular about these two processes.

*

Usually such feelings of emptiness [*in the body*] come when the identification with the body is lessening and the consciousness is preparing to take its seat either above or in a cosmic wideness or in some beginning of that wideness.

*

An emptiness in the mind or vital may be spiritual without emptiness being an essential characteristic of the higher consciousness. If it were, there could be no Force, Light or Ananda in the higher consciousness. Emptiness is only a result produced by a certain action of the higher Force on the system in order that the higher consciousness may be able to come into it. It is a spiritual emptiness as opposed to the dull and inert emptiness of complete tamas which is not spiritual.

*

If it is the spiritual emptiness then it will not be felt as interfering with the sadhana.

*

If it is real emptiness, one can last in it for years together, — it is because the vital is restless and full of desires (not empty) that it is like that [*difficult to remain empty*]. Also the physical mind is by no means at rest. If the desires were thrown out and the ego less active and the physical mind at rest knowledge would come from above; in place of the physical mind's stupidities, the vital mind could be calm and quiet and the Mother's Force take up the action and the higher consciousness begin to come down. That is the proper sequel of emptiness. But nothing of this has happened because the "emptiness" could not complete itself, that is to say, the true silence and peace.

Emptiness — A Transitional State

The emptiness that you described in your letter yesterday was not a bad thing — it is this emptiness inward and outward that often in Yoga becomes the first step towards a new consciousness. Man's nature is like a cup of dirty water — the water has to be thrown out, the cup left clean and empty for the divine liquor to be poured into it. The difficulty is that the human physical consciousness feels it difficult to bear this emptiness — it is accustomed to be occupied by all sorts of little mental and vital movements which keep it interested and amused or even if in trouble and sorrow still active. The cessation of these things is hard to bear for it. It begins to feel dull and restless and eager for the old interests and movements. But by this restlessness it disturbs the quietude and brings back the things that had been thrown out. It is this that is creating the difficulty and the obstruction for the moment. If you can accept emptiness as a passage to the true consciousness and true movements, then it will be easier to get rid of the obstacle.

All in the Asram are not suffering from the sense of dullness and want of interest, but many are because the Force that is descending is discouraging the old movements of the physical and vital mind which they call life and they are not accustomed to accept the renunciation of these things, or to admit the peace or joy of silence.

*

There is a certain truth in what you say about the empty cup — a certain emptying of the consciousness of old things is necessary before anything positive can settle itself. It is what is happening in your physical consciousness, the old movements are being emptied out and you fall quiet, but they press in again and the cup has to be repeatedly emptied. If there is a firm and persistent rejection, then this repeated return of these old movements will cease to be so persistent; the periods of quiet and its intensity will increase until the peace and quietude can be established and permanent.

It is not however a fact that the whole nature has to be emptied of the old things before there can be the Light and Grace. It is done usually in different parts of the nature at different times. You had your former experiences because the mind and higher vital were sufficiently emptied and quiet to receive some experiences of a new consciousness. Now it is the physical mind, physical vital and body that have to be emptied — these always take longer than the others because the physical is more full of old habits, more obstinate in keeping and always repeating them, more slow to receive anything new or to change. But by the detachment and steady rejection and reliance on the Mother's force, this obstinacy can be overcome and the cup emptied for filling with the Divine Light.

*

There is nothing out of the normal in what you describe — it happens in the course of the change of consciousness. What has to be remedied is that you feel the stillness, emptiness, but seem to have no joy of it or the satisfied peace of the self or sense of wideness or quiet release and freedom. Usually the cessation of the lower activities brings a sense of freedom, release, repose. The inner consciousness does not miss the mental jumpings or the vital swirl — it feels as if the silence were its native element.

*

Emptiness is not in itself a bad condition, only if it is a sad and restless emptiness of the dissatisfied vital. In sadhana emptiness is very usually a necessary transition from one state to another. When mind and vital fall quiet and their restless movements, thoughts and desires cease, then one feels empty. This is at first often a neutral emptiness with nothing in it, nothing in it either good or bad, happy or unhappy, no impulse or movement. This neutral state is often or even usually followed by the opening to inner experience. There is also an emptiness made of peace and silence, when the peace and silence come out from the psychic within or descend from the higher consciousness above. This is not neutral, for in it there is the sense of peace, often also of wideness and freedom. There is also a happy emptiness with the sense of something close or drawing near which is not yet there, e.g. the closeness of the Mother or some other preparing experience. What you describe is the neutral quiet. There is no need for anxiety. When it comes, one has only to remain quiet and open and turned to the Mother till something develops from within.

*

What you describe is the same neutral condition that you had before. It is a transitional state in which the old consciousness has ceased to be active, the new is preparing behind a neutral quietude. One must take it quietly and wait for it to turn into the spiritual peace and the psychic happiness which is quite different from vital joy and grief. To have neither vital joy nor vital grief is considered by the Yogins to be a very desirable release, — it makes it possible to pass from the ordinary human vital feelings to the true and constant inner peace, joy or happiness. I suppose you have no time just now for sitting in meditation. The pressure of sleep is a pressure to go inside and the habit of meditation makes it possible to turn the sleep that comes into a kind of sleep-samadhi in which one is conscious of various experiences and progresses in the inner being.

*

If you mean that after this kind of samadhi [*during the afternoon rest*], you feel a greater emptiness or voidness, it is quite natural. To void the being of the old consciousness and its movements and to fill the mind from above are the two main processes now by the Force from above.

*

When you feel empty like that, you have only to remain very still and open yourself to receive the Light and Force. Emptiness is a bad condition only when it is dull or when you receive into it wrong movements. But often one has to be empty in order to receive what is to be given.

*

In itself this emptiness and quietude free from all anxiety or trouble or thought about people or things is not a bad sign or an undesirable state. It is a state of what the Yogis call *udāsīnatā*, a separateness from all things and indifference, an untroubled neutral quietude. In many Yogas it is considered a very advanced and desirable condition — a state of liberation from the world, though not yet of realisation of the Divine, — but they consider it a necessary passage to the realisation. In our Yoga it is only a passage through which one arrives at a more positive spiritual calm consciousness in which all experiences and all realisations become possible. The feeling of dullness is due probably not to this state which is in itself a condition of ease and release, but to the depressed condition of the bodily health and strength. That also is probably the cause why the more positive state does not come quickly. The forgetfulness you speak of comes sometimes in the period of change, but passes away afterwards; a new force of memory comes.

Voidness

The voidness is the best condition for a full receptivity.

*

The voidness (if by that you mean silence and emptiness of thoughts, movements etc.) is the basic condition into which the higher consciousness can flow.

*

The usual result of voidness is to quiet down any vital tumult although it does not, unless it is complete, stop the mechanical recurrent action of the mind.

*

Yes, it becomes like that.[1] In the end you feel as if you had no body, but were spread out in the vastness of space as an infinite consciousness and existence — or as if the body were only a dot in that consciousness.

*

There is no reason why the void should be a dull or unhappy condition. It is usually the habit of the mind and vital to associate happiness or interest only with activity, but the spiritual consciousness has no such limitations.

*

Voidness can come from anywhere, mind, vital or from above.

*

Voidness may be of different kinds — a certain kind of spiritual voidness or the emptiness that is a preparation for new experience. But an exhaustion of life energy is a very different thing. It may arise from fatigue, from somebody or something drawing away the vital force or from an invasion of tamas.

Blankness

In the course of the sadhana a state of blankness, of "neutral quiet" like this often comes — especially when the sadhana is in the physical consciousness. It is not that the aspiration is gone, but that it does not manifest for the time being, because all has become neutrally quiet. This condition is trying for the human mind and vital which are accustomed to be in some kind of activity always and regard this as a lifeless state. But one must not feel disturbed or disappointed when this comes, but remain calm in the full confidence that it is a stage only, a ground that

---

[1] *The correspondent wrote that in the state of voidness his body felt as light as cotton.* — Ed.

has to be crossed in the sadhana. In whatever condition, the faith and the fixed idea of surrender must be kept before the mind. As for the brief movements of restlessness, they will still down if this is kept and the quiet mind and vital reassert themselves quickly.

*

The physical does not get tired of the blankness. It may feel tamasic because of its own tendency to inertia, but it does not usually object to voidness. Of course it may be the vital physical — you have only to reject it as a remnant of the old movements.

*

Blankness is only a condition in which realisation has to come. If aspiration is needed for that, it has to be used; if the realisation comes of itself, then of course aspiration is not necessary.

Emptiness, Blankness and Silence

Silence of the being is the first natural aim of the Yoga. You and some others do not find satisfaction in it because you have not overcome the vital mind which wants always some kind of activity, change, doing something, making something happen. The eternal immobility of the silent Brahman is a thing it does not relish. So when emptiness comes, it finds it dull, inert, monotonous.

*

I do not quite gather what is the nature of this silence and this heat which makes you feel like that. An inner silence is a condition favourable to the sadhana even if for a time it means the cessation of all activity within, all thoughts, emotions or mental perceptions. But it is possible and it does happen that the unaccustomed physical consciousness feels the silence to be dull and a deprivation of intelligence rather than a release and repose, and the strangeness of this inactive condition causes it apprehension and an alarmed perplexity. As for the heat that also may be troublesome and difficult to bear to the physical consciousness because it is unaccustomed and gets alarmed and troubled. If it is that we must try to slow down and diminish the intensity of the force that is acting.

But in any case try to dismiss any alarm that may be suggested to you and keep the faith which you express in the last part of the letter.

*

I cannot have written that it is only you who feel the silence as empty, as there are plenty who do so feel it at first. One feels it empty because one is accustomed to associate existence with thought, feeling and movement or with forms and objects, and there are none of these there. But it is not really empty.

*

Certainly, the vital cannot take an interest in a blank condition. If you depend on your vital you cannot prolong it. It is the spirit that feels a release in the silence empty of all mental or other activities, for in that silence it becomes self-aware. For the blankness to be real one must have got into the Purusha or Witness consciousness. If you are looking at it with your mind or vital, then there is not blankness, — for even if there are no distinct thoughts then there must be a mental attitude or mental vibrations — e.g. the not feeling interest.

*

The silence can remain when the blankness has gone. All sorts of things can pour in and yet the silence still remains, but if you become full of force, light, Ananda, knowledge etc. you can't call yourself blank any longer.

*

Every kind of realisation — infinite self, cosmic consciousness, the Mother's Presence, Light, Force, Ananda, Knowledge, Sachchidananda realisation, the different layers of consciousness up to the Supermind — all these can come in the silence which remains but ceases to be blank.

*

The emptiness, silence and peace are the basic condition for the spiritual siddhi — it is the first step towards it. It enables the Purusha to be free from the movements of Prakriti, to see and know where they come from since they no longer rise from within the mind, heart etc., these being in a state of quietude, and to reject the lower movements and to call in the knowledge, will etc. of the higher Consciousness which is above.

Emptiness, Voidness and the Self

Emptiness is a state of quietude of the mental or vital or all the consciousness not visited by any mind or vital movements, but open to the Pure Existence and ready or tending to be that or already that but not yet realised in its full power of being. Which of these conditions it happens to be depends on the particular case. The Self state or the state of pure Existence is sometimes also called emptiness, but only in the sense that it is a state of sheer static rest of being without any contacts of mobile Nature.

*

Emptiness as such is not a character of the higher consciousness, though it often looks like that to the human vital when one has the pure realisation of the Self, because all is immobile, and for the vital all that is not full of action appears empty. But the emptiness that comes to the mind, vital or physical is a special thing intended to clear the room for the things from above.

*

The void is the condition of the Self — free, wide and silent. It seems void to the mind, but in reality is simply a state of pure existence and consciousness, Sat and Chit with Shanti.

*

There is no such thing as *néant*. By "void" is meant emptiness clear of all contents except existence pure and simple. Without that one cannot realise the silent Brahman.

Part Two

The Opening of the Inner Senses

Section One

Visions, Sounds, Smells and Tastes

Chapter One
The Value of Visions

Vision, Experience and Realisation

When you see Light, that is vision; when you feel Light entering into you, that is experience; when Light settles in you and brings illumination and knowledge, that is a realisation. But ordinarily visions are also called experiences.

*

Sometimes a vision accompanies an experience and is as it were a visual rendering of it or accompaniment to it, but the experience itself is a separate thing.

*

Vision is something *seen* in the conscious state (whether with closed or open eyes) which is not of the physical plane. In "conscious state" I include the consciousness of Samadhi when one is unaware of outward things but conscious of things going on within.
    Experience is a wide term which covers almost everything that happens in the inner consciousness — usually it indicates either a spiritual happening, e.g. the descent of peace, the feeling of the presence of the Mother, or an occult experience, e.g. a going into the other worlds in dream and seeing and doing things there. There are thousands of different kinds of experience. Visions are a special kind of experience in which the inner eye is active.

*

Visions do not come from the spiritual plane — they come from the subtle physical, the vital, the mental, the psychic or from planes above the Mind. What comes from the spiritual planes are experiences of the Divine, e.g. the experience of self everywhere, of the Divine in all etc.

*

The Infinite is in all things and can be seen through them when the vision opens.

*

By going deep [*in meditation*] one person may see visions; another may fall in deeper consciousness but see no vision — and so on. The result varies with the nature.

*

Yes, it [*the higher consciousness*] can come down into the mind planes bringing peace, wideness, the cosmic consciousness, the realisation of the Divine, the sense of the cosmic forces and other things — without any breaking of the veil through vision. Ordinarily, however, with most people the inner vision comes first.

*

I said [*in the preceding letter*] the realisation of the Divine in the mind. If there is to be the total realisation, the breaking of the veil is indispensable.

*

Usually the visions precede realisation, in a way they prepare it.

*

Visions and voices have their place when they are the genuine visions and the true voices. Naturally, they are not the realisation but only a step on the way and one has not to get shut up in them or take all as of value.

*

The vision of the higher planes or the idea of what they are can be had long before the transformation. If that were not possible, how could the transformation take place — the lower nature cannot change of itself, it changes by the growing vision, perception, descent of the higher consciousness belonging to the higher planes? It is through aspiration, through an increasing opening that these visions and perceptions begin to come — the realisation comes afterwards.

Sensing Supraphysical Things

No, it was neither optical illusion nor hallucination nor coincidence nor auto-suggestion nor any of the other ponderous and vacant polysyllables by which physical science tries to explain away or rather avoid explaining the scientifically inexplicable. In these matters the scientist is always doing what he is always blaming the layman for doing when the latter lays down the law on things about which he is profoundly ignorant, without investigation or experiment, without ascertained knowledge — simply by evolving a theory or *a priori* idea out of his own mind and plastering it as a label on the unexplained phenomena.

There is, as I have told you, a whole range or many inexhaustible ranges of sensory phenomena other than the outward physical which one can become conscious of, see, hear, feel, smell, touch, mentally contact — to use the new established Americanism — either in trance or sleep or an inward state miscalled sleep or simply and easily in the waking state. This faculty of sensing supraphysical things internally or externalising them, so to speak, so that they become visible, audible, sensible to the outward eye, ear, even touch, just as are gross physical objects, this power or gift is not a freak or an abnormality; it is a universal faculty present in all human beings, but latent in most, in some rarely or intermittently active, occurring as if by accident in others, frequent or normally active in a few. But just as anyone can with some training learn science and do things which would have seemed miracles to his forefathers, so almost anyone, if he wants, can with a little concentration and training develop the faculty of supraphysical vision. When one starts Yoga, this power is often though not invariably — for some find it difficult — one of the first to come out from its latent condition and manifest itself, most often without any effort, intention or previous knowledge on the part of the sadhak. It comes more easily with the eyes shut than with the eyes open, but it does come in both ways. The first sign of its opening in the externalised way is very often that seeing of "sparkles" or small luminous dots, shapes etc. which was your first introduction to the matter; a second is, often enough, the seeing of circles of light or colour round objects, most easily round luminous objects like a star; seeing of colours is a third initial experience — but they do not always come in that order. The Yogis in India very often in order to develop the power use the method of *trāṭak*, concentrating the vision on a single point or object — preferably a luminous object. Your looking at the star was precisely an exercise in *trāṭak* and had the effect which any Yogi in India would have told you is normal. For all this is not fancy or delusion; it is part of an occult science which has been practised throughout the historic and prehistoric ages in all countries and it has always been known to be not merely auto-suggestive or hallucinatory in its results, but, if one can get the key, veridical and verifiable. Your first scepticism may be natural in a "modern" man plunging into these lasting things of the past, present and future, — natural but not justifiable because very obviously inadequate to the facts observed; but once you have seen, the first thing you should do is to throw all this vapid pseudo-science behind you, this vain attempt to stick physical explanations on supraphysical things, and take the only rational course. Develop the power, get more and more experience — develop the consciousness by which these things come: as the consciousness develops, you will begin to understand and get the intuition of the significances. Or if you want their science too, then learn and apply the occult science which can alone deal with supraphysical phenomena. As for what showed itself to you, it was not mere curious phenomena, not even merely symbolic colours, but things that have a considerable importance.

    Develop this power of inner sense and all that it brings you. These first seeings are only an outer fringe — behind lie whole worlds of experience which fill what seems to the material man the gap (your Russell's inner void) between the earth-consciousness and the Eternal and Infinite.

The Importance of Visions

All visions have a significance of one kind or another. This power of vision is very important for the Yoga and should not be rejected although it is not the most important thing — for the most important thing is the change of the consciousness. All other powers like this of vision should be developed without attachment as parts and aids of the Yoga.

*

The particular things seen may be of no importance, but the power of seeing is of importance and can be of great help in the Yoga. It enables you to see things belonging to other planes (other than the physical) and get knowledge that is useful for sadhana — also to have concrete contact with the Mother in those planes (mental, vital, psychic worlds) etc.

*

Visions come from all planes and are of all kinds and different values. Some are of very great value and importance, others are a play of the mind or vital and are good only for their own special purpose, others are formations of the mind and vital plane, some of which may have truth, while others are false and misleading, or they may be a sort of artistry of that plane. They can have considerable importance in the development of the first Yogic consciousness, that of the inner mind, inner vital, inner physical or for an occult understanding of the universe. Visions which are real can help the spiritual progress, I mean, those which show us inner realities: one can for instance meet Krishna, speak with him and hear his voice in an inner "real" vision, quite as real as anything on the outer plane. Merely seeing his image is not the same thing, any more than seeing his picture on the wall is the same thing as meeting him in person. But the picture on the wall need not be useless for the spiritual life. All one can say is that one must not attach oneself too much to this gift and what it shows us, but neither is it necessary to belittle it. It has its value and sometimes a considerable spiritual utility. But, naturally, it is not supreme, — the supreme thing is the realisation, the contact, the union with the Divine, bhakti, change of the nature etc.

*

Visions and experiences (especially experiences) are all right; but you cannot expect every vision to translate itself in a corresponding physical fact. Some do, the majority don't, others belong to the supraphysical entirely and indicate realities, possibilities or tendencies that have their seat there. How far these will influence the life or realise themselves in it or whether they will do so at all depends upon the nature of the vision, the power in it, sometimes on the will or formative power of the seer.

People value visions for one thing because they are one key (there are others) to contact with the other worlds or with the inner worlds and all that is there and these are regions of immense riches which far surpass the physical plane as it is at present. One enters into a larger freer self and a larger more plastic world; of course individual visions only give a contact, not an actual entrance, but the power of vision accompanied with the power of the other subtle senses (hearing, touch, etc.) as it expands does give this entrance. These things have not the effect of a mere imagination (as a poet's or artist's, though that can be strong enough) but if fully followed out bring a constant growth of the being and the consciousness and its richness of experience and its scope.

People also value the power of vision for a greater reason than that: it can give a first contact with the Divine in his forms and powers; it can be the opening of a communion with the Divine, of the hearing of the Voice that guides, of the Presence as well as the Image in the heart, of many other things that bring what man seeks through religion or Yoga.

Farther, vision is of value because it is often a first key to inner planes of one's own being and one's own consciousness as distinguished from worlds or planes of the cosmic consciousness.

The Value of Visions

Yoga experience often begins with some opening of the third eye in the forehead (the centre of vision in the brows) or with some kind of beginning and extension of subtle seeing which may seem unimportant at first, but is the vestibule to deeper experience. Even when it is not that, — for one can go to experience direct, — it can come in afterwards as a powerful aid to experience; it can be full of indications which help to self-knowledge or knowledge of things or knowledge of people; it can be veridical and lead to prevision, premonition and other openings of less importance but very useful to a Yogi.

In short, vision is a great instrument though not absolutely indispensable.

But, as I have suggested, there are visions and visions just as there are dreams and dreams, and one has to develop discrimination and a sense of values and kinds and know how to understand and make use of these powers. But that is too big and intricate a matter to be pursued now.

*

The visions he has between the eyebrows are not imaginations — they could be so only if he thought them first and his thoughts took shape, but as they came independent of his thoughts, they are not visual imagination but vision. This faculty is a useful one in Yoga and it can be allowed to develop; it should not be discouraged. I do not know what he means by not having *śraddhā* in them. What he sees now are probably only images of subtle (*sūkṣma*) scenes and objects; but, when developed, this can become a power of symbolic, representative or real vision, showing the truths of things or realities of this or other worlds or representations of the past, present or future.

If the concentration goes naturally to the centre between the eyebrows which is the centre of inner mind and its thought, will and vision, there is no harm in that.

*

These lights and visions are not hallucinations. They indicate an opening of the inner vision whose centre is in the forehead between the eyebrows. Lights are very often the first thing seen. Lights indicate the action or movement of subtle forces belonging to the different planes of being, — the nature of the force depending on the colour and shade of the light. The sun is the symbol and power of the inner or higher Truth — to see it in meditation is a good sign. The sea is also often symbolic, indicating usually the vital nature, sometimes the expanse of consciousness in movement. The opening of vision must be allowed to develop, but too much importance need not be given to the individual visions unless or until they become evidently symbolic or significant or shed light on things in the sadhana etc.

*

What was developed in you is a power of true inner vision — this will help you to enter through it into touch with the Divine; you have only to let it develop. Two other things have to develop — the feeling of the Divine Presence and power and inspiration behind your actions, and the inner contact with myself and the Mother. Aspire with faith and sincerity and these will come. I do not wish to give any more precise instructions until I see what happens in you during your stay here; for although the path is common to all, each man has his own way of following it.

*

The frequent seeing of lights such as those he writes of in his letter is usually a sign that the seer is not limited by his outward surface or waking consciousness but has a latent capacity (which can be perfected by training and practice) for entering into the experiences of the inner consciousness of which most people are unaware but which opens by the practice of Yoga. By this opening one becomes aware of subtle planes of experience and worlds of existence other than the material. For the spiritual life a still farther opening is required into an inmost consciousness by which one becomes aware of the Self and Spirit, the Eternal and the Divine.

*

From what he writes it is apparent that he has a capacity [*for Yoga*], and it is probable that he would have made more progress if he had not shut the door that was opening. Evidently, he made a mistake when he stopped the visions that were coming. Vision and hallucination are not the same thing. The inner vision is an open door on higher planes of consciousness beyond the physical mind which gives room for a wider truth and experience to enter and act upon the mind. It is not the only or the most important door, but it is one which comes readiest to very many if not most and can be a very powerful help. It does not come easily to intellectuals as it does to men with a strong life-power or the emotional and the imaginative. It is true that the field of vision, like every other field of activity of the human mind, is a mixed world and there is in it not only truth but much half-truth and error. It is also true that for the rash and unwary to enter into it may bring confusion and misleading inspirations and false voices, and it is safer to have some sure guidance from those who know and have spiritual and psychic experience. One must look at this field calmly and with discrimination, but to shut the gates and reject this or other supraphysical experiences is to limit oneself and arrest the inner development.

*

Visions and voices are not meant for creating faith; they are effective only if one has faith already.

Visions Not the Most Important Thing

Visions are not indispensable — they are a help, that is all, when they are of the right kind.

*

Anybody with a predisposition can develop the power of seeing visions like that. People are mistaken in thinking it is a sign of great Yogashakti. Apposite and effective visions, those that reveal movements in the occult workings of the nature or help the spiritual growth, are another matter.

*

Well, it is difficult to explain [*what kind of visions help one's spiritual growth*]. I might give the example of St. Paul's vision on the way to Damascus as an example of a vision which really meant business. You have yourself given the Kurukshetra example. But all visions need not be so stupendous as that — small ones can also be useful.

But the predisposition I spoke of was for visionary display, not for spiritual growth. There are people who can see visions by the hundred and there are those who cannot. But it does not follow that the non-visionary cannot have decisive spiritual experiences or the realisation.

*

The kind of vision you want comes only if the general visual power opens and develops. It is not the greatest form of experience; many advance very far and have high experiences and change of consciousness without it. The important thing is to feel the Presence of the Mother with one and in one, her Light, her Power working, her Ananda. The form can be there, if the vision develops, but only as one element of the experience.

*

I did not quite understand from your letter what is the nature of these sights and objects that pass like a cinema film before you. If they are things seen by the inner vision, then there is no need to drive them away — one has only to let them pass. When one does sadhana an inner mind which is within us awakes and sees by an inner vision images of all things in this world and other worlds — this power of vision has its use, though one has not to be attached to it; one can let them pass with a quiet mind, neither fixing on them nor driving them away.

*

This kind of vision [*seeing water, a rose, a tiger*] almost anybody can have except those who live too much in the mind. For others it is very near to the surface, this faculty of vision. Many have it in this elementary way without doing any Yoga at all.

*

The power of occult seeing is there in everyone, mostly latent, often near the surface, sometimes but much more rarely already on the surface. If one practises *trāṭak*, it is pretty certain to come out sooner or later, — though some have a difficulty and with them it takes time; those in whom it comes out at once have had all the time this power of occult vision near the surface and it emerges at the first direct pressure.

No Reason to Fear Visions

Such visions [*of human figures*] often happen when the inner sight is open. These were evidently two powers of the supraphysical world. One has to see quietly whatever comes of this kind — there is no reason to fear them, any more than if you saw a picture or moving figures in the cinema.

Wrong Visions and Voices

When the sadhana progresses, one almost always gets the power of vision; what one sees is true if one remains in the right consciousness. There are also wrong voices and experiences. The people who have gone mad, went mad because they were egoistic, began to think themselves great sadhaks and attach an exaggerated importance to themselves and their experiences; this made them get a wrong consciousness and wrong voices and visions and inspirations. They attached so much importance to them that they refused to listen to the Mother and finally became hostile to her because she told them they were in error and checked their delusions. Your visions and experiences are very true and good and I have explained to you what they signify — the wrong ones tried to come but you threw them away, because you are not attached to them and are fixed on the true aim of sadhana. One must not get attached to these things, but observe them simply and go on; then they become a help and cannot be a danger.

Chapter Two

Kinds of Vision

The Inner Vision

There is an inner vision that opens when one does sadhana and all sorts of images rise before it or pass. Their coming does not depend upon your thought or will; it is real and automatic. Just as your physical eyes see things in the physical world, so the inner eye sees things and images that belong to the other worlds and subtle images of things of this physical world also.

*

Everything not physical is seen by an inner vision.

*

When the inner vision opens, there can come before it all that ever was or is now in the world, even it can open to things that will be hereafter — so there is nothing impossible in seeing thus the figures and the things of the past.

*

The inner vision can see objects — but it can also see instead the vibration of the forces which act through the object.

*

This realm (whose centre is between the eyebrows) is the realm of inner thought, will, vision — the motor-car indicates a rapid progress in this part of the consciousness. The motor-car is a symbolic image, these images do not refer to anything physical.
    These things take place in the inner mind or inner vital and usually there is a truth behind them, but the form in which they come into the mind may be imperfect — i.e. the meaning may be something not perfectly revealed in the words.

*

Things inside can be seen as distinctly as outward things whether in an image by the subtle vision or in their essence by a still more subtle and powerful way of seeing; but all these things have to develop in order to get their full power and intensity.

Stages in the Development of the Inner Vision

It is the inner vision that is opened or opening in you. When that opens, the first thing that you see is colours or lights moving or small or vague shapes or objects — afterwards flowers etc., then figures of people, scenes, landscapes, things happening etc. Often by the power of this subtle vision the sadhak can see the image of the Divine he worships in his heart and so feel more concretely the presence.

*

The seeing of colours is the beginning of inner vision, what is called *sūkṣmadṛṣṭi*. Afterwards this vision opens and one begins to see figures and scenes and people. It is good that the seeing began with an image of the Mother.

*

When one tries to meditate, the first obstacle in the beginning is sleep. When you get over this obstacle, there comes a condition in which, with the eyes closed, you begin to see things, people, scenes of all kinds. This is not a bad thing, it is a good sign and means that you are making progress in the Yoga. There is, besides the outer physical sight which sees external objects, an inner sight in us which can see things yet unseen and unknown, things at a distance, things belonging to another place or time or to other worlds; it is the inner sight which is opening in you. It is the working of the Mother's force which is opening it in you, and you should not try to stop it. Remember the Mother always, call on her and aspire to feel her presence and her power working in you; but you do not need, for that, to reject this or other developments that may come in you by her working hereafter. It is only desire, egoism, restlessness and other wrong movements that have to be rejected.

*

The visions you describe are those which come in the earliest stages of sadhana. At this stage most of the things seen are formations of the mental plane and it is not always possible to put on them a precise significance, for they depend on the individual mind of the sadhak. At a later stage the power of vision becomes important for the sadhana, but at first one has to go on without attaching excessive importance to the details — until the consciousness develops more. The opening of the consciousness to the Divine Light and Truth and Presence is always the one important thing in the Yoga.

The Diverse Nature and Significance of Visions

Your visions are not mental images but significant symbols. The white dove is the higher divine or spiritual Consciousness above the mental surrounded by the golden lightnings of the Truth. The lamb is the psychic aspiring to the Truth. When one has a thought or feeling and creates a mental form of it, that is a mental image — or when not so positively or consciously self-created forms arise either in meditation or sleep, which correspond to mental thoughts or vital feelings, one's own or those of others, those also are simply mental images or vital formations. The true significant ones are those that come of themselves and correspond to things, states of consciousness or a play of forces that are actual and not determined mainly by one's ideas, will or feelings.

*

Visions are of all kinds — some are merely suggestions of what wants to be or is trying to be, some indicate some approach of the thing or movement towards it, some indicate that the thing is being done.

*

Nothing has to be done to develop them [*images seen in vision*]. They develop of themselves by the growing practice of seeing, — what was faint becomes clear, what was incomplete becomes complete. One cannot say in a general way that they are real or unreal. Some are formations of the mind, some are images that come to the sight of themselves, some are images of real things that show themselves directly to the sight — others are true pictures, not merely images.

*

No rule of a general character can be given. Each vision or dream has to be taken by itself; some are mental constructions, symbols or indications, some are vital possibilities truly or falsely represented, some are representations of physical facts — but this last is more rare.

*

The seeing of the body (at least one's own) in its internal parts is a Yogic power developed by the Raja and Hathayogins — I suppose it could be extended to the body of others. There is also the sense of subtle smells and I have noticed that sometimes one smell persists.

*

Subtle images can be images of all things in all worlds.

*

There is no criterion [*for distinguishing visions from dreams of a deeper origin*], but one can easily distinguish if one is in the inward condition, not sleep, in which most visions take place by the nature of the impression made. A vision in dream is more difficult to distinguish from a vivid dream-experience, but one gets to feel the difference.

*

Vision in trance is vision no less than vision in the waking state. It is only the condition of the recipient consciousness that varies

— in one the waking consciousness shares in the vision, in the other it is excluded for the sake of greater facility and range in the inner experience. But in both it is the inner vision that sees.

*

The physical things[1] are simply an occasion or starting-point for the inner vision to work through the open eyes and bring in the significant inner things.

Representative and Dynamic Visions

It depends on the nature of the symbolic vision whether it is merely representative, offering to the inner vision and nature (even though the outer mind has not the understanding, the inner can receive its effect) the thing symbolised in its figure or whether it is dynamic. The Sun symbol, for instance, is usually dynamic. Again among the dynamic symbols some may bring simply an influence of the thing symbolised, some indicate what is being done but not yet finished, some a formative experience that visits the consciousness, some a prophecy of something that may or will or is soon about to happen. There are others that are not merely symbols but present actualities seen by the vision in a symbolic figure.

*

When the colours begin to take definite shapes [*in one's visions*], it is a sign of some dynamic work of formation in the consciousness — a square for instance means that some kind of creation is in process in some field of the being; the square indicates that the creation is to be complete in itself while the rectangle indicates something partial and preliminary. The waves of colour mean a dynamic rush of forces and the star may in such a context indicate the promise of the new being that is to be formed. The blue colour must here be the Krishna light — so it is a creation under the stress of the Krishna light. All these are symbols of what is

---

[1] *The correspondent saw the lights on a pier at night as sparkling diamonds.* — Ed.

going on in the inner being, in the consciousness behind, and the results well up from time to time in the external or surface consciousness in such feelings as the awareness of a softening and opening which you had, devotion, joy, peace, Ananda etc. When the opening is complete, there is likely to be a more direct consciousness of the working that is going on behind till it is no longer behind but in the front of the nature.

*

When you see a square, that is a symbol of complete creation; when you see a buffalo rushing upon you and missing and feel you have escaped a great danger, that is a transcription. Something actually happened of which the buffalo's ineffectual rush was your mind's transcription — the rush of some hostile force represented by the buffalo.

Seeing Forms of the Divine and Other Beings

Subjective visions can be as real as objective sight — the only difference is that one is of real things in material space, while the others are of real things belonging to other planes down to the subtle physical; even symbolic visions are real insofar as they are symbols of realities. Even dreams can have a reality in the subtle domain. Visions are unreal only when these are merely imaginative mental formations not representing anything that is true or was true or is going to be true.

In this case the thing seen [*a vision of Krishna, silvery blue in colour, standing in a dance pose playing the flute*] can be taken as true since it has been seen by many and always in the same relation and still more because it has been confirmed by what was seen by Yashodabai and Krishnaprem. It means obviously that your singing by the power of the bhakti it expresses can and does bring the presence of Krishna there. It is not that Krishna "shows himself", but simply that he is there and some who have the power of vision catch sight of him and others who have not the power fail to do so. This power of vision is sometimes inborn and habitual even without any effort of development, sometimes it wakes up of itself and becomes abundant or needs only a little practice to develop; it is not necessarily a sign of spiritual attainment, but usually when by practice of Yoga one begins to go inside or live within, the power of subtle vision awakes to a greater or less extent; but this does not always happen easily, especially if one has been habituated to live much in the intellect or in an outward vital consciousness.

I suppose what you are thinking of is "darshan", the self-revelation of the Deity to the devotee; but that is different, it is an unveiling of his presence, temporary or permanent, and may come as a vision or may come as a close feeling of his presence which is more intimate than sight and a frequent or constant communication with him; that happens by deepening of the being into its inner self and growth of consciousness or by growth of the intensity of bhakti. When the crust of the external consciousness is sufficiently broken by the pressure of increasing and engrossing bhakti, the contact comes.

*

It is quite usual at a certain stage of the sadhana for people who have the faculty to see or hear the Devata of their worship and to receive constant directions from him or her with regard either to action or to sadhana. Defects and difficulties may remain, but that does not prevent the direct guidance from being a fact. The necessity of the Guru in such cases is to see that it is the right experience, the right voice or vision — for it is possible for a false guidance to come as it did with X and Y.

*

These things [*the seeing of Buddha, Ramakrishna, Vivekananda, Shankaracharya in vision*] are the result of past thoughts and influences. They are of various kinds — sometimes merely thought-forms created by one's own thought-force to act as a vehicle for some mental realisation — sometimes Powers of different planes that take these forms as a support for their work through the individual, — but sometimes one is actually in communion with that which had the name and form and personality

of Buddha or Ramakrishna or Vivekananda or Shankara.
It is not necessary to have an element akin to these personalities — a thought, an aspiration, a formation of the mind or vital are enough to create the connection — it is sufficient for a vibration of response anywhere to what these Powers represent.

Cosmic, Inner and Psychic Vision

Cosmic vision is the seeing of the universal movements — it has nothing to do with the psychic necessarily. It can be in the universal mind, the universal vital, the universal physical or anywhere.

What do you mean here by psychic vision? Inner vision means the vision with the inner seeing as opposed to outer vision, the external sight with the surface mind or the surface eyes. Psychic in the language of this Yoga is confined to the soul, the psychic being — it is not as in the ordinary language in which if you see a ghost it is called a psychic "vision": we speak of the inner vision or the subtle sight or the occult sight — not the psychic vision.

*

The "sight" spoken of [*in passages of the Upanishads*] is not a sense vision but an experience in the inner consciousness which is more true and living and dynamic than the experiences given to the external consciousness by the material senses.

There is also a psychic vision by which one can see the forms of the Gods or one of the many forms in which the Ishwara reveals himself to the Bhakta.

There is too an inner or subtle sense and sight by which one can see and experience forms and happenings which are not present to the physical eye and also those which belong to other planes than that of the physical world. There are many supraphysical worlds and one can get into contact with these worlds and their beings only by an awakening or developing of this inner sense.

Mental Visions

The mental visions are meant to bring in the mind the influence of the things they represent.

*

Inner vision is vivid like actual sight, always precise and contains a truth in it. In mental vision the images are invented by the mind and are partly true, partly a play of possibilities. Or a mental vision like the vital may be only a suggestion, — that is a formation of some possibility on the mental or vital plane which presents itself to the sadhak in the hope of being accepted and helped to realise itself.

*

The visions and experiences you have described are all of the mental plane and show a great openness and purity of the inner mental being free from unfavourable influences. But it is difficult to tell the precise significance of those that are in the nature of colours, lights, a star etc., because they depend on contacts which are personal to the sadhaka. The first five are of this kind and appear to indicate contact with powers, influences, personalities (godheads), etc. of the higher mental plane. E.g. the light of pink colour might be that of some influence or godhead of love or bhakti in contact with the mental being. In some cases it may be the figure of a formation of the mental being itself. The flowers, diamonds and gems etc. would seem to indicate contact with Radha, Mahalakshmi and Mahakali influences. The vision of writing is also frequent on the mental plane — it is known by us as the *lipi*, and if it organises itself so as to be legible and intelligible, it can embody many things such as intuitions, messages from one or other of the mental planes — the voice you heard was probably one of these messages. There is no necessity to explain the vision of the form of the Mother and mine — for that is clear.

Vital Visions

The dream was on the vital plane. Dreams or visions on the vital plane are usually either
 (1) symbolic vital visions
 (2) actual occurrences on the vital plane
 (3) formations of the vital mind, either of the dreamer or of someone else with whom he contacts in sleep or of powers or beings of that plane. No great reliance can be put on this kind of experience.

*

These are visions of the vital world and the vital planes and one sees hundreds of them there.[2] Those of the type of the first have no significance; they are only things seen just as on earth you may see a man bathing in water. The other seems to indicate a being or else simply a Force given form entering into the consciousness. All the parts of the consciousness are like fields into which forces from the same planes of consciousness in the universal Nature are constantly entering or passing. The best thing is to observe without getting affected in either way or without attaching too much importance — for these are minor experiences and one's concentration must call the major ones.

*

Most of these visions are the result of your getting into contact with a certain field of forces in the vital world which are at present creating the pressure for war and revolution and all catastrophic things in Europe. It was from here that these menacing visions were coming. There is no coherence or reality in them. Chhinnamasta is a symbol of this kind of force, feeding as it were the world with her own blood.

They have to be at once rejected. It was not meant that you should be inactive, but that there was sufficient Force gathering

---

[2] *The correspondent had two visions in dream — one of a young lad standing waist deep in water, another of a woman's face which looked at the correspondent and then entered his chest. — Ed.*

to carry on the sadhana as if by an automatic action. But the consent of the sadhak, his rejection of all that comes against is always necessary.

*

It is the vital plane — probably the vital physical. It is mostly there that the beings of the vital world appear with animal heads or features. A human figure with a dog's face means a very coarse and material sexual energy. Of course, all such energies can be transformed and cease to be sexual — turned into material strength of some kind, just as the seminal force can be turned by brahmacharya into ojas.

*

This gazing on a flame or a bright spot is the traditional means used by Yogis for concentration or for awakening of the inner consciousness and vision. You seem to have gone by the gazing into a kind of surface (not deep) trance, which is indeed one of its first results, and begun to see things probably on the vital plane. I do not know what were the "dreadful objects" you saw but that dreadfulness is the character of many things first seen on that plane, especially when crossing its threshold by such means. You should not employ these means, I think, for they are quite unnecessary and besides, they may lead to a passive concentration in which one is open to all sorts of things and cannot choose the right ones.

Subtle Physical Visions

All that can be seen with closed eyes can be seen with open eyes also; it is sufficient that the inner sight should extend to the subtle physical consciousness for that to happen.

*

One can see [visions] either with open or closed eyes or both. It is a matter of temperament or idiosyncrasy which one starts with.

*

The world you see is in some subtle physical plane where men see the gods according to their own ideas and images of them.

*

As you were concentrating your attention on the electric light, it may have been the god of electricity you saw, Vaidyuta Agni. There is no reason why he should have many faces — the many-headed or many-armed figures belong usually to the vital plane — and it may not have been in his vital form that he was manifesting. As for the colours, colours are symbols of forces and Agni need not be pure red — the principle of Fire can manifest all the colours and the pure white fire is that which contains in itself all the colours.

*

The gods in the overmental plane have not many heads and arms — this is a vital symbolism, it is not necessary in other planes. This figure [*of Vaidyuta Agni, mentioned in the preceding letter*] may have belonged to the subtle physical plane.

*

(1) It [*the vision of a flower*] was seen through the physical eyes but by the subtle physical consciousness; in other words there was an imposition of one consciousness upon another. After a certain stage of development, this capacity of living in the ordinary physical consciousness and yet having superadded to it another and more subtle sense, vision, experience becomes quite normal. A little concentration is enough to bring it; or, even, it happens automatically without any concentration.

As the flower was a subtle physical object, not entirely material in the ordinary sense of the word (though quite substantial and material in its own plane, not an illusion), a camera would not be able to detect it — except in the case of one of those abnormal interventions by which a subtle form has been thrown upon the material plate.

It could be sensed in a dark room, though not so easily, and it would not then have so vivid an appearance — unless you are able to bring out something of the light of the subtle physical plane to surround it and give it its natural medium.

If seen with the eyes shut, it would be no longer a subtle physical form, but an object or formation of the vital, mental or other plane. Unless, indeed, the inner consciousness had progressed so far as to be able to project itself into the physical planes; but this is a rare and, in most cases, a late development.

(2) It is not, usually, the object that vanishes; it is the consciousness that changes. Owing to lack of sustained capacity or lack of training, one is not able to keep the subtle physical vision which is what was really seeing the object. This subtle physical vision comes easiest in the moment between light sleep and waking — either when one just comes out of the sleep or when one is just going into it. But one can train oneself to have it when one is quite wide awake.

At first when one begins to see, it is quite usual for the more ill-defined and imprecise figures to last longer while those which are successful, complete, precise in detail and outline are apt to be quite momentary and disappear in an instant. It is only when the subtle vision is well developed that the precise and full seeing lasts for a long time. This results from the difficulty of keeping what is still an abnormal consciousness and also, in this case, from the difficulty of keeping the two momentarily superimposed consciousnesses together.

(3) There are all kinds in the experiences of each plane — symbolic forms, figures of suggestion, thought-figures, desire-formations or will-formations, constructions of all kinds, things real and lasting in the plane to which they belong and things fictitious and misleading. The haphazardness belongs to the consciousness that sees with its limited and imperfect way of cognizing the other worlds, not to the phenomena themselves. Each plane is a world or a conglomeration or series of worlds, each organised in its own way, but organised, not haphazard; only, of course, the subtler planes are more plastic and less rigid in their organisation than the material plane.

Chapter Three

Subtle Sights, Sounds, Smells and Tastes

Sights and Sounds of Other Planes

The sounds of bells and the seeing of lights and colours are signs of the opening of the inner consciousness which brings with it an opening also to sights and sounds of other planes than the physical. Some of these things, like the sound of bells, crickets etc., seem even to help the opening. The Upanishad speaks of them as *brahmavyaktikarāṇi yoge*. The lights represent forces — or sometimes a formed light like that you saw may be the Light of a being of the supraphysical planes.

*

When the inner senses open, or any of them, one sees or hears things belonging to the other planes automatically. What one sees or hears depends on the development of the inner sense. It depends on what you hear whether these are the symbol sounds only which have a connection with the sadhana or simply other-plane sounds of an ordinary character.

*

It depends on the nature of the sounds. Some have a connection [*with sadhana*], others are merely sounds of the other planes.

Subtle Sounds

When the mind becomes quiet, there are certain sounds that are heard, which are supposed to be signs of the awakening of the subtle senses and the inner consciousness.

*

Sounds in the ear indicate a pressure to open the inner consciousness.

*

The sound is a very good sign. It comes when the inner consciousness is opening or preparing to open to the Yoga-force and the deeper experiences it brings.

*

They [*subtle sounds*] are the signs of a working going on to prepare something — but as that is a general thing, it cannot be said from the sounds themselves what the preparation is.

*

The sounds or voices you hear are like the sights (persons, objects) you see. As there is an inner sight other than the physical, so there is an inner hearing other than that of the external ear, and it can listen to voices and sounds and words of other worlds, other times and places, or those which come from supraphysical beings. But here you must be careful. If conflicting voices try to tell you what to do or not to do, you should not listen to them or reply. It is only myself and the Mother who can tell you what you should or should not do or guide or advise you.

*

Such sounds (bells, bees, crickets etc.) are stated in the Upanishad to be signs of realisation approaching. They come very commonly when the inner or subtle consciousness is awake.

*

The hearing of the bells has always been considered a sign or a premonition of the opening of the inner being to spiritual experience.

*

It [*the sound of the conch*] is one of the many symbol sounds one hears in Yoga. The conch shell is the sound of victory.

*

Both of these [*the sound of OM and of church bells*] are usually sounds that indicate the opening or attempt to open to the cosmic consciousness.

*

The music you heard was the music of the divine call to the soul — like the flute of Krishna.

Subtle Smells and Tastes

It [*experiencing subtle smells and tastes*] was not an opening of occult knowledge and powers, but simply an opening of the inner consciousness.

*

Subtle smells of that kind [*sweet smells*] are a common feature of occult experience. Their exact nature and *provenance* varies, but they have no gross physical cause.

*

The smell [*coming from a person*] is due to something in the person's vital-physical. That something may not be prominent at all times. When it is, the smell is there.

*

I wrote [*in the preceding letter*] that the something may be of different kinds in different cases and one cannot give a rule that it is this or it is that. What has the dirtiest smell is sex.

*

Every man has a different smell; also there is a particular smell that goes with different states of the vital-physical. Animals (like the dogs) recognise a man and his character by the smell. The human sense has lost this acuteness, but it can be recovered by a development in the sense consciousness. That is what probably has happened in your case. There are others in the Asram who have the same experience.

Section Two

Lights and Colours

Chapter One
Light

Seeing Light

Light is always seen in Yoga with the inner eye and even with the outer eye, but there are many lights; all are not and all do not come from the *paraṁ jyotiḥ*.

*

Lights of various colours are one of the first things people see when they meditate.

*

There is no imagination in the seeing of these lights — it is when the inner vision is open or active that one sees them — for they themselves are subtle and not physical lights.

*

A concentrated mind is not always necessary for seeing the light — if there is an opening anywhere in the consciousness, that is sufficient.

*

It is not necessary to have the mind quiet in order to see the lights — that depends only on the opening of the subtle vision in the centre which is in the forehead between the eyebrows. Many people get that as soon as they start sadhana. It can even be developed by effort and concentration without sadhana by some who have it to a small extent as an inborn faculty. The quietude of the mind is needed for other things, such as the feeling of the presence of the Mother etc.

*

Light between the eyebrows indicates some opening of the Ajnachakra, which is there — it is the centre of the inner mind, inner will and occult vision.

*

The light outside means a touch or influence of the Force indicated by the light (golden is truth-light, blue is some spiritual force from the upper planes), while within means that it has penetrated and is established or is frequently active in the nature itself. Light above means a Force descending upon the mind, light around a general enveloping influence.

*

The golden and blue lights are both of them lights of Krishna. It was intimated to you by your seeing them once that they are there within you waiting to manifest. But it is by a psychic and spiritual, not a physical pressure that it must be done. If the mind can become silent and not interfere and if the nature can become more pure and both open to what is above the mind, these lights descend into the body and with them the divine influence.

Light and the Illumination of the Consciousness

Light or rays of light are always light of the higher consciousness working in the being to illumine or to purify or to awaken the consciousness or attune it to the Truth.

*

It [*Light*] is the power that enlightens whatever it falls upon — the result may be vision, memory, knowledge, right will, right impulse etc.

*

There are many lights of various planes — there is also the Divine Light that comes down from the higher planes and illumines the Adhar.

*

It is not necessary or possible to define [*the Divine Light*].

Light is light just like the light you see, only subtle — it clarifies the consciousness and works as a force and makes knowledge possible.

*

It [*the Divine Light*] has no function — it is just Light of Divine Consciousness. If you mean the result, it is supposed to illumine, to remove darkness and obscurity, to make the nature fit for true consciousness, Knowledge etc.

*

Light is a general term. Light is not knowledge but the illumination that comes from above and liberates the being from obscurity and darkness. But this Light also assumes different forms such as the white light of the Mother, the pale blue light of Sri Aurobindo, the golden light of Truth, the psychic light (pink and rose) etc.

*

The light, colours, flowers are always seen when there is a working of the forces within at a certain stage of the sadhana. The light of course indicates an illumination of the consciousness, the colour the play of forces mental (yellow), physical and vital, but forces making for enlightenment of these parts of the being. The flowers usually indicate a psychic activity.

Different Forms of Light

One sometimes sees the Light in masses, sometimes in forms — and the most common forms are sun, moon, star or fire.

*

The Light is often seen in front before the centre of inner vision, mind and will which is between the eyebrows in the forehead. The Sun means the formed Light of the Divine Truth, the starry light is the same Light acting as a diffused Power on the ordinary consciousness which is seen as the night of Ignorance. The call brought the Light etc. streaming down into the inner being.

*

It is not balls or flashes of light [*seen around the Mother*], but a flow or sea of Light entering into the body and surrounding it and illumining the whole field of consciousness. There can also be a vivid sense of Light and illumination without the vision. It can be seen or felt usually as an intense white or diamond or golden Light or something like sunlight or, for many, a blue or bluish white light.

*

What you saw was the procession of the chariots of the gods (Divine Powers) bringing light flashes into the air and the other was the corresponding movement of lightning flashes of the Truth in the heart lighting up the consciousness. These lightning flashes do not as yet bring knowledge — as the sunlight from above the mind does, — but they prepare the consciousness for realisation and knowledge.

*

Sparks or movements of light indicate the play of forces in the consciousness or around it.

*

Any well-formed illumined thought can be seen as a spark of light.

*

A glow means a subdued but rich light or else a sort of warm exhilaration of a luminous kind.

Two Visions Explained

(1) The lid of the skull opening means that the mental being has opened to the Divine Light and the flames indicate aspiration filled with the Light arising to join the mental part to what is above Mind.

(2) The Divine Light from above is of various colours. White is the Divine Power of purity, blue the light of the spiritual consciousness, gold the hue of the supramental knowledge or of knowledge from the intermediate planes.

(3) OM golden rising to the sky = the cosmic consciousness supramentalised and rising towards the Transcendent consciousness.

(1) and (2) indicate either something that is happening at present or a potentiality that is trying to materialise. (3) symbolises the process of the Yoga which will be followed if this potentiality is realised and pursued to its natural goal.

*

About your vision. It came as an answer to your call for the removal of ugly things in your own nature and you were shown how it would be effectively done.

First a vivid realisation was given of what the lower nature is, its terrible darkness and ugliness in which men contentedly live. But having realised its true nature a cry came from your lower nature itself for the change.

You were then shown the light of the higher nature by whose descent the change could come — the white light of the Mother's consciousness and a flame of it descended into you by the usual path and filled you with the light. From there it descended into the subconscient and brought the light there. As a result the consciousness (it was the inner consciousness) became like a crystal pillar connecting the heights with the depths, the superconscient with the subconscient. In it the image of the Mother filled with the light in her.

You were then shown a symbol of the *rūpāntar*, the change in the universal Nature. This change was only in seed and in symbol. Afterwards this part of the vision disappeared and you saw again the darkness of the lower Nature. But in you the light was there still and the assurance that it brings. For it is in the individual that the change must first come and it is with the light and the faith in the individual as a support that the wider change can be made.

Chapter Two
Colours

The Symbolism of Colours

Colour and light are always close to each other — colour being more indicative, light more dynamic. Colour incandescent becomes light.

*

As for the exact symbolism of colours, it is not always easy to define exactly, because it is not rigid and precise, but complex, the meaning varying with the field, the combinations, the character and shades of the colour, the play of forces. A certain kind of yellow, for instance, is supposed by many occultists to indicate the *buddhi*, the intellect, and it often has that sense, but occurring among a play of vital forces it could not always be so interpreted — that would be too rigid. Here all one can say is that the blue (the particular blue seen, not every blue) indicated the response to the Truth; the green — or *this* green — is very usually associated with Life and a generous emanation or action of forces — often of emotional life-force, and it is probably this that it would indicate here.

*

The rays which you saw the trees giving out are there always, only they are veiled to the ordinary material vision. I said the blue and gold together indicated the combined presence of Krishna and Durga-Mahakali; but gold and yellow have different significances. Yellow in the indication of forces signifies the thinking mind, *buddhi*, and the pink (modified here into a light vermilion) is a psychic colour; the combination probably meant the psychic in the mental.

In interpreting these phenomena you must remember that all depends on the order of things which the colours indicate in any particular case. There is an order of significances in which they indicate various psychological dynamisms, e.g., faith, love, protection, etc. There is another order of significances in which they indicate the aura or the activity of divine beings, Krishna, Mahakali, Radha or else of other superhuman beings; there is another in which they indicate the aura around objects or living persons — and that does not exhaust the list of possibilities. A certain knowledge, experiences, growing intuition are necessary to perceive in each case the true significance. Observation and exact description are also very necessary; for sometimes people say, for instance, yellow when they mean gold or *vice versa*; there are besides different possible meanings for different shades of the same colour. Again, if you see colour near or round a person or by looking at him or her, it does not necessarily indicate that person's aura; it may be something else near him or around him. In some cases it may have nothing to do with the person or object you look at, which may serve merely the purpose of a background or a point of concentration — as when you see colours on a wall or by looking at a bright object.

*

There are no separate colours of the beings. There is a characteristic colour of mind, yellow, of the psychic, pink or pale rose, of the vital, purple; but these are colours corresponding to the forces of mind, psychic, vital — they are not the colours of the beings. Also other colours can play, e.g. in the vital, green and deep red as well as purple and there are other colours for the hostile vital forces.

*

The lights one sees in concentration are the lights of various powers or beings or forces and often lights that come down from the higher consciousness.

The violet light is that of the Divine Compassion (*karuṇā* — Grace) — the white light is the light of the Mother (the Divine Consciousness) in which all others are contained and from which they can be manifested.

Purple is the colour of vital power. "Red" depends on the character of the colour, for there are many reds — this may be the colour of the physical consciousness.

*

As for the tricoloured ball of energy, I am not quite sure, but it may mean the triple force, Love, Light, Life which are contained and constrained in the inconscient sleep of the Shakti in the Muladhara. Possibly an observation of the colours might determine the significance; but this is not sure, as the colours on these lower planes have various meanings.

*

The four lights were the lights of the Truth, — white the purity and power of the divine Truth, green its active energy for work, blue the spiritual consciousness of the divine Truth, the gold its knowledge.

*

The silver temple is that of the spiritualised mind — the golden is that of the divine Truth. Yellow is the colour of the light of the thinking mind — white is that of the divine consciousness.

White Light

White light indicates the divine consciousness.

*

White indicates a force of purity.

*

The forces that come with white light are usually those of purity and peace.

*

The important experience is that of the white ray in the heart — for that is a ray of the Mother's light, the white light, and the illumining of the heart by this light is a thing of great power for this sadhana.

*

The white light is, as you know, the Mother's light — it is the light of the Force of the Divine Consciousness; the sun of white light is symbolic of that Force in its origin and fullness of manifestation. It is a very good sign and if one feels its power in the being or mind or body it can have a strong influence.

*

What you saw was the Light (the white Light is the Mother's) which is always there in a mass; but it is seen only when the inner (Yogic) eye is open and the consciousness in some part of it at least can enter into touch with the Light.

*

The diamond light is the Mother's own light (that of divine Consciousness) at its most intense.

White Light with Light of Other Colours

The white light is that of the Pure Conscious Force from which all the rest come. The golden light is that of the Divine Truth on the higher planes.

*

The pale blue light is mine — the white light is the Mother's. The world you saw above the head was the plane of the illumined Mind which is a level of consciousness much higher than the human intelligence. It is there that the Divine Light and Power come down to be transmitted to the human consciousness and from there they work and prepare the transformation of the human consciousness and even the physical nature.

*

The two first [*bright white and whitish blue*] are the Mother's light and mine — the golden red is the touch of the Truth in the physical.

Whitish Blue Light

The pale whitish blue light is "Sri Aurobindo's light" — it is the blue light modified by the white light of the Mother.

*

The snake form is a symbol of Energy and the white blue light may be that of the Mother's consciousness in the higher mind, or if it is not two separate colours but whitish blue then it is Sri Aurobindo's light. The light is a manifestation of Force, the nature of the force being indicated by the colour of the Light.

*

The lights indicate the action of certain forces, usually indicated by the colour of the light. Whitish blue is known as Sri Aurobindo's light or sometimes Sri Krishna's light.

*

Whitish blue is Krishna's light or mine; deeper blues often indicate light from the higher consciousness.

*

There are two pale blues, one which is whitish blue and is known as Sri Aurobindo's light, the other quite blue which is that of the higher consciousness just above mind.

*

The meaning of blue light depends on the exact character of the colour, its shade and nature. A whitish blue like moonlight is known as Krishna's light or Sri Aurobindo's light — light blue is often that of the Illumined Mind — there is another deeper blue that is of the Higher Mind; another, near to purple, which is the light of a power in the vital.

Blue Light

Blue light, according to the shades, means several different things.

*

If the blue lights [*seen in vision*] were of different shades it might mean the overhead planes, Overmind, Intuition, Illumined Mind, Higher Mind.

*

The light from the higher planes of consciousness just above the mind is blue.

*

The light indicates an action of force (bluish probably indicates the spiritual-mind-force), the rest was a working to open the higher spiritual centre (*sahasradala*).

*

Blue is the normal colour of the spiritual planes; moonlight indicates the spiritual mind and its light.

*

Moonlight indicates spirituality — the blue light may be that of the higher or illumined mind.

*

The plane with the blue light is the Higher Mind which is just above the ordinary human intelligence, the first of several planes of higher consciousness through which one has to pass in order to reach the Divine Truth. Something from your mind (thinking willing mind) is trying to rise up into the blue light of the Higher Mind so as to join and become one with it.

*

There is one blue that is the higher mind, a deeper blue that belongs to the mind — Krishna's light in the mind.

*

There are different Krishna lights — pale diamond blue, lavender blue, deep blue etc. It depends on the plane in which it manifests.

*

Diamond blue is Krishna's light in the overmind — lavender blue in intuitive mind.

*

There is the whitish moonlight blue of Krishna's light — lavender blue of devotion, deep blue of the physical mind, sapphire blue of the higher mind and many others.

*

All blue is not Krishna's light.

*

Blue is also the Radha colour.

Violet Light

The violet is the light of the Divine grace and compassion.

*

"Violet" is the colour of benevolence or compassion, but also more vividly of the Divine Grace — represented in the vision as flowing from the heights of the spiritual consciousness down on the earth. The golden cup is I suppose the Truth consciousness.

*

Violet is indeed the colour or light of Divine Compassion, so also of Krishna's grace.

Golden Light

Golden Light is the light of the divine Truth descending from above.

*

The golden light is the light of the Divine Truth which comes out from the supramental sunlight and, modified according to the level it crosses, creates the ranges from Overmind to higher Mind.

*

The golden light is usually a light from the supermind — a light of Truth-Knowledge (it may sometimes be the supramental Truth-Knowledge turned into overmind or intuitive Truth).

*

It [*golden light*] always means the light of Truth — but the nature of the Truth varies according to the plane to which it belongs. Light is the light of consciousness, truth, knowledge — the Sun is the concentration or source of the Light.

*

The sunlight is the light of the Truth itself — whatever power of Truth it may be — while the other lights derive from the Truth.

*

The Light of the Sun descending into the heart (the Sun of the Knowledge) turns upon the physical and purifies it.

*

The golden light is the promise of the higher knowledge. For the coming of that knowledge the silence of the frontal exterior mind is necessary.

*

Gold is always the symbol of the higher Truth.

*

The hand with the gold pen writing golden letters was perhaps an indication of the Mother writing the things of the Divine Truth in you, — for gold in these visions is the symbol of the Divine Truth.

*

The spiritual Power is naturally more free on its own level than in the body. The golden colour indicates here Mahakali force which is the strongest for the working in the body.

*

The different parts [*mind, life and body*] are naturally coloured by the lights of the powers that come down (golden of Overmind and Intuition, blue of higher, illumined and intuitive mind) while keeping their own characteristic shade as an element.

Gold-Green Light

Gold-green: gold indicates at its most intense something from the supramental, otherwise overmind truth or intuitive truth deriving ultimately from the supramental Truth consciousness. Green has much to do with the vital and indicates here, I think, the emotional forces in their outpouring. The play of the emotional forces in the divine Truth is, obviously, very pertinent to the working of the Krishna lights.

*

Sunlight is the direct light of the Truth; when it gets fused into the vital, it takes the mixed colour — here gold and green — just as in the physical it becomes golden red or in the mental golden yellow.

Golden Red or Red Gold Light

Golden red is the colour of the supramental physical light — so this yellow red may indicate some plane of the Overmind in which there is a nearer special connection with that. The golden red light has a strong transforming power.

*

The golden Light is that of the modified (overmentalised) Supramental, i.e., the Supramental Light passing through the Overmind, intuition etc. and becoming the Light of Truth in each of these planes. When it is golden red it means the same modified supramental-physical Light — the Light of divine Truth in the physical.

*

"Red gold" is rather the light of the Truth in the physical.

*

Orange or red gold is supposed by the way to be the light of the supramental in the physical.

Orange Light

Orange is the true light manifested in the physical consciousness and being.

*

Orange is the colour of occult knowledge or occult experience.

Yellow Light

Yellow is the thinking mind. The shades indicate different intensities of mental light.

*

Yellow is light of the mind — golden is light from above the mind.

*

It is again the ascent into one of the higher planes of mind illumined with the light of the Divine Truth. Yellow is the light of mind growing brighter as one goes higher till it meets the golden light of the Divine Truth.

Pink or Rose Light

The rosy light is that of love — so probably you entered the psychic worlds — or at least one of them.

*

The colour of the psychic light is according to what it manifests — e.g., psychic love is pink or rose, the psychic purity is white etc.

Green Light

Green is the higher light in the vital, especially the emotional vital.

*

The green light is a vital force, a dynamic force of the emotional vital which has the power to purify, harmonise or cure.

*

Green is a vital energy of work and action.

*

Green light can signify various things according to the context — in the emotional vital it is the colour of a certain form of emotional generosity, in the vital proper an activity with vital abundance or vital generosity behind it — in the vital physical it signifies a force of health.

Purple and Crimson Light

It [*purple light*] is a light of vital power.

*

Purple is the colour of the vital force — crimson is usually physical.

*

Both [*purple and crimson*] are vital lights, but when seen above they represent the original forces of which the vital are the derivations.

*

The crimson colour is the light of Love in the vital and physical.

Red Light

Red is the colour of the physical, — touched by the higher Light it becomes golden red.

*

It seems to be an opening of various powers and the peace, light and wideness of the spiritual consciousness. The red Purusha may be the power of the true physical — red being the colour of the physical.

*

It depends on the nature of the red. Red (when it does not mean the light of the physical consciousness) indicates always some kind of Force or Power, but what power it is depends on the shade.

*

Deep red is the Divine Love — rosy is the psychic love.

*

The deep red is the light of the Power that descended before the 24th [*November 1933*] for the transformation of the physical.

*

The deep red light is a Light that came down into the physical for its change just before the 24th [*November 1933*]. It is associated with the sunlight and the golden Light.

Red and Black

Red is the colour of rajas, black is the colour of tamas.

Section Three

Symbols

Chapter One
Symbols and Symbolic Visions

Different Kinds of Symbols

A symbol, as I understand it, is the form on one plane that represents a truth of another. For instance, a flag is the symbol of a nation. But generally all forms are symbols. This body of ours is a symbol of our real being and everything is a symbol of some higher reality. There are, however, different kinds of symbols:

(1) Conventional symbols, such as the Vedic Rishis formed with objects taken from their surroundings. The cow stood for light because the same word *go* meant both ray and cow, and because the cow was their most precious possession which maintained their life and was constantly in danger of being robbed and concealed. But once created, such a symbol becomes alive. The Rishis vitalised it and it became a part of their realisation. It appeared in their visions as an image of spiritual light. The horse also was one of their favourite symbols, and a more easily adaptable one, since its force and energy were quite evident.

(2) What we might call Life-symbols, such as are not artificially chosen or mentally interpreted in a conscious deliberate way, but derive naturally from our day-to-day life and grow out of the surroundings which condition our normal path of living. To the ancients the mountain was a symbol of the path of Yoga, level above level, peak upon peak. A journey involving the crossing of rivers and the facing of lurking enemies, both animal and human, conveyed a similar idea. Nowadays I dare say we would liken Yoga to a motor ride or a railway trip.

(3) Symbols that have an inherent appositeness and power of their own. Akasha or etheric space is a symbol of the infinite all-pervading eternal Brahman. In any nationality it would convey the same meaning. Also, the Sun stands universally for the

supramental Light, the divine Gnosis.

(4) Mental symbols, instances of which are numbers or alphabets. Once they are accepted, they too become active and may be useful. Thus geometrical figures have been variously interpreted. In my experience the square symbolises the Supermind. I cannot say how it came to do so. Somebody or some force may have built it before it came to my mind. Of the triangle, too, there are different explanations. In one position it can symbolise the three lower planes, in another the symbol is of the three higher ones: so both can be combined together in a single sign. The ancients liked to indulge in similar speculations concerning numbers, but their systems were mostly mental. It is no doubt true that supramental realities exist which we translate into mental formulas such as Karma, psychic evolution etc. But they are, so to speak, infinite realities which cannot be limited by these symbolic forms, though they may be somewhat expressed by them; they might be expressed as well by other symbols, and the same symbol may also express many different ideas.

The Effect of Symbolic Visions

It is the same with the symbols in Yoga [*as with images in mystic poetry*]. One puts an intellectual label on the "White Light" and the mind is satisfied and says, "Now I know all about it; it is the pure divine Consciousness light," and really it knows nothing. But if one allows the Divine White Light to manifest and pour through the being, then one comes to know it and get all its results. Even if there is no labelled knowledge there is the luminous experience of all its significance.

*

The vision of the moon and the rain of flowers means always the falling of the light of spirituality on the consciousness (the moon) and the descent of a psychic influence (flowers). These things are symbols to the mind, but in the inner experience they have a reality and can produce a tangible effect.

Some Symbolic Visions and Dreams Interpreted

The depth of the sleep in your experience was intended to make you go deep inside and, as soon as you did so, you entered into the psychic and spiritual state which takes the figure of the beautiful *maidān* and the flow of white light and the coolness and peace. The staircase was a symbol of the ascent from this psychic and spiritual state into higher and higher levels of the spiritual consciousness where is the source of the light. The Mother's hand was the symbol of her presence and help which will draw you up and lead you to the top of the ladder.

*

The separate images [*in a mystic poem submitted by the correspondent*] are very usual symbols of the inner experience, but they have been combined together here in a rather difficult way. The fire of course is the psychic fire which wells up from the veiled psychic source. The bird is the soul and the flower is the rose of love and surrender. The moon is the symbol of spirituality. As the star is within it is described as piercing through the knots of the inner darkness and worsting the vital growths that are like clouds enwrapping it. The boat also is a usual symbol in the inner visions. The elephant is the spiritual strength that removes obstacles and the horse the force of tapasya that gallops to the summits of the spiritual realisation. The sun is the symbol of the higher Truth. The lotus is the symbol of the inner consciousness.

*

The vision you saw was a symbol of the outward physical consciousness obscured by the ordinary movements (clouds), but with the spirituality (the moon) still spreading its light everywhere from behind the ordinary human ignorance. The dog indicates something in the physical (the part that is faithful, obedient etc.) waiting confidently for the Light to come.

The fire you felt was the fire of purification and the heat came because it was burning up some resistance, — after that was burnt out there was coolness and peace and quietude. The voices and sounds and impression of X being there indicate a confused activity of the occult sense in the vital which hears things other than the physical. When this kind of thing comes, there has to be a quiet rejection in the being and the thing will pass away. Some people get interested and have a lot of trouble because they get into the habit of hearing voices and seeing and feeling things which are only partly or sometimes true but mixed with much that is false and misleading. It is good that there was something in your vital being which rejected it.

*

The dream is evidently an indication of the difficulty you are experiencing. The sea is the sea of the vital nature whose flood is pursuing you (desires are the sea water) on your road of sadhana. The Mother is there in your heart but sleeping — i.e. her power has not become conscious in your inner consciousness because she is surrounded by the thin curtain of skin (the obscurity of the physical nature). It is this (it is not thick any longer but still effective to veil her from you) which has to go so that she may awake. It is a matter of persistence in the will and the endeavour — the response from within, the awaking of the Mother in the heart will come.

*

It is probably a symbol of three stages or developments or planes of spiritualised life. A star means creation, the triangle a triple principle. The tree is life in a new creation. Green is the colour of the emotional vital, the moon governs a spiritualised emotional life; blue is the colour of the higher mind, the moon there governs a spiritualised higher mind life; the gold colour is that of the Divine Truth, whether intuitive or overmind — the moon here is the spiritualised Truth-life. As the star is *sphaṭika*-coloured, the triangle may indicate Sachchidananda principle. The butterflies and birds are of course life forces and soul forces, powers or beings. Probably it indicates three stages of transformation before the supramental can reign altogether or else three that will exist as the steps towards the supramental.

*

Symbols and Symbolic Visions   141

Your dreams were very beautiful and, symbolically, very true. By the way, let me repeat, they were not really dreams; the state between sleep and waking or which is neither sleep nor waking is not a dozing but an inward gathered consciousness, quite as much awake as the waking mind, but awake in a different plane of experience.

As for the dream of the cobras it could be taken as an answer to your complaints against the Divine being grim and solemn and refusing to play and your remark that if you could have the faith that the troubles were a part of the Divine plan leading you through them to the Divine, you would be more at ease. The answer of the symbolic experience was that the Divine can play if you know how to play with him — and bear his play on your shoulders; the cobras and the bite indicate that what seems to you in the vital painful and dangerous may be the very means of bringing you the ecstasy of the Divine Presence.

Less generally the cobras are the forces of the evolution, the evolution towards the Divine. Their taking the place of the legs means that their action here takes place in the physical or external consciousness, in the evolution of the external mind, vital, physical towards the experience of the Divine and of the Divine Nature. The bite of the cobras (Shiva's cobras!) does not kill, or it only kills the "old Adam" in the being; their bite brings the ecstasy of the presence of the Divine — that which you felt coming upon your head as trance waves. It is this trance ecstasy that has descended upon you each time you went inside or were even on the point of going inside in meditation. It is the universal experience of sadhaks that a force or consciousness or Ananda like this first comes from above — or around — and presses on or surrounds the head, then it pierces the skull as it were and fills first the brain and forehead, then the whole head and descends occupying each centre till the whole system is full and replete. (Of course there are or can be preliminary rushes occupying the whole body for a time or some other part of the system most open and least resistant to the influence.)

Chapter Two
Sun, Moon, Star, Fire

Sun

Fire, lights, sun, moon are usual symbols and seen by most in sadhana. They indicate movement or action of inner forces. The Sun means the inner truth.

*

The sun is the symbol of the concentrated light of Truth.

*

The Sun is the Truth-Light of the One Existence and the flame the dynamic power of action (Yogic) of that Truth-Light.

*

The Sun is the divine Truth-Light on whatever plane of consciousness. It is, I suppose, the original cosmic Truth that is here indicated.

*

The Sun is the Truth from above, in the last resort the Supramental Truth.

*

The sun is the symbol of the Supermind.

*

The sun in the Yoga is the symbol of the supermind and the supermind is the first power of the Supreme which one meets across the border where the experience of spiritualised mind ceases and the unmodified divine Consciousness begins the domain of the supreme Nature, *parā prakṛti*. It is that Light of which the Vedic mystics got a glimpse and it is the opposite of the intervening darkness of the Christian mystics, for the supermind is all light and no darkness. To the mind the Supreme is *avyaktāt param avyaktam* but if we follow the line leading to the supermind, it is an increasing affirmation rather than an increasing negation through which we move.

*

Supermind is not mind at all, it is something different. The Sun indicates Truth directly perceived in whatever plane it may be. It is the symbol of Supermind but the Truth may come down into the other planes and then that is no longer supramental but modified to the substance of the other planes — still it is the direct Light of Truth.

*

The sun rising on the horizon is the direct light of the Divine Truth rising in the being — the ray upwards opens the being to the Truth as it is above mind, the ray in front opens it to what we call the cosmic consciousness, it becomes released from the personal limitation and opens and becomes aware of the universal mind, universal physical, universal vital. The action on the heart was the pressure of this Sun on it to have this direct opening, so that the consciousness may become free, wide and wholly at peace.

*

There are different suns in the different planes, each with its own colour. But there are also suns of a similar colour above, only more bright, from which these minor suns derive their light and power.

*

The golden [*Sun*] is the Light of the Truth on the higher planes. The white [*Sun*] is the Sun of the Mother's consciousness (the Divine Consciousness) which manifests on all the planes.

*

The white sun indicates the purity and peace of the Divine Consciousness.

*

The red sun is a symbol of the true, illumined physical consciousness which is to replace the obscure and ignorant physical consciousness in which men now live. Red is the colour of the physical; the red diamond is the Mother's consciousness in the physical.

*

In the experience the disc of the sun indicates the supramental consciousness with the Divine Being in it (the supramental Divine who can bridge by his light the gulf between the higher and the lower consciousness and unify them). But the smoky appearance, the veil etc. indicated that there was something in the (human) nature that made rapid realisation difficult. This was what was also said by the voice that the time was not yet. Obviously the supramental cannot be achieved except by a long sadhana — the experience should not be taken as meaning anything more than that.

Moon

The moon signifies the light of spirituality or of the spiritual consciousness.

*

The moonlight indicates the light of the spiritual consciousness.

*

The moonlit *maidān* is the spiritual consciousness at the doors of which you are standing as it were and feeling its peace and ease.

*

The moon generally indicates spiritual realisation in the mind.

*

The moon indicates different things according to circumstances — most often spiritual consciousness in the mind.

*

The light above the head is never an imagination in Yoga; if it is felt, it is because it is there. If it is the moon, it means the light of the spiritual consciousness in the mind.

*

The moon as a symbol in vision signifies usually spirituality in the mind or, simply, the spiritual consciousness. It can also indicate the flow of spiritual Ananda (nectar is in the moon according to the old tradition).

*

The moon indicates spirituality, sometimes also spiritual Ananda.

*

It [*spiritual mind, symbolised by the moon*] is Mind in contact with truths of the spirit and reflecting them. The Sun is the light of the Truth, the Moon only reflects the light of the Truth — that is the difference.

*

Golden light means the light of the higher Truth — the moon is the symbol of spirituality. A golden moon means a power of spirituality full of the light of the higher Truth.

*

The moon, as I have already written, indicates spirituality — the crescent form means a commencement of the spiritual light. The position near the knee would indicate an action on the physical consciousness — for all below the Muladhara down to the feet is the physical province.

*

The moon is sometimes a symbol of the Light in the mind, — if it is a full moon. The crescent moon may be a symbol of growing spirituality of the mind centre.

Star

The star signifies a creation or formation or the promise or power of a creation or formation.

*

The star is always a promise of the Light to come; the star changes into a sun when there is the descent of the Light. It is not possible to fix the actual value of these signs for the future; they indicate a turn or a possibility, but everything depends on herself and the future orientation she gives to her being.

*

Stars in such visions[1] indicate points of light or of higher experience in the consciousness. The earth means the physical consciousness.

*

Stars indicate points of light in the ignorant mental consciousness.
    Moon = spiritual light
    Sun = the higher Truth light

*

They [*gold stars in the sky*] are simply indications of divine Truth in the mind — the sky is a symbol of mind very often.

*

The sky is always some mental plane. The stars indicate beginnings or promises of Light — the various lights indicating various powers of the consciousness: gold = Truth, blue = higher

---

[1] *In one vision the correspondent saw stars in the sky, in another stars upon earth.* — Ed.

spiritualised mind, violet = sympathy, unity or universal compassion.

Fire and Burning

The fire indicates a dynamic action.

*

The white fire is the fire of aspiration, the red fire is the fire of renunciation and tapasya, the blue fire is the fire of spirituality and spiritual knowledge which purifies and dispels the Ignorance.

*

The fire is always the fire of purification — it is very red when it is acting on the vital; when the vital no longer covers the psychic, then the rose colour of the psychic comes out more and more.

*

It is the purification of the physical that is usually indicated in the symbol of burning.

Chapter Three

Sky, Weather, Night and Dawn

Sky

The sky usually symbolises a plane of consciousness mental or higher than the ordinary mental — stars are formations of light on that plane.

*

The sky is a symbol of the mental consciousness (or the psychic) or other consciousnesses above the mind — e.g. the higher mind, intuition, overmind etc. Akasha as the ether indicates also the infinite.

*

The sky in the heart is the chidakash. It is seen usually above the head, but when it is seen in the heart, that means the opening of the heart to the higher consciousness.

*

The blue sky is that of the Higher Mind — the nearest of the planes between human mentality and the Supermind. The moon here [*in a vision*] is the symbol of spirituality in the mental planes. The world of the Higher Mind is above those directly connected with the body consciousness.

*

The higher consciousness on any of its levels is seen usually as a sky or ether, but when felt through the vital it is often perceived as a sea.

*

Sat, Chit, Ananda, Supermind, Mind, Life, Matter are the seven [*seas of consciousness mentioned in the Veda*]. But in this Yoga one sees many levels of consciousness which appear as skies or else as seas.

Rain, Snow, Clouds, Lightning, Rainbow

The rain is the symbol of the descent of Grace or of the higher consciousness which is the cause of the riches — the spiritual plenty.

*

The vision you saw of the snow is probably a symbol of the consciousness in a condition of purity, silence and peace like a snowy ground; in that a new life (psychic, spiritual as indicated by the flowers) appears in place of the old mental and vital life which has been covered by that mantle of snowy whiteness.

*

Clouds are a symbol of obscurity.

*

The lightning is a symbol of the dynamic force of the higher consciousness acting at intervals to enlighten the rest of the being.

*

The rainbow is the sign of peace and deliverance.

Night and Dawn

The Night is the symbol of the Ignorance or Avidya in which men live just as Light is the symbol of Truth and Knowledge.

*

Dawn always means an opening of some kind — the coming of something that is not yet fully there.

Chapter Four
Water and Bodies of Water

Water

Water is the symbol of a state of consciousness or a plane.

Sea or Ocean

The sea with the sun over it is a plane of consciousness lit by the Truth. To enter into the rays is to be no longer merely lit by it, but in one's own conscious being to begin to become part of the Truth.

*

A sea in tumult usually indicates a vital upheaval or a period of strain and stress and struggle.

*

The blue ocean is often a symbol of the spiritual consciousness in higher Mind one and indivisible.

*

Normally, the ocean of higher consciousness is above the head (mind) and all below is that of the lower consciousness. Your seeing of the two oceans rather means that in the descent the influence of the higher consciousness reaches down to the heart (emotional being with the psychic behind it), but does not yet reach below in the lower vital and physical — but it is dissolving the knot in the heart centre which prevents the descent into the lower vital and physical centres. The joy in the *śānta svarūpa* is indeed a sign of the release of the heart centre. But the phrase in the Upanishads refers more particularly to the breaking of the knots of desire, attachment, sanskara, ego in the heart, which stand in the way of spiritual liberation and ascension — not to the knot which prevents the descent.

Pond, Lake, River

When the water is symbolic [*it is a plane of consciousness*] and here it is a big expanse of water — but a river or a pond are not large enough to symbolise a plane. It may be an actual experience in another world — or it may be the symbol of a particular movement in the sadhana.

It is not from dreams that you can know what plane of consciousness you are living in; it is by an observation of your condition.

*

Sometimes a part of the consciousness is seen in the image of a pond, lake or sea. The fish must be the vital mind.

*

The lake is the being in its individual consciousness, the sea is the same being with a universalised consciousness which can hold the universe and its cosmic forces in itself — the one (individual) merges into the other (the universal). The boat is the formation of the Mother's consciousness in you in which you are preparing to sail on this sea.

*

The river represents some movement of the consciousness. All these are images of the vital plane.

Chapter Five
Earth

Mountain

The mountain is the symbol of the embodied consciousness based upon earth but rising up towards the Divine.

*

The mountain always represents the ascending hill of existence with the Divine to be reached on the summits.

*

The mountain always means the same thing — it is the ascending consciousness.

*

The mountain is an image of the ascending consciousness.

*

The mountain is a very usual symbol of the consciousness with its ascending levels. The flowing of water from the peak indicates some flow from the higher consciousness above.

*

The mountain represents the ascending planes of the higher consciousness. The journey in the train is the passage from one consciousness to another.

*

The bucket is the physical consciousness; milk is always a symbol of the flow of consciousness from Above; the mountain is the Adhar with its ascending levels from the physical to the Above.[1]

---

[1] *In a vision during meditation, the correspondent saw a stream of milk flowing down a mountain and filling a bucket at its base.* — Ed.

The golden mountain is a symbol of the ascent to the Truth.

*

The Golden Mountain is always the mountain of the Divine Truth which one has to ascend — at its summit is the dwelling place of the Divine.

*

The experience of the great expanse of golden light on a mountain-top came because I had asked X to aspire for the higher experiences of the consciousness from above. The symbolic image of the mountain with the light on its top comes to most sadhaks who have the power of vision at all. The mountain is the consciousness rising from earth (the physical) through the successive heights (vital, mental, above-mental) towards the spiritual heaven. The golden light is always the light of the higher Truth (Supermind, Overmind or a little lower down the pure Intuition) and it is represented as a great luminous expanse on the summits of the being. X by concentrating on the light entered into contact with the higher reaches and that always gives these results, peace, joy, strength, a consciousness secure in the power of the Divine. It is of course through the psychic that she got into this contact, but in itself it is more an experience of the higher spiritual consciousness above mind than a psychic experience.

*

The silvery narrow way upward is the path of the spiritual consciousness.

Earth and Patala

Patala simply means the subconscient below the Earth — the Earth being the conscious physical plane.

*

You had asked the other day about the subconscient, what it was. In the vision you describe you were shown the universal subconscient in the figure of Patala, a place without light of consciousness and, because universal, therefore without bounds or end — the dark unconscious infinite out of which this material universe has arisen — it is walled with darkness on all sides, it seems also to have no bottom. The Light comes from above from the higher consciousness and coming down through the mind and heart and vital and physical has to pour down into this subconscient and make it luminous.

*

"Patala" is a name for the subconscient — the beings there [*in a dream*] had no heads, that is to say, there is there no mental consciousness; men have all of them such a subconscient plane in their own being and from there rise all sorts of irrational and ignorant (headless) instincts, impulses, memories etc. which have an effect upon their acts and feelings without their detecting the real source. At night many incoherent dreams come from this world or plane. The world above is the superconscient plane of being — above the human consciousness — there are many worlds of that kind; they are divine worlds.

Chapter Six
Gods, Goddesses and Semi-Divine Beings

Agni

There are many forms of Agni, — the solar fire, the vaidyuta fire and the nether fire are one Trinity — the fivefold fire is part of the Vedic symbolism of sacrifice.

*

The vision you saw of the man and the fire at his feet was probably a vision of the God Agni from whom flows the fire of tapasya and purification in the sadhana.

Shiva

The vision you had was of the way to the goal. Shiva on the way is the Power that pours the light but also scrutinises the sadhak to see whether he is ready for the farther advance. When he lets him pass, then is the rush of new and higher experiences, the march and progress of the divine forces, the Gods and their powers, the transformation of the nature into a higher consciousness. It was these powers that you saw passing in your vision.

Parvati-Shankara

It is probably the realm of the dynamic creative Spirit on the highest mental plane which you saw as the world of Parvati-Shankara.

Narayana, Vishnu, Brahma, Lakshmi, Saraswati, Ananta

Narayana is usually taken as a name of Vishnu — to the Vaishnavas he is the Supreme as Shiva is to the Shaivas. Both are cosmic Personalities of the Divine and both like Brahma have their original plane in the Overmind, although they take different forms to the human consciousness in the mental, vital and subtle physical planes.

Lakshmi is usually golden, not white. Saraswati is white.

The snake is simply a symbol of Energy or Power. Narayana in your dream is clearly Vishnu as is shown by the presence of Lakshmi and the single many-hooded snake.

Vishnu or Narayana in this image which is a normal Puranic image is the Lord of the waters of Space and Time — the Preserver of the principle of the Universe which he maintains as a seed in himself even in the intervals between one creation and another. Out of that seed in his navel (the navel is the central seat of the Vital, the Life-Principle) Brahma the Creator arises in the Lotus (cosmic consciousness) which grows from it when Vishnu awakens from the inter-cyclic sleep. The Snake Ananta is the Energy of the cosmic manifestation of the Infinite in Space-Time.

Krishna

This is the Krishna of the Gita[1] (the boy Krishna is the Krishna of Brindavan), — Krishna bringing the spiritual knowledge, will, bhakti — and not love and bhakti alone.

The eye indicates the vision of the higher spiritual consciousness and the blue expanse indicates that consciousness.

*

The boy with the flute is Sri Krishna, the Lord descended into the world-play from the divine Ananda; his flute is the music of the call which seeks to transform the lower ignorant play of mortal life and bring into it and establish in its place the lila of his divine Ananda. It was the psychic being in you that heard the call and followed after it.

*

---

[1] *In a dream the correspondent saw Sri Krishna in the prime of manhood. This image disappeared and gave way to a large eye seen in a vast expanse of blue. — Ed.*

It is, I suppose, the image of Sri Krishna as Lord of the divine Love and Ananda — and his flute calls the physical being to awake out of the attachments of the physical world and turn to that Love and Ananda.

*

Krishna with Radha is the symbol of the Divine Love. The flute is the call of the Divine Love; the peacock is victory.

*

The green circular disc you saw round Venus must indeed have been the aura of Venus which is of that colour; but this was only an introduction, a first application of the suddenly developed power of vision. Afterwards what came, the blue and the violet, were another kind of seeing more important for your Yoga; both are closely associated with Krishna. Blue is his especial and significant colour, the colour of his aura when he manifests, — that is why he is called *Nil Krishna*; the adjective does not mean that he was blue or dark in his physical body whether in Brindavan or Mathura or Dwarka! Violet is the radiance of Krishna's protection, — that was why, very naturally, it brought to you a sense of peace. The Mother says that she always saw it when she was in communion with Krishna and now too constantly sees it enveloping the Asram. That this should be the first thing shown when the power of vision broke through its state of latency is very significant; it proves that you are in contact, the touch already there in your inner being and this force of presence and protection is already around you or over you as an environing influence.

Hanuman

Hanuman stands for Bhakti.

*

Hanuman = complete bhakti.

*

Hanuman is a symbol of Shakti and devotion.

Narada

Narada stands for the expression of the Divine Love and Knowledge.

Mahakali and Kali

Mahakali and Kali are not the same, Kali is a lesser form. Mahakali in the higher planes appears usually with the golden colour.

*

These — Kali, Shyama, etc. — are ordinary forms seen through the vital; the real Mahakali form whose origin is in the Overmind is not black or dark or terrible, but golden of colour and full of beauty, even when formidable to the Asuras.

Durga on a Lion

The lion with Durga on it is the symbol of the Divine Consciousness acting through a divinised physical-vital and vital-material force.

*

The lion is the attribute of the Goddess Durga, the conquering and protecting aspect of the Universal Mother.
    The Death's Head is the symbol of the Asura (the adversary of the gods) vanquished and killed by the Divine Power.

Ganesh

It is according to the need or else the condition of the consciousness that these figures [*of the Gods*] appear in sadhana. Ganesh is at once the god of wisdom and the remover of obstacles.

*

Ganesh (among other things) is the devata of spiritual Knowledge — so as you are getting this knowledge, you saw yourself in this form, identified with Ganesh.

Kartikeya

The peacock is the bird of victory and Kartikeya the leader of the divine forces.

Sanatkumar

Sanatkumar is, I believe, one of the four mind-born sons of Brahma; he cannot therefore be identical with Skanda who is a son of Shiva.

Buddha

Buddha stands for the conquest over the Ignorance of the lower Nature.

Apsaras

Apsaras generally indicate sexual desire.

Chapter Seven
The Human World

Child

The child is usually the symbol of the psychic being.

*

A dream like this of a child — especially a newborn child — usually signifies the birth (i.e. the awakening) of the soul or psychic being in the outward nature.

*

The child usually signifies the psychic being — newborn in the sense that it at last comes to the surface. The colour of the cloth [*bright yellow*] would mean that it comes with health (internal or external or both) and the spiritual riches.

*

The infant in the Mother's arms is the symbol of the psychic being.

*

It is not a fact that the psychic being always appears as a baby — it is sometimes seen symbolically as a newborn baby; many see it as a child of varying ages — it is a very common and usual experience; it is not peculiar to emotional natures. It has several significances such as the new birth of the consciousness into the true psychic nature, the still young growth of this new being, the trust, reliance, dependence of the child on the Mother.

*

The child (when it does not mean the psychic being) is usually the symbol of something newborn in some part of the consciousness.

*

I suppose the golden child is the Truth-Soul which follows after the silver light of the spiritual. When it plunges into the black waters of the subconscient, it releases from it the spiritual light and the sevenfold streams of the Divine Energy and, clearing itself of the stains of the subconscient, it prepares its flight towards the supreme Divine (the Mother).

Parents and Relatives

In these dreams the parents or relatives mean the ordinary forces of the physical consciousness (the old nature).

*

A relative is generally a symbol of some element of the hereditary nature (the external being so far as it is created by heredity).

*

Mother, sister or other relatives are usually in such dreams symbols of forces of ordinary nature. The exact meaning depends on the context. But all such dreams are not symbolical — a sex dream for instance may bring up the form of any woman known or unknown.

*

These vital dreams are not interpretable unless there is an evident clue. Aunt or mother usually indicates the ordinary physical nature, a closed room would be some part of the physical nature that was not open to the light, bats would mean forces of the night, i.e. ignorant movements finding a lodging in the obscurity of the unenlightened nature.

*

It [*seeing relatives in dreams*] is the impression left by the past life and its sanskaras that come up in these dreams from the subconscient. They have to be rejected till the impressions are rooted out.

Robbers

The robbers are, as in the Veda, vital beings who come to steal away the good condition or else to steal the gains of the sadhana.

Journeying

The image of journeying always signifies a movement in life or a progress in sadhana.

*

Journeying on a horse or in a conveyance, if symbolic, means a progress or a movement in life, work or sadhana.

*

A journey in a boat or other conveyance means always a movement in the Yoga — often an advance or progress.

*

A journey in a carriage, train, motor car, steamer, boat, aeroplane etc. indicates a movement in the sadhana. The white horse may be the sattwic mind and the red horse the vital rajas giving energy and both combining to make a progress.

*

Aeroplane, steamer and train are always symbols of a rapid progress or forward movement.

*

The railway train at full speed means rapid progress.

*

The railway line is a symbol of rapid progress and the three stars are a symbol of Divine Grace in the mind, life and body.

*

The moving on the sands — it frequently happens in these

dreams — is usually a sign of an easier movement in the sadhana.

Running Away

The running away [*in dream*] is a symbol of the inertia in part of the being which allows the forces to invade, drawing back from them and losing ground instead of facing and destroying them.

Flying

When you find yourself flying it is always the vital being in the subtle body in the vital world that is doing it.

*

Flying during sleep over houses, streets, etc. simply means that the consciousness in the vital sheaths has gone out and is moving over places in the vital or subtle physical world (even sometimes the material); it is always in the vital sheath that one flies like that.

The ascending movement is different — in that it is the consciousness that goes high up to other planes or levels and comes down again to the body.

Ears

The ears signify usually the place of inspired knowledge or else of inspired expression — red and gold mean truth and power joined together.

Teeth

Symbolically, if the dream is symbolic, the falling of teeth means the disappearance of old fixed mental habits belonging to the physical mind.

*

The breaking or falling of teeth [*in dream*] is symbolic usually of the breaking or falling off of habitual formations or sanskaras in the physical mind.

Flesh

The piece of flesh indicates something restless in the physical being which stands by its restlessness and excessive materiality in the way of the full flow of the Ananda. In the dream this became active and was eliminated by the pressure of the psychic.

Being Dead

The feeling of being dead in a vision or dream experience comes when something in the being is to be silenced into entire inactivity and ceases to exist as a part of the nature. It may be a very small part, but as during the process the consciousness is concentrated in it and identified with it for the purpose of the working, the feeling is that "I am dead". When you said, "I am dead, now let me get up and go", it simply meant, "The thing is done and the process is over. There is no need to identify myself with this part any longer." There is no indication in the experience as to what the thing was that passed through this experience.

Chapter Eight
The Animal World

Cow

The cow in the occult symbolism indicates Light or the consciousness — white indicates the purified or spiritual consciousness — the white Light.

*

It is quite clear; it is the Vedic image. In the Veda the Cow is the Divine Light — the white Cow is the pure Consciousness in which there is the Light. The milk is the Knowledge and Power descending from the divine Consciousness.

*

The Cow usually means the Higher Consciousness. Perhaps the calf indicates the truth of the higher consciousness (white) in the physical (red).

*

The white calf is the sign of a pure and clear consciousness, — the cow or calf being the symbol of Light in the consciousness, something psychic or spiritual that you felt natural and intimate to you and inseparable.

*

The vision of the cows must have taken place in the psychic world. It has also a symbolic significance. The sun is the symbol of the Divine Truth, the cows are its powers, rays of the sun, sources of true knowledge, true feeling, true experience.

The descent you felt must have been into some depth of light, probably in the psychic nature.

*

Milk is always the symbol of the flow of the higher consciousness.

Bull

The bull is an emblem of strength and force. It is also in the Veda an image of the Gods, the male powers in Nature. Again the bull is the *vāhana* of Shiva. It may in a dream or an experience be any of these symbols — but it is probably the first here.

Horse

A horse always indicates some power.

*

The Horse is the symbol in dream or vision of a Power or Energy.

*

The Horse is Power — white is pure. It is the pure Power.

*

The Horse is Power, usually Life-Power, but also it may mean Mind-Power in Tapas if it is dynamic and mobile.

*

The Horse is the symbol of Power in motion — often of the Power that makes for rapid progress in sadhana.

*

The horse is a force acting for progress.

*

The horse is always the symbol of Power; it must be then a Power which you were trying to catch and make your own while sometimes it was trying to come up with you, perhaps to use you. This is what happens in the vital where there are these uncertain and elusive movements. The high platform was evidently the level of a higher Consciousness which stilled this fluctuating movement and made control of the Power more possible, as it became still and near.

*

The ass is the symbol of the inertia and obstruction in the body. The horse is the symbol of force or power. The tunnel of water must be the vital physical and the arch is a passage out, by which, if the ass can cross it or rather be pulled across, then it becomes a horse. In other words, the inertia and obstruction in the physical will be changed into Power and Force of Progress.

Lion

The Lion is the vital force.

*

The lion means vital force, strength, courage — here full of the light, illumined by the spiritual consciousness.[1]

*

The lion indicates force and courage, strength and power. The lower vital is not lionlike.

Tiger

It all depends on the attitude of the tiger. If fierce and hostile, it may be a form of an adverse force, otherwise it is simply a power of vital nature which may be friendly.

Elephant

The elephant is Strength — sometimes Strength illumined with Wisdom.

*

---

[1] *In the correspondent's vision, the lion's face was full of shining light and the hairs of its mane were like rays of spreading light.* — Ed.

The elephant is Strength — sometimes Strength removing obstacles.

*

The blue elephant is the strength of the Higher Consciousness fulfilling itself and removing obstacles.

Giraffe

The Giraffe symbolises aspiration.

Camel

[*Camel manifesting violet light*] Patient progress and endurance as a gift of the Divine Grace.

Deer and Antelope

The deer = speed in the spiritual path.

*

The deer is perhaps a symbol of speed in the spiritual progress.

*

The deer is Immortality, the antelope is Rapid Movement.

Boar

It [*the boar*] is rajasic strength and vehemence. Much however depends upon the context, — these figures have also other meanings.

*

The wild boar points to attacks of the crude vital rajas.

Buffalo

A buffalo conveys the idea often of an obscure violence in the nature — here [*in the correspondent's dream*] it seems tied up — i.e. under control but not eliminated. But it is not clear to what it refers — if it is symbolic at all.

*

The buffalo is a symbol of unnecessary or blind anger — perhaps it meant that that was still somewhere in your nature.

*

[*Buffaloes:*] Rash and obscure vital forces.

Goat

The goat in vision is often symbolic of lust.

*

Goats usually indicate sex tendencies.

Monkey

The monkey is a symbol of the leaping restless mind; these monkeys are the doubts and suggestions that have been assailing you.

*

The monkey is a symbol of the restless vital consciousness or of one or other of its movements.

Dog

The dog is the symbol of devoted affection and obedience.

*

The dog generally signifies devoted obedience — so it[2] may indicate the action of a devoted obedience spiritualised in the

---

[2] In a vision the correspondent saw a dog's face bathed in blue light, with its eyes full of white light. — Ed.

higher consciousness.

*

The dog usually indicates fidelity and as it is yellow, it would be fidelity in the mind to the Divine — but the other black and white one is difficult to interpret — it is something in the vital, but the meaning of the black spots is not clear.

Black Cat

The black cat is usually the symbol of magic of an evil kind or of an evil influence of the vital world acting on the physical as magic does. It is effective so long as its nature and mode of action are not discovered, so long as it can act invisibly — when it is seen it can be dealt with. The others had not seen it and were not aware that it was taking the life of the sick person and that she was not dead and need not die if this force could be destroyed or prevented from acting; you saw it and were therefore able to fight and catch it and kill it. That it took long to kill shows that it was not representing a particular process of magic which can be annulled quickly and decisively, but a Force of evil magic from the vital plane.

Snake or Serpent

The serpent is the symbol of energy, it may be a bad or hostile energy — but it may also be a good, even a divine energy.

*

The snake indicates some kind of energy always — oftener bad, but also it can indicate some luminous or divine energy. It is [*in this case*] the ascent of some such force from the physical upwards. The other details are not clear.

*

About the snake you saw in your meditation — serpents indicate always energies of Nature and very often bad energies of the vital plane; but they can also indicate luminous or divine energies like the snake of Vishnu. The one you saw was evidently of this latter type — a luminous divine energy and therefore there was no cause for alarm, it was a good sign.

*

A snake is a bad symbol only when it comes from the vital or other lower plane.

*

What you saw was not what is in yourself, but a symbol of the things that are in vital Nature. Scorpions and usually snakes also are symbols of harmful energies; the vital nature of earth is full of these energies and that is why the purification of man's outer vital nature also is so difficult and there are so many wrong movements and happenings in him, — because his vital is easily open to all these earth movements. In order to get rid of them, the inner being must wake and grow and its nature replace the outer nature. Sometimes serpents indicate energies simply, not harmful ones; but more often it is the other way. On the other hand the peacocks you saw were powers of victory, the victory of the energies of light over the energies of darkness.

*

The serpent Ananta is the infinite energy in infinite Time-Space which supports the universe.

*

It is in answer to your aspiration that the Mahakali force descended — the Serpent is the Energy from above working in the vital answering to the Serpent Kundalini which rises from below.

*

The Serpent is the symbol of energy — especially of the Kundalini Shakti which is the divine Force coiled up in the lowest (physical) centre, Muladhara — and when it rises it goes up through the spine and joins the higher consciousness above.

Energies are of all kinds and the snakes can also symbolise the evil powers of the unregenerate vital nature — but here it is not that.

*

The serpent symbolises an energy good or bad, divine or undivine according to its nature. Here, it looks as if it were the Kundalini trying to ascend to the Brahmarandhra, but it has not yet reached beyond the vital and is stopped — probably because the time has not yet come.

*

This [*vision*] is the symbol of the opening of the centres to the Light.

The swan is the Indian symbol of the individual soul, the central being, the divine part which is turned towards the Divine, descending from there and ascending to it.

The two serpents interlaced are the two channels in the spine, through which the Shakti moves upward and downward.

The serpent with the six hoods is the Kundalini Shakti, the divine Power asleep in the lowest physical centre which, awakened in the Yoga, ascends in light through the opening centres to meet the Divine in the highest centre and so connect the manifest and the unmanifested, joining Spirit and Matter.

*

The golden serpent in the Muladhara is a symbol of the energy of the transformed physical consciousness.

*

The cobra is a symbol of the Energy in Nature — the upraised hood and light indicate the illumination and victorious position of the emerged Energy.

*

The opening of the hood indicates the victorious or successful activity of the Energy indicated by the snake.

*

The serpent with the hood over the head generally indicates future siddhi.

*

Snakes and scorpions always indicate attacks or threats of attack of one kind or another, more often threats from the vital plane or hostile influences on the physical.

*

The serpent is a symbol of force, very often a hostile or evil force of the vital plane. The sea is a symbol of a plane of consciousness. The white light is a manifestation of pure divine force descending from one of the truth-planes leading to the supramental.

The indication is that of a hostile vital force being expelled and the purifying light from above descending to illumine and deliver the part of the plane formerly occupied by it.

Crocodile

The crocodile signifies greed, *lobha*, of some kind.

Frog

Frog = modest usefulness.

Fish

The fish is the always moving vital mind making all sorts of formations.

*

Fish might be formations in the vital consciousness — for water most often indicates the vital consciousness.

Bird

The bird is often a symbol of the being.

*

The bird is a symbol of the individual soul.

*

A bird is a very frequent symbol of the soul, and the tree is the standing image of the universe — the Tree of Life.

*

Birds often indicate either mind-powers or soul-powers.

*

The bird is usually a symbol of some soul power when it is not the soul itself — here it is a power (awakened in the soul) of the whitish blue light — Sri Aurobindo's light.

*

The Blue Bird is always a symbol of aspiration towards something Beyond.

*

The blue bird is the symbol of aspiration to the heights.

Swan or Hansa

The swan is a symbol of the soul on the higher plane.

*

The swan is the liberated soul.

*

Both [*the goose and the swan*] are symbols of the beings in a man — but the goose or ordinary Hansa usually refers to the *manomaya puruṣa*.

*

The Hansa is the symbol of the being — it regains its original purity as it rises until it becomes luminous in the Highest Truth.

*

The Hansa is a symbol of the soul or the self — the peacock is the bird of victory. The golden Hansa is the soul living in the Truth, the golden peacock is the victory of the Truth.

Duck

The duck is the symbol of the soul — silvery colour = the spiritual consciousness — golden wings = the power of the Divine Truth.

*

The duck is usually a symbol of the soul or inner being; perhaps it was the four beings — mental, psychic, vital and physical — that you saw.[3]

Crane

The crane is the messenger of happiness.

Peacock

The peacock is the Bird of Victory.

*

A peacock is the symbol of spiritual victory.

*

The peacock signifies victory — in Yoga the divine victory. The clear sky would indicate perhaps the mental part cleared of obscurities. Seeing the higher part of the bodies [*of the peacocks*] would mean a victory in the higher parts of the consciousness, in the mental (head and neck) and perhaps also in vital mind and in emotional.

---

[3] *The correspondent saw four ducks with uplifted necks, illuminated with white light, advancing in a row. — Ed.*

Dove or Pigeon

The dove signifies peace. The colours indicate the vital — green would be self-giving in the vital; blue the higher consciousness in the vital. So it must be peace casting its influence from above on the vital.

*

The white pigeon must be Peace.

Crow, Eagle, Kite

The crow signifies practical cleverness, the eagle Intelligence. The kite is Krishna's *vāhana*.

Ostrich

The ostrich may mean rapidity of movement.

Spider

The image of the spider in the Upanishads is used for the Brahman creating the world out of itself, dwelling in it and withdrawing it into itself. But what matters in a symbol is what it means for you. It may mean for you success or successful formations.

White Ants

Obviously it [*white ants seen in a dream*] must have been symbolic of small but destructive forces in the lower vital or physical.

Flies

Something small in the smaller vital.

Chapter Nine
The Plant World

Aswattha or Peepul Tree

The aswattha usually symbolises the cosmic manifestation.

*

It [*the peepul tree*] is the symbol of the cosmic existence.

Jungle

The jungle must be some unregenerated part of the vital nature and the serpent a wrong force emerging from it.

Leaves

Images of leaves and plants usually indicate vital strength or energy.

*

A green leaf means vital strength or energy or vitality.

Fruits

The fruits are the results of the sadhana.

Flowers

Flowers indicate a blossoming in the consciousness, sometimes with special reference to the psychic or the psychicised vital, mental and physical consciousness.

*

The vision of flowers is a symbol usually of psychic qualities or movements whether a potentiality or promise or an actual state of development.

*

It is usually when the psychic is active that this seeing of flowers becomes abundant.

*

The flowers indicate always an opening (usually psychic) in some part of the consciousness.

*

The flowers[1] are the symbols of psychic movements. The sun is the Divine Consciousness. It is the awakening of the psychic consciousness and its activity under the Divine Influence.

*

Red flowers would ordinarily indicate an opening of the consciousness either in the physical or some part of the vital according to the shade.

Lotus

A lotus flower indicates open consciousness.

*

A lotus signifies the opening of the (true) consciousness.

*

The lotus is always the sign of the consciousness opening somewhere — when the consciousness opened from above, you became aware of a new plane of being of which you were not aware before.

*

---

[1] *In a vision the correspondent saw a luminous sun sending forth a multitude of flowers. — Ed.*

It [*the lotus*] means consciousness. The opening of the lotus is the opening of some part of the consciousness.

*

The opening of the lotuses[2] means, I suppose, the opening of the true vital and physical consciousness in which the spiritual being (the Swan) can manifest with all the consequences of that opening.

*

The lotus must represent owing to its numerous petals the "thousand petalled" lotus above the head which is the seat of the higher consciousness above the thinking intelligence. The vision may mean the opening of the consciousness there and in it the adoration of the Divine.

*

A lotus usually indicates an opening into the spiritual. The white and red are symbols of the Mother and the incarnating Divine.

*

The white lotus is the symbol of the Mother's consciousness, — it does not indicate any part of the individual consciousness.

*

The red lotus is the flower of the Divine Presence.

*

The red lotus is the presence of the Divine on earth — the sun is the Divine Truth. It indicates the Divine manifestation on earth raising earth consciousness towards the Truth.

*

The red lotus signifies the presence of the Divine on the Earth.

*

---

[2] *The correspondent wrote about a vision in which two lotuses blossomed in his body, one at the navel region, the other at the base of the spine.* — Ed.

It [*the blue lotus*] can be taken as the (Avatar) incarnation on the mental plane.

Other Flowers

The red rose is the flower of love and surrender, the white is the purity of psychic love.

*

Reddish pink rose = psychic love or surrender.
White rose = pure spiritual surrender.

*

The java [*red hibiscus*] is the flower of the Divine Power.

*

The [*flower named*] eternal smile[3] means the self-existent joy and gladness of the Spirit.

*

I told you saffron meant purification — so if it has any significance, it can only mean that the Mother gave you a power of purification to use.[4]

---

[3] Hibiscus micranthus, *a very small white hibiscus.* — Ed.
[4] *The correspondent wrote that in a dream the Mother put a large packet of saffron in her hand.* — Ed.

Chapter Ten
Constructions

Building

The building is the symbol of a new creation — the white indicating spiritual consciousness, the coloured lights the different powers.

Workshop

The workshop is probably a symbol of the activity of the ordinary nature which is so full of formations and activities of the ordinary kind that it is difficult to pass through it to the inner or the inmost being.

The walls with the spaces between indicate the different parts of the being to which the outer mind has no access — possibly, the inner vital (the women may be the occult vital nature), emotional etc. The ceiling (yellow) may be the intellect or thinking mind which walls one in and prevents from getting into the open spaces of the higher consciousness. But through all a way lies to the open way of the higher consciousness full of peace, light and Ananda.

Temple

The temple means religious feeling, worship, adoration, consecration.

*

It is a temple and the temple is the symbol of spiritual aspiration. This one being complex meant a rich and many-sided aspiration.

Pyramid and Sphinx

The pyramid is usually a symbol of aspiration — reddish perhaps because it is in the physical.

*

The Sphinx is a symbol of the eternal quest that can only be answered by the secret knowledge.

Chapter Eleven
Objects

Cross and Shield

The cross is the sign of the triple being, transcendent, universal and individual.

*

The cross indicates the triple Divine (transcendent, universal, individual) — the shield means protection.

Crown

The crown is the sign of fulfilment (here in the intuitive consciousness) and the going up means an ascent to higher planes.

*

The crown indicates the higher consciousness in its static condition, the wheel its dynamic action. The red light is the Power sent down to change the physical.

Diamond

The diamond is the symbol of the Mother's light and energy — the diamond light is that of her consciousness at its most intense.

*

Diamonds may indicate the Mother's Light at its intensest, for that is diamond white light.

*

The diamond in your heart was a formation of the light of Mother's consciousness there, — for the Mother's light is of a white and at its most intense of a diamond radiance. The light is a sign of the Mother's presence in your heart and that is what you saw once and felt for a moment.

Pearl

It [*a pearl*] may be a representation of the "bindu", which is a symbol of the infinite in the exceedingly small, the individual point which is yet the Universal.

Flute

The flute is the symbol of a call — usually the spiritual call.

*

The flute is the call of the Divine.

*

The flute is the call of the Divine which descends into you from above and awakes the psychic yearning (the tears) and ends by bringing a vast peace and shows to you the clear sky of the higher consciousness in which there are the Truth-formations (golden stars) some of which begin to descend in a rain upon the physical consciousness (the earth).

Conch

The conch is often the symbol of call or aspiration.

*

The conch is the symbol of the spiritual call.

*

The conch is the call to realisation.

*

The conch is perhaps the proclamation of victory.

*

The lotus is the opened consciousness — the conchshell is the call to victory.

Bells

Bells heard are usually a sign of progress in sadhana, progress to come.

Vina

Harmony.

Wheel, Disc or Chakra

The wheel is the sign of an action of Force (whatever force may be indicated by the nature of the symbol) and as it was surging upwards it must be the fire of aspiration rising from the vital (navel centre) to the Higher Consciousness above.

*

A revolving disc means a force in action on the nature. The whitish blue light is known as Krishna's light, also as Sri Aurobindo's light. White is the Mother's. Perhaps here it is a combination.

*

The [*Sudarshan*] Chakra symbolises the action of Sri Krishna's force.

*

The chakra is the energy at work and it brings the first opening of the consciousness in the gross physical plane, i.e. of the mental physical, psychic physical, vital physical and the material.

*

Yes, the circular movement and the Chakra are always signs of energy in action, generally creative action.

Bow and Arrow

The bow is a symbol of the force sent out to reach its mark.

*

The arrow is the symbol of the Force which goes to its aim. Gold = the Truth, Yellow = the mind, Green = the vital energy. The arrow of the spiritual Truth using the mind and the vital energy.

Key

Is it a key you saw?[1] If so the meaning is clear; it is the key to the divine realisation; the Mother is the key because it is her light (white is her colour) that enables us to open the gate of realisation.

Book

The book indicates some kind of knowledge.

Mirror, Square and Triangle

The mirror between the eyebrows indicates that something in the inner mind has become able to reflect the Truth from above (golden light) — a square is a symbol of the truth beyond the mind as a triangle is the symbol of mind, life, body.

Incense Stick and Tobacco

The incense stick is the symbol of self-consecration.

*

Tobacco is associated with tamas and incense sticks with adoration.

---

[1] *The correspondent wrote that in a vision he saw a key with the word "MOTHER" written on it in white letters, with white light around it. — Ed.*

Gramophone

The gramophone is obviously symbolic of the mechanical mind.

Chapter Twelve
Numbers and Letters

Numbers

In one form or another all these ideas [*such as the significance of numbers*] have existed in the past. The significance of numbers was one of the chief elements in the teaching of Pythagoras 5 centuries before Christ.

*

The number 7 is the number of realisation — when there are four 7's it indicates perfect realisation.

*

7 is the figure of realisation. 3 x 3 means the descent from above and the answer from below.

*

There is no unlucky number. Numbers all have their powers and why should 13 not have its chance?

Letters (Writing)

The writing [*floating before the eyes*] is often seen by sadhaks either in meditation and sleep or with the waking eyes or in both states. But if you see it only in sleep or an inward condition, it is not so easy to remember when waking unless you train yourself to remember.

OM

OM there [*above the crown of the head*] indicates the realisation of the Brahman on that level of the (higher) consciousness.

Part Three

Experiences of
the Inner Consciousness
and the Cosmic Consciousness

Section One

Experiences on the Inner Planes

Chapter One

Experiences on the Subtle Physical, Vital and Mental Planes

Subtle Physical Experiences

Is it [*a strong and rapid heartbeat that shakes the whole body*] the physical nerves and heart — or in the subtle body? Often one feels a shaking and vibration of the subtle body and can feel as if heartbeats there, but if not experienced, it impresses as if it were a material phenomenon.

*

It is evidently in a subtle world, not the physical that you move; that is evident from the different arrangement of things, by such details as the third arm and the book marker removed yet there; but they show also that it is a subtle world very near to the physical; it is either a subtle physical world or a very material vital domain. In all the subtle domains the physical is reproduced with a change, the change growing freer and more elastic as one gets farther away. Such details as the lameness show the same thing, — the hold of the physical is still there. It is possible to move about in the physical world, but usually that can only be done by drawing on the atmosphere of other physical beings for a stronger materialisation of the form — when that happens one moves among them and sees them and all the surroundings exactly as they are at that time in the physical world and can verify the accuracy of the details if immediately after returning to the body (which is usually done with a clear consciousness of the whole process of getting into it) one can traverse the same scene in the physical body. But this is rare; the subtle wandering is on the contrary a frequent phenomenon, only when it is near to the physical world, all seems very material and concrete and the association of physical habits and physical mental movements with the subtle events is closer.

Vital Experiences

The place where you were [*in a dream*] is as much a world of fact and reality as is the material world and its happenings have sometimes a great effect on this world. What an ignorant lot of disciples you all are! Too much modernisation and Europeanisation by half!

These things are meetings on the vital plane, but very often in the transcription of what happened some details get in that are contributed by the subconscient mind. I rather suspect all that about X was such a contribution. The rest seems all right. The writing on the forehead means of course something that is fixed in you in the vital plane and has to come out hereafter in the physical consciousness.

*

You are too physically matter of fact. Besides you are quite ignorant of occult things. The vital is part of what European psychologists sometimes call the subliminal and the subliminal, as everybody ought to know, can do things the physical cannot do — e.g. solve a problem in a few minutes over which the physical has spent days in vain etc. etc.

What is the use of the same things happening on both planes; it would be superfluous and otiose. The vital plane is a field where things can be done which for some reason or other can't be done now on the physical.

There are of course hundreds of varieties of things in the vital as it is a much richer and more plastic field of consciousness than the physical, and all are not of equal validity and value. I am speaking above of the things that are valid. By the way, without this vital plane there would be no art, poetry or literature — these things come through the vital before they can manifest here.

*

Experiences: Subtle Physical, Vital and Mental 195

At this stage you have only to watch the experiences and observe their significance. It is only when the experiences are in the vital realm that some are likely to be false formations. These of which you write are simply the common experiences of an opening Yogic consciousness and they have to be understood, simply.

Here it is the breaking up of the small surface vital into the largeness of the true or inner vital being which can at once open to the Higher Consciousness, its power, light and Ananda. There is also begun a similar breaking of the small physical mind and sense into the wideness of the inner physical consciousness. The inner planes are always wide and open into the Universal while the outer surface parts of the being are shut up in themselves and full of narrow and ignorant movements.

*

It is plain. The lower being (vital and physical) was receiving an influence (mental light, yellow) from the thinking mind and higher vital which was clearing it of the old habitual lower vital reactions: very often in the sadhana one feels the inner being speaking to the outer or the mind or higher vital speaking to the lower so as to enlighten it.

*

These things that come [*in dreams*] to frighten you are merely impressions thrown on you by small vital forces which want to prevent you (by making you nervous) pushing on the sadhana. They can really do nothing to you, only you must reject all fear. Keep always this thought when these things come, "The Mother's protection is with me, nothing bad can happen"; for when there is the psychic opening and one puts one's faith in the Mother, that is sufficient to ward these things off. Many sadhaks learn, when they have alarming dreams, to call the Mother's name in the dream itself and then the things that menace them become helpless or cease. You must therefore refuse to be intimidated and reject these impressions with contempt. If there is anything frightening, call down the Mother's protection.

The heat you felt was probably due to some difficulty in the force coming down below the centre between the eyes where it has been working up till now. When such sensations or the unease you once felt or similar things come, you must not be alarmed, but remain quiet and let the difficulty pass.

What you had before that, the moonlight in the forehead, was this working in the centre there between the eyebrows, the centre of the inner mind, will and vision. The moonlight you saw is the light of spirituality and it was this that was entering into your mind through the centre, with the effect of the widening in the heart like a sky filled with moonlight. Afterwards came some endeavour to prepare the lower part of the mind whose centre is in the throat and join it with the inner mind and make it open; but there was some difficulty, as is very usually the case, which caused the heat. It was probably the fire of tapas, Agni, trying to open the way to this centre.

The experience of being taken up into the sky is a very common one and it means an ascent of the consciousness into a higher world of light and peace.

The idea that you must go more and more within and turn wholly to the Mother is quite right. It is when there is no attachment to outward things for their own sake and all is only for the Mother and the life through the inner psychic being is centred in her that the best condition is created for the spiritual realisation.

*

Your series of experiences are very interesting by the constant (though interspaced) development they illustrate. Here two new significant elements have been added to the previous substance of the experience. The first is the very precise localisation of the uprush of the consciousness from the pit of the stomach — that is to say, from above the navel, the movement itself starting from the navel or even below it. The navel-centre (*nābhi-padma*) is the main seat of the centralised vital consciousness (dynamic centre) which ranges from the heart level (emotional) to the centre below the navel (lower vital, sensational desire centre). These three mark the domain of the vital being. It is therefore

Experiences: Subtle Physical, Vital and Mental

clear that it was your inner vital being which had this experience, and its intensity and vehemence was probably due to the whole vital (or most of it) being awake and sharing in it this time. The experience itself was psychic in its origin, but was given a strong emotional-vital form in its expression. I may add, for completeness, that the centre of the psychic is behind the heart and it is through the purified emotions that the psychic most easily finds an outlet. All from the heart above is connected with the mental-vital and above it is the mind with its three centres, one in the throat (the outward-going or externalising mind), one between the eyes or rather in the middle of the forehead (the centre of vision and will) and one above, communicating with the brain, which is called the thousand-petalled lotus and where are centralised the highest thought and intelligence communicating with the greater mind planes (illumined mind, intuition, overmind) above.

The second new significant feature is the self-manifestation of the inner mind; for it was your inner mind that was watching, observing and criticising the vital being's psychic experience. You found this clear division in you curious, but it will no longer seem curious once you know the perfectly normal divisibility of the different parts of the being. In the outer surface nature mind, psychic, vital, physical are all jumbled together and it needs a strong power of introspection, self-analysis, close observation and disentanglement of the threads of thought, feeling and impulse to find out the composition of our nature and the relation and interaction of these parts upon each other. But when one goes inside as you have done, we find the sources of all this surface action and there the parts of our being are quite separate and clearly distinct from each other. We feel them indeed as different beings in us, and just as two people in a group can do, they too are seen to observe, criticise, help or oppose and restrain each other; it is as if we were a group-being, each member of the group with its separate place and function, and all directed by a central being who is sometimes in front above the others, sometimes behind the scenes. Your mental being was observing the vital and not quite easy about its vehemence, —

for the natural base of the mental being is calm, thoughtfulness, restraint, control and balance, while the natural turn of the vital is dynamism, energy thrown into emotion, sensation and action. All therefore was perfectly natural and in order.

*

As for the experience stated it was probably in the vital plane and such suddennesses and vividnesses of experience are characteristic of the vital — but they are not lasting, they only prepare. It is when one has got into contact with what is beyond mind and vital and body and risen there that the great lasting fundamental realisations usually come.

Influence or Possession by Beings of Other Planes

The case of the girl in question seems to be of a fairly common kind. In one way or another a certain subtle faculty is awakened by which there is contact with some other plane of consciousness and its beings, usually with the vital or larger "life" worlds behind the material plane. These experiences are often of little value, trivial and full of misleading conceptions, messages or suggestions; the inexperienced *voyant* or seer adds to them the formations and delusions of his own subliminal mind. It is only by training and experience that one can arrive at an elimination of these errors and establish the true use of the subtle faculties. These powers are often enough dangerous to their unexperienced or indisciplined possessor and the hysteria of the girl in question was obviously the result (a result that happens in many cases) of her allowing some being of the vital plane to delude and influence her. This kind of thing has no connection at all with the spiritual or psychic experience of the Rishis and sages; it is rather akin to the experiences of mediums and others in Europe.

*

It seems that you do not pay sufficient attention to the instructions that are sent to you from here. You were specially warned not to allow anything to take possession of you. But in relating one of your experiences repeated for several days you speak of something that was taking possession of you, even obliging you to make incoherent noises, and yet you say you do not know whether it was good or bad or what kind of force it was! It is evident from your description that it was a vital force trying to take violent possession of the body. Nothing can be more dangerous than to allow this kind of loss of control and intrusion of an alien influence. In your present condition of ignorance, the vital being not yet sufficiently open, the psychic not yet sufficiently awake, a hostile power can easily intrude and pass itself off as the divine Force. Remember that no personality and no power is to be allowed to possess you. The divine Force will not act in this way; it will work first to purify, to widen and enlighten and transform the consciousness, to open it to Light and Truth, to awaken the heart and the psychic being. Only afterwards will it take gradual and quiet control through a pure and conscious surrender.

*

I have omitted all this time to reply to your letter forwarding your friend's statement about his experiences. I am not very sure of its significance. The "double" voice is a frequent phenomenon; it happens very often when one has been long repeating a mantra that a voice or consciousness within begins to repeat it automatically — also prayer can be taken up in the same way from within. It is usually by an awakening of the inner consciousness or by the going in of the consciousness more deeply within from its outward poise that this happens. This is supported in his case by the fact that he feels himself halfway to trance, his body seems to melt away, he does not feel the weight of the book etc.; all these are well-known signs of the inner consciousness getting awake and largely replacing the outer. The moral effects of his new condition would also indicate an awakening of the inner consciousness, the psychic or psychic-mental perhaps. But on the other hand, he seems to feel this other voice as if outside him and to have the sense of another being than himself, an invisible presence in the room. The inner being is often felt as someone separate from or other than the ordinary self, but it is not usually felt outside. So it may be that in this state of withdrawal he comes into contact with another plane or world and attracts to himself one of its beings who wants to share in his sadhana and govern it. This last is not a very safe phenomenon, for it is difficult to say from the data what kind of being it is and the handing over of the government of one's inner development to any other than the Divine, the Guru or one's own psychic being may bring with it serious peril. That is all I can say at present.

*

All the other circumstances which you relate[1] are normal and would be the phenomena of an invasion of Ananda occupying the whole instrumental being while the silent inner being within remains separate as it does usually from all that comes from outside. The circumstance that is not clear is the Presence. There is nothing to indicate who or what it is. If it were an undesirable vital Presence producing a vital joy, there would usually be vital phenomena which would enable you to detect their origin, but these are not apparent here. In the circumstances the only course is to observe the experience without accepting any occupation of the being by what comes, taking it as only an experience which the inner being looks on as a witness, until the point that remains veiled is made clear.

P.S. There are several possible explanations but I do not speak of them as that might influence and interfere with the pure observation of the experience by bringing in a mental suggestion.

*

I have read your letter and I have also read it to the Mother. My conclusion about the experience — I had suspended judgment till now — is the same as hers.

We consider that it will be wiser for you to be on your guard

---

[1] *This letter and the four that follow it were written to the same person. — Ed.*

Experiences: Subtle Physical, Vital and Mental 201

about it in future. In the first place it cannot be the Buddha — the Buddha's presence would bring peace but could never give this kind of Ananda. Next, the suggestion based on an old subjective feeling of yours seems to be thrown on you to make you more readily admit some *emprise* that the experience is a means of establishing on you. Again the feeling you have that the Ananda is more than you can bear is a sign not favourable to the experience; you suppose that it is a want of adaptation that gives you the feeling, but it is more likely that it is because it is something foreign thrown on you through the vital with which the psychic being in you does not feel at home. Finally, it is not safe to admit while you are doing the Yoga here another influence, *whatever it may be*, which is not ours or part of the movement of this sadhana. If that takes place anything might happen and we would not be able to protect you against it because you would have stepped out of the circle of protection. You have hitherto been proceeding on a very sound line of development; a diversion of this kind which seems to be on the vital level might be a serious interference. No trust can be put on the beauty of the eyes or the face. There are many Beings of the inferior planes who have a captivating beauty and can enthral with it and they can give too an Ananda which is not of the highest and may on the contrary by its lure take away from the path altogether. When you have reached the stage of clear discernment where the highest Light is turned on all things that come, then experiences of many kinds may be safely faced, but now a strict vigilance must be exercised and all diversions rejected. It is necessary to keep one's steps firmly on the straight road to the Highest; all else must wait for the proper time.

*

For the eyes, that experience had got a certain hold and it was not to be expected that it would altogether disappear all at once. These things try to persist, but if the refusal is firm and unchanging, they fade away after a time or cease. The lessening of the intensity of the ananda is already a sign that the rejection is having its effect. You have only to persist and after a time the vital consciousness will be free.

*

I have no doubt that the action of this force once rejected will disappear in time. It is something with which you have been brought into contact, not something intimate to yourself to which part of your being is naturally responsive. That is shown by the inability to catch what the being who manifested wanted to convey to you. It seems to have been an onslaught, as you say, an attempted invasion by force and ruse. It is quite true that when there is the opening to the Light, the adverse Forces as well as the lower forces become active when they can do so. The consciousness of the seeker has come out of its normal limits and is opening to the universal as well as upwards to the Self above and they take advantage of that to attempt an entrance. Such onslaughts however are not inevitable and you are probably right in thinking that you caught it in the atmosphere of X. He has made experiments of many kinds in the occult field and there one comes easily into contact with forces and beings of a darker nature and one needs a great power and light and purity — one's own or a helping Power's — to face them and overcome. There are also deficiencies or errors in one's own nature which can open the door to these beings. But the best is if one can have nothing to do with them; for the conquest of the forces of the lower nature is a sufficiently heavy task without that complication. If the work one has to do necessitates the contact and conflict with them, that is another matter. In your case I think this has been something of an accident and not a necessity of the development of your sadhana.

*

No, there was no special concentration or call from the Mother at that time. It was at a time when she never sees anyone, so evidently she would not have put such a force upon you, nor does she usually exercise her power in this way. You did well to resist the impulsion. It is always necessary to keep the inner perception and will clear, conscious and in perfect balance and never to allow any force of impulsion, however it may present itself, to sweep without their discerning consent the vital or the body into action. Whatever appearance they may assume, such forces cannot be trusted; once the discriminating intelligence gives up its control, any kind of force can intervene in this way and a path is opened for unbalanced vital impulses to be used to the detriment of the sadhana. A psychic or spiritual control replacing the mental would not act in this way, but whatever intensity or ardour it may give, would maintain a clear perception of things, a perfect discrimination, a harmony between the inward and the outward reality. It is only the vital that is swept by these impulses; the vital must always be kept under the control of the intelligence, the psychic or when that becomes dynamic, the higher spiritual consciousness.

An Experience on the Mental Plane

The vision you had was of the mental plane and symbolic. It symbolised not so much your own position as the general difficulties which lie in the way of one's going deep inside into the psychic centre and living there. The *maidān* full of light was the inmost psychic centre; the dark place in between represents the veil of ignorance created by the gulf between this inmost psychic and the outer nature. The chakra turning round and round which prevents the approach from one side (the mental side) is the activity of the ordinary mind; when the mind becomes quiet, then it is easier. The serpent is the vital energy which covers up the psychic and prevents approach from another (the vital) side. Here again if the vital becomes quiet, then the approach is easier.

The blows on the forehead were perhaps the working of a force to open the centre there — for there between the eyes is the centre of the inner mind, will and vision. All these centres are closed in the ordinary consciousness or else only very slightly open on the surface. If the inner mind centre opens, then the peace etc. from above can enter easily into the mind and afterwards into the vital and both mind and vital will become quiet.

The difficulty about the two parts of the mind is one that everybody has when the tendency to go within begins. It is solved in this sadhana by a sort of harmony being established by which even in doing one's work and keeping the necessary outer activities one can still live within in the fullness of the inner life and experience.

Rely on the Mother always. These things are the first beginnings of Yogic experience and the difficulties of the mind and vital (which are not the old ones you had but simply the ordinary difficulties of the adjustment and harmonisation of the different parts of the being) will get solved of themselves.

Chapter Two
Exteriorisation or Going Out of the Body

The Experience of Exteriorisation

The experience you had was that of exteriorisation or going out of the body. The consciousness went up and remained above the body for a time. The feeling or vision of oneself in the form of an egg is frequent in such cases. It is not always so, for many go out in an individualised consciousness with an awareness of a subtle body, subtle thought, subtle sensation etc. and move about in the vital or even in the physical world till they come back to the body. But when one begins, the vital body is at first a little vague and the consciousness also with the result that all is at first dim and unorganised. The serpent must be the Kundalini force which had left its coiled sleeping position in the Muladhara and taken the lengthened one in which it joins the embodied consciousness with the consciousness above.

The power of exteriorisation is one that can be used for many purposes by the Yogi when it has been developed.

*

It was a partial exteriorisation, part of the consciousness going out to the scene and surroundings described by you while the rest remained in the body and was aware both of the normal surroundings and, by communication or indirect participation, of what the other was experiencing. This is quite possible and for that no form of trance or loss of external consciousness is necessary. As for the cause of such an experience, it does not depend at all on one's own ordinary mental or other interests; it comes by a sort of attraction or touch from someone who is there on the scene and who feels the need of sympathy, support or help of some kind, a need so strong that it forms a sort of call; it is very usually somebody quite unknown and it just depends on whom the call happens to touch because he is open at the time and receives the vibration and has the capacity to answer. Usually there is a sort of identification of consciousness with that of the person calling so that one can see the surroundings and the things happening through him. It is the physical that becomes nervous at these experiences and this must be overcome; as the inner mental, vital, physical consciousness opens to things behind the thick physical veil all kinds of experiences may happen that are strange to the physical mind and its tendency to be apprehensive or nervous at these things must disappear. It must be able to face even formidable things without fear.

*

A feeling like that of the shock and the stopping of the breath for a second and as if of falling down comes to many when the consciousness for a moment or a longer time exteriorises itself (goes up out of the body); the shock comes from the going up of the consciousness or from the return into the body. The Mother used to have that hundreds of times. It is not anything physical (the Doctor, as you say, found nothing). When this movement of the consciousness is more normal, the feeling will probably disappear.

*

You must have gone out of your body leaving it unprotected and there was an attack which you got rid of after coming into the body. This part of the head from the ears down to the neck is the seat of the physical mind — the centre of the physical or externalising mind is in the throat joining the spine at the back. It was an attack on the physical mind.

Going Out in the Vital Body

It looks as if it were an exteriorisation[1] in which she goes out in

---

[1] *The correspondent reported the case of a woman who, without willing it, entered into a state of trance at any time, even while writing or talking with someone.* — Ed.

her vital body. When one does so consciously and at will, it is all right, but this unconscious exteriorisation is not always safe. The important question is what effect it has on her. If she comes out of it strong and refreshed or quite normal, there is no cause for distress or anxiety; if she comes out exhausted or depressed, then there are forces that are pulling her out into the vital world to the detriment of her vital sheath and it should not continue.

*

It is clear that when you go out of your body like that you pass into a vital plane and as you are constantly attacked there and have fear, it is not desirable.

It seems to me I have explained all that to you before. Everybody goes out into the vital world in that way, but it is not indispensable to the sadhana to have these experiences and it is better to postpone them till you have the truly helpful experiences — such as those narrated in a recent letter — and can build up a strong consciousness which can enter any plane without fear or danger.

*

As to your experience about the inkstand. When the vital being goes out, it moves on the vital plane and in the vital consciousness, and, even if it is aware of physical scenes and things, it is not with a physical vision. It is possible for one who has trained his faculties to enter into touch with physical things although he is moving about in the vital body, to see and sense them accurately, even to act on them and physically move them. But the ordinary sadhaka who has no knowledge or organised experience or training in these things cannot do it. He must understand that the vital plane is different from the physical and that things that happen there are not physical happenings, though, if they are of the right kind and properly understood and used, they may have a meaning and value for the earth life. But also the vital consciousness is full of false formations and many confusions and it is not safe to move among them without knowledge and without a direct protection and guidance.

*

Your three experiences related in your letter mean that you are going out in your vital body into the vital worlds and meeting the beings and formations of these worlds. The old man of the temple and the girls you saw are hostile beings of the vital plane.

It is better not to go out in this way, unless one has the protection of someone (physically present) who has knowledge and power over the vital world. As there is no one there who can do this for you, you should draw back from this movement. Aspire for perfect surrender, calm, peace, light, consciousness and strength in the mind and the heart. When the mental being and psychic being are thus open, luminous and surrendered, then the vital can open and receive the same illumination. Till then premature adventures on the vital plane are not advisable.

If the movement cannot be stopped, then observe the following instructions:

(1) Never allow any fear to enter into you. Face all you meet and see in this world with detachment and courage.

(2) Ask for the protection of Sri Aurobindo and the Mother before you sleep or meditate. Use their names when you are attacked or tempted.[2]

(3) Do not indulge in this world in any kind of sympathy such as you felt for the old man in the temple or accept such suggestions, e.g., that he was your spiritual preceptor, which was obviously false since you could have no other spiritual preceptor than Sri Aurobindo and the Mother. It was because of this sympathy and the accepted suggestion that he was able to go inside you and create the pain you felt.

(4) Do not allow any foreign personality to enter into you, only the Light, Power etc. from above.

---

[2] *Sri Aurobindo refers to himself in the third person here and below; he wrote this letter to be sent over the signature of his secretary.* — Ed.

Section Two

Experiences of the Inner Being and the Inner Consciousness

Chapter One
The Inward Movement

The Importance of Inner Experiences

The outer work is only half the matter. There is also the consciousness within which does the work and that must develop from the mental-vital to the spiritual-psychic. How can it do that without experiences? Also one can develop an intuitive consciousness which is helpful to the work.

*

What you say about the outer being is correct; it must change and manifest what is within in the inner nature. But for that one must have experiences in the inner nature and through these the power of the inner nature grows till it can influence wholly and possess the outer being. To change the outer consciousness entirely without developing this inner consciousness would be too difficult. That is why these inner experiences are going on to prepare the growth of the inner consciousness. There is an inner mind, an inner vital, an inner physical consciousness which can more easily than the outer receive the higher consciousness above and put itself into harmony with the psychic being; when that is done the outer nature is felt as only a fringe on the surface, not as oneself, and is more easily transformed altogether.

Whatever difficulties there may still be in the outer nature, they will not make any difference to the fact that you are now awake within, the Mother's force working in you and you her true child destined to be perfectly that in all ways. Put your faith and your thought entirely on her and you will go through all safely.

*

What you express in the letter is the right way of thinking and seeing. The self-will of the mind wanting things in its own way and not in the Divine's way was a great obstacle. With that gone the way should become much less rough and hard to follow.

The outer consciousness can grow in faith, fidelity to the Divine, reverence, love, worship and adoration, great things in themselves, — though in fact these things too come from within, — but realisation can only take place when the inner being is awake with its vision and feeling of things unseen. Till then, one can feel the results of the divine help and, if one has faith, know that they are the work of the Divine; but it is only then that one can feel clearly the Force at work, the divine Presence, the direct communion.

*

So long as you live only in thoughts and other movements of the surface consciousness, you cannot be conscious in the Yogic sense. It is when the mind becomes quiet that the real (inner) consciousness comes out or the higher consciousness above the mind comes down. It is only then also that the inner physical being becomes active and brings an alert consciousness and an intuitive sense into the body. Also the higher thought and the inner will comes then only.

*

The exterior being has to become aware of the inner — the veil between the inner and outer consciousness has to be removed, it is only then that a real Yogic consciousness begins. The outer has to be merely an instrument or channel for the inner to express itself and communicate with the outer physical world. The inner again has to have free communication with the universal on all the planes — it has to enter into the cosmic consciousness. The outer consciousness has to be remoulded and reshaped through the inner consciousness and the processes that must do it are the psychic by its influence and the higher consciousness by its descent. Naturally, in the process the outer being also will lose its separativeness and become aware of and, in a way, unified with the universal.

Becoming Aware of the Inner Being

It is not that anything has been taken from you, but as you say at the end, your being is seen by you in two parts. That is a thing that happens as the sadhana proceeds and must happen in order that one may have completely the knowledge of oneself and the true consciousness. These two parts are the inner being and the outer being. The outer being (mind, vital and physical) has now become capable of quietude and it sits in meditation in a free, happy, vacant quietude which is the first step towards the true consciousness. The inner being (inner mind, vital, physical) is not lost but gone inside — the outer part does not know where — but probably gone inside into union with the psychic. The only thing that can have gone is something of the old nature that was standing in the way of this experience.

*

The silence descends into the inner being first — as also other things from the higher consciousness. One can become aware of this inner being, calm, silent, strong, untouched by the movements of Nature, full of knowledge or light, and at the same time be aware of another lesser being, the small personality on the surface which is made up of the movements of Nature or else still subject to them or else, if not subject to them, still open to invasion by them. This is a condition that any number of sadhaks and Yogis have experienced. The inner being means the psychic, the inner mind, the inner vital, the inner physical. In this condition none of these can be even touched, so there has been an essential purification. All need not feel this division into two consciousnesses, but most do. When it is there, the will that decides the action is in the inner being, not in the outer — so the invasion of the outer by vital movements can in no way compel the action. It is on the contrary a very favourable stage in the transformation because the inner being can bring the whole force of the higher consciousness in it to change the nature wholly, observing the action of Nature without being affected by it, putting the force for change wherever needed and setting the whole being right as one does with a machine. That is if one wants a transformation. For many Vedantins don't think it necessary — they say the inner being is *mukta*, the rest is simply a mechanical continuation of the impetus of Nature in the physical man and will drop away with the body so that one can depart into Nirvana.

*

In fact all these ignorant vital movements originate from outside in the ignorant universal nature; the human being forms in his superficial parts of being, mental, vital, physical a habit of certain responses to these waves from outside. It is these responses that he takes as his own character (anger, desire, sex etc.) and thinks he cannot be otherwise. But that is not so; he can change. There is another consciousness deeper within him, his true inner being, which is his real self, but is covered over by the superficial nature. This the ordinary man does not know, but the Yogi becomes aware of it as he progresses in his sadhana. As the consciousness of this inner being increases by sadhana, the surface nature and its responses are pushed out and can be got rid of altogether. But the ignorant universal Nature does not want to let go and throws the old movements on the sadhak and tries to get them inside him again; owing to a habit the superficial nature gives the old responses. If one can get the firm knowledge that these things are from outside and not a real part of oneself, then it is easier for the sadhak to repel such notions, or if they lay hold, he can get rid of them sooner. That is why I say repeatedly that these things are not in yourself, but from outside.

The Piercing of the Veil

The cry you heard was not in the physical heart, but in the emotional centre. The breaking of the wall meant the breaking of the obstacle or at least of some obstacle there between your inner and your outer being. Most people live in their ordinary outer ignorant personality which does not easily open to the

Divine; but there is an inner being within them of which they do not know, which can easily open to the Truth and the Light. But there is a wall which divides them from it, a wall of obscurity and unconsciousness. When it breaks down, then there is a release; the feelings of calm, Ananda, joy which you had immediately afterwards were due to that release. The cry you heard was the cry of the vital part in you overcome by the suddenness of the breaking of the wall and the opening.

*

The piercing of the veil between the outer consciousness and the inner being is one of the crucial movements in Yoga. For Yoga means union with the Divine, but it also means awaking first to your inner self and then to your higher self, — a movement inward and a movement upward. It is, in fact, only through the awakening and coming to the front of the inner being that you can get into union with the Divine. The outer physical man is only an instrumental personality and by himself he cannot arrive at this union, — he can only get occasional touches, religious feelings, imperfect intimations. And even these come not from the outer consciousness but from what is within us.

There are two mutually complementary movements; in one the inner being comes to the front and impresses its own normal motions on the outer consciousness to which they are unusual and abnormal; the other is to draw back from the outer consciousness, to go inside into the inner planes, enter the world of your inner self and wake in the hidden parts of your being. When that plunge has once been taken, you are marked for the Yogic, the spiritual life and nothing can efface the seal that has been put upon you.

This inward movement takes place in many different ways and there is sometimes a complex experience combining all the signs of the complete plunge. There is a sense of going in or deep down, a feeling of the movement towards inner depths; there is often a stillness, a pleasant numbness, a stiffness of the limbs. This is the sign of the consciousness retiring from the body inwards under the pressure of a force from above, — that pressure stabilising the body into an immobile support of the inner life, in a kind of strong and still spontaneous *āsana*. There is a feeling of waves surging up, mounting to the head, which brings an outer unconsciousness and an inner waking. It is the ascending of the lower consciousness in the Adhara to meet the greater consciousness above. It is a movement analogous to that on which so much stress is laid in the Tantrik process, the awakening of the Kundalini, the Energy coiled up and latent in the body and its mounting through the spinal cord and the centres (*cakras*) and the Brahmarandhra to meet the Divine above. In our Yoga it is not a specialised process, but a spontaneous uprush of the whole lower consciousness sometimes in currents or waves, sometimes in a less concrete motion, and on the other side a descent of the Divine Consciousness and its Force into the body. This descent is felt as a pouring in of calm and peace, of force and power, of light, of joy and ecstasy, of wideness and freedom and knowledge, of a Divine Being or a Presence — sometimes one of these, sometimes several of them or all together. The movement of ascension has different results: it may liberate the consciousness so that one feels no longer in the body, but above it or else spread in wideness with the body either almost non-existent or only a point in one's free expanse. It may enable the being or some part of the being to go out from the body and move elsewhere, and this action is usually accompanied by some kind of partial *samādhi* or else a complete trance. Or it may result in empowering the consciousness, no longer limited by the body and the habits of the external nature, to go within, to enter the inner mental depths, the inner vital, the inner (subtle) physical, the psychic, to become aware of its inmost psychic self or its inner mental, vital and subtle physical being and, it may be, to move and live in the domains, the planes, the worlds that correspond to these parts of the nature. It is the repeated and constant ascent of the lower consciousness that enables the mind, the vital, the physical to come into touch with the higher planes up to the supramental and get impregnated with their light and power and influence. And it is the repeated and constant descent of the Divine Consciousness and its Force that is the means for the transformation of the whole being and the whole nature. Once this descent becomes habitual, the Divine Force, the Power of the Mother begins to work, no longer from above only or from behind the veil, but consciously in the Adhara itself, and deals with its difficulties and possibilities and carries on the Yoga.

Last comes the crossing of the border. It is not a falling asleep or a loss of consciousness, for the consciousness is there all the time; only, it shifts from the outer and physical, becomes closed to external things and recedes into the inner psychic and vital part of the being. There it passes through many experiences and of these some can and should be felt in the waking state also; for both movements are necessary, the coming out of the inner being to the front as well as the going in of the consciousness to become aware of the inner self and nature. But for many purposes the ingoing movement is indispensable. Its effect is to break or at least to open and pass the barrier between this outer instrumental consciousness and that inner being which it very partially strives to express, and to make possible in future a conscious awareness of all the endless riches of possibility and experience and new being and new life that lie untapped behind the veil of this small and very blind and limited material personality which men erroneously think to be the whole of themselves. It is the beginning and constant enlarging of this deeper and fuller and richer awareness that is accomplished between the inward plunge and the return from this inner world to the waking state.

The sadhak must understand that these experiences are not mere imaginations or dreams but actual happenings, for even when, as often occurs, they are formations only, of a wrong or misleading or adverse kind, they have still their power as formations and must be understood before they can be rejected and abolished. Each inner experience is perfectly real in its own way, although the values of different experiences differ greatly, but it is real with the reality of the inner self and the inner planes. It is a mistake to think that we live physically only or only with the outer mind and life. We are all the time living and acting on other planes of consciousness, meeting others there and acting upon them, and what we do and feel and think there, the forces we gather, the results we prepare have an incalculable importance and effect, unknown to us, upon our outer life. Not all of it comes through, and what comes through takes another form in the physical — though sometimes there is an exact correspondence; but this little is at the basis of our outward existence. All that we become and do and bear in the physical life is prepared behind the veil within us. It is therefore of immense importance for a Yoga which aims at the transformation of life to grow conscious of what goes on within these domains, to be master there and be able to feel, know and deal with the secret forces that determine our destiny and our internal and external growth or decline.

It is equally important for those who want that union with the Divine without which the transformation is impossible. The aspiration could not be realised if you remained bound by your external self, tied to the physical mind and its petty movements. It is not the outer being which is the source of the spiritual urge; the outer being only undergoes the inner drive from behind the veil. It is the inner psychic being in you that is the bhakta, the seeker after the union and the Ananda, and what is impossible for the outer nature left to itself becomes perfectly possible when the barrier is down and the inner self in the front. For the moment this comes strongly to the front or draws the consciousness powerfully into itself, peace, ecstasy, freedom, wideness, the opening to light and a higher knowledge begin to become natural, spontaneous, often immediate in their emergence.

Once the barrier breaks by the one movement or the other, you begin to find that all the processes and movements necessary to the Yoga are within your reach and not as it seems in the outer mind difficult or impossible. The inmost psychic self in you has already in it the Yogin and the bhakta and if it can fully emerge and take the lead, the spiritual turn of your outer life is predestined and inevitable. In the initially successful sadhak it has already built a deep inner life, Yogic and spiritual, which is veiled only because of some strong outward turn the education and past activities have given to the thinking mind and lower vital parts. It is precisely to correct this outward orientation and take away the veil that he has to practise more strenuously the Yoga. Once the inner being has manifested strongly whether by the inward-going or the outward-coming movement, it is bound to renew its pressure, to clear the passage and finally come by its kingdom. A beginning of this kind is the indication of what is to happen on a greater scale hereafter.

The Movement Inward

The movement inward is all to the good — for going inward if one goes far enough brings one to the psychic. The more peace there is the better; even if it is only a little at first, that is so much gained. If the inward-drawing movement is held to, it will grow and the power to reject anger and other such movements will increase. It is this peace and inward psychic movement in you that we shall try for till it is done.

*

It is rather a pity that the fear came in and spoiled the inward movement — for this inward movement is exceedingly important for the sadhana. The increasing frequency and completeness of the psychic consciousness in you coming in and replacing the ordinary one has hitherto been the most hopeful sign of progress — but the establishment of an inward movement would be a still greater thing; for its natural result would be to liberate the soul within and to give you a stand in the inner being so that you would be able to regard any fluctuations in the outer consciousness without being subjugated by them and without any interruption of the inner poise and freedom. But the movement is bound to come back and fulfil itself. It is very good that the help comes when you call and that you can shake yourself free — it is another sign of the psychic growth.

*

It takes time of course to make the transition from one state of consciousness to another. The depth of feeling will come more and more as your consciousness draws back from the claim of external things and goes deeper in into the heart region seeing and feeling from there with the psychic to prompt and enlighten it. Faith also will increase with that movement — for it is the outer intellect that is infirm or deficient in faith, the inner being in the heart has it always.

*

That is quite natural [*an inward movement during the afternoon nap*]. The usual movement does not take place, but there is still a pressure habitual at the time under which the consciousness goes inside not into sleep but into some kind of samadhi in which a working takes place in the inner consciousness. As yet you have not developed the power of being conscious in this state nor the power of remembering what took place.

*

It was probably not so much a sleep as a going inward under the pressure of the influence at the Pranam. In any case it was not a dream but an experience, an ascent into one of the higher ranges of consciousness above the mind — all of which have this character of vastness and peace everywhere.

*

X's experiences are those which usually attend the withdrawal from the outer consciousness into an inner plane of experience. The feeling of coldness of the body in the first is one of the signs — like the immobility and stiffness of Y's experience — that the consciousness is withdrawing from the outer or physical sheath and retiring inside. The crystallisation was the form in which he felt the organisation of an inner consciousness which could receive at once firmly and freely from above. The crystals at once indicate organised formation and a firm transparence in which the greater vision and experience descending from the higher planes could be clearly reflected.

As for the other experience, his rejection of the waking consciousness evidently had the result of throwing him into an inner awareness in which he began to have contact with the supraphysical planes. What was meant by the sea of red colour and stars depends on the character of the red colour. If it was crimson, what he saw was the sea of the physical consciousness and physical life as it is represented to the inner symbolic vision; if it was purple red, then it was the sea of the vital consciousness and the vital life-force. Perhaps, if he had not stopped his sense of the Mother's presence, it would have been better, — he should rather, if he can, take it with him into the inner planes, then he would have had no occasion to fear.

In any case, if he wants to go into the inner consciousness and move in the inner planes — which will inevitably happen if he shuts off the waking consciousness in his meditation — he must cast away fear. Probably he expected to get the silence or the touch of the divine consciousness by following out the suggestion of the Gita. But the silence or the touch of the divine consciousness can be equally and for some more easily got in the waking meditation through the Mother's presence and the descent from above. The inward movement, however, is probably unavoidable and he should try to understand and, not shrinking or afraid, to go to it with the same confidence and faith in the Mother as he has in the waking meditation. His dreams are of course experiences on the inner (vital) plane.

P.S. The dream about the Mahadeva image may mean that someone (not of this world, of course) wanted to mislead him and make him confuse some narrower traditional form of the past with the greater living Truth that he is seeking.

*

The difficulty indicated by you in your last (long) letter indicates that you enter into the inner being and begin to have experiences there, but there is a difficulty in organising them or seeing them coherently. The difficulty is because the inner mind is not yet sufficiently habituated to act and see the inside things and therefore the ordinary outer mind interferes and tries to arrange them; but the outer mind is unable to see the meaning of inner things. When the outer mind is left outside altogether, the things inside begin to be seen vividly and clearly, but the inner mind not being active, either their coherence is not seen or the consciousness lingers in the confused experiences of the lower vital plane and does not get through to the deeper, more coherent and significant experiences. A development of the inner consciousness is needed — when that development takes place, then all will become more clear and coherent. This development will take place if, without getting disturbed, you quietly aspire and go on calling the Mother's Force to do what is needed.

Your call will always reach the Mother. If you remain quiet and confident, you will in time become aware of the answer. The more the mind becomes quiet, the clearer will it become to you and you will feel her working. From time to time you can write of your experiences; wherever an answer is needed, I will answer.

The Inner Consciousness and the Body

It is the inner consciousness that you felt separated from the body, liberated from the identification with the body, and yet in touch with all the material surroundings. It is a very helpful experience — indispensable for the Yoga.

*

It is that the consciousness is detaching itself from the body.[1] Usually in men it is identified with the body and bound to it — in Yoga it detaches itself and becomes free. The body is no longer felt as oneself, but as something not oneself, something that one carries with oneself or else as an instrument which one uses for certain purposes.

*

If you went inside and lost consciousness of the outer world, it would be called a kind of samadhi — but this experience can

---

[1] *The correspondent wrote that sometimes he felt raindrops or sunlight falling on his body as if they were touching something other than himself; at other times he felt very light, as if he had no body at all.* — Ed.

be got in the waking state also. It is a liberation from body consciousness and an awakening into the spiritual wideness. At first it is usually felt as a void of all other things but consciousness alone or existence alone.

*

The feeling [*in meditation*] of having no head usually means that the mental consciousness is no longer imprisoned in the head at the time — but silent and extended.

A Transitional State of Inwardness

The condition which you feel is one which is very well known in sadhana. It is a sort of passage or transition, a state of inwardness which is growing but not yet completed — at that time to speak or throw oneself outward is painful. What is necessary is to be very quiet and remain within oneself all the time until the movement is completed; one should not speak or only a little and in a low quiet way nor concentrate the mind on outward things. You should also not mind what people say or question; although they are practising sadhana, they know nothing about these conditions and if one becomes quiet or withdrawn they think one must be sad or ill. The Mother did not find you at all like that, sad or ill; it is simply a phase or temporary state in the sadhana that she has experience of and knows very well.

*

The condition [*of inwardness*] lasts often for a number of days, sometimes many, until something definite begins. Remain confident and quiet.

The Growth of the Inner Being and the Inner Consciousness

What you feel as the new life is the growth of the inner being in you; the inner being is the true being and as it grows the whole consciousness begins to change. This feeling and your new attitude towards people are signs of the change. The seeing of inner things also usually comes with this growth of the inner being and consciousness; it is an inner vision which awakes in most sadhaks when they enter this stage.

It is also a characteristic of this inner consciousness that even when it is active, there is felt behind the action or containing it a complete quietude or silence. The more one concentrates, the more this quietude and silence increases. That is why there seems to be all quiet within even though all sorts of things may be taking place within.

It is also quite usual that what takes place in the inner consciousness should not express itself at present in the outer physical. It at first creates changes inside, but takes possession of the outer instruments only afterwards.

*

The things you feel are due to the fact that the consciousness goes inside, so physical things are felt as if they were at a distance. The same phenomenon can happen when one goes into another plane of consciousness and sees physical things from there. But it is probably the first that is happening with you. When one goes quite inside, then physical things disappear, — when some connection is kept, then they become distant. But this is a transitory change. Afterwards you will be able to have the two consciousnesses together, be in your psychic in one part of yourself with all the experience and activities of the psychic being and nature and yet with your surface self fully awake and active in physical things with the psychic support and influence behind this outer action.

*

It is a very good sign that when the thoughts and the attempt at disturbance come there is something that remains calm and cool — for that, like the psychic reply from within, shows that the inner consciousness is fixed or fixing itself in part of the being. This is a well-recognised stage of the inner change in sadhana. Equally good is the emerging of the self-existent Ananda from within not dependent on outward things. It is a fact that this inner gladness and happiness is something peaceful and happy at once — it is not an excited movement like the vital outward pleasure, though it can be more ardent and intense. Another good result is the fading out of the feeling that "the work is mine" and the power to do it with the outward consciousness not engaging the inner being.

The sense of release as if from jail always accompanies the emergence of the psychic being or the realisation of the self above. It is therefore spoken of as a liberation, *mukti*. It is a release into peace, happiness, the soul's freedom not tied down by the thousand ties and cares of the outward ignorant existence.

It was of course the Mother's face you saw in your vision, but probably in one of her supraphysical, not her physical form and face — that is also indicated by the great light that came from the form and rendered it invisible.

*

I am glad to hear of the development you speak of in your dealing with others. It is a power proper to the Yoga consciousness that is developing in you, because the Mother's force is at work and is developing the inner consciousness. For it is one of the powers of this inner consciousness to bring about what it sees to be the right thing by simply communicating in entire silence to the consciousness of another. That is the true way of acting — through the power of the inner consciousness, its knowledge, vision and will. The other thing, the coming of what you want to see on the street, is another form of the same action of the inner conscious force. As for the anger it is evidently in process of control and elimination and its recurrences cannot fail to disappear after a time as the new consciousness increases.

Living Within

There is an inner being in man of which he is not usually conscious; he lives in a superficial consciousness which he calls himself and which is normally concerned with outer things; one is aware of the inner being either not at all or only as something behind from which feelings, ideas, impulses, imperatives etc. come occasionally into the outer. When one ceases to be mainly concerned with outer and surface things one can go more inside nearer to this inner being and become aware of things other than the ego and the outer nature. One can become aware of the inner being and live in it and get detached from the hold of outer things, dealing with them from an inner consciousness (felt as separate from the outer consciousness) according to an inner truth of the soul and spirit and no longer according to the demands of the outer Nature.

*

If one lives within, then it is the inner consciousness that one depends on, not the outer. The inner consciousness can then always go on independent of the outer state to which it gives attention only when it chooses.

*

It is good. Fasten on the true thing, the concentration in the inner being and the inner life. All these outer things are of minor importance and it is only when the inner life is well established that the difficulties with which they are hampered can get their true solution. That you have seen several times when you went inside. To be too much occupied in mind with the outer difficulties keeps it externalised. Living inwardly you will find the Mother close to you and realise her will and her action.

*

Do not allow outward events to disturb you or be the cause of suggestions. It is as with the words of people and the suggestions they raise which disturb uselessly the consciousness. Both should be rejected. Live in the inner consciousness which can remain in its own calm and light whatever happens outside.

*

To remain within, above and untouched, full of the inner consciousness and the inner experience, — listening, when need be, to X or another with the surface consciousness, but with even that undisturbed, not either pulled outwards or invaded, that is the perfect condition for the sadhana.

*

You must gather yourself within more firmly. If you disperse yourself constantly, go out of the inner circle, you will constantly move about in the pettinesses of the ordinary outer nature and under the influences to which it is open. Learn to live within, to act always from within, from constant inner communion with the Mother. It may be difficult at first to do it always and completely, but it can be done if one sticks to it — and it is at that price, by learning to do that that one can have the siddhi in the Yoga.

*

It is a very serious difficulty in one's Yoga — the absence of a central will always superior to the waves of the Prakriti forces, always in touch with the Mother, imposing its central aim and aspiration on the nature. That is because you have not yet learned to live in your central being; you have been accustomed to run with every wave of Force, no matter of what kind, that rushed upon you and to identify yourself with it for the time being. It is one of the things that has to be unlearned; you must find your central being with the psychic as its basis and live in it.

*

To be aware of one's central consciousness and to know the action of the forces is the first definite step towards self-mastery.

*

In the things of the subtle kind having to do with the working of consciousness in the sadhana, one has to learn to feel and observe and see with the inner consciousness and to decide by the intuition with a plastic look on things which does not make set definitions and rules as one has to do in outward life.

*

Yes. When one is in the right consciousness, then there is the right movement, the right happiness, everything in harmony with the Truth.

When there is the wrong consciousness, there is demand, dissatisfaction, doubt, all kinds of disharmony.

*

It [*calmness*] is only the proper condition for receptivity. Naturally, it is the proper thing to do if you want to be receptive or become conscious of inner things. So long as the mind is jumping about or rushing out to outside things, it is not possible to be inward, collected, conscious within.

*

Obviously to live in the silent Brahman, the best way is to live within where one can have the silence and resist all outward pulls. As much avoidance of outer pulls — contact does not matter, if there is no pull outward — as will help that, can be very helpful. It is only an entire seclusion that for occult rather than mental reasons is not altogether desirable unless one has already a great inner strength and poise.

Living Within and the External Being

It is the past habit of the vital that makes you repeatedly go out into the external part; you must persist and establish the opposite habit of living in your inner being which is your true being and of looking at everything from there. It is from there that you get the true thought, the true vision and understanding of things and of your own self and nature.

*

You must have somehow externalised yourself too much. It is only by living in one's inner consciousness and doing everything from there that the right psychic condition can be kept. Otherwise it goes inside and the external covers it up. It is not lost, but hidden — one must go inside again to recover it.

*

When one comes out of the inner condition, one gets externalised in the outer consciousness. It is difficult for the outer nature to remain always within, its nature is to pull outward. But when this happens, one must learn to look quietly at what is happening, observe what the outer nature does but not identify with it, not feel that it is oneself that is doing that, but only something that one is observing, while one's real self is that which observes and that which goes within. If one can do that, then there is no disturbance and it is easier to go back again inward.

*

As for the activity going on, it is so with everybody. What has to be done, is not to be upset by it, but to learn to live inside where one always feels the force — or even if one does not feel because the consciousness is covered up, it is still there and after a time dispels the covering and is visible again. Outside the imperfect activities will go on till the whole being is changed and that cannot be done in a day.

Your mistake is to get upset because the exterior being is still there with its imperfections. What you ought to do is not to mind too much, to aspire for changing it but not get upset, to have confidence that it will change in time and meanwhile to stand back from it, to live in the part of you that is open to the force and to regard the rest as you would a cut that has to be cleaned or anything else belonging to you but external.

*

The large inner mind and the true vital having shown themselves are bound to get the mastery; but the old lower nature, especially the vital part of it, is bound to struggle for reaffirming its hold on the consciousness. To remain very firm and repel its attacks till they lose their strength, is necessary.

*

The difficulty is that you attach so much importance to things that are of quite a small value. You behave as if to have or have not a table is something of supreme importance and worry and excite yourself so much about the rights and wrongs of the matter that you allow it to upset your whole peace of mind and make you fall from the true condition. These things are small and relative — you may have a new table or you may not have a new table, neither way is of any very great importance and it makes no difference to the Divine Purpose in you. The one thing important is to increase calm and peace and the descent of the Divine Force, to grow in equality and inward light and consciousness. Outward things have to be done with a great quiet, doing whatever is necessary but not exciting or upsetting yourself about anything. It is only so that you can advance steadily and quickly. When you feel the Mother's Force about you, the peace closely round you that is the one thing of importance — these small outward things can be settled in a hundred different ways, it does not really matter.

*

The entire dependence on the inner realisation and not on outward things for their own sake and the seeking of the Divine for the sake of the Divine and without any tinge of ego motive is indeed the most difficult thing for the mind even of the Sadhak to learn; but it is the essence of the highest realisation and the condition of a perfect self-finding.

*

When you come to the Divine, lean inwardly on the Divine and do not let other things affect you.

Acting from Within on the Outer Being

Detach yourself from the outer being; live in the inner; let the Force work from the inner being — it will change the outer being.

*

It is on the surface that the transformation is done. One comes up to the surface with what one has gained in the depths, to change it. It may be you need to go in again and find it difficult to make the movement back quickly. When the whole being becomes plastic you will be able to make whatever movement is needed more quickly.

*

Yes, that is right. Relying on outer methods mainly never succeeds very well. It is only when there is the inner poise that the outer movement is really effective — and then it comes of itself.

*

The difference [*in learning something*] is when a thing is done with the inner mind and when it is done only with the outer brain. What you feel is the inner mind taking it up — then it becomes part of the consciousness and things are really learned — the working of the outer mind is always difficult and superficial.

It is evident that the inner being in you is beginning to come more and more forward. As it does so, these outer difficulties will be more and more pushed out and the consciousness will keep the peace and force at first in the greater part of it, afterwards in the whole.

*

It is a wall of consciousness that one has to build [*against undesirable things*]. Consciousness is not something abstract, it is like existence itself or ananda or mind or prana, something very concrete. If one becomes aware of the inner consciousness one can do all sorts of things with it, send it out as a stream of force, erect a circle or wall of consciousness around oneself, direct an idea so that it shall enter somebody's head in America etc. etc.

*

It is simply that you became conscious of the inner being and the inner world and rose up to a higher plane of being where the outer difficulties do not exist. The object of Yoga is to establish the inner consciousness and the higher being in you and by their strength change the outer existence.

The Double Consciousness

The condition you describe in your work shows that the inner being is awake and that there is now the double consciousness. It is the inner being which has the inner happiness, the calm and quiet, the silence free from any ripple of thought, the inwardly silent repetition of the name. The automatic repetition of the mantra is part of the same phenomenon — that is what ought to happen to the mantra, it must become a conscious but spontaneous thing repeating itself in the very substance of the consciousness itself, no longer needing any effort of the mind. All these doubts and questionings of the mind are useless. What has to happen is that this inner consciousness should be always there not troubled by any disturbance with the constant silence, inner happiness, calm quietude, etc., while the outer consciousness does what is necessary in the way of work etc. or, what is better, has that done through it — it is the latter experience that you have some days as someone pushing the work with so much continuous force without your feeling tired.

If you feel more quiet and the surrender feels more intense, then that is a good, not a bad condition — and if it makes the mind an empty room receiving the light, so much the better. Experiences and descents are very good for preparation, but change of the consciousness is the thing wanted — it is the proof that the experiences and descents have had an effect. Descents of peace are good, but an increasingly stable quietude and silence of the mind is something more valuable. When that is there then other things can come — usually one at a time, light or strength and force or knowledge or ananda. It is not necessary to go on for ever having always the same preparatory experiences — a time comes when the consciousness begins to take a new poise and another state.

The Inner Being and Calmness, Silence, Peace

The calmness you feel is that of the inner being which remains the same whatever the surface experience. But the use to be made of these things is to liberate oneself from the desires and mental or vital sanskaras of the past so that one may be free to reach that greater Truth consciousness in which there is no need of an Adesh, for all one's action there is the direct conscious movement of the self-knowing Truth and the Mother herself is the doer.

*

The absence of thought is quite the right thing — for the true inner consciousness is a silent consciousness which has not to think out things, but gets the right perception, understanding and knowledge in a spontaneous way from within and speaks or acts according to that. It is the outer consciousness which has to depend on outside things and to think about them because it has not this spontaneous guidance. When one is fixed in this inner consciousness, then one can indeed go back to the old action by an effort of will, but it is no longer a natural movement and, if long maintained, becomes fatiguing. As for the dreams, that is different. Dreams about old bygone things come up from the subconscient which retains the old impressions and the seeds of the old movements and habits long after the waking consciousness has dropped them. Abandoned by the waking consciousness, they still come up in dreams; for in sleep the outer physical consciousness goes down into the subconscient or towards it and many dreams come up from there.

The silence in which all is quiet and one remains as a witness while something in the consciousness spontaneously calls down the higher things is the complete silence which comes when the full force of the higher consciousness is upon mind and vital and body.

*

All experiences come in the silence[2] but they do not come all pell-mell in a crowd at the beginning. The inner silence and peace have first to be established.

*

---

[2] *The correspondent wrote that although he was sometimes able to achieve silence of mind, experiences were not coming in the silence.* — Ed.

The consciousness from which these experiences come [*such as the division of the mind into an active surface mind and a silent inner mind*] is always there pressing to bring them in. The reason why they don't come in freely or stay is the activity of the mind and vital always rushing about, thinking this, wanting that, trying to perform mountaineering feats on all the hillocks of the lower nature instead of nourishing a strong and simple aspiration and opening to the higher consciousness that it may come in and do its own work. Rasa of poetry, painting or physical work is not the thing to go after. What gives the interest in Yoga is the rasa of the Divine and of the divine consciousness which means the rasa of Peace, of Silence, of inner Light and Bliss, of growing inner Knowledge, of increasing inner Power, of the Divine Love, of all the infinite fields of experience that open to one with the opening of the inner consciousness. The true rasa of poetry, painting or any other activity is truly found when these activities are part of the working of the Divine Force in you and you feel it as that and you feel in it the joy of that working.

This condition you had of the inner being and its silence, separated from the surface consciousness and its little restless workings, is the first liberation, the liberation of Purusha from Prakriti, and it is the fundamental experience. The day when you can keep it, you can know that the Yogic consciousness has been founded in you. This time it has increased in intensity, but it must also increase in duration.

These things do not "drop" — what you have felt was there in you all the time, but you did not feel it because you were living on the surface altogether and the surface is all crowd and clamour. But in all men there is this silent Purusha, base of the true mental being, the true vital being, the true physical being. It was by your prayer and aspiration that the thing came, to show you in what direction you must travel in order to have the true rasa of things, for it is only when one is liberated that one can get the real rasa. For after this liberation come others and among them the liberation and Ananda in action as well as in the static inner silence.

*

I don't think it is at all owing to the suggestion from what I wrote in the letter that you got the experience [*of a deep spiritual peace*]. The fundamental reason of these things does not belong to the surface, it is in the depths — or on the heights, at any rate, in the inner being behind the veil of the frontal consciousness. The actual occasional cause of the spiritual experience, — the match that sets the fire, so to say, — may be something very slight and looking accidental on the surface, a chance word or happening or something else quite fortuitous in its appearance. The person also through whom it comes may seem very much like a fortuitous instrument. It is true that this is only in appearance; for things slight and seemingly fortuitous have a reason for happening as they do, but that reason too is not on the surface.

As for the experience itself it takes up the movement which had started in you a long time ago and was interrupted by the vital upheaval that brought you so much trouble and struggle. Only, there has been since a widening of the consciousness and a step forward which made this form of the experience possible. At that time you had not much appreciation for calm and peace — you hankered only after bhakti and Ananda. But calm, peace, shanti are the necessary basis for any establishment of other things. Otherwise there is no solid foundation in the consciousness; if there is only unrest and movement, bhakti, Ananda and everything else can only come and go in starts and fits and find no ground to live on. It must, however, be not a mere mental quiet, but the deep spiritual peace of the shantimaya Shiva. It was this that touched you (descending through the head) in this experience. For the rest it is a resumption of the piercing of the veil, the beginning of the power of inner experience as opposed to the lesser experiences of the surface, the opening of the inner being, which is necessary for bringing the Yogic consciousness. A certain amount of vital purification has taken place which made the resumption of this kind of experience possible.

You certainly need not be afraid of going into unconsciousness, for it is not unconsciousness that you would go into, but simply the *inner* consciousness, — that going quite inward which is the result of intense *dhyāna* and the beginning of a certain kind of *samādhi*.

The Inner Being and the Inmost or Psychic Being

There is an inner being and an inmost being which we call the psychic. When one meditates, one tries to go into the inner being. If one does it, then one feels very well that one has gone inside. What can be realised in meditation can also become the ordinary consciousness in which one lives. Then one feels what is now the ordinary consciousness to be something quite external and on the surface, not one's real self.

*

The inner being is composed of the inner mental, the inner vital, the inner physical. The psychic is the inmost — supporting all the others. Usually it is in the inner mental that this separation first happens and it is the inner mental Purusha who remains silent observing the Prakriti as separate from himself. But it may also be the inner vital Purusha or inner physical or else without location simply the whole Purusha consciousness separate from the whole Prakriti. Sometimes it is felt above the head — but then it is usually spoken of as the Atman and the realisation is that of the silent Self.

*

It is not possible to distinguish the psychic being at first. What has to be done is to grow conscious of an inner being which is separate from the external personality and nature — a consciousness or Purusha calm and detached from the outer action of the Prakriti.

*

The reason why she remembers nothing when she comes out of her meditation is that the experience is taking place in the inner being and the outer consciousness is not ready to receive it. Formerly her sadhana was mainly on the vital plane which is often the first to open and the connection of that plane with the body consciousness is easy to establish because they are nearer to each other. Even then however her body was suffering because of attacks from the hostile elements in the vital plane. Now the sadhana seems to have gone inward into the psychic being. This is a great advance and she need not mind the want of connection with the most external consciousness at present. The work goes on all the same and it is probably necessary that it should be so just now. Afterwards, if she keeps steadily to the right attitude, it will descend into the outer consciousness.

Chapter Two

Inner Detachment and the Witness Attitude

Inner Detachment

It [*the individual consciousness*] is not by its nature detached from the mental and other activities. It can be detached, it can be involved. In the human consciousness it is as a rule always involved, but it has developed the power of detaching itself — a thing which the lower creation seems unable to do. As the consciousness develops, this power of detachment also develops.

*

Detachment means standing back with part of the consciousness and observing what is being done without being involved in it. There is no "how" to that; you do it or try it until it succeeds.

*

That sense of separate being and concentration behind the frontal consciousness is very good. It helps to liberate the inner being and make it stand back from the movements of the outer nature.

*

That is the condition of progress, — if, whenever there is an attempt to cloud the consciousness, you can stand back, remain quiet and prevent the clouding. Do that always and the progress is sure.

*

All that you have written here is perfectly correct. It is so, by standing back from these forces [*in the surrounding world*], neither attracted nor disturbed by them, that one gets freedom,

Inner Detachment and the Witness Attitude

perceives their falsity or imperfection and is able to rise above and overcome them. The consciousness that comes forward may be either the psychic or the spiritualised mind — it is probably the former.

*

Well, but it [*the need for detachment*] is not individual to you. Everyone has to do that with his difficulties. Detach means that the Witness in oneself has to stand back and refuse to look on the movement as his own (the soul's own) and look on it as a habit of past nature or an invasion of general Nature. Then to deal with it as such. It may seem difficult, but it comes perfectly well by trying persistently.

*

One must get the power to quiet the mental and vital, if not at first at all times, yet whenever one wills — for it is the mind and vital that cover up the psychic being as well as the self (Atman) and to get at either one must get in through their veil; but if they are always active and you are always identified with their activities, the veil will always be there. It is also possible to detach yourself and look at these activities as if they were not your own but a mechanical action of Nature which you observe as a disinterested witness. One can then become aware of an inner being which is separate, calm and uninvolved in Nature. This may be the inner mental or vital Purusha and not the psychic, but to get at the consciousness of the inner *manomaya* and *prāṇamaya* Purusha is always a step towards the unveiling of the psychic being.

*

The condition in which all movements become superficial and empty with no connection with the soul is a stage in the withdrawal from the surface consciousness to the inner consciousness. When one goes into the inner consciousness, it is felt as a calm, pure existence without any movement, but eternally tranquil, unmoved and separate from the outer nature. This comes as a result of detaching oneself from the movements, standing back from them and is a very important movement of the sadhana. The first result of it is an entire quietude, but afterwards that quietude begins (without the quietude ceasing) to fill with the psychic and other inner movements which create a true inner and spiritual life behind the outer life and nature. It is then easier to govern and change the latter.

At present there are fluctuations in your consciousness because this inner state is not yet fully developed and established. When it is, there will still be fluctuations in the outer consciousness, but the inner quiet, force, love etc. will be constant and the superficial fluctuations will be watched by the inner being without its being shaken or troubled, until they are removed by the complete outer change.

As for X, it is best to let it pass and try to remain steady within and detached; one cannot separate from all contacts; one must become more and more superior to their customary reactions.

*

Detachment is the beginning of mastery, but for complete mastery there should be no reactions at all. When there is something within undisturbed by the reactions that means the inner being is free and master of itself, but it is not yet master of the whole nature. When it is master, it allows no wrong reactions — if any come they are at once repelled and shaken off, and finally none come at all.

*

The experience you have of a division in the being with the inner void and indifferent, *udāsīna*, — not sorrowful, but neutral and indifferent, — is an experience which many pass through and is highly valued by the Sannyasis. For us it is a passage only to something larger and more positive. In it the old small human feelings fall away and a sort of calm neutral void is made for a higher nature to manifest. It must be fulfilled and replaced by a sense of large silence and freedom into which the Mother's consciousness can flow from above.

*

In the ordinary consciousness one takes a personal interest in what is done, feels joy or feels sorrow. When one does sadhana, a condition may come in which the consciousness draws back from these reactions of joy and sorrow and does work and action impersonally as a thing that ought or has to be done but without desire or reactions. The Yogis value this condition of complete detachment very highly. In our Yoga it is a passage only, if it comes, through which one goes from the ordinary consciousness to a deeper one in which one acts out of a deep peace and union with the Divine or else of a self-existent Ananda not depending on anything but the presence of the Divine, in which all works are done not out of personal interest or satisfaction but for the sake of the Divine.

The Witness Attitude

A man with a very developed introspective mind often identifies himself with the witness part of his mind and observes his own thoughts and studies their nature. That is a beginning which makes it easy for the full detachment to come. For others it is less easy, but it can be done by all.

*

There is a stage in the sadhana in which the inner being begins to awake. Often the first result is the condition made up of the following elements:

(1) A sort of witness attitude, in which the inner consciousness looks at all that happens as a spectator or observer, observing things but taking no active interest or pleasure in them.

(2) A state of neutral equanimity in which there is neither joy nor sorrow, only quietude.

(3) A sense of being something separate from all that happens, observing it but not part of it.

(4) An absence of attachment to things, people or events.

It seems as if this condition were trying to come in you; but it is still imperfect. For instance in this condition (1) there should be no disgust or impatience or anger when people talk, only indifference and an inner peace and silence. Also (2) there should not be a mere neutral quiet and indifference, but a positive sense of calm, detachment and peace. Again (3) there should be no going out of the body so that you do not know what is happening or what you are doing. There may be a sense of not being the body but something else, — that is good; but there should be a perfect awareness of all that is going on in or around you.

Moreover this condition even when it is perfect is only a transitional stage — it is intended to bring a certain state of freedom and liberation. But in that peace there must come the feeling of the Divine Presence, the sense of the Mother's power working in you, the joy or Ananda.

If you can concentrate in the heart as well as in the head, then these things can more easily come.

*

The mind can become quiet only when you detach yourself from it and see the thoughts as things that pass. Then you don't think yourself but see thoughts passing through your mind. Afterwards you can stop attending to these passers-by and concentrate on the Mother.

Thoughts and feelings are passing from one human being to another all the time, only people don't know or observe it. Especially if people live together the same life, as in the Asram, a sort of atmosphere is formed in which the same thoughts and feelings are moving about and constantly passing from one to another.

You have to become conscious — that is to say, there must be something in you which is not carried away by thoughts and feelings, but looks at them and observes how they work and how they affect you. The part that observes and knows is called the Witness *sākṣī* in man. It is always possible to develop this in oneself.

It is not by thinking and reading that consciousness comes. There are many who read and think a great deal but are not conscious, have not the witness developed in them. There are others who work all day like X, yet are very strongly conscious. When one has the power of stopping thinking altogether and only looking, then the Witness becomes very strong and conscious. This consciousness can come by practice, but it can also come by turning to the Mother and thinking of her always and offering to her everything. The being opens, the Mother's force begins to work and one becomes more and more conscious.

*

It is indeed a great thing that you can keep this calm and this unaffected witness attitude. It is always the sign of a strong inner foundation in the consciousness and that even the physical being shares in this result of the realisation.

*

As for the "spectator" and the coils of the dragon, it is the Chino-Japanese image for the world-force extending itself in the course of the universe and this expresses the attitude of the Witness seeing it all and observing in its unfolding the unrolling of the play of the Divine, Lila. It is this attitude that gives the greatest calm, peace, samata in face of the riddle of the cosmic workings. It is not meant that action and movement are not accepted but they are accepted as the Divine Working which is leading to ends which the mind may not always see at once, but the soul divines through all the supreme purpose and the hidden guidance.

Of course there is afterwards an experience in which the two sides of the Divine Whole, the Witness and the Player, blend together; but this poise of the spectator comes first and leads to that fuller experience. It gives the balance, the calm, the increasing understanding of soul and life and their deeper significances without which the full supramental experience cannot come.

The Witness Purusha or Witness Consciousness

By itself the Purusha is impersonal, but by mixing itself with the movements of Prakriti it makes for itself a surface ego or personality. When it appears in its own separate nature then it is seen to be detached and observing.

*

The consciousness you speak of would be described in the Gita as the witness Purusha. The Purusha or basic consciousness is the true being or at least, on whatever plane it manifests, represents the true being. But in the ordinary nature of man it is covered up by the ego and the ignorant play of the Prakriti and remains veiled behind as the unseen Witness supporting the play of the Ignorance. When it emerges, you feel it as a consciousness behind, calm, central, unidentified with the play which depends upon it. It may be covered over, but it is always there. The emergence of the Purusha is the beginning of liberation. But it can also become slowly the Master — slowly because the whole habit of the ego and the play of the lower forces (which also you describe correctly here) is against that. Still it can dictate what higher play is to replace the lower movement and then there is the process of that replacement, the higher coming, the lower struggling to remain and push away the higher movement. You say rightly that the offering to the Divine shortens the whole thing and is more effective, but usually it cannot be done completely at once owing to the past habit and the two methods continue together until the complete surrender is possible.

*

The attitude of the witness consciousness within — I do not think it necessarily involves an external seclusion, though one may do that also — is a very necessary stage in the progress. It helps the liberation from the lower prakriti — not getting involved in the ordinary nature movements; it helps the establishment of a perfect calm and peace within, for there is then one part of the being which remains detached and sees without

Inner Detachment and the Witness Attitude

being disturbed the perturbations of the surface; it helps also the ascent into the higher consciousness and the descent of the higher consciousness, for it is through this calm, detached and liberated inner being that the ascent and descent can easily be done. Also, to have the same witness look on the movements of Prakriti in others, seeing, understanding but not perturbed by them in any way is a very great help towards both the liberation and the universalisation of the being. I could not therefore possibly object to this movement in a sadhak.

As for the surrender it is not inconsistent with the witness attitude. On the contrary by liberating from the ordinary Prakriti, it makes easier the surrender to the higher or divine Power. Very often when this witness attitude has not been taken but there is a successful calling in of the Force to act in one, one of the first things the Force does is to establish the witness attitude so as to be able to act with less interference or immixture from the movements of the lower Prakriti.

There remains the question of the avoidance of contact with others and there there is some difficulty or incertitude. Part of your nature has a strong turn towards contact with others, action on others, interchange, almost a need of it. This brings about some fluctuation between the turn to an inner isolation and the turn towards contact and action. There is the same double and fluctuating movement in others here like X. In such cases I generally do not stress upon either tendency but leave the consciousness to find its own poise, because I have seen that to press too much on the isolation tendency when the nature is not mainly contemplative does not succeed very well — unless of course the sadhak himself gets a strong and fixed determination that way. This may be the cause of what you felt. But the question between witness attitude and surrender does not arise, for the reason I have explained — one can very well aid or lead to the other as ours is a Yoga which joins these things together and does not keep them always separate.

*

It is by a constant repetition and development of the experience [*that the witness consciousness can become constant*]. But the witness being does not always remain as a point. It becomes something extended supporting the rest.

The Purusha and Change of the Prakriti

That is the old Vedantic idea — to be free and detached within and leave the Prakriti to itself. When you die, the Purusha will go to glory and the Prakriti drop off — perhaps into Hell. This theory is a source of any amount of self-deception and wilful self-indulgence.

*

The witness attitude is not meant as a convenient means for disowning the responsibility of one's defects and thereby refusing to mend them. It is meant for self-knowledge and, in our Yoga, as a convenient station (detached and uninvolved, therefore not subject to Prakriti) from which one can act on the wrong movements by refusal of assent and by substituting for them the action of the true consciousness from within or above.

*

You can certainly go on developing the consciousness of the Witness Purusha above, but if it is only a witness and the lower Prakriti is allowed to have its own way, there would be no reason why it [*an unquiet and disturbed condition*] should ever stop. Many take that attitude — that the Purusha has to liberate itself by standing apart, and the Prakriti can be allowed to go on till the end of the life doing its own business, — it is *prārabdha karma*; when the body falls away, the Prakriti will drop also and the Purusha go off into the featureless Brahman! This is a comfortable theory, but of more than doubtful truth; I don't think liberation is so simple and facile a matter as that. In any case, the transformation which is the object of our Yoga would not take place.

The Purusha above is not only a Witness, he is the giver (or withholder) of the sanction; if he persistently refuses the sanction to a movement of Prakriti, keeping himself detached, then, even if it goes on for a time by its past momentum, it usually loses its hold after a time, becomes more feeble, less persistent, less concrete and in the end fades away. If you take the Purusha consciousness, it should be not only as the Witness but as the Anumanta, refusing sanction to the disturbing movements, sanctioning only peace, calm, purity and whatever else is part of the divine nature. This refusal of sanction need not mean a struggle with the lower Prakriti; it should be a quiet, persistent, detached refusal leaving unsupported, unassented to, without meaning or justification the contrary action of the nature.

Chapter Three
Inner Experiences in the State of Samadhi

Samadhi or Trance

The experience you had is of course the going inside of the consciousness which is usually called trance or *samādhi*. The most important part of it however is the silence of the mind and vital which is fully extended to the body also. To get the capacity of this silence and peace is a most important step in the sadhana. It comes at first in meditation and may throw the consciousness inward in trance, but it has to come afterwards in the waking state and establish itself as a permanent basis for all the life and action. It is the condition for the realisation of the Self and the spiritual transformation of the nature.

*

The experience you relate, the stillness, the emptiness of mind and vital and cessation of thoughts and other movements, was the coming of the state called "samadhi" in which the consciousness goes inside in a deep stillness and silence. This condition is favourable to inner experience, realisation, the vision of the unseen truth of things, though one can get these in the waking condition also. It is not sleep but the state in which one feels conscious within, no longer outside.

*

It [*the experience of samadhi*] is not indispensable at this stage; but if it comes of itself, it can be allowed to develop. But experience in the waking state is more important for this Yoga. Samadhi is a help for reaching the inner depths of the consciousness. One is able to go more easily by it inward below the surface being, to get into direct contact with other supraphysical planes of experience, to pass into other worlds and return, to contact happenings distant in space and time, to see what is in the supraconscient and to enter into what is supraconscient to our mental status.

*

What she speaks of as losing the body consciousness is probably a tendency of the consciousness to go inside — into Samadhi of some kind. Samadhi means a state in which one is not awake and aware of outward things, but also one is not asleep, one is conscious inwardly with another than the waking consciousness. If this comes, it is not to be avoided, as Yogic realisation can take place in this condition as well as in the waking state.

*

It is a state of inner immobile silence that one gets in Samadhi when the outer mind is stilled and there is only some inner or some higher consciousness which may itself be either in silent concentration or else experiencing some state of Knowledge or Ananda or Peace.

*

Going inside does not bring always Ananda. There are many kinds of samadhi and many sorts of experience in each kind. What happens when one goes in is that one enters into the inner planes of consciousness, it may be the subconscient, it may be the mental, vital or subtle physical plane. From there one goes into the corresponding worlds or else one rises up into higher planes superconscious to us — to the ranges above our mind or to the spiritual mental plane in which one can unite with the Sachchidananda consciousness or to the Supramental. What you describe seems to be the subconscient, but that may be only a first step in the going inside.

*

In samadhi it is the inner mental, vital, physical which are separated from the outer, no longer covered by it — therefore they can freely have inner experiences. The outer mind is either quiescent or in some way reflects or shares the experience. As for the central consciousness being separated from all mind that would mean a complete trance without any recorded experiences.

*

It is the subtle parts of the physical that go up. The external consciousness can also go up, but then there is a complete trance. There is not much utility for the complete trance in this sadhana.

*

Trance in English is usually used only for the deeper kinds of samadhi; but, as there is no other word, we have to use it for all kinds.

*

Samadhi is not a thing to be shunned — only it has to be made more and more conscious.

Trance Not Essential

It is not necessary to be in samadhi to be in contact with the Divine.

*

Yes, they [*all the stages of higher realisation*] can be attained even in full activity. Trance is not essential — it can be used, but by itself it cannot lead to the change of consciousness which is our object, for it gives only an inner subjective experience which need not make any difference in the outer consciousness. There are plenty of instances of sadhaks who have fine experiences in trance but the outer being remains as it was. It is necessary to bring out what is experienced and make it a power for transformation both of the inner and the outer being. But it can be done without going into Samadhi in the waking consciousness itself. Concentration of course is indispensable.

Kinds of Samadhi

Nirvikalpa Samadhi according to tradition is simply a trance from which one cannot be awakened even by burning or branding — i.e. a trance in which one has gone completely out of the body. In more scientific parlance it is a trance in which there is no formation or movement of the consciousness and one gets lost in a state from which one can bring back no report except that one was in bliss. It is supposed to be a complete absorption in the Sushupti or the Turiya.

*

"Nirvikalpa samadhi" properly means a complete trance in which there is no thought or movement of consciousness or awareness of either inward or outward things — all is drawn up into a supracosmic Beyond. But here it cannot mean that — it probably means a trance in a consciousness beyond the Mind.

*

As to the dream, it was not a dream but an experience of the inner being in a conscious dream state, *svapna-samādhi*. The numbness and the feeling of being about to lose consciousness are always due to the pressure or descent of a Force to which the body is not accustomed but feels strongly. Here it was not the physical body that was being directly pressed, but the subtle body, the *sūkṣma śarīra* in which the inner being more intimately dwells and in which it goes out in sleep or trance or in the moment of death. But the physical body in these vivid experiences feels as if it were itself that was having the experience; the numbness was the effect on it of the pressure. The pressure on the whole body would mean a pressure on the whole inner consciousness, perhaps for some modification or change which would make it more ready for knowledge or experience; the 3rd or 4th rib would indicate a region which belongs to the vital nature, the domain of the life-force, some pressure for a change there.

*

It [*the kind of samadhi one has*] depends on the nature of the physical consciousness you keep. When there is the descent of consciousness into the body one becomes aware of a subtle physical consciousness and that can remain in samadhi — one seems to be aware of the body, but it is really the subtle body and not the outward physical. But also one can go deep within and yet be aware of the physical body also and of working upon it, but not of outward things. Finally one can be absorbed in a deep concentration but strongly aware of the body and the descent of the Force in it. This last is accompanied with consciousness of outward things, though no attention may be paid to them. This last is not usually called samadhi, but it is a kind of waking samadhi. All conditions from the deep samadhi of complete trance to the working of the Force in the fully waking consciousness are used in this Yoga; one need not insist on complete trance always, for the others also are necessary and without them the complete change cannot take place.

It is good that the higher consciousness and its powers are descending into the parts below the head and heart. That is absolutely necessary for the transformation, since the lower vital and the body must also be changed into stuff of the higher consciousness.

*

For this Yoga these divisions [*the classifications of samadhi in Vedanta*] are not so important.

Samadhi and the Waking State

Trance is a going inside away from the waking state. What corresponds to trance in the waking state would be a complete concentration indifferent to outward movements or else a silence of the whole being in Brahman realisation, the *samāhita* state of the Gita.

*

Immersion in Sachchidananda is a state one can get in the waking condition without Samadhi — dissolution can come only after the loss of the body on condition that one has reached the highest state and does not will to return here to help the world.

*

On the contrary it is in the waking state that this realisation must come and endure in order to be a reality of the life. If experienced in trance it would be a superconscient state true for some part of the inner being, but not real to the whole consciousness. Experiences in trance have their utility for opening the being and preparing it, but it is only when the realisation is constant in the waking state that it is truly possessed. Therefore in this Yoga most value is given to the waking realisation and experience.

What you write about the work is correct; to work in this calm ever-widening consciousness is at once a *sādhanā* and a *siddhi*.

*

The entire oblivion of the experience means merely that there is still no sufficient bridge between the inner consciousness which has the experience in a kind of samadhi and the exterior waking consciousness. It is when the higher consciousness has made the bridge between them that the outer also begins to remember.

Samadhi and Sleep

It [*a tendency to fall asleep while meditating*] is the result of the attempt to go above. It is not sleep that comes, but a tendency to go inside under the pressure — the old Yogas did this going above precisely in this way, by going into samadhi. For us, it has to come in the waking condition — for until it does, it cannot be made the basis for a new consciousness governing the life.

*

It [*the tendency to fall asleep during meditation*] is a common obstacle with all who practise Yoga at the beginning. The sleep disappears gradually in two ways — (1) by the intensifying of the force of concentration, (2) by the sleep itself becoming a kind of swapna samadhi in which one is conscious of inner experiences that are not dreams (i.e. the waking consciousness is lost for the time, but it is replaced not by sleep but by an inward conscious state in which one moves in the supraphysical of the mental or vital being).

*

There is no reason why one should not have a burning aspiration in sleep, provided one is conscious in sleep. In fact, the condition you describe was not sleep — it was simply that the consciousness was trying to go inside in a sort of indrawn condition (a kind of half-samadhi) while the external mind was constantly coming out of it. What you have, if you go into this indrawn condition, is not dreams but spiritual experiences or visions or experiences in other supraphysical planes of consciousness. Your burning aspiration was just such a spiritual experience.

*

No, it was not sleep. You went inside into an inner consciousness; in this inner consciousness one is awake inside, but not outside, not conscious of external things but of inner things only. Your inner consciousness was busy doing what your outer mind had been trying to do, that is to work upon the thoughts and suggestions that bring restlessness and to put them right; it can be done much more easily by the inner consciousness than by the outer mind.

As for the things that are necessary to be done, they can be done much more easily by the Force and Peace descending (bringing the solid strength) than by your own mental effort.

*

It was not half sleep or quarter sleep or even one-sixteenth sleep that you had; it was a going inside of the consciousness, which in that state remains conscious but shut to outer things and open only to inner experience. You must distinguish clearly between these two quite different conditions, one is *nidrā*, the other the beginning at least of *samādhi* (not *nirvikalpa* of course!). This drawing inside is necessary because the active mind of the human being is at first too much turned to outward things; it has to go inside altogether in order to live in the inner being (inner mind, inner vital, inner physical, psychic). But with training one can arrive at a point when one remains outwardly conscious and yet lives in the inner being and has at will the indrawn or the outpoured condition; you can then have the same dense immobility and the same inpouring of a greater and purer consciousness in the waking state as in that which you erroneously call sleep.

*

About your experiences:

(1) The sleep which you felt when meditating was not sleep but an inward condition of the consciousness. When this inward condition is not very deep one can be aware of various scenes, voices etc. which belong not to the physical but to some inner plane of consciousness — their value or truth depends on the plane to which one reaches. Those of the surface are of no importance and one has simply to pass through them till one gets deeper.

(2) The fear, anger, depression etc. which used to rise when making the japa of the names came from a vital resistance in the nature (this resistance exists in everyone) which threw up these things because of the pressure on the vital part to change which is implied in sadhana. These resistances rise and then, if one takes the right attitude, slowly or quickly clear away. One has to observe them and separate oneself from them, persisting in the concentration and sadhana till the vital becomes quiet and clear.

(3) The things you saw (moon, sky etc.) are due to the opening of the inner vision; this usually comes when the concentration begins to open up the inner consciousness of which this subtle vision is a part. This faculty of vision has its importance in the development of the inner being, and need not be discouraged, even though too much importance should not be attached to the

things seen in the earlier stages.

(4) There are some however that are part of the growing spiritual experience, such as the sun you saw overhead and the piece of golden light — for these are signs of an opening within and symbolic. Both are symbols of the Divine Truth and Light and of one action of their influence.

(5) The most important experience, however, is that of the peace and quiet which comes with a good concentration. It is this that must grow and fix itself in the mind and vital and body — for it is this peace and quiet that make a firm basis for the sadhana.

*

The starting of the body happens very often when it is in a kind of sleep of samadhi and something touches whether from within or without.

The Trance of Mediums

The medium trance is of a different kind — they get not into touch with Sachchidananda but with the beings of the lower vital plane. To develop the power of going into this higher kind of trance, one must have done some sadhana. As to purification, entire purification is not necessary, but some part of the being must have turned to higher things.

Chapter Four

Three Experiences of the Inner Being

Opening into the Inner Mental Self

The three experiences of which you speak belong all to the same movement or the same stage of your spiritual life; they are initial movements of the consciousness to become aware of your inner being which was veiled, as in most, by the outer waking self. There are, we might say, two beings in us, one on the surface, our ordinary exterior mind, life, body consciousness, another behind the veil, an inner mind, an inner life, an inner physical consciousness constituting another or inner self. This inner self once awake opens in its turn to our true real and eternal self. It opens inwardly to the soul, called in the language of this Yoga the psychic being which supports our successive births and at each birth assumes a new mind, life and body. It opens above to the Self or spirit which is unborn and by conscious recovery of it we transcend the changing personality and achieve freedom and full mastery over our nature.

You did quite right in first developing the sattwic qualities and building up the inner meditative quietude. It is possible by strenuous meditation or by certain methods of tense endeavour to open doors on to the inner being or even break down some of the walls between the inner and outer self before finishing or even undertaking this preliminary self-discipline, but it is not always wise to do it as that may lead to conditions of sadhana which may be very turbid, chaotic, beset with unnecessary dangers. By adopting the more patient course you have arrived at a point at which the doors of the inner being have begun almost automatically to swing open. Now both processes can go on side by side, but it is necessary to keep the sattwic quietude, patience, vigilance, — to hurry nothing, to force nothing, not to be led away by any strong lure or call of the intermediate stage which is now beginning before you are sure that it is the right call. For there are many vehement pulls from the forces of the inner planes which it is not safe to follow.

Your first experience is an opening into the inner mental self — the space between the eyebrows is the centre of the inner mind, vision, will and the blue light you saw was that of a higher mental plane, a spiritual mind, one might say, which is above the ordinary human mental intelligence. An opening into this higher mind is usually accompanied by a silence of the ordinary mental thought. Our thoughts are not really created within ourselves independently in the small narrow thinking machine we call our mind; in fact, they come to us from a vast mental space or ether either as mind-waves or waves of mind-force that carry a significance which takes shape in our personal mind or as thought-formations ready-made which we adopt and call ours. Our outer mind is blind to this process of Nature; but by the awakening of the inner mind we can become aware of it. What you saw was the receding of this constant mental invasion and the retreat of the thought-forms beyond the horizon of the wide space of mental Nature. You felt this horizon to be in yourself somewhere, but evidently it was in that larger self-space which even in its more limited field just between the eyebrows you felt to be bigger than the corresponding physical space. In fact, though the inner mind spaces have horizons, they stretch beyond those horizons — illimitably. The inner mind is something very wide projecting itself into the infinite and finally identifying itself with the infinity of universal Mind. When we break out of the narrow limits of the external physical mind we begin to see inwardly and to feel this wideness, in the end this universality and infinity of the mental self-space. Thoughts are not the essence of mind-being, they are only an activity of mental nature; if that activity ceases, what appears then as a thought-free existence that manifests in its place is not a blank or void but something very real, substantial, concrete we may say — a mental being that extends itself widely and can be its own field of existence silent or active as well as the Witness, Knower, Master of that field and its action. Some feel it first as a void, but that is because their observation is untrained and insufficient and loss of activity gives them the sense of blank; an emptiness there is, but it is an emptiness of the ordinary activities, not a blank of existence.

The recurrence of the experience of the receding away of thoughts, the cessation of the thought-generating mechanism and its replacement by the mental self-space, is normal and as it should be; for this silence or at any rate the capacity for it has to grow until one can have it at will or even established in an automatic permanence. For this silence of the ordinary mind-mechanism is necessary in order that the higher mentality may manifest, descend, occupy by degrees the place of the present imperfect mentality and transform the activities of the latter into its own fuller movements. The difficulty of its coming when you are at work is only at the beginning — afterwards when it is more settled one finds that one can carry on all the activities of life either in the pervading silence itself or at least with that as the support and background. The silence remains behind and there is the necessary action on the surface or the silence is our wide self and somewhere in it an active Power does the works of Nature without disturbing the silence. It is therefore quite right to suspend the work while the visitation of the experience is there — the development of this inner silent consciousness is sufficiently important to justify a brief interruption or pause.

In the case of the other two experiences, on the contrary, it is otherwise. The dream-experience must not be allowed to take hold of the waking hours and pull the consciousness within; it must confine its operation to the hours of sleep. So too there should be no push or pressure to break down the wall between the inner self and the outer "I" — the fusion must be allowed to take place by a developing inner action in its own natural time. I shall explain why in another letter.

The Awakening of the Inner Being in Sleep

Your second experience is a first movement of the awakening of the inner being in sleep. Ordinarily when one sleeps a complex phenomenon happens. The waking consciousness is no longer there, for all has been withdrawn within into the inner realms of which we are not aware when we are awake, though they exist; for then all that is put behind a veil by the waking mind and nothing remains except the surface self and the outward world — much as the veil of the sunlight hides from us the vast worlds of the stars that are behind it. Sleep is a going inward in which the surface self and the outside world are put away from our sense and vision. But in ordinary sleep we do not become aware of the worlds within either; the being seems submerged in a deep subconscience. On the surface of this subconscience floats an obscure layer in which dreams take place, as it seems to us, but, more correctly it may be said, are recorded. When we go very deeply asleep, we have what appears to us as a dreamless slumber; but in fact dreams are going on, but they are either too deep down to reach the recording surface or are forgotten, all recollection of their having existed even is wiped out in the transition to the waking consciousness. Ordinary dreams are for the most part or seem to be incoherent, because they are either woven by the subconscient out of deep-lying impressions left in it by our past inner and outer life, woven in a fantastic way which does not easily yield any clue of meaning to the waking mind's remembrance, or are fragmentary records, mostly distorted, of experiences which are going on behind the veil of sleep — very largely indeed these two elements get mixed up together. For in fact a large part of our consciousness in sleep does not get sunk into this subconscious state; it passes beyond the veil into other planes of being which are connected with our own inner planes, planes of supraphysical existence, worlds of a larger life, mind or psyche which are there behind and whose influences come to us without our knowledge. Occasionally we get a dream from these planes, something more than a dream, — a dream experience which is a record direct or symbolic of what happens to us or around us there. As the inner consciousness grows by sadhana, these dream experiences increase in number, clearness, coherence, accuracy and after some growth of experience and consciousness, we can, if we observe, come to understand them and their significance to our inner life. Even we can by training become so conscious as to follow our own passage, usually veiled to our awareness and memory, through many realms and the process of the return to the waking state. At a certain pitch of this inner wakefulness this kind of sleep, a sleep of experiences, can replace the ordinary subconscient slumber.

It is of course an inner being or consciousness or something of the inner self that grows aware in this way, not, as usually it is, behind the veil of sleep, but in the sleep itself. In the condition which you describe, it is just becoming aware of sleep and dream and observing them — but as yet nothing farther — unless there is something in the nature of your dreams that has escaped you. But it is sufficiently awake for the surface consciousness to remember this state, that is to say, to receive and keep the report of it even in the transition from the sleep to the waking state which usually abolishes by oblivion all but fragments of the record of sleep-happenings. You are right in feeling that the waking consciousness and this which is awake in sleep are not the same — they are different parts of the being.

When this growth of the inner sleep consciousness begins, there is often a pull to go inside and pursue the development even when there is no fatigue or need of sleep. Another cause aids this pull. It is usually the vital part of the inner being that first wakes in sleep and the first dream experiences (as opposed to ordinary dreams) are usually in the great mass experiences of the vital plane, a world of supraphysical life, full of variety and interest, with many provinces, luminous or obscure, beautiful or perilous, often extremely attractive, where we can get much knowledge too both of our concealed parts of nature and of things happening to us behind the veil and of others which are of concern for the development of our parts of nature. The vital being in us then may get very much attracted to this range of experience, may want to live more in it and less in the outer life. This would be the source of that wanting to get back to something interesting and enthralling which accompanies the desire to fall into sleep. But this must not be encouraged in waking hours, it should be kept for the hours set apart for sleep where it gets its natural field. Otherwise there may be an unbalancing, a tendency to live more and too much in the visions of the supraphysical realms and a decrease of the hold on outer realities. The knowledge, the enlargement of our consciousness of these fields of inner Nature is very desirable, but it must be kept in its own place and limits.

A Touch of the Inner Self

In my last letter I had postponed the explanation of your third experience. What you have felt is indeed a touch of the Self, — not the unborn Self above, the Atman of the Upanishads, for that is differently experienced through the silence of the thinking mind, but the inner being, the psychic supporting the inner mental, vital, physical being, of which I have spoken. A time must come for every seeker of complete self-knowledge when he is thus aware of living in two worlds, two consciousnesses at the same time, two parts of the same existence. At present he lives in the outer consciousness, the outer being and sees within the inner self — but he will go more and more inward, till the position is reversed and he lives within in this new inner consciousness, inner self and feels the outer as something on the surface formed as an instrumental personality for the inner's self-expression in the material world. Then from within a Power works on the outer to make it a conscious plastic instrument so that finally the inner and the outer may become fused into one. The wall you feel is indeed the wall of the ego which is based on the insistent identification of oneself with the outer personality and its movements. It is that identification which is the keystone of the limitation and bondage from which the outer being suffers, preventing expansion, self-knowledge, spiritual freedom. But still the wall must not be prematurely broken down, because that may lead to a disruption or confusion or invasion of either part by the movements of the two separated worlds before they are ready to harmonise. A certain separation is necessary for some time after one has become aware of these two parts of the being as existing together. The force of the Yoga must be given time to make the necessary adjustments and openings, and to take the being inward and then from this inward poise to work on the outer nature.

This does not mean that one should not allow the consciousness to go inward so that as soon as possible it should live in the inward world of being and see all anew from there. That inward going is most desirable and necessary and that change of vision also. I mean only that all should be done by a natural movement without haste. The movement of going inward may come rapidly, but even after that something of the wall of ego will be there and it will have to be steadily and patiently taken down so that no stone of it may abide. My warning against allowing the sleep world to encroach on the waking hours is limited to that alone and does not refer to the inward movement in waking concentration or ordinary waking consciousness. The waking movement carries us finally into the inner self and by that inner self we grow into contact with and knowledge of the supraphysical worlds, but this contact and knowledge need not and should not lead to an excessive preoccupation with them or a subjection to their beings and forces. In sleep we actually enter into these worlds and there is the danger, if the attraction of the sleep consciousness is too great and encroaches on the waking consciousness, of this excessive preoccupation and influence.

It is quite true that an inner purity and sincerity, in which one is motived only by the higher call, is one's best safeguard against the lures of the intermediate stage. It keeps one on the right track and guards from deviation until the psychic being is fully awake and in front and, once that happens, there is no farther danger. If in addition to this purity and sincerity there is a clear mind with a power of discrimination, that increases the safety in the earlier stages. I do not think I need or should specify too fully or exactly the forms the lure or pull is likely to take. It may be better not to call up these forces by an attention to them which may not be necessary. I do not suppose you are likely to be drawn away from the path by any of the greater perilous attractions. As for the minor inconveniences of the intermediate stage, they are not dangerous and can easily be set right as one goes by the growth of consciousness, discrimination and sure experience.

As I have said, the inward pull, the pull towards going inward is not undesirable and need not be resisted. At a particular stage it may be accompanied by an abundance of visions due to the growth of the inner sight which sees things belonging to all the planes of existence. That is a valuable power helpful in the sadhana and should not be discouraged. But one must see and observe without attachment, keeping always the main object in front, realisation of the inner Self and the Divine — these things should only be regarded as incidental to the growth of consciousness and helpful to it, not as objects in themselves to be followed for their own sake. There should also be a discriminating mind which puts each thing in its place and can pause to understand its field and nature. There are some who become so eager after these subsidiary experiences that they begin to lose all sense of the true distinction and demarcation between different fields of reality. All that takes place in these experiences must not be taken as true — one has to discriminate, see what is mental formation or subjective construction and what is true, what is only suggestion from the larger mental and vital planes or what has reality only there and what is of value for help or guidance in inner sadhana or outer life.

Section Three

Experiences of the Cosmic Consciousness

Chapter One

The Universal or Cosmic Consciousness

The Terms "Universal" and "Cosmic"

There is no difference between the terms "universal" and "cosmic" except that "universal" can be used in a freer way than "cosmic". Universal may mean "of the universe", cosmic in that general sense. But it may also mean "common to all", — e.g., "This is a universal weakness" — but you cannot say, "This is a cosmic weakness."

*

Universal applies to everything in the universe — there are individual beings everywhere, but not physical in the terrestrial sense — the composition being different.

The Nature of the Cosmic Consciousness

Man is shut up at present in his surface individual consciousness and knows the world (or rather the surface of it) only through his outward mind and senses and by interpreting their contacts with the world. By Yoga there can open in him a consciousness which becomes one with that of the world; he becomes directly aware of a universal Being, universal states, universal Force and Power, universal mind, life, matter and lives in conscious relations with these things. He is then said to have the cosmic consciousness.

*

Men are usually shut up in the sense of their separate existence and know of the world and of other beings only what they see, hear, feel by their senses and their mental images and inferences. By Yoga one can get free of this limitation and become directly aware of the Cosmic Self, the self of other beings, of their movements, of the movements of the cosmic forces, etc. etc. That is the cosmic consciousness.

*

Everyone has a universal consciousness standing concealed behind the individualised personality. When one becomes aware of it one feels in contact with the universal self and forces or one with them.

*

When one has the cosmic consciousness, one can feel the cosmic self as one's own self, one can feel one with other beings in the cosmos, one can feel all the forces of Nature as moving in oneself, all selves as one's own self.

There is no why except that it is so, since all is the One.

*

The ordinary consciousness of man is confined to his own individuality — he can enter into the consciousness of others and of the universe only by indirect means or a superficial and incomplete apprehension, by sense experience, contacts of emotional sympathy, mental concepts, analogy with his own movements, inference. In Yoga at a certain point this limitation breaks down, the consciousness enlarges itself, becomes directly aware of the Cosmic Self and knows the individual self to be one with it; of the Cosmic Energy and meets directly the action of the cosmic forces; of the cosmic mind, life, matter and feels first a contact of its individual mind, life, body with them, then a unity in which one's own individual mentality, vitality, physicality is felt as only a part of the universal, a wave of the ocean, a dynamo receiving and formulating the universal forces. Finally, the individual melts into the cosmic consciousness, the whole world is felt in oneself and oneself suffused through the world — it is the cosmic Consciousness, Mind, Life, material Energy that works through the individual function. The separate ego either does not exist or is only a convenience for the universal Spirit and its action. This is the complete consummation of the cosmic Consciousness, but in its fullness it is not common, belonging properly to what we may call the Overmind realisation; but a constant partial and growing experience of it or an increasing contact with the cosmic Consciousness is a normal part of Yoga.

The Cosmic Consciousness and the Overmind

The cosmic consciousness does not belong to overmind in especial; it covers all the planes.

*

The overmind is the basis of the total cosmic consciousness, but the cosmic consciousness itself can be felt on any plane, not only above mind, but in mind, life, matter.

The Cosmic Consciousness and the Transcendent

The consciousness in the individual widens itself into the cosmic consciousness outside and can have any kind of dealing with it, penetrate, know its movements, act upon it or receive from it, even become commensurate with or contain it — which was what was meant in the language of the old Yogas by having the *brahmāṇḍa* within you.

The cosmic consciousness is that of the universe, of the cosmic Spirit and cosmic Nature with all the beings and forces within it. All that is as much conscious as a whole as the individual separately is, though in a different way. The consciousness of the individual is part of this, but a part feeling itself as a separate being. Yet all the time most of what he is comes into him from the cosmic consciousness. Only there is a wall of separative ignorance between. Once it breaks down he becomes aware of the cosmic Self, of the consciousness of the cosmic Nature, of the forces playing in it etc. He feels all that as he now feels physical things and impacts. He finds it all to be one with his larger or universal self.

There is the universal mental, the universal vital, the universal physical nature, and it is out of a selection of their forces and movements that the individual mind, vital and physical are made. The soul comes from beyond this nature of mind, life and body. It belongs to the Transcendent and because of it we can open to the higher Nature beyond.

The Divine is always One that is Many. The individual spirit is part of the "Many" side of the One, and the psychic being is what it puts forth to evolve here in the earth-nature. In liberation the individual self realises itself as the One (that is yet Many). It may plunge into the One and merge or hide itself in its bosom — that is the Laya of the Adwaita; it may feel its oneness and yet as part of the Many that is One enjoy the Divine, that is the Dwaitadwaita liberation; it may lay stress on its Many aspect and be possessed by the Divine, the Visishtadwaita, or go on playing with Krishna in the eternal Vrindavan, the Dwaita liberation. Or it may, even being liberated, remain in the Lila or manifestation or descend into it as often as it likes. The Divine is not bound by human philosophies — it is free in its play and free in its essence.

*

One has to get above the cosmic consciousness of the mind, life and matter by entering into the spiritual levels above the ordinary mind, into the higher consciousness. This does not cut one off from the cosmic consciousness, but one sees it without being involved in it.

*

It [*the correspondent's experience*] is the release from the limitations by the body consciousness and the opening into the wider being which is universal although it has an individual centre. As this develops one becomes aware of the true Self silent and illimitable and the cosmic consciousness. The concentration at the apex above the head is the station in the thousand-petalled lotus. There one becomes aware of states of mind above the ordinary human *buddhi*, the higher mind, the illumined mind, the intuition, the overmind — finally when one has achieved the overmind one opens directly to the supramental consciousness.

*

The cosmic consciousness has many levels — the cosmic physical, the cosmic vital, the cosmic Mind, and above the higher planes of cosmic Mind there is the Intuition and above that the Overmind and still above that the Supermind where the Transcendental begins. In order to live on the Intuitive plane (not merely to receive intuitions), one has to live in the cosmic consciousness because there the cosmic and individual run into each other as it were, and the mental separation between them is already broken down, so nobody can reach there who is still in the separative ego.

A reflected static realisation of Sachchidananda is possible on any of the cosmic planes, but the full entering into it, the entire union with the Supreme Divine dynamic as well as static, comes with the transcendence.

*

It [*realisation of the Cosmic Divine*] is sufficient if only a static Consciousness is aimed at — but if transformation and the dynamic Divine is the aim, then the whole must be known. To realise the Cosmic Divine is after all impossible without entering into or opening to the cosmic consciousness — but one has to know the cosmic Prakriti as well as the cosmic Purusha.

Spiritual, Cosmic and Ordinary Consciousness

1. The spiritual consciousness is that in which we enter into the awareness of Self, the Spirit, the Divine and are able to see in all things their essential reality and the play of forces and phenomena as proceeding from that essential Reality.

2. The cosmic consciousness is that in which the limits of ego, personal mind and body disappear and one becomes aware of a cosmic vastness which is or is filled by a cosmic Spirit and aware also of the direct play of cosmic forces, universal

mind forces, universal life forces, universal energies of Matter, universal Overmind forces. But one does not become aware of all these together; the opening of the cosmic consciousness is usually progressive. It is not that the ego, the body, the personal mind disappear, but one feels them as only a small part of oneself. One begins to feel others too as part of oneself or varied repetitions of oneself, the same self modified by Nature in other bodies or, at the least, as living in the larger universal self which is henceforth one's own greater reality. All things in fact begin to change their value and appearance; one's whole experience of the world is radically different from that of those who are shut up in their personal selves. One begins to know things by a different kind of experience, more direct, not depending on the external mind and the senses. It is not that the possibility of error disappears, for that cannot be so long as mind of any kind is one's instrument for transcribing knowledge, but there is a new vast and deep way of experiencing, seeing, knowing, contacting things, and the confines of knowledge can be rolled back to an almost immeasurable degree. The things one has to be on guard against in the cosmic consciousness are the play of a magnified ego, the vaster attacks of the hostile forces — for they too are part of the cosmic consciousness — and the attempt of the cosmic Illusion (Ignorance, Avidya) to prevent the growth of the soul into the cosmic Truth. These are things that one has to learn by experience; mental teaching or explanation is quite insufficient. To enter safely into the cosmic consciousness and to pass safely through it, it is necessary to have a strong central unegoistic sincerity and to have the psychic being, with its divination of truth and unfaltering orientation towards the Divine, already in front in the nature.

3. The ordinary consciousness is that in which one knows things only or mainly by the intellect, the external mind and the senses and knows forces etc. only by their outward manifestations and results and the rest by inferences from these data. There may be some play of mental intuition, deeper psychic seeing or impulsions, spiritual intimations etc. — but in the ordinary

consciousness these are incidental only and do not modify its fundamental character.

The Widening of the Consciousness

It is very good. The widening of the consciousness so as to be in touch with the Universal Infinite is an important stage in the sadhana.

*

The ordinary man lives in his own personal consciousness knowing things through his mind and senses as they are touched by a world which is outside him, outside his consciousness. When the consciousness subtilises, it begins to come into contact with things in a much more direct way, not only with their forms and outer impacts but with what is inside them, but still the range may be small. But the consciousness can also widen and begin to be first in direct contact with an immense range of things in the world, then to contain them as it were, — as it is said to see the world in oneself, — and to be in a way identified with it. To see all things in the self and the self in all things — to be aware of one being everywhere, aware directly of the different planes, their forces, their beings — that is universalisation.

*

Opening is when it [*the consciousness*] receives the higher forces — widening is when it is no longer limited to the body but widens to meet the cosmic consciousness.

*

The widening of the consciousness beyond the body means that there is a preparation to pass out of the limitation by the body consciousness and feel oneself either in the cosmic consciousness or in contact with it. If one has this feeling of enlargement or wideness above the head one is in contact with the universal Self; below it is according to the level with the cosmic Mind, the cosmic vital or the cosmic physical consciousness. When one is entirely freed from the body limitation, then one feels the consciousness as infinite with the body only as something very small within it.

*

It [*separation of the consciousness from the body*] means the liberation from the body sense in which one can truly say, "I am not the body." This liberation is part of the cosmic consciousness — as is also the realisation of the cosmic Will.

It is the liberation from the body sense only. That is quite different from the control of the body.

*

Yes, your experience was a very good one and your feeling about it was correct. When the consciousness is narrow and personal or shut in the body, it is difficult to receive from the Divine — the wider it expands, the more it can receive. A time comes when it feels as wide as the world and able to receive all the Divine into itself.

*

If you feel the barrier in which you lived broken down and an inner ocean of wideness, then a great thing has happened in you. For it is this wideness that comes when the consciousness opens to the Divine. Into this wideness the Divine's peace, love, light and joy can pour and fix themselves there.

Go on calling the Mother and opening yourself to her. All the rest will come.

*

By a widening of all the parts of the being, a sense of largeness and liberation of the mind, vital and physical, an opening to the Divine everywhere and many other signs [— *so the Divine's wideness manifests itself*].

*

Yes — it [*wideness*] is felt as if a great substantial vastness full of power and giving the sense of oneness free and infinite and the same from top to bottom.

*

The emptiness and wideness in the brain is a very good sign. It is a condition for the opening horizontally into the cosmic consciousness and upward into the Self and higher spiritual Mind above the head.

*

The lightness, the feeling of the disappearance of the head and that all is open is a sign of the wideness of the mental consciousness which is no longer limited by the brain and its body sense — no longer imprisoned but wide and free. This is felt in the meditation only at first or with closed eyes, but at a later stage it becomes established and one feels always oneself a wide consciousness not limited by any feeling of the body. You felt something of this wideness of your being in the second experience when the Mother's foot pressed down your physical mind (head) till it went below and left room for this sense of an infinite Self. This wide consciousness not dependent on the body or limited by it is what is called in Yoga the Atman or Self. You are only having the first glimpses of it, but later on it becomes normal and one feels that one was always this Atman infinite and immortal.

*

It is an experience of the extension of consciousness. In Yoga experience the consciousness widens in every direction, around, below, above, in each direction stretching to infinity. When the consciousness of the Yogin becomes liberated, it is not in the body, but in this infinite height, depth and wideness that he lives always. Its basis is an infinite void or silence, but in that all can manifest — Peace, Freedom, Power, Light, Knowledge, Ananda. This consciousness is usually called the consciousness of the Self or Atman, for it is a pure existence or self that is the source of all things and contains all things.

*

You must dismiss the fear of the concentration. The emptiness you feel coming on you is the silence of the great peace in which you become aware of your self, not as the small ego shut up in the body, but as the spiritual self wide as the universe. Consciousness is not dissolved; it is the limits of the consciousness that are dissolved. In that silence thoughts may cease for a time, there may be nothing but a great limitless freedom and wideness, but into that silence, that empty wideness descends the vast peace from above, light, bliss, knowledge, the higher Consciousness in which you feel the oneness of the Divine. It is the beginning of the transformation and there is nothing in it to fear.

*

If these were imaginations, you would be able to reproduce them exactly each time you thought of them. The idea that it is imagination comes from the physical mind which cannot believe in anything supraphysical.

This opening of the chest into the void (not really the void, but the infinite Akash of the Chit universal and illimitable) is always the sign of an opening of the emotional being into the wideness of the Universal Divine. The image of the Akash is often seen by sadhaks in Dhyana. When the consciousness is liberated, whether in the mind or other part, there is always this sense of the wide infinite emptiness. From the top of the head to the throat is the mental plane of the being — a similar opening and emptiness or wideness here is the sign of the mind being freed into the Universal. From the throat to the stomach is the higher vital or emotional region. Below is the lower vital plane.

*

It is of course the inner wideness in which you were absorbed so that outward things went on of themselves without engaging the interest. In the meditation it was the same descent into the head — when it fills the head, there is often this feeling of there being no head, only that which is coming down or else a wideness in which that is acting. In the end one gets the feeling of being not something confined in the head and body, but a wide consciousness with the body only as something comparatively small inside it. The vision was a figure of this wider consciousness with the Mother's inner presence always there.

*

Yes, what you see is right.[1] It is why the former Yogins preferred to remain in the wide consciousness aloof from the play of the energies — they regarded the latter as something belonging to the life of illusion which would fall away only by the rejection of the physical life through knowledge. It is when you oscillate from one consciousness to another that you seem to lose the higher one or feel as if it were lost. By keeping it within always, one is able to regard both sides and change the recalcitrant lower nature.

*

The wideness comes when one exceeds or begins to exceed the individual consciousness and spread out towards the universal. But the psychic can be active even in the individual consciousness.

*

At the beginning the experience of wideness like other experiences comes only from time to time. It is only afterwards that it becomes frequent and remains long, till finally it settles and the consciousness remains always wide.

The Cosmic Consciousness and the Cosmic Self

In the cosmic consciousness the personal I disappears into the one Self of all. The I which alone exists is not that of the person, the individualised I, but the universalised I identical with all and with the cosmic Self (Atman).

*

---

[1] *The correspondent said that when he lived in the wide consciousness above, he could remain undisturbed by the energies of the lower nature. But when he tried to change those energies, he became troubled and confused by their downward pull. — Ed.*

It is what it represents itself to be — an experience of the universal consciousness aspiring to the Divine Truth and beginning to receive its light. It is not your own consciousness, although you feel it in yourself, but a symbolic experience of this universal Vishwa-Purusha. These things one sees when one opens to the Cosmic Consciousness. Observed, felt and taken rightly they help to liberate, universalise and impersonalise. But keep the ego out of it — *everybody* opening to the Cosmic Divine will have these or similar experiences. Observe and go forward.

*

There is no doubt that you will succeed in your endeavour — all that is needed is firm persistence till the success is complete.

What you saw in the vision was the wide and luminous infinite of what is called the universal Self or spirit. It is that which is one of the fundamental things into which one enters when one reaches the higher consciousness and goes above. The personal being naturally feels itself as something very small and insignificant in that Infinite. But in that Infinite there are higher and higher levels and it is to these levels that the Mother was leading you when she took you by the hand. This often happens in meditation or trance when one has once gone upward into the spiritual infinity. The reason why you did not see the Mother's form was not that the Mother hid herself, or anything in you came between, but that you were both moving in the formless Infinite as spiritual beings and so it was easier to feel the presence than to see any physical form. Not that the form cannot be there, but it is less insistent and therefore not so soon seen as on the physical plane.

The silence in the head and heart and the emptiness are both necessary and desirable. When they are there, the consciousness finds them natural and they give it the sense of lightness and release; that is why the thoughts or speech of the old kind are foreign to it and when they come give fatigue. This silence and emptiness must grow, so that the higher consciousness with its knowledge, light, Ananda, peace can come down in it and progressively replace the old things. They must indeed occupy not only head and heart but the whole body.

The Cosmic Consciousness and Self-Realisation

Liberation is the first necessity — to live in the peace, silence, purity, freedom of the Self. Along with that or afterwards if one wakens to the cosmic consciousness, then one can be free, yet one with all things.

To have the cosmic consciousness without the liberation etc. is possible, but then there is no freedom anywhere in the being from the lower nature and one may become in one's extended consciousness the playground of all kinds of forces without being able to be either free and detached from the Prakriti or free and master.

On the other hand, if there has been self-realisation, there is one part of the being that remains untouched amid the play of the cosmic forces — while if the peace and purity of the self has been established in the whole inner consciousness, then the outer touches of the lower nature cannot come in or overpower. This is the advantage of self-realisation preceding the cosmic consciousness and supporting it.

*

When there is the development of the Self-realisation or of the cosmic consciousness or if there is the emptiness which is the preliminary condition for these things, there comes an automatic tendency for a unity with all — their affections, mental, vital, physical may easily touch. One has to keep oneself free.

*

Affections here [*in the preceding letter*] has not the ordinary sense — it means "ways in which they are affected by things", e.g. joy, grief, pleasure, pain, illness etc.

*

What you feel is the normal condition when the liberation takes place. The work of the senses etc. goes on as before, but the consciousness is different, so that one feels not only the sense of liberation, separation etc., but that one is living in quite another world than that of the ordinary mind, life or senses. It is another consciousness with another knowledge and way of looking at things that begins. Afterwards as this consciousness takes possession of the instruments, there is a harmony of it with the sense and life; but these too become different, with a changed outlook, seeing the world no more as before but as if made of another substance with another significance.

*

It is when you feel the universal or divine beauty or presence in things that the senses are open to the Divine.

Chapter Two
Aspects of the Cosmic Consciousness

The Cosmic Ignorance and the Cosmic Truth

I think you are speaking of two different sides of the cosmic Consciousness, that which is behind all Cosmos and that which is expressed in the apparent universe.

*

There are in the cosmic consciousness two sides — one the contact with and perception of the ordinary cosmic forces and the beings behind these forces, that is what I call the cosmic Ignorance — the other is the perception of the cosmic Truths, the realisation of the one universal, the one universal Force, all the Vedantic truths of the One in all and all in one; all the various aspects of the Divine in the cosmic and a host of other things can come which do help to realisation and knowledge — provided they are taken in the right way. However all that can be best dealt with when it actually comes. It does not always come as soon as there is the widening — many pass through the widening of the consciousness to what is beyond the cosmic and take the cosmic in detail afterwards — and it is perhaps the safest order.

*

Each defect of the nature of the Ignorance is a deformation of something in the higher nature — a deformation which amounts to a contradiction even. It is a concretised perception of this that you got in your experience.

*

There is no ignorance that is not part of the cosmic Ignorance — only in the individual it becomes a limited formation and movement, while the cosmic Ignorance is the whole movement of world-consciousness separated from the supreme Truth and acting in an inferior motion in which the Truth is perverted, diminished, mixed and clouded with falsehood and error. The cosmic Truth is the view on things of a cosmic Consciousness in which things are seen in their true essence and their true relation to the Divine and to each other.

*

The Yogi's cosmic experiences are spiritual experiences — experience of the play of the Forces and its relation with the self, the action of the Guide, what is behind the appearance of things, occurrences etc. etc., the actual relations of the workings of Purusha and Prakriti etc. The Divine Truth is the truth of the divine Essence, Consciousness, Self-Knowledge, Light, Power, Bliss. It is something from which the cosmos derives with all its movements, but it is more than the cosmos.

*

The cosmic Truth is the truth of things as they are at present expressed in the universe. The Divine Truth is independent of the universe, above it and originates it.

The Cosmic Harmony and Discords

A cosmos or universe is always a harmony, otherwise it could not exist, it would fly to pieces. But as there are musical harmonies which are built out of discords partly or even predominantly, so this universe (the material) is disharmonious in its separate elements — the individual elements are at discord with each other to a large extent, — it is only owing to a sustaining divine Will behind that the whole is still a harmony to those who look at it with the cosmic vision. But it is a harmony in evolution, in progress — that is, all is combined to strive towards a goal which is not yet reached, and the object of our Yoga is to hasten the arrival to this goal. When it is reached, there will be a harmony of harmonies substituted for the present harmony built up on discords. This is the explanation of the present appearance of things.

*

This harmony of the lower consciousness is a harmony of discords brought about by a clash and mixture of forces.

*

It [*a rhythmic word like a song*][1] is a representation in sound of the cosmic harmony from which the Ignorance is a fall and a discord.

*

There is a rhythm in everything unheard by the physical ear and by that rhythm things exist.

The Cosmic Will

It is not possible for the individual mind, so long as it remains shut up in its personality, to understand the workings of the Cosmic Will, for the standards made by the personal consciousness are not applicable to them. A cell in the body, if conscious, might also think that the human being and its actions are only the resultant of the relations and workings of a number of cells like itself and not the action of a unified self. It is only if one enters into the Cosmic Consciousness that one begins to see the forces at work and the lines on which they work and get a glimpse of the Cosmic Self and the Cosmic Mind and Will.

*

Everything here is not perfect, but all works out the cosmic Will in the course of the ages.

---

[1] *The correspondent heard a rhythmic word entering into his ears from above. The word was like a song and its rhythm sustained the universe, though it worked through destruction. — Ed.*

Opening to the Cosmic Mind

What is happening is that you have got into touch with the cosmic Mind where all sorts of ideas, possibilities, formations are moving about. The individual mind takes up those which appeal to it or perhaps come into distinct form when they touch it. But these are possibilities, not truths, so it is better not to let them run free like that.

*

One [*who is open to the cosmic Mind*] is aware of the cosmic Mind and the mental forces that move there and how they work on one's mind and that of others and one is able to deal with one's own mind with a greater knowledge and effective power. There are many other results, but this is the fundamental one. This is of course if one opens in the right way and does not merely become a passive field of all sorts of ideas and mental forces.

*

The opening to cosmic mind makes the experience of the Divine everywhere for instance more easy — but it is not essentially spiritual; if there is not a coming of wider spiritual experiences, then it need not be spiritual at all.

Opening to the Cosmic Life

One [*who is open to the cosmic Life*] becomes aware of all the life-forces and of how they act upon oneself and others, upon mind, upon body — also the force movements behind events. One becomes too directly aware of the vital plane, its worlds, its beings, and the direct action of their formations on the earth-life. One has to become aware also at the same time of one's own true vital being and act from it and not from the surface or desire vital in relation to all these things. All this effect does not come at once, — it develops as the contact with the cosmic Life increases.

*

In the universal vital especially there is a deceptive attraction and an exhilarating rush of power (not true quiet power but mere force) which those who yield to it cling to as a drunkard to his intoxicants. It gives them a sense of being strong and great and full of interesting things — when it is taken from them, they feel "like ordinary people" and ask for it back again.

*

You had a mental and the beginning of a vital opening to the cosmic consciousness — kept on the spiritualised level, the vision or feeling of the Divine Ananda without seeking for possession or a gross outer enjoyment, it would have established a Yogic consciousness and made a base for knowledge and peace and power and psychic love and surrender to come down.

The Cosmic Consciousness and the Physical

One cannot be high in the cosmic consciousness unless one has taken one's station above the body in a cosmic wideness which envelops the whole being. What you did was to open to it to a certain extent and then, instead of plunging into it at once as some do, your sadhana took the turn of coming down into the physical to prepare it. That is not altogether an undesirable turn — for many suffer by not having taken it. X for instance got a very evident opening into the cosmic, but he lost his way in it altogether because neither his vital nor his physical were cleared of certain very serious imperfections.

*

Yes, it is the psychising and purification that have been going on, but you had some openings of contact with the cosmic consciousness which did not prolong themselves when you came into the physical. X's ascents, I suppose, are more a going out of the body in his mind and vital than any stationing of his consciousness above. The latter would have brought a calm and peace and liberation which he does not possess as yet. This kind of ascent brings a conscious contact with cosmic forces of the mental and vital planes (in his case more the vital) and some extraordinary experiences which are not altogether safe. There is great danger there of entering into and getting perplexed in the intermediate zone. I would rather see him liberated from these things than pursuing them any farther. A descent from above of the higher forces would be far more helpful to him than these ascensions.

Chapter Three

The Universal or Cosmic Forces

The Nature of the Universal or Cosmic Forces

Universal forces means all forces good or bad, favourable or hostile, of light or of darkness that move in the cosmos.

*

The cosmic forces here whether good or bad are forces of the Ignorance. Above them is the Truth-Consciousness that can only manifest when ego and desire are overcome — it is the force from the Divine Truth-Consciousness that must descend — the higher Peace, Light, Knowledge, Purity, Power, Ananda must work upon the cosmic forces in the individual so as to change them and substitute the Truth-Forces in place of the ordinary working.

*

They [*the cosmic forces*] act on everyone, according to the person's nature — and his will and consciousness.

*

It [*knowledge of the working of the cosmic forces*] is necessary — it comes of itself as one gets more and more forward in the cosmic consciousness.

*

They [*pain and misery*] are perhaps rather the result of the action of universal forces — but in a certain sense grief and pain may be said to be universal forces — for there are waves of these things that arrive and invade the being often without apparent cause.

*

The universal forces move by their own force and the consciousness within them — but there is also the Cosmic Spirit who supports them and determines by his onlook and disposing will their play — although the direct action is left to the forces — it is the play of universal Prakriti with the universal Purusha watching behind it. In the individual also there is the individual Purusha who can, if he wills, not merely assent to the play of Prakriti, but accept or reject or will for its change. All that is in the play itself as we see it here. There is something above — but the action of that is an intervention rather than a moment to moment control; it can become a constant direct control only when one replaces the play of the forces by the government of the Divine.

*

One can live in contact with the Divine even amidst the universal forces — but to live in the Divine one must be able to rise beyond the lower universal nature or to call down the Divine consciousness here. The beginnings are difficult for most — and at no time is it really easy.

The Universal Energies and the Divine Force

There is only one Force or Energy here in reality; what is called the individual energy does not belong to the individual, but to the one universal Power.

In the one infinite Energy itself a distinction has to be made between the Divine Force that descends from above the mind and the inferior universal Energy with all its different forms, movements, waves and currents that come into you from outside. The inferior Energy proceeds from the Divine Shakti, but it has fallen from the truth of its source and has no longer its direct guidance.

When these universal energies come into touch with the Divine Force, rise to meet it and allow it to take hold of them and occupy and change them, then they are purified and uplifted and transformed and become a movement of the Divine Force.

When they are not in touch with the Divine Force, not obedient to it, but act for themselves, they are unenlightened, erring, impure, mixed and confused — powers of the Ignorance.

Always, therefore, keep in touch with the Divine Force. The best thing for you is to do that simply and allow it to do its own work; wherever necessary, it will take hold of the inferior energies and purify them; at other times it will empty you of them and fill you with itself. But if you let your mind take the lead and discuss and decide what is to be done, you will lose touch with the Divine Force and the lower energies will begin to act for themselves and all go into confusion and a wrong movement.

It is still worse to try to draw these lower universal energies from those around you and keep up with them a vital interchange; what gain can there be in that? On the contrary, it will lead to greater confusion and even bring in all kinds of mischief and trouble.

Often the association of these universal energies with others is a mistake of your mind. Your mind is seeking always to fix them on to somebody, and often it fixes on one or another at random or else according to old experiences which are no longer valid. For instance, what you call X's force was not his, but a universal hostile force which used X at one time and, owing to a continued association in your mind, still presents itself to you as his, but may now no longer have anything to do with him. By keeping up the old association, you simply give greater opportunity for this undesirable energy to come upon you.

Follow always the one rule, to open yourself directly to the Divine Force and not to others; if you keep in touch with it, all else will progressively arrange itself.

The Cosmic Force and the Overmind

The cosmic Force is under the control of the Overmind. The Supermind does not act on it directly — whatever comes down from there is modified so as to pass through the Overmind and takes a lesser form suitable to the plane on which it acts, mental, vital or physical. But this intervention is exceptional in the ordinary play of the cosmic forces.

The Entry of the Universal Forces

There is no rule for that [*the points at which the universal forces enter one*]. The human being is ordinarily conscious only on the surface — but the surface records only the results of subliminal agencies at work. It is often through the centres that the forces come in, for then they get the greatest power to act on the nature — but they can enter anywhere.

*

The universal forces act very often through the subconscient — especially when the force they send is something the person has been in the habit of obeying and of which the seeds, impressions, "complexes" are strongly rooted in the subconscient — or, even if that is no longer the case, of which there is a memory still in the subconscient.

The Universal Forces and the Individual

Egoism is part of the machinery — a chief part — of universal Nature, first to develop individuality out of indiscriminate force and substance of Nature and, secondly, to make the individual (through the machinery of egoistic thought, feeling, will and desire) a tool of the universal forces. It is only when one gets into touch with a higher Nature that it is possible to get free of this rule of ego and subjection to these forces.

*

Yes, certainly, there is nothing in the individual that is not in the cosmic Energy. For all ordinary purposes the individual is only a differentiated centre of the universal forces — although his soul comes from beyond.

Time Vision and the Cosmic Movement

Time vision is the perception of the cosmic movement of things developing from state to state and in that the individual movements which make it up. There is also possible a sense of the All as Time in flow or of Time as a dimension interwoven with Space like warp and woof of a cloth etc.

Section Four

The Dangers of Inner and Cosmic Experiences

Chapter One
The Intermediate Zone

The Nature of the Intermediate Zone

I mean by it [*the intermediate zone*] that when the sadhak gets beyond the barriers of his own embodied personal mind he enters into a wide range of experiences which are not the limited solid physical truth of things and not yet either the spiritual truth of things. It is a zone of formations, mental, vital, subtle physical, and whatever one forms or is formed by the forces of these worlds in us becomes for the sadhak for a time the truth — unless he is guided and listens to his guide. Afterwards if he gets through he discovers what it was and passes on into the subtle truth of things. It is a borderland where all the worlds meet, mental, vital, subtle physical, pseudo-spiritual — but there is no order or firm foothold — a passage between the physical and the true spiritual realms.

*

The intermediate zone means simply a confused condition or passage in which one is getting out of the personal consciousness and opening into the cosmic (cosmic Mind, cosmic vital, cosmic physical, something perhaps of the cosmic higher Mind) without having yet transcended the human mind levels. One is not in possession of or direct contact with the divine Truth *on its own levels*, but one can receive something from them, even from the Overmind, indirectly. Only, as one is still immersed in the cosmic Ignorance, all that comes from above can be mixed, perverted, taken hold of for their purposes by lower, even by hostile Powers.

It is not necessary for everyone to struggle through the intermediate zone. If one has purified oneself, if there is no abnormal vanity, egoism, ambition or other strong misleading element, or if one is vigilant and on one's guard, or if the psychic is in front, one can either pass rapidly and directly or with a minimum of trouble into the higher zones of consciousness where one is in direct contact with the Divine Truth.

On the other hand the passage through the higher zones — higher Mind, illumined Mind, Intuition, Overmind — is obligatory; they are the true Intermediaries between the present consciousness and the Supermind.

*

All these experiences are of the same nature and what applies to one applies to another. Apart from some experiences of a personal character, the rest are either idea-truths, such as pour down into the consciousness from above when one gets into touch with certain planes of being, or strong formations from the larger mental and vital worlds which, when one is directly open to these worlds, rush in and want to use the sadhak for their fulfilment. These things, when they pour down or come in, present themselves with a great force, a vivid sense of inspiration or illumination, much sensation of light and joy, an impression of widening and power. The sadhak feels himself freed from the normal limits, projected into a wonderful new world of experience, filled and enlarged and exalted: what comes associates itself, besides, with his aspirations, ambitions, notions of spiritual fulfilment and Yogic siddhi; it is represented even as itself that realisation and fulfilment. Very easily he is carried away by the splendour and the rush and thinks that he has realised more than he has truly done, something final or at least something sovereignly true. At this stage the necessary knowledge and experience are usually lacking which would tell him that this is only a very uncertain and mixed beginning; he may not realise at once that he is still in the cosmic Ignorance, not in the cosmic Truth, much less in the Transcendental Truth, and that whatever formative or dynamic idea-truths may have come down into him are partial only and yet farther diminished by their presentation to him by a still mixed consciousness. He may fail to realise also that if he rushes to apply what he is realising or receiving as if it were something definitive, he may either fall into confusion and error or else get shut up in some partial formation in which there may be an element of spiritual Truth but it is likely to be outweighed by more dubious mental and vital accretions that deform it altogether. It is only when he is able to draw back (whether at once or after a time) from his experiences, stand above them with the dispassionate witness consciousness, observe their real nature, limitations, composition, mixture that he can proceed on his way towards a real freedom and a higher, larger and truer siddhi. At each step this has to be done. For whatever comes in this way to the sadhak of this Yoga, whether it be from Overmind or Intuition or illumined Mind or some exalted Life-Plane or from all these together, it is not definitive and final; it is not the supreme Truth in which he can rest, but only a stage. And yet these stages have to be passed through, for the Supramental or the Supreme Truth cannot be reached in one bound or even in many bounds; one has to pursue a calm patient steady progress through many intervening stages without getting bound or attached to their lesser Truth or Light or Power or Ananda.

This is in fact an intermediary state, a zone of transition between the ordinary consciousness in mind and the true Yoga knowledge. One may cross without hurt through it, perceiving at once or at an early stage its real nature and refusing to be detained by its half-lights and tempting but imperfect and often mixed and misleading experiences; one may go astray in it, follow false voices and a mendacious guidance, and that ends in a spiritual disaster; or one may take up one's abode in this intermediate zone, care to go no farther and build there some half-truth which one takes for the whole truth or become the instrument of the Powers of these transitional planes, — that is what happens to many sadhaks and Yogis. Overwhelmed by the first rush and sense of power of a supernormal condition, they get dazzled with a little light which seems to them a tremendous illumination or a touch of force which they mistake for the full Divine Force or at least a very great Yoga Shakti, or they accept some intermediate Power (not always a Power of the Divine) as the Supreme and an intermediate consciousness as the supreme realisation. Very readily they come to think that they are in the full cosmic consciousness when it is only some front or small part of it or some larger Mind, Life-Power or subtle physical ranges with which they have entered into dynamic connection. Or they feel themselves to be in an entirely illumined consciousness, while in reality they are receiving imperfectly things from above through a partial illumination of some mental or vital plane; for what comes is diminished and often deformed in the course of transmission through these planes; the receiving mind and vital of the sadhak also often understands or transcribes ill what has been received or throws up to mix with it its own ideas, feelings, desires which it yet takes to be not its own but part of the Truth it is receiving because they are mixed with it, imitate its form, are lit up by its illumination and get from this association and borrowed light an exaggerated value.

There are worse dangers in this intermediate zone of experience. For the planes to which the sadhak has now opened his consciousness, — not as before getting glimpses of them and some influences, but directly, receiving their full impact, — send a host of ideas, impulses, suggestions, formations of all kinds, often the most opposite to each other, inconsistent or incompatible, but presented in such a way as to slur over their insufficiencies and differences, with great force, plausibility and a wealth of argument or a convincing sense of certitude. Overpowered by this sense of certitude, vividness, appearance of profusion and richness the mind of the sadhak enters into a great confusion which it takes for some larger organisation and order; or else it whirls about in incessant shiftings and changes which it takes for a rapid progress but which lead nowhere. Or there is the opposite danger that he may become the instrument of some apparently brilliant but ignorant formation; for these intermediate planes are full of little Gods or strong Daityas or smaller beings who want to create, to materialise something or to enforce a mental and vital formation in the earth life and are eager to use or influence or even possess the thought and will of the sadhak and make him their instrument for the purpose. This is quite apart from the well-known danger of actually hostile beings whose sole purpose is to create confusion, falsehood, corruption of the sadhana and disastrous unspiritual error. Anyone allowing himself to be taken hold of by one of these beings, who often take a divine Name, will lose his way in the Yoga. On the other hand, it is quite possible that the sadhak may be met at his entrance into this zone by a Power of the Divine which helps and leads him till he is ready for greater things; but still that itself is no surety against the errors and stumblings of this zone; for nothing is easier than for the powers of these zones or hostile powers to imitate the guiding Voice or Image and deceive and mislead the sadhak or for himself to attribute the creations and formations of his own mind, vital or ego to the Divine.

For this intermediate zone is a region of half-truths — and that by itself would not matter, for there is no complete truth below the Supermind; but the half-truth here is often so partial or else ambiguous in its application that it leaves a wide field for confusion, delusion and error. The sadhak thinks that he is no longer in the old small consciousness at all, because he feels in contact with something larger or more powerful, and yet the old consciousness is still there, not really abolished. He feels the control or influence of some Power, Being or Force greater than himself, aspires to be its instrument and thinks he has got rid of ego; but this delusion of egolessness often covers an exaggerated ego. Ideas seize upon him and drive his mind which are only partially true and by overconfident misapplication are turned into falsehoods; this vitiates the movements of the consciousness and opens the door to delusion. Suggestions are made, sometimes of a romantic character, which flatter the importance of the sadhak or are agreeable to his wishes and he accepts them without examination or discriminating control. Even what is true, is so exalted or extended beyond its true pitch and limit and measure that it becomes the parent of error. This is a zone which many sadhaks have to cross, in which many wander for a long time and out of which a great many never emerge. Especially if their sadhana is mainly in the mental and vital, they have to meet here many difficulties and much danger; only those who follow scrupulously a strict guidance or have the psychic being prominent in their nature pass easily as if on a sure and clearly marked road across this intermediate region. A central sincerity, a fundamental humility also save from much danger and trouble. One can then pass quickly beyond into a clearer Light where if there is still much mixture, incertitude and struggle, yet the orientation is towards the cosmic Truth and not to a half-illumined prolongation of Maya and Ignorance.

I have described in general terms with its main features and possibilities this state of consciousness just across the border of the normal consciousness, because it is here that these experiences seem to move. But different sadhaks comport themselves differently in it and respond sometimes to one class of possibilities, sometimes to another. In this case it seems to have been entered through an attempt to call down or force a way into the cosmic consciousness — it does not matter which way it is put or whether one is quite aware of what one is doing or aware of it in these terms, it comes to that in substance. It is not the Overmind which was entered, for to go straight into the Overmind is impossible. The Overmind is indeed above and behind the whole action of the cosmic consciousness, but one can at first have only an indirect connection with it; things come down from it through intermediate ranges into a larger mind-plane, life-plane, subtle physical plane and come very much changed and diminished in the transmission, without anything like the full power and truth they have in the Overmind itself on its native levels. Most of the movements come not from the Overmind, but down from higher mind ranges. The ideas with which these experiences are penetrated and on which they seem to rest their claim to truth are not of the Overmind, but of the higher Mind or sometimes of the illumined Mind; but they are mixed with suggestions from the lower mind and vital regions and badly diminished in their application or misapplied in many places. All this would not matter; it is usual and normal, and one has to pass through it and come out into a clearer atmosphere where things are better organised and placed on a surer basis. But the movement was made in a spirit of excessive hurry and eagerness, of exaggerated self-esteem and self-confidence, of a premature certitude, relying on no other guidance than that of one's own mind or of the "Divine" as conceived or experienced in a stage of very limited knowledge. But the sadhak's conception and experience of the Divine, even if it is fundamentally genuine, is never in such a stage complete and pure; it is mixed with all sorts of mental and vital ascriptions and all sorts of things are associated with this Divine guidance and believed to be part of it which come from quite other sources. Even supposing there is any direct guidance, — most often in these conditions the Divine acts mostly from behind the veil, — it is only occasional and the rest is done through a play of forces; error and stumbling and mixture of Ignorance take place freely and these things are allowed because the sadhak has to be tested by the world-forces, to learn by experience, to grow through imperfection towards perfection — if he is capable of it, if he is willing to learn, to open his eyes to his own mistakes and errors, to learn and profit by them so as to grow towards a purer Truth, Light and Knowledge.

The result of this state of mind is that one begins to affirm everything that comes in this mixed and dubious region as if it were all the Truth and the sheer Divine Will; the ideas or the suggestions that constantly repeat themselves are expressed with a self-assertive absoluteness as if they were Truth entire and undeniable. There is an impression that one has become impersonal and free from ego, while the whole tone of the mind, its utterance and spirit are full of vehement self-assertiveness justified by the affirmation that one is thinking and acting as an instrument and under the inspiration of the Divine. Ideas are put forward very aggressively that can be valid to the mind, but are not spiritually valid; yet they are stated as if they were spiritual absolutes. For instance, equality, which in that sense — for Yogic Samata is a quite different thing — is a mere mental principle, the claim to a sacred independence, the refusal to accept anyone as Guru, the opposition made between the Divine and the human Divine etc., etc. All these ideas are positions that can be taken by the mind and the vital and turned into principles which they try to enforce on the religious or even the spiritual life, but they are not and cannot be spiritual in their nature. There also begin to come in suggestions from the vital planes, a pullulation of imaginations romantic, fanciful or ingenious, hidden interpretations, pseudo-intuitions, would-be initiations into things beyond, which excite or bemuse the mind and are often so turned as to flatter and magnify ego and self-importance, but are not founded on any well-ascertained spiritual or occult realities of a true order. This region is full of elements of this kind and, if allowed, they begin to crowd on the sadhak; but if he seriously means to reach the Highest, he must simply observe them and pass on. It is not that there is never any truth in such things, but for one that is true there are nine imitative falsehoods presented and only a trained occultist with the infallible tact born of long experience can guide himself without stumbling or being caught through the maze. It is possible for the whole attitude and action and utterance to be so surcharged with the errors of this intermediate zone that to go farther on this route would be to travel far away from the Divine and from the Yoga.

Here the choice is still open whether to follow the very mixed guidance one gets in the midst of these experiences or to accept the true guidance. Each man who enters the realms of Yogic experience is free to follow his own way; but this Yoga is not a path for anyone to follow, but only for those who accept to seek the aim, pursue the way pointed out upon which a sure guidance is indispensable. It is idle for anyone to expect that he can follow this road far, much less go to the end by his own inner strength and knowledge without the true aid or influence. Even the ordinary long-practised Yogas are hard to follow without the aid of the Guru; in this which as it advances goes through untrodden countries and unknown entangled regions, it is quite impossible. As for the work to be done it also is not a work for any sadhak of any path; it is not, either, the work of the "impersonal" Divine — who, for that matter, is not an active Power but supports impartially all work in the universe. It is a training ground for those who have to pass through the difficult and complex way of this Yoga and none other. All work here must be done in a spirit of acceptance, discipline and surrender, not with personal demands and conditions, but with a vigilant conscious submission to control and guidance. Work done in any other spirit only results in an unspiritual disorder, confusion and disturbance of the atmosphere. In it too difficulties, errors, stumblings are frequent, because in this Yoga people have to be led patiently and with some field for their own effort, by experience, out of the ignorance natural to Mind and Life to a wider spirit and a luminous knowledge. But the danger of an unguided wandering in the regions across the border is that the very basis of the Yoga may be contradicted and the conditions under which alone the work can be done may be lost altogether. The transition through this intermediate zone — not obligatory, for many pass by a narrower but surer way — is a crucial passage; what comes out of it is likely to be a very wide or rich creation; but when one founders there, recovery is difficult, painful, assured only after a long struggle and endeavour.

The Dangers of the Intermediate Zone

As for the letter, I suppose you will have to tell the writer that his father committed a mistake when he took up Yoga without a Guru — for the mental idea about a Guru cannot take the place of the actual living influence. This Yoga especially, as I have written in my books, needs the help of the Guru and cannot be done without it. The condition into which his father got was a breakdown, not a state of siddhi. He passed out of the normal mental consciousness into a contact with some intermediate zone of consciousness (not the spiritual) where one can be subjected to all sorts of voices, suggestions, ideas, so-called inspirations which are not genuine. I have warned against the dangers of this intermediate zone in one of my books.[1] The sadhak can avoid entering into this zone — if he enters, he has to look with indifference on all these things and observe them without lending any credence; by so doing he can safely pass into the true spiritual light. If he takes them all as true or real without discrimination,

---

[1] *The Riddle of This World. Sri Aurobindo is referring to the preceding letter (pp. 296–303), which appeared in this book. — Ed.*

he is likely to land himself in a great mental confusion and if there is in addition a lesion or weakness of the brain — the latter is quite possible in one who has been subject to apoplexy — it may have serious consequences and even lead to a disturbance of the reason. If there is ambition or other motive of the kind mixed up in the spiritual seeking, it may lead to a fall in the Yoga and the growth of an exaggerated egoism or megalomania — of this there are several symptoms in the utterances of his father during the crisis. In fact one cannot or ought not to plunge into the experiences of this sadhana without a fairly long period of preparation and purification (unless one has already a great spiritual strength and elevation). Sri Aurobindo himself does not care to accept many into his path and rejects many more than he accepts. It would be well if he can get his father to pursue the sadhana no farther — for what he is doing is not really Sri Aurobindo's Yoga but something he has constructed in his own mind and once there has been an upset of this kind, the wisest course is discontinuance.

*

All these experiences of yours belong to what I have called the intermediate zone; a large proportion of them are of the vital plane. In the vital plane there are all kinds of things, good and bad, helpful and dangerous, true, half true and false, genuine and deceptive. One has therefore to be very careful and be always vigilant and turned towards the true source of Light. The difficulty is that here one may have a true spiritual experience and afterwards all sorts of imitative deceptions come in and bring with them the danger of a false experience. One has to watch, observe one's experiences and try to discriminate and understand, — waiting for two things, the opening of a wider higher consciousness from above and the coming forward of the psychic being from behind. When these two things happen, then the chance of error is diminished and the true inner guidance begins to make itself more and more felt in the sadhana.

Lights are of all kinds, supramental, mental, vital, physical, divine or Asuric — one has to watch, grow in experience and learn to know one from another. The true lights however are by their clarity and beauty not difficult to recognise.

The current from above and the current from below are familiar features of Yogic experience. It is the energy of the higher Nature and the energy of the lower Nature that become active and turned towards each other and move to meet, one descending, the other ascending. What happens when they meet, depends on the sadhaka. If his constant will is for the purification of the lower by the higher consciousness, then the meeting results in that and in spiritual progress. If his mind and vital are turbid and clouded, there is a clash, an impure mixture and much disturbance.

The division of the being into two parts — one a large consciousness behind, the other a smaller consciousness in front, is also a familiar feature of sadhana. In itself it is a necessary movement; it should naturally result in the growth of a larger Yogic consciousness prevailing over the small external consciousness and becoming a means for transformation under the pressure of the Divine Shakti. But here too it is possible for errors to take place — especially an outside Force may come in and replace the larger consciousness behind by a larger vital ego which pretends to be that. One must be on one's guard against any such intrusion; for many sadhaks suffer long and severely owing to such an intrusion which spoils the course of the sadhana.

On the whole aspire for the growth of the psychic and its control of the rest of the nature and for the opening, not to a larger vital consciousness, but to the higher consciousness above. And at all stages open yourself to the protection of the Mother and her grace and call on that for your safeguard and your guidance.

*

There is no utility in such experiences; they may happen on the vital plane so long as one has still to pass through the vital range of experiences, but the aim should be to get beyond them and live in a pure psychic and spiritual experience. To admit or call the invasion of others into one's own being is to remain always in the confusions of the intermediate zone. Only the Divine should be called into one's personal adhar — by which is not meant the loss of one's personal being or any idea of becoming the Divine, for that should be avoided. The ego has to be overcome, but the central personal being (which is not the ego but the individual self, soul, a portion of the Divine) has to remain a channel and instrument of the Divine Shakti. As for others, sadhaks etc. one can feel them in one's universalised consciousness, be aware of their movements, live in harmony with them in the Divine All, but not allow or call their presence within the personal adhar. Very often that leads to the invasion of the consciousness by vital powers or presences which assume the forms of those who are so admitted — and that is most undesirable. The sadhak must make his basic consciousness silent, calm, pure, peaceful and preserve or attain an absolute control over what he shall or shall not admit into it — otherwise, if he does not keep this control, he is in danger of becoming a field of confused and disorderly experiences or a plaything of all sorts of mental and vital beings and forces. Only one rule or influence other than one's own should be admitted, the rule of the Divine Shakti over the adhar.

Avoiding the Dangers of the Intermediate Zone

You are taking the first steps towards the cosmic consciousness in which there are all things good and bad, true and false, the cosmic Truth and the cosmic Ignorance. I was not thinking so much of ego as of these thousand voices, possibilities, suggestions. If you avoid these, then there is no necessity of passing through the intermediate zone. By avoid I mean really not admit — one can take cognizance of their nature and pass on.

*

Anybody passing the border of the ordinary consciousness can enter into this [*intermediate*] zone, if he does not take care to enter into the psychic. In itself there is no harm in passing through, provided one does not stop there. But ego, sex, ambition etc., if they get exaggerated, can easily lead to a dangerous downfall.

*

It [*the breaking of the veil*] comes of itself with the pressure of the sadhana. It can also be brought about by specific concentration and effort.

It is certainly better if the psychic is conscious and active before there is the removing of the veil or screen between the individual and the universal consciousness which comes when the inner being is brought forward in all its wideness. For then there is much less danger of the difficulties of what I have called the intermediate zone.

Chapter Two
Inner Voices and Indications

The Nature of Voices

There are many voices, and all are not divine; this may be only a voice of desire. All that keeps one faithful to the Truth and insists on peace, purity, devotion, sincerity, a spiritual change of the nature can be listened to with profit; the rest must be observed with discrimination and not followed blindly. Keep the fire of aspiration burning, but avoid all impatient haste.

*

Anybody can get "voices" — there are first the movements of one's nature that take upon themselves a voice — then there are all sorts of beings who either for a joke or for a serious purpose invade with their voices.

*

These voices are sometimes one's own mental formations, sometimes suggestions from outside. Good or bad depends on what they say and on the quarter from which they come.

*

This kind of manifestation [*hearing voices*] comes very often at a certain stage of the practice of Yoga. My experience is that it does not come from the highest source and cannot be relied upon and it is better to wait until one is able to enter a higher consciousness and a greater truth than any that these communications represent. Sometimes they come from beings of an intermediate plane who want to use the sadhak for some work or purpose. Many sadhaks accept and some, though by no means all, succeed in doing something, but it is often at the cost of the greater aims of Yoga. In other cases they come from beings who are hostile to the sadhana and wish to bring it to nothing by exciting ambition, the illusion of a great work or some other form of ego. Each sadhak must decide for himself (unless he has a guru to guide him) whether to treat it as a temptation or a mission.

*

It is possible to have a guiding Voice, but it is also easy to make a mistake in this matter. For the mind imitates the guiding voice and, if there are demands and desires in the vital, these also put themselves in the same form and are mistaken for a guiding voice. Make yourself pure of demand and desire, full only of psychic aspiration, surrendered, and in time a real guidance from within will come.

*

An inner voice is a voice only — it may give the direction, but not the force. A voice speaks, it does not act. There is a great difference between reading a book [*for guidance*] and receiving the inner direction.

The Danger of Following Inner Voices

No, these indications of time and these voices were not commands from the Mother. I have indicated to you the truth of this matter; you must follow the rules laid down by the Mother for the physical life; if any change has to be made, either she herself will let you know or you have to get sanction for it from her. No voice heard within can prevail against her word and no intimation that comes through your mind can be accepted as binding unless it is confirmed by her.

You have made a confusion which is often made at the beginning of this kind of experience. It is no doubt the Mother's Force that was working within you or upon you, and some of the experiences, such as that of feeling the Mother in your heart, were perfectly genuine. But when the pressure of the Force works upon the consciousness, then in the plane on which it happens to be working, a great activity of different forces is set in play, e.g. if it is the mind, various mental forces, if it is the vital, various vital forces. It is not safe to take all these for true things, to be accepted without question and followed as commands of the Mother. You received a pressure of a force so strong that it made your head shake for a long time; if the head shook like that, it is a sign that the mind or at least the mental physical was not able yet to receive all the force and assimilate it; if it had done so, there would have been no movement of the head, all would have been perfectly at ease, calm and still. But your mind started working, interpreting, beginning to put its own meaning on this particular phenomenon and again on others, trying to make a system by which to regulate your conduct and to give it authority, put it as the command of the Mother. The action of the Force was a fact, the interpretation you put on its details of coming and going was a mental formation and had no very positive value.

If you look at it carefully — as I have looked at the details reported by you — you will see that these suggestions were of a very shifting and changeful character, now one thing, now the other; only your mind adapted itself to the changes, adjusted its interpretation to suit them and tried to keep the consistency of a system. But in fact all was irregular and chaotic and it tended to make your action and conduct irregular and chaotic. True intuition would not do that; it would at least tend to balance, harmony, order.

You speak of intuition as regards the indication of time. There is an intuition of Time which is not of the mind and when it plays is always accurate to the very minute and if need be to the very second; but this was not that Intuition, — for it was not always accurate; it came right perhaps several times, then it began to be deceptive, it made you late for Pranam; it began to push towards lateness for the noon meal, make you clash with the convenience of the dining-room workers. It pushed you to be late for the evening and abandoned you altogether, so that in the end you had no evening meal. But your mind had got attached to its own formations and tried to justify, to put a meaning on these chaotic caprices, to explain them by the (very changeful) will of the Mother. All this is well-known to those experienced in Yoga, and it means that these things were not intuitions, but constructions of the mind, mental formations. If there was an intuition at all, it was movements of the intuitive mind, but what the intuitive mind gives to us is the intuition of possibilities, some of which realise themselves, some do not or do it partly only, others miss altogether. Behind these mental constructions are Forces that want to realise themselves and try to use men as their instruments for realisation. These Forces need not be hostile, but they play for their own hand, they want to rule, use, justify themselves, create their own results. If they can do it by getting the Mother's sanction or passing themselves off as commands of the Mother, they are ready to do so; if they cannot get the embodied Mother's sanction, they are ready to represent themselves as sanctions of the Mother in her subtle unseen universal Form or Presence. Some they persuade to make not only a distinction but an opposition between their inner Mother who always tells them what they want to hear and the embodied Mother who, they find, is not so complaisant, checks them, corrects their fancies and their errors. At this stage there is the danger of a more serious invasion of Falsehood, of a hostile vital Force coming in, taking advantage of the mind's errors, which either tries to take the place of the Mother using her name or else creates revolt against her. A persuasion not to come to Pranam, not to keep her acquainted with your experiences and submit to correction, not to accord the life with her expressed will is a danger-signal at this stage, — for it means that the intruding Force wants space to work free from all control — and that was why I felt compelled to call your attention to the peril of a hostile Maya.

As for voices, there are many voices; each Force, each movement of the mental, vital, physical plane may equip itself with a voice. Your voices were not even at one with each other; one said one thing, when it did not work out another said something inconsistent with it; but you were attached to your mental formation and still tried to follow.

All this happens because the mind and vital in these exaltations of the stress of the sadhana become very active. That is why it is necessary, first, to found your sadhana on a great calm, a great equality, not eagerly rushing after experiences or their fruit, but looking at them, observing, calling always for more and more Light, trying to be more and more wide, open, quietly and discerningly receptive. If the psychic being is always at the front, then these difficulties are greatly lessened, because there is here a light which the mind and vital have not, a spontaneous and natural psychic perception of the divine and the undivine, the true and the false, the imitation and the genuine guidance. It is also the reason why I insist on your referring your experiences to us, because, apart from anything else, we have the knowledge and experience of these things and can immediately put a check on any tendency to error.

Keep yourself open to the Mother's Force, but do not trust all forces. As you go on, if you keep straight, you will come to a time when the psychic becomes more predominantly active and the Light from above prevails more purely and strongly so that the chance of mental constructions and vital formations mixing with the true experience diminishes. As I have told you, these are not yet and cannot be the supramental Forces; it is a work of preparation which is only making things ready for a future Yoga-siddhi.

*

How can the people in this Asram judge whether a man has progressed in Yoga or not? They judge from outward appearances — if a sadhak secludes himself, sits much in meditation, gets voices and experiences, etc. etc. they think he is a great sadhak! X was always a very poor Adhar. He had a few experiences of an elementary kind — confused and uncertain, but at every step he was getting into trouble and going off on a side path and we had to pull him up. At last he began to get voices and inspirations which he declared to be ours — I wrote to him many letters of serious warning and explanation but he refused to listen, was too much attached to his false voices and inspirations and, to avoid rebuke and correction, ceased to write or inform us. So he went wholly wrong and finally became hostile. You can tell this by my authority to anybody who is puzzled like yourself about this matter.

*

Higher experiences hurt nobody — the question is what is meant by higher? X for instance thought his experiences to be the highest Truth itself — I told him they were all imaginations but only with the result that he became furious with me. There are imitation higher experiences when the mind or vital catches hold of an idea or suggestion and turns it into a feeling, and while there is a rush of forces, a feeling of exultation and power etc. All sorts of "inspirations" come, visions, perhaps "voices". There is nothing more dangerous than these voices — when I hear from somebody that he has a "voice", I always feel uneasy, though there can be genuine and helpful voices, and feel inclined to say, "No voices please, — silence, silence and a clear discriminating brain." I have hinted about this region of imitation experiences, false inspirations, false voices into which hundreds of Yogis enter and some never get out of it in my letter about the intermediate zone. If a man has a strong clear head and a certain kind of spiritual scepticism, he can go through and does — but people without discrimination like X or Y get lost. Especially ego enters in and makes them so attached to their splendid (?) condition that they absolutely refuse to come out. Now a retirement into seclusion gives free scope for this kind of action, as it makes one live entirely in one's own subjective being without any control except what one's own native discernment can bring in — and if that is not strong? Ego is of course the strong support of these subjective falsehoods, but there are other supports also. Work and mixing with others — with the contact of the objective that that brings — is not an absolute defence against these things, but it is a defence and serves as a check and as a kind of corrective balance. I notice that those who enter into this region of the intermediate zone usually make for retirement and seclusion and insist on it. These are the reasons why I prefer usually that sadhaks should not take to an absolute retirement, but keep a certain poise between silence and action, the inner and the outer together.

Part Four

The Fundamental Realisations
of the Integral Yoga

Section One

Three Stages of Transformation: Psychic, Spiritual, Supramental

Chapter One

The Psychic and Spiritual Realisations

The Fundamental Realisations[1]

1. The psychic change so that a complete devotion can be the main motive of the heart and the ruler of thought, life and action in constant union with the Mother and in her Presence.

2. The descent of the Peace, Power, Light etc. of the Higher Consciousness through the head and heart into the whole being, occupying the very cells of the body.

3. The perception of the One and Divine infinitely everywhere, the Mother everywhere and living in that infinite consciousness.

Four Bases of Realisation

You know the four things on which the realisation has to be based — (1) on a rising to a station above the mind, (2) on the opening out of the cosmic consciousness, (3) on the psychic opening, (4) on the descent of the higher consciousness with its peace, light, force, knowledge, Ananda etc. into all the planes of the being down to the most physical. All this has to be done by the working of the Mother's force aided by your aspiration, devotion and surrender. That is the Path. The rest is a matter of the working out of these things for which you have to have faith in the Mother's working.

Three Realisations for the Soul

When one speaks of the Divine spark, one is thinking of the soul

---

[1] *The letter under this heading is Sri Aurobindo's reply to the question, "What are the fundamental realisations in the Yoga?" — Ed.*

as a portion of the Divine which has descended from above into the manifestation rather than of something which has separated itself from the cosmos. It is the nature that has formed itself out of the cosmic forces — mind out of cosmic mind, life out of cosmic life, body out of cosmic matter.

For the soul there are three realisations — (1) the realisation of the psychic being and consciousness as the divine element in the evolution, (2) the realisation of the cosmic Self which is one in all, (3) the realisation of the supreme Divine from which both individual and cosmos have come and of the individual being (Jivatma) as an eternal portion of the Divine.

Foundations of the Sadhana

What you are experiencing is the true foundation of the spiritual life and realisation. It has three elements — first, the love which is the heart of Bhakti; then the descent of peace and equanimity which is the first necessary basis for realisation of self and the higher knowledge — what comes with it is the descent of the force which will work out in you the whole sadhana; thirdly, the feeling of a guiding presence or power which is the basis of Karma — of work and action founded in the spiritual consciousness.

*

You can reply to X that the three experiences he is having are the right ones — viz. the opening of the psychic through the heart, the descent of peace and the consciousness of his true being as the witness. But these experiences must be developed, deepened, completed and made the ordinary state of the consciousness. So established they become the triple foundation of the sadhana.

*

If you keep the wideness and calm as you are keeping it and also the love for the Mother in the heart, then all is safe — for it means the double foundation of the Yoga — the descent of the higher consciousness with its peace, freedom and security from above and the openness of the psychic which keeps all the effort or all the spontaneous movement turned towards the true goal.

*

To quiet the mind in such a way that no thoughts will come is not easy and usually takes time. The most necessary thing is to feel a quietude in the mind so that if thoughts come they do not disturb or hold the mind or make it follow them, but simply cross and pass away. The mind first becomes the witness of the passage of thought and not the thinker, afterwards it is able not to watch the thoughts but lets them pass unnoticed and concentrates in itself or on the object it chooses without trouble.

There are two main things to be secured as the foundations of sadhana — the opening of the psychic being and the realisation of the Self above. For the opening of the psychic being, concentration on the Mother and self-offering to her are the direct way. The growth of Bhakti which you feel is the first sign of the psychic development. A sense of the Mother's presence or force or the remembrance of her supporting and strengthening you is the next sign. Eventually, the soul within begins to be active in aspiration and psychic perception guiding the mind to the right thoughts, the vital to the right movements and feelings, showing and rejecting all that has to be put away and turning the whole being in all its movements to the Divine alone. For the self-realisation, peace and silence of the mind are the first condition. Afterwards one begins to feel release, freedom, wideness, to live in a consciousness silent, tranquil, untouched by any or all things, existing everywhere and in all, one with or united with the Divine. Other experiences come on the way, or may come, such as the opening of the inner vision, the sense of the Force working within and various movements and phenomena of the working etc. One may also be conscious of ascents of the consciousness and descents of Force, Peace, Bliss or Light from above.

*

I do not know why you doubt your experiences — you should

accept them as genuine unless we expressly say anything to the contrary. In all the experiences you have sent me up to now, I have never found any that were not perfectly genuine; moreover, your observation of them is quite sound and accurate.

Your first experience was that of the opening of the psychic; you became aware of the psychic being and its aspirations and experiences and of the external being in front, as two separate parts of your consciousness. You were not able to keep this experience because the vital was not purified and pulled you out into the ordinary external consciousness. Afterwards, you got back into the psychic and were at the same time able to see your ordinary vital nature, to become aware of its defects and to work by the power of the psychic for its purification. I wrote to you at the beginning that this was the right way; for if the psychic is awake and in front, it becomes easy to remain conscious of the things that have to be changed in the external nature and it is comparatively easy too to change them. But if the psychic gets veiled and retires into the background, the outer nature left to itself finds it difficult to remain conscious of its own wrong movements and even with great effort cannot succeed in getting rid of them. You can see yourself, as in the matter of the food, that with the psychic active and awake the right attitude comes naturally and whatever difficulty there was soon diminishes or even disappears.

I told you also at that time that there was a third part of the nature, the inner being (inner mind, inner vital, inner physical) of which you were not yet aware, but which must also open in time. It is this that has happened in your last experience. What you felt as a part of you, yourself but not your physical self, rising to meet the higher consciousness above, was this inner being; it was your (inner) higher vital being which rose in that way to join the highest Self above — and it was able to do so, because the work of purifying the outer vital nature had begun in earnest. Each time there is a purification of the outer nature, it becomes more possible for the inner being to reveal itself, to become free and to open to the higher consciousness above.

When this happens, several other things can happen at the

same time. First, one becomes aware of the silent Self above — free, wide, without limits, pure, untroubled by the mental, vital and physical movements, empty of ego and limited personality, — this is what you have described in your letter. Secondly, the Divine Power descends through this silence and freedom of the Self and begins to work in the Adhara. This is what you felt as a pressure; its coming through the top of the head, the forehead and eyes and nose meant that it was working to open the mental centres — especially the two higher centres of thought and will and vision in the inner mental being. These two centres are called the thousand-petalled lotus and the *ājñā-cakra* between the eyebrows. Thirdly, by this working the inner parts of the being are opened and freed; you are liberated from the limitations of the ordinary personal mind, vital and physical and become aware of a wider consciousness in which you can be more capable of the needed transformation. But that is necessarily a matter of time and long working and you are only taking the first steps in this way.

When one goes into the inner being, the tendency is to go entirely inside and lose consciousness of the outside world — this is what people call Samadhi. But it is also necessary to be able to have the same experiences (of the Self, the workings in the inner consciousness etc.) in the waking state. The best rule for you will be to allow the entire going inside only when you are alone and not likely to be disturbed, and at other times to accustom yourself to have these experiences with the physical consciousness awake and participating in them or at least aware of them. You did therefore quite right in stopping the complete going inside while you were at X's place. There was no harm in having these experiences there or anywhere, but there should be nothing to draw the attention of others — especially of those who are not in the Yoga or in the atmosphere.

The Central Process of the Yoga

I have said that the most decisive way for the Peace or the Silence to come is by a descent from above. In fact, in reality though not always in appearance, that is how they always come; — not in appearance always, because the sadhak is not always conscious of the process; he feels the peace settling in him or at least manifesting, but he has not been conscious how and whence it came. Yet it is the truth that all that belongs to the higher consciousness comes from above, not only the spiritual peace and silence, but the Light, the Power, the Knowledge, the higher seeing and thought, the Ananda come from above. It is also possible that up to a certain point they may come from within, but this is because the psychic being is open to them directly and they come first there and then reveal themselves in the rest of the being from the psychic or by its coming into the front. A disclosure from within or a descent from above are the two sovereign ways of the Yoga-siddhi. An effort of the external surface mind or emotions, a tapasya of some kind may seem to build up something of these things, but the results are usually uncertain and fragmentary compared to the result of the two radical ways. That is why in this Yoga we insist always on an "opening" — an opening inwards of the inner mind, vital, physical to the inmost part of us, the psychic, and an opening upwards to what is above the mind — as indispensable for the fruits of the sadhana.

The underlying reason for this is that this little mind, vital and body which we call ourselves is only a surface movement and not our "self" at all. It is an external bit of personality put forward for one brief life and for the play of the Ignorance. It is equipped with an ignorant mind stumbling about in search of fragments of truth, an ignorant vital rushing about in search of fragments of pleasure, an obscure and mostly subconscious physical receiving the impacts of things and suffering rather than possessing a resultant pain or pleasure. All that is accepted until the mind gets disgusted and starts looking about for the real Truth of itself and things, the vital gets disgusted and begins wondering whether there is not such a thing as real bliss and the physical gets tired and wants liberation from itself and its pains and pleasures. Then it is possible for this little ignorant bit of surface personality to get back to its real Self and with it to these greater things — or else to extinction of itself, Nirvana.

The real Self is not anywhere on the surface but deep within and above. Within is the soul supporting an inner mind, inner vital, inner physical in which there is a capacity for universal wideness and with it for the things now asked for, — direct contact with the Truth of self and things, taste of a universal bliss, liberation from the imprisoned smallness and sufferings of the gross physical body. Even in Europe the existence of something behind the surface is now very frequently admitted, but its nature is mistaken and it is called subconscient or subliminal, while really it is very conscious in its own way and not subliminal but only behind the veil. It is, according to our psychology, connected with the small outer personality by certain centres of consciousness of which we become aware by Yoga. Only a little of the inner being escapes through these centres into the outer life, but that little is the best part of ourselves and responsible for our art, poetry, philosophy, ideals, religious aspirations, efforts at knowledge and perfection. But the inner centres are, for the most part, closed or asleep — to open them and make them awake and active is one aim of Yoga. As they open, the powers and possibilities of the inner being also are aroused in us; we awake first to a larger consciousness and then to a cosmic consciousness; we are no longer little separate personalities with limited lives but centres of a universal action and in direct contact with cosmic forces. Moreover, instead of being unwilling playthings of the latter, as is the surface person, we can become to a certain extent conscious and masters of the play of nature — how far this goes depending on the development of the inner being and its opening upward to the higher spiritual levels. At the same time the opening of the heart centre releases the psychic being which proceeds to make us aware of the Divine within us and of the higher Truth above us.

For the highest spiritual Self is not even behind our personality and bodily existence but is above it and altogether exceeds it. The highest of the inner centres is in the head, just as the deepest is the heart; but the centre which opens directly to the Self is above the head, altogether outside the physical body, in what is called the subtle body, *sūkṣma śarīra*. This Self has two aspects and the results of realising it correspond to these two aspects. One is static, a condition of wide peace, freedom, silence: the silent Self is unaffected by any action or experience; it impartially supports them but does not seem to originate them at all, rather to stand back detached or unconcerned, *udāsīna*. The other aspect is dynamic and that is experienced as a cosmic Self or Spirit which not only supports but originates and contains the whole cosmic action — not only that part of it which concerns our physical selves but also all that is beyond it, this world and all other worlds, the supraphysical as well as the physical ranges of the universe. Moreover, we feel the Self as one in all, but also we feel it as above all, transcendent, surpassing all individual birth or cosmic existence. To get into the universal Self — one in all — is to be liberated from ego; ego either becomes a small instrumental circumstance in the consciousness or disappears from our consciousness altogether. That is the extinction or *nirvāṇa* of the ego. To get into the transcendent self above all makes us capable of transcending altogether even the cosmic consciousness and action — it can be the way to that complete liberation from the world-existence which is called also extinction, *laya*, *mokṣa*, Nirvana.

It must be noted however that the opening upward does not necessarily lead to peace, silence and Nirvana only. The sadhak becomes aware not only of a great, eventually an infinite peace, silence, wideness above us, above the head as it were and extending into all physical and supraphysical space, but also he can become aware of other things — a vast Force in which is all power, a vast Light in which is all knowledge, a vast Ananda in which is all bliss and rapture. At first they appear as something essential, indeterminate, absolute, simple, *kevala*; a Nirvana into any of these things seems possible. But we can come to see too that this Force contains all forces, this Light all lights, this Ananda all joy and bliss possible. And all this can descend into us. Any of them and all of them can come down, not peace alone; only the safest is to bring down first an absolute calm and peace for that makes the descent of the rest more secure; otherwise it may be difficult for the external nature to contain or bear so much Force, Light, Knowledge or Ananda. All these things together make what we call the higher, spiritual or divine consciousness. The psychic opening through the heart puts us primarily into connection with the individual Divine, the Divine in his inner relations with us; it is especially the source of love and bhakti. This upward opening puts us into direct relation with the whole Divine and can create in us the divine consciousness and a new birth or births of the spirit.

For when the Peace is established, this higher or Divine Force from above can descend and work in us. It descends usually first into the head and liberates the inner mind centres, then into the heart centre and liberates fully the psychic and emotional being, then into the navel and other vital centres and liberates the inner vital, then into the Muladhara and below and liberates the inner physical being. It works at the same time for perfection as well as liberation; it takes up the whole nature part by part and deals with it, rejecting what has to be rejected, sublimating what has to be sublimated, creating what has to be created. It integrates, harmonises, establishes a new rhythm in the nature. It can bring down too a higher and yet higher force and range of the higher Nature until, if that be the aim of the sadhana, it becomes possible to bring down the supramental force and existence. All this is prepared, assisted, farthered by the work of the psychic being in the heart centre; the more it is open, in front, active, the quicker, safer, easier the working of the Force can be. The more love and bhakti and surrender grow in the heart, the more rapid and perfect becomes the evolution of the sadhana. For the descent and transformation imply at the same time an increasing contact and union with the Divine.

That is the fundamental rationale of the sadhana. It will be evident that the two most important things here are the opening of the heart centre and the opening of the mind centres to all that is behind and above them. For the heart opens to the psychic being and the mind centres open to the higher consciousness and the nexus between the psychic being and the higher consciousness is the principal means of the siddhi. The first opening is effected by a concentration in the heart, a call to the Divine to manifest within us and through the psychic to take up and lead the whole nature. Aspiration, prayer, bhakti, love, surrender are the main supports of this part of the sadhana — accompanied by a rejection of all that stands in the way of what we aspire for. The second opening is effected by a concentration of the consciousness in the head (afterwards, above it) and an aspiration and call and a sustained will for the descent of the divine Peace, Power, Light, Knowledge, Ananda into the being — the Peace first or the Peace and Force together. Some indeed receive Light first or Ananda first or some sudden pouring down of knowledge. With some there is first an opening which reveals to them a vast infinite Silence, Force, Light or Bliss above them and afterwards either they ascend to that or these things begin to descend into the lower nature. With others there is either the descent, first into the head, then down to the heart level, then to the navel and below and through the whole body, or else an inexplicable opening — without any sense of descent — of peace, light, wideness or power or else a horizontal opening into the cosmic consciousness or, in a suddenly widened mind, an outburst of knowledge. Whatever comes has to be welcomed — for there is no absolute rule for all, — but if the peace has not come first, care must be taken not to swell oneself in exultation or lose the balance. The capital movement however is when the Divine Force or Shakti, the power of the Mother comes down and takes hold, for then the organisation of the consciousness begins and the larger foundation of the Yoga.

The result of the concentration is not usually immediate — though to some there comes a swift and sudden outflowering; but with most there is a time longer or shorter of adaptation or preparation, especially if the nature has not been prepared already to some extent by aspiration and tapasya. The coming of the result can sometimes be aided by associating with the concentration one of the processes of the old Yogas. There is the Adwaita process of the way of knowledge — one rejects from oneself the identification with the mind, vital, body, saying continually "I am not the mind", "I am not the vital", "I am not the body", seeing these things as separate from one's real self — and after a time one feels all the mental, vital, physical processes and the very sense of mind, vital, body becoming externalised, an outer action, while within and detached from them there grows the sense of a separate self-existent being which opens into the realisation of the cosmic and transcendent Spirit. There is also the method — a very powerful method — of the Sankhyas, the separation of the Purusha and the Prakriti. One enforces on the mind the position of the Witness — all action of mind, vital, physical becomes an outer play which is not myself or mine, but belongs to Nature and has been enforced on an outer me. I am the witness Purusha who am silent, detached, not bound by any of these things. There grows up in consequence a division in the being; the sadhak feels within him the growth of a calm silent separate consciousness which feels itself quite apart from the surface play of the mind and the vital and physical Nature. Usually when this takes place, it is possible very rapidly to bring down the peace of the higher consciousness and the action of the higher Force and the full march of the Yoga. But often the Force itself comes down first in response to the concentration and call and then, if these things are necessary, it does them and uses any other means or process that is helpful or indispensable.

One thing more. In this process of the descent from above and the working it is most important not to rely entirely on oneself, but to rely on the guidance of the Guru and to refer all that happens to his judgment and arbitration and decision. For it often happens that the forces of the lower nature are stimulated and excited by the descent and want to mix with it and turn it to their profit. It often happens too that some Power or Powers undivine in their nature present themselves as the Supreme Lord or as the Divine Mother and claim the being's service and surrender. If these things are accepted, there will be an extremely disastrous consequence. If indeed there is the assent of the sadhak to the Divine working alone and the submission or surrender to that guidance, then all can go smoothly. This assent and a rejection of all egoistic forces or forces that appeal to the ego are the safeguard throughout the sadhana. But the ways of Nature are full of snares, the disguises of the ego are innumerable, the illusions of the Powers of Darkness, Rakshasi Maya, are extraordinarily skilful; the reason is an insufficient guide and often turns traitor; vital desire is always with us tempting to follow any alluring call. This is the reason why in this Yoga we insist so much on what we call *samarpaṇa* — rather inadequately rendered by the English word surrender. If the heart centre is fully opened and the psychic is always in control, then there is no question; all is safe. But the psychic can at any moment be veiled by a lower upsurge. It is only a few who are exempt from these dangers and it is precisely those to whom surrender is easily possible. The guidance of one who is himself by identity or represents the Divine is in this difficult endeavour imperative and indispensable.

What I have written may help you to get some clear idea of what I mean by the central process of the Yoga. I have written at some length but, naturally, could cover only the fundamental things. Whatever belongs to circumstance and detail must arise as one works out the method, or rather as it works itself out, — for the last is what usually happens when there is an effective beginning of the action of the sadhana.

Chapter Two
Conditions of Transformation

Realisation and Transformation

Transformation is something progressive, but certainly there must be realisation before the complete transformation is possible.

The Three Transformations

There are three stages of the sadhana, psychic change, transition to the higher levels of consciousness — with a descent of their conscious forces — the supramental. In the last even the control over death is a later, not an initial stage. Each of these stages demands a great length of time and a high and long endeavour.

*

To be *sthitaprajña* merely means to have one's thinking mind settled in the spiritual consciousness in the realisation of Self. That does not necessarily transform the other parts of the nature. The bringing down of the Force and Light of the higher consciousness, the opening of the psychic and the centres of the mind, vital and physical, the consent and receptive opening of the nature to the workings of the psychic and the higher consciousness, finally the opening to the supramental are the conditions of transformation. What do you mean by "attaining" the higher consciousness? The higher consciousness is something above the mind, vital and body of the human being. It is wholly spiritual. To attain may mean only to be able to go into it at will or to remain in it with a part of one's consciousness, while the rest goes on in the old way. Psychic transformation is when the whole being is remoulded into the nature of the psychic; spiritual transformation is when the whole being is spiritualised; supramental transformation is when the whole being is supramentalised —

that cannot be done automatically by merely being aware of the higher consciousness or attaining it in the ordinary limited sense.

The physical is of course the basis — that of the Overmind is in between the two hemispheres. The lower hemisphere must contain all the mind including its higher planes, the vital, the physical. The upper hemisphere contains the Divine existence-consciousness-bliss, with the Supermind as its means of self-formulation. The Overmind is at the head of the lower hemisphere and is the intermediate or transitional plane between the two.

The psychic being stands behind the heart supporting the mind, life and body. In the psychic transformation there are three main elements: (1) the opening of the occult inner mind, inner vital, inner physical, so that one becomes aware of all that lies behind the surface mind, life and body; (2) the opening of the psychic being or soul by which it comes forward and governs the mind, life and body turning all to the Divine; (3) the opening of the whole lower being to the spiritual truth — this last may be called the psycho-spiritual part of the change. It is quite possible for the psychic transformation to take one beyond the individual into the cosmic. Even the occult opening establishes a connection with the cosmic mind, cosmic vital, cosmic physical. The psychic realises the contact with all existence, the oneness of the Self, the universal love and other realisations which lead to the cosmic consciousness.

But all that is a result of the opening to the spiritual above and it comes by an infiltration or reflection of the spiritual light and truth in mind, life and body. The spiritual transformation proper begins or becomes possible when one rises above the mind and lives there governing all from above. Even in the psychic transformation one can rise above by a sort of going above of the mental, vital, physical being and a return, but one does not yet live above in the summit consciousness where Overmind has its seat with the other planes that are above the human Mind.

The supramental transformation can only come when the lid

between the lower and higher hemispheres or halves of existence is removed and the Supermind instead of the Overmind becomes the governing power of the existence — but of that nothing can be spoken now.

Preparation for the Supramental Change

Get the psychic being in front and keep it there, putting its power on the mind, vital and physical — so that it shall communicate to them its force of single-minded aspiration, trust, faith, surrender, direct and immediate detection of whatever is wrong in the nature and turned towards ego and error, away from Light and Truth.

Eliminate egoism in all its forms; eliminate it from every movement of your consciousness.

Develop the cosmic consciousness — let the egocentric outlook disappear in wideness, impersonality, the sense of the cosmic Divine, the perception of universal forces, the realisation and understanding of the cosmic manifestation, the play.

Find in place of ego the true being — a portion of the Divine, issued from the World-Mother and an instrument of the manifestation. This sense of being a portion of the Divine and an instrument should be free from all pride, sense or claim of ego or assertion of superiority, demand or desire. For if these elements are there, then it is not the true thing.

Most, even in doing Yoga, live in the mind, vital, physical, lit up occasionally or to some extent by the higher mind and by the illumined mind; but to prepare for the supramental change it is necessary (as soon as, personally, the time has come) to open up to the Intuition and the Overmind, so that these may make the whole being and the whole nature ready for the supramental change. Allow the consciousness quietly to develop and widen, and the knowledge of these things will progressively come.

Calm, discrimination, detachment (but not indifference) are all very important, for their opposites impede very much the transforming action. Intensity of aspiration should be there, but it must go along with these. No hurry, no inertia — neither rajasic over-eagerness nor tamasic discouragement—a steady and persistent but quiet call and working. No snatching or clutching at realisation, but allowing realisation to come from within and above and observing accurately its field, its nature, its limits.

Let the power of the Mother work in you, but be careful to avoid mixture or the substitution in its place of either a magnified ego-working or a force of Ignorance presenting itself as Truth. Aspire especially for the elimination of all obscurity and unconsciousness in the nature.

These are the main conditions of preparation for the supramental change, but none of them is easy, and they must be complete before the nature can be said to be ready. If the true attitude (psychic, unegoistic, open only to the Divine Force) can be established, then the process can go on much more quickly. To take and keep the true attitude, to further the change in *oneself*, is the help that can be given, the one thing needed to assist the general change.

*

1. Loss of egoism — including all ambition (even "spiritual" ambition), pride, desire, self-centred life, mind, will.
2. Universalisation of the consciousness.
3. Absolute surrender to the transcendental Divine.

Section Two

The Psychic Opening, Emergence and Transformation

Chapter One
The Psychic Being and Its Role in Sadhana

The Importance of the Psychic Change

What is meant in the terminology of the Yoga by the psychic is the soul element in the nature, the pure psyche or divine nucleus which stands behind mind, life and body (it is not the ego) but of which we are only dimly aware. It is a portion of the Divine and permanent from life to life, taking the experience of life through its outer instruments. As this experience grows it manifests a developing psychic personality which insisting always on the good, true and beautiful, finally becomes ready and strong enough to turn the nature towards the Divine. It can then come entirely forward, breaking through the mental, vital and physical screen, govern the instincts and transform the nature. Nature no longer imposes itself on the soul, but the soul, the Purusha, imposes its dictates on the nature.

*

The soul, the psychic being, is in direct touch with the divine Truth, but it is hidden in man by the mind, the vital being and the physical nature (*manas, prāṇa, anna* of the Taittiriya Upanishad). One may practise Yoga and get illuminations in the mind and the reason; one may conquer power and luxuriate in all kinds of experiences in the vital; one may establish even surprising physical siddhis; but if the true soul-power behind does not manifest, if the psychic nature does not come into the front, nothing genuine has been done. In this Yoga, the psychic being is that which opens the rest of the nature to the true supramental light and finally to the supreme Ananda. Mind can open by itself to its own higher reaches; it can still itself and widen into the Impersonal; it may too spiritualise itself in some kind of static liberation or Nirvana; but the supramental cannot find a sufficient base in spiritualised mind alone. If the inmost soul is awakened, if there is a new birth out of the mere mental, vital and physical into the psychic consciousness, then this Yoga can be done; otherwise (by the sole power of the mind or any other part) it is impossible. If there is a refusal of the psychic new birth, a refusal to become the child new born from the Mother, owing to attachment to intellectual knowledge or mental ideas or to some vital desire, then there will be a failure in the sadhana.

*

It seems to me that you must know by this time about the psychic being — that it is behind the veil and its consciousness also; only a little comes out into the mind and vital and physical. When that consciousness is not concealed, when you are aware of your soul (the psychic being), when its feelings and aspirations are yours, then you have got the consciousness of the psychic being. The feelings and aspirations of the psychic being are all turned towards truth and right consciousness and the Divine; it is the only part that cannot be touched by the hostile forces and their suggestions.

*

Everything is dangerous in the sadhana or can be, except the psychic change.

*

That [*feeling the Mother's Presence, Love, Joy, Beauty*] is one part of the psychic experience — the other is a complete self-giving, absence of demand, a prominence of the psychic being by which all that is false, wrong, egoistic, contrary to the Divine Truth, Divine Will, Divine Purity and Light is shown, falls away, cannot prevail in the nature. With all that the increase of the psychic qualities, gratitude, obedience, unselfishness, fidelity to the true perception, true impulse etc. that comes from the Mother or leads to the Mother. When this side grows, then the other, the Presence, Love, Joy, Beauty, can develop and be permanently there.

The Role of the Psychic in Sadhana

The contribution of the psychic being to the sadhana is: (1) love and bhakti, a love not vital, demanding and egoistic but without conditions or claims, self-existent; (2) the contact or the presence of the Mother within; (3) an unerring guidance from within; (4) a quieting and purification of the mind, vital and physical consciousness by their subjection to the psychic influence and guidance; (5) the opening up of all this lower consciousness to the higher spiritual consciousness above for its descent into a nature prepared to receive it with a complete receptivity and right attitude — for the psychic brings in everything right thought, right perception, right feeling, right attitude.

One can raise up one's consciousness from the mental and vital and bring down the power, ananda, light, knowledge from above; but this is far more difficult and uncertain in its result, even dangerous if the being is not prepared or not pure enough. To ascend with the psychic for the purpose is by far the best way. If you are thus rising from the psychic centre, so much the better.

What you say indicates that the psychic and mental centres are in communication and through them you are able to bring down things from the higher consciousness. But you have not changed your head centre for the above-head centre or for the above-head wideness. That usually comes by a gradual rising of the consciousness first to the top of the head and then above it. But this must not be strained after or forced; it will come of itself.

*

The psychic being not only helps openly, when it is strong and in front, but can govern the mind and vital and physical nature, give it the clear intimation of what is true and false, divine or undivine, right or wrong and repel all invasion of the hostile forces.

*

It is true that if the consciousness remains quiet, the psychic will manifest more and more from deep inside and a clear feeling will come of what is true and spiritually right and what is wrong or untrue and with it also will come the power to throw away what is hostile, wrong or untrue.

*

If the psychic is active — or in so far as it is active, there is something in it which is like an automatic test for the universal forces — warning against (not by thought so much as by an essential feeling) and rejecting what should not be, accepting and transmuting what should be.

*

That is the special work of the psychic being, to receive the true things from above and to send away the false things from below.

*

This is the function of the psychic — it has to work on each plane so as to help each to awaken to the true truth and the divine reality.

*

You are right in thinking that this psychic attitude is your true need; it is that which can make the progress simple, happy and easy.

Persevere; there is no reason for giving up. Let no uprising of difficulties discourage you. At the end there is victory and lasting peace.

The Psychic Deep Within

The place of the psychic is deep within the heart, — but *deep within*, not on the surface where the ordinary emotions are. But it can come forward and occupy the surface as well as be within, — then the emotions themselves become no longer vital things, but psychic emotions and feelings. The psychic so standing in front can also extend its influence everywhere, to the mind for instance so as to transform its ideas or to the body so as to transform its habits and its reactions.

*

The psychic being is in the heart centre in the middle of the chest (not in the physical heart, for all the centres are in the middle of the body), but it is deep behind. When one is going away from the vital into the psychic, it is felt as if one is going deep deep down till one reaches that central place of the psychic. The surface of the heart centre is the place of the emotional being; from there one goes deep to find the psychic. The more one goes, the more intense becomes the psychic happiness which you describe.

*

If it was something in the heart, it must be the psychic being which is often felt as if deep down somewhere or rising out of a depth. If one goes to it, it is felt often as if one were going into a deep well.

The shock must have been the psychic force trying to open the mental and vital lid which covers the soul.

*

It is evidently the psychic — it is often seen as a deep well or abyss into which one plunges and finds no end; but here it is evidently the psychic penetrating down into all the lower planes and also rising up to the higher planes above.

*

The empty condition by itself is not called samadhi — it is when one goes inside, is conscious within but not conscious of outside things. What you describe yourself as doing involuntarily is this going inside and being conscious there. It was into the psychic centre inside that you were going, the place that you saw as a luminous *maidān* in a former experience. When one goes there it is just this peace and sweetness that one feels and also this sense of the Mother being there not far away or very near. So it is a very good development of the sadhana.

The Psychic and the Mental, Vital and Physical Nature

The mind, life and body are the instruments for manifestation. Of course the psychic can manifest things by itself inwardly or in its own plane, but for manifestation in the physical plane the instrumentality of the other parts is needed.

*

These [*questions about the transformation of the lower worlds*] are questions with which we need not concern ourselves at present. To answer them would be to stimulate merely the curiosity of the mind — what is important now is to liberate the psychic from its veils and to open the mind and vital and body to the higher consciousness. Until that is done, there can be no individual transformation and so long as there is not the individual transformation what is the use of speculating about the transformation of worlds and its results?

*

The soul is the witness, upholder, inmost experiencer, but it is master only in theory, in fact it is not-master, *anīśa*, so long as it consents to the Ignorance. For that is a general consent which implies that the Prakriti gambols about with the Purusha and does pretty well what she likes with him. When he wants to get back his mastery, make the theoretical practical, he needs a lot of tapasya to do it.

The psychic has always been veiled, consenting to the play of mind, physical and vital, experiencing everything through them in the ignorant mental, vital and physical way. How then can it be that they are bound to change at once when it just takes the trouble to whisper or say, "Let there be Light"! They have a tremendous negating power and can refuse and do refuse point-blank. The mind resists with an obstinate persistency in argument and a constant confusion of ideas, the vital with a fury of bad will aided by the mind's obliging reasonings on its side, the physical resists with an obstinate inertia and crass fidelity to old habit, and when they have done, the general Nature comes in and says, "What, you are going to get free from me so easily? Not if I know it," and it besieges and throws back the old nature on you again and again as long as it can.

*

You should never listen to these suggestions of unfitness or anything else that denies the possibility of progress and fulfilment. Whatever the difficulties or the slowness or periods of emptiness, keep before you the firm idea that succeed you must and will. Do not be discouraged by the time taken. There are people who have laboured for many years together thinking they were making no progress and yet finally the opening has come. The Force is there working behind the veil to remove difficulties and prepare the Adhar — if one is constant, finally the result will appear.

It does not matter with what motive you or anyone began the sadhana. There are always two elements, the psychic within which wants the Divine, and the mind, vital, physical which are pushed to enter the way through some idea, desire or feeling — it may be the feeling of *vairāgya* with the ordinary life, disgust of it and a desire for freedom and peace, or it may be something else, the idea of a greater knowledge or joy or calm which mind and life cannot give, or the seeking of Yoga power for one object or another. All that does not matter — for as the psychic pushes one farther on the way, these things drop away and the one longing for the Divine takes their place, or else they themselves are transformed and put in their proper place. The only thing you must be careful about is that, when the experience develops, you do not replace the first motives by Yogic ambition or desire for greatness or get misled by vital desires; but this can always be avoided if your mind knows and holds to it firmly that union with the Divine alone is the true central object of sadhana.

The Psychic Awakening

The psychic being is always there, but is not felt because it is covered up by the mind and vital; when it is no longer covered up, it is then said to be awake. When it is awake, it begins to take hold of the rest of the being, to influence it and change it so that all may become the true expression of the inner soul. It is this change that is called the inner conversion. There can be no conversion without the awakening of the psychic being.

*

The experiences that are coming cannot be permanent at the beginning; they come and go and do their work and afterwards there is a permanent result. What must be permanent is the psychic awakening, the psychic condition and attitude and what you have written in your letter is an exact description of this psychic condition and psychic attitude. One has to keep this and see what happens and the Mother's Force will do the rest.

*

Let the sweetness and the happy feeling increase, for they are the strongest sign of the soul, the psychic being awake and in touch with us. Let not mistakes of thought or speech or action disturb you — put them away from you as something superficial which the Power and Light will deal with and remove. Keep to the one central thing — your soul and these higher realities it brings with it.

*

That is good — the awakening of the psychic consciousness and its control over the rest is one of the most indispensable elements of the sadhana.

Living in the Psychic

The division of the being of which you speak is a necessary stage in the Yogic development and experience. One feels that there

The Psychic Being and Its Role in Sadhana 345

is a twofold being, the inner psychic which is the true one and the other, the outer human being which is instrumental for the outward life. To live in the inner psychic being and in union with the Divine while the outer does the outward work, as you feel, is the first stage in Karmayoga. There is nothing wrong in these experiences; they are indispensable and normal at this stage.

If you feel no bridge between the two, it is probably because you are not yet conscious of what connects the two. There is an inner mental, an inner vital, an inner physical which connect the psychic and the external being. About this, however, you need not be anxious at present.

The important thing is to keep what you have and let it grow, to live always in the psychic being, your true being. The psychic will then in due time awaken and turn to the Divine all the rest of the nature, so that even the outer being will feel itself in touch with the Divine and moved by the Divine in all it is and feels and does.

*

If it is the sense of the presence that you have, then you are living in the consciousness of the psychic centre. Thinking with the mind is good because it leads towards that but it is not in itself that living in the psychic centre.

*

It is necessary [*in order to be constantly aware of the psychic*] to accustom oneself to do things from within, not to let the consciousness be thrown outward. If it is thrown outward, then to step back inwardly and regard the action or movement from within. Of course there must be the habit of self-offering too or turning all to the Divine.

*

It [*the psychic being*] has to be surrendered consciously and with more and more knowledge. The psychic aspires to the Divine or answers to things divine, it is surrendered in principle, but it has to develop its surrender in detail carrying with it the surrender of all the being.

*

There are always unregenerate parts tugging people backwards and who is not divided? But it is best to put one's trust in the soul, the spark of the Divine within and foster that till it rises into a sufficient flame.

Chapter Two
The Psychic Opening

The Meaning of Psychic Opening

The psychic in the ignorant human being is always behind a veil and can act on the mind or vital but not in its own power, for that is limited and obscured by the instruments. A psychic opening means the removal of the veil and the increasingly direct action of the psychic.

*

The present nature is ignorant and full of wrong actions and reactions. But there is a being within you, the psychic, which answers to the Truth and not to the Ignorance. If one turns to the Divine and becomes open, then this psychic being shows itself and gives to the nature the true thoughts, feelings, will, action. This is the first change to be made.

*

What you feel is the true psychic opening and it is that for which you should always aspire and reject other things until it becomes your normal base of consciousness. Once that is there, it is possible to call down through it a strength from above which will make the vital strong and remove the weakness. Your sadhana is still too mental and therefore difficult and slow; it is the psychic opening that makes a more satisfying and rapid progress possible.

*

It does not matter if strenuous meditation leads to experiences or not. Remember what I told you that it is the psychic growth and not experiences that are the road for you just now. That means three things — 1st, the drawing back from the vital ego and its perturbations to a quiet attitude of faith and surrender; 2nd, the growth of something within that sees what is to be changed in the nature and gives the impulse to change it; 3rd, the psychic feeling in sadhana which presses towards the growth of bhakti, feels it a joy simply to think, feel, write, speak of, remember the Divine, grows full of a quiet self-upliftment towards the Divine and lives in that more than in outward things. When the consciousness is full of these things altogether, i.e. when there is the full psychic state or opening, then experiences begin to come of themselves. The first two at least had started of themselves in you — let them grow and the third should necessarily follow. The psychic opening first, the higher consciousness and its experiences afterwards.

*

What you desire about the self-giving free from demand is sure to fulfil itself when there is the full opening of the psychic.

*

X has been always like that. It is the activity of his mind which is very restless; sometimes he gets a psychic opening and is all right, then the mind comes across and he becomes confused and miserable. Going away will not cure him; "thinking over things" will only make him more confused and lost. He is a man who can be rescued from all that only by a complete and permanent psychic opening, through the heart not the mind.

Conditions for the Psychic Opening

It is good that you go back from this struggle towards the quiet foundation that helps the opening. All this struggling and confusion and harassing self-depreciation is the old wrong way of proceeding; it is mental and vital and cannot succeed; it is in the quiet mind that the opening must come. Then the psychic being, the soul in you, begins to come forward. The soul knows and sees the Truth; the mind and vital do not — until they are enlightened by the soul's knowledge.

*

Then only can the psychic being fully open when the sadhaka has got rid of the mixture of vital motives with his sadhana and is capable of a simple and sincere self-offering to the Mother. If there is any kind of egoistic turn or insincerity of motive, if the Yoga is done under a pressure of vital demands, or partly or wholly to satisfy some spiritual or other ambition, pride, vanity or seeking after power, position or influence over others or with any push towards satisfying any vital desire with the help of the Yogic force, then the psychic cannot open, or opens only partially or only at times and shuts again because it is veiled by the vital activities; the psychic fire fails in the strangling vital smoke. Also, if the mind takes the leading part in the Yoga and puts the inner soul into the background, or, if the bhakti or other movements of the sadhana take more of a vital than of a psychic form, there is the same inability. Purity, simple sincerity and the capacity of an unegoistic unmixed self-offering without pretension or demand are the conditions of an entire opening of the psychic being.

*

If desire is rejected and no longer governs the thought, feeling or action and there is the steady aspiration of an entirely sincere self-giving, the psychic usually after a time opens of itself.

An Experience of Psychic Opening

It was certainly an experience and as X very accurately described it an experience of great value, a psychic experience par excellence. A feeling of velvety softness within — an *ineffable plasticity within* is a psychic experience and can be nothing else. It means a modification of the substance of the consciousness especially in the vital emotional part, and such a modification prolonged or repeated till it became permanent would mean a great step in what I call the psychic transformation of the being. It is just these modifications in the inner substance that make transformation possible. Farther, it was a modification that made a beginning of knowledge possible — for by knowledge we mean in Yoga not thought or ideas about spiritual things but psychic understanding from within and spiritual illumination from above. Therefore the first result was this feeling "that there was no ignominy in not understanding it, that the true understanding would come only when one realised that one was completely impotent". This was itself a beginning of true understanding, a psychic understanding, something felt within which sheds a light or brings up a spiritual truth that mere thinking would not have given, also a truth that is effective bringing both the enlightenment and solace you needed — for what the psychic being brings with it always is light and happiness, an inner understanding and relief and solace.

Another very promising aspect of this experience is that it came as an immediate response to an appeal to the Divine. You asked for the understanding and the way out and at once Krishna showed you both — the way out was the change of the consciousness within, the plasticity which makes the knowledge possible and also the understanding of the condition of mind and vital in which the true knowledge or power of knowledge could come. For the inner knowledge comes from within and above (whether from the Divine in the heart or from the Self above) and for it to come the pride of the mind and vital in the surface mental ideas and their insistence on them must go. One must know that one is ignorant before one can begin to know. This shows that I was not wrong in pressing for the psychic opening as the only way out. For as the psychic opens, such responses and much more also become common and the inner change also proceeds by which they are made possible.

*

What was meant [*by "plasticity within"*], I suppose, was the psychic plasticity which makes surrender possible along with a free openness to the Divine working from above — plasticity within as opposed to the rigidity which insists on maintaining one's own ideas, feelings, habitual ways of consciousness as opposed to the higher things from above or from the psychic within.

The Psychic Opening and the Inner Centres

There is no doubt that the inner being and the psychic in you are opening and that the psychic is influencing all including the physical centre.

As to the centres. The psychic is placed behind the heart-lotus, the centre of the emotional being, the Anahata chakra — it is therefore the opening of the Anahata that is most important for the unveiling of the psychic. The Manipura (navel centre) and the Swadhisthana below it are the seats of the vital being, the Muladhara is the seat of the physical. The opening of the Manipura gives one the free play of the inner vital consciousness and it is very helpful, no doubt, for the influence of the psychic on the vital, but it is not the direct or first condition of the psychic opening itself. But so also the opening of the higher centres is helpful for the influence of the psychic on the mental being. All the centres have to open, because otherwise the inner consciousness is not opened out and liberated to its full working in all its parts.

There is however no invariable rule as to the order of the opening. By concentration on the heart centre that can open first liberating the psychic action, which is veiled by the emotional, into free play. In many there is first some opening of the vital centre and for a long time there is an abundant but unpurified play of experiences on the vital plane. In the Tantric discipline there is a process of opening all the centres from the Muladhara upward. In our Yoga very often the Power descends from above and opens the Ajnachakra first, then the others in order. But it is perhaps the safest to open by concentration the heart-lotus first so as to have the psychic influence from the beginning.

The psychic cannot lose its consciousness in the enjoyment of experiences; when it is in free action, it has the unfailing discrimination of which you speak. It has besides no push to outward enjoyment, though it has Ananda. It is the vital that is carried away by enjoyment and carries away with it the mind and other lower parts — and it can also cover up the psychic; but then what happens is not that the psychic loses its own consciousness, which is impossible, but that the sadhak loses for the time being the full possession of the psychic consciousness. But it can always be recovered by a rectification of the wrong movement. But if one lives firmly in the psychic, there is not much danger of this aberration. What one must not do is to throw oneself out into the mind and vital; one must live within and from there command one's experience.

"Opening" and "Coming in Front"

In using the expression "opening of the psychic" I was thinking not of an ordinary psychic opening producing some amount of psychic (as opposed to vital) love and bhakti, but of what is called the coming in front of the psychic. When that happens one is aware of the psychic being with its simple spontaneous self-giving and feels its increasing direct control (not merely a veiled or half-veiled influence) over mind, vital and physical. Especially there is the psychic discernment which at once lights up the thoughts, emotional movements, vital pushes, physical habits and leaves nothing there obscure, substituting the right movements for the wrong ones. It is this that is difficult and rare, more often the discernment is mental and it is the mind that tries to put all in order. In that case, it is the descent of the higher consciousness through the mind that opens the psychic, instead of the psychic opening directly.

*

Nobody said it [*the opening of the psychic*] must be done necessarily from above. Naturally it is done direct and is most effective then. But when it is found difficult to do direct, as it is in certain natures, then the change begins from above, and the consciousness descending from there has to liberate the heart centre. As it acts on the heart centre, the psychic action becomes more possible.

*

The direct opening of the psychic centre is easy only when

the ego-centricity is greatly diminished and also if there is a strong bhakti for the Mother. A spiritual humility and sense of submission and dependence is necessary.

Chapter Three

The Emergence or Coming Forward of the Psychic

The Meaning of "Coming to the Front"

What is meant by [*the psychic's*] coming to the front is simply this. The psychic ordinarily is deep within. Very few people are aware of their souls — when they speak of their soul, they usually mean the vital + mental being or else the (false) soul of desire. The psychic remains behind and acts only through the mind, vital and physical wherever it can. For this reason the psychic being except where it is very much developed has only a small and partial, concealed and mixed or diluted influence on the life of most men. By coming forward is meant that it comes from behind the veil, its presence is felt clearly in the waking daily consciousness, its influence fills, dominates, transforms the mind and vital and their movements, even the physical. One is aware of one's soul, feels the psychic to be one's true being, the mind and the rest begin to be only instruments of the inmost within us.

The inner mental, vital, physical are also veiled, but much nearer to the surface and much of their movements or inspirations get through the veil (but not in any fullness or purity) in the lives of developed human beings, something even in the lives of ordinary people. But these too in Yoga throw down the veil after a time and come in front and their action predominates in the consciousness while the external is no longer felt as one's own self but only as a front or even a fringe of the being.

*

Awakening [*of the psychic being*] is a different thing [*from its coming to the front*], it means the conscious action of the psychic from behind. When it comes to the front it invades the mind and vital and body and psychicises their movements. It comes best by aspiration and an unquestioning and entire turning and surrender to the Mother. But also it sometimes comes of itself when the Adhar is ready.

*

That is what we speak of as the psychic being coming in front — to psychicise the whole consciousness, i.e. make it subject to the psychic truth and full of the psychic nature. At the same time the ordinary vital being has to disappear and be changed into the true vital.

*

The soul in itself contains all possible strength, but most of it is held behind the veil and it is what comes forward in the nature that makes the difference. In some people the psychic element is strong and in others weak; in some people the mind is the strongest part and governs, in others the vital is the strongest part and leads or drives. But by sadhana the psychic being can be more and more brought forward till it is dominant and governs the rest. If it were already governing, then the struggles and difficulties of the mind and vital would not at all be serious; for each man in the light of the psychic would see and feel the truth and more and more follow it.

Signs of the Psychic's Coming Forward

It is the psychic being in you that has come forward — and when the psychic being comes forward all is happiness, the right attitude, the right vision of things. Of course in one sense it is the same I that puts forward different parts of itself. But when these different parts are all under the control of the psychic and turned by it towards the reception of the higher consciousness, then there begins the harmonisation of all the parts and their progressive recasting into moulds of the higher consciousness growing in peace, light, force, love, knowledge, Ananda which is what we call the transformation.

*

The psychic being in you is open always to the Divine Power, and when it comes in front, your spiritual capacity awakens and you are fully within the protection and can be moved by the Mother's force. The other parts are divided and can be carried away by the wrong movements of the ordinary nature. Especially if you trust your physical mind and mistake its ideas and suggestions for the true inspiration, you are liable to fall into serious errors both in your attitude and your choice of action and may lose the results of the protection and of the Force. Aspire to live always in your psychic being and to be open to the Mother; let the psychic part in you dominate the instruments, mind, life and body. Then the habit of the true intuition and the true impulse to action will come and you will be able to live in conscious communion, to feel her presence and be moved only by her Force. This is your true way in the Yoga.

*

A central love, bhakti, surrender, giving everything, a sight within that sees always clearly what is spiritually right or wrong and automatically rejects the latter — a movement of entire consecration and dedication of all in one to the Mother [*are the signs of the psychic's coming forward*].

*

It is your psychic being which came in front, probably, or else it is the true vital being in you which was able to come in front because you took the psychic attitude. When the psychic being comes in front, then there is an automatic perception of the true and untrue, the divine and the undivine, the spiritual right and wrong of things and the false vital and mental movements and attacks are immediately exposed and fall away and can do nothing; gradually the vital and physical as well as the mind get full of this psychic light and truth and sound feeling and purity and such violent attacks as you have are impossible. When the true vital being comes forward, it is something wide and strong and calm, an unmoved and powerful warrior for the Divine and the Truth repelling all enemies, bringing in a true strength and force and opening the vital to the greater Consciousness above. It has to be seen which of the two it is you feel within you.

*

That is good. It means that the psychic has come up again. When the psychic is in the front, the sadhana becomes natural and easy and it is only a question of time and natural development. When the mind or the vital or the physical consciousness is on the top, then the sadhana is a tapasya and a struggle.

*

Excuse me, — if it [*the soul*] goes on with its karma, then it does not get liberation. If it wants only farther experience, it can just stay there in the ordinary nature. The aim of Yoga is to transcend karma. Karma means subjection to lower Nature; through Yoga the soul goes towards freedom.

You are describing the action of the ordinary existence, not the Yoga. Yoga is a seeking (not a mental searching), it is not experimenting in contraries and contradictories. It is the mind that does that and the mind that analyses. The soul does not search, analyse, experiment — it seeks, feels, experiences.

The only grain of truth is that the Yoga is very usually a series of ups and downs till you get to a certain height. But there is a quite different reason for that — not the vagaries of the soul. On the contrary when the psychic being gets in front and becomes master, there comes in a fundamentally smooth action and although there are difficulties and undulations of movement, these are no longer of an abrupt or dramatic character.

*

It is very good; all you write is a strong sign of the psychic emergence of which I spoke in yesterday's letter. There is at once the deep plunge into the psychic and the emergence of the psychic influence in mind and heart. The depth of the plunge is the reason why action has become so slow, because the consciousness is too much inside to act swiftly on outside things. This is a stage which one passes through in the process of the inner change. At the same time the ideas in the mind and the perceptions and the mental and vital attitude towards things and happenings and people are becoming more and more of a psychic character. Love and devotion to the Divine is the central feeling of the psychic nature and that is growing in you towards the Mother, pervading your being. A psychic love towards all is also emerging; this love is a thing inward and does not seek to express itself outwardly like the vital love which men usually have. The psychic and spiritual attitude is also not dependent on the good and bad in beings, but is self-existent regarding them as souls who carry the Divine in them however thickly concealed and are children of the Mother.

*

Once the condition has come in which the thoughts that cross are not believed, accepted or allowed to govern the conduct, it must be understood that the vital mind is no longer dominant — for the nature of the vital mind is always to cloud the true mind's perception and drive it towards action. Neither the vital mind nor the physical mind are things that have to be got rid of, but they must be quietened, purified, controlled and transformed. That will take place fully when the thinking mind becomes fully conscious and when the psychic comes forward and leads and governs both it and the vital and physical being. Your thinking mind is becoming more and more conscious; that is shown by what you write, for the perceptions there expressed are quite clear-seeing and correct and show an increasingly right understanding. Moreover what is making you conscious is the increasing pressure of the psychic behind to come forward. For what you felt as trying to come out from behind was the psychic itself. The feeling of flowers and fragrance and a coolness and peace are always sure signs that the psychic is becoming active. It has been developing in you for some time past, only it was covered over by rushes of the old vital mind which did not want to lose its hold or its place. Now that the vital mind is quiet, it is again the psychic that is pressing to come forward and establish its influence.

The thoughts that came afterwards about the defects of your action towards others, repentance and the reasons why you could not establish proper relations with others were the result of this psychic emergence. For when the psychic comes forward or when it strongly influences mind or vital, then one begins to see clearly and rightly about one's own nature and action and about things and about others and to have the right feelings. It was under this pressure of the psychic also that while the mind got these right thoughts and perceptions, the vital felt repentance for what had been done and wished to ask forgiveness. But while this readiness to ask forgiveness was in itself a right feeling, to do so physically would not have been quite the wisest or best action. So the psychic itself at once told you what was the true thing to do, to ask forgiveness instead from the Mother. What was necessary having been done in the mind and vital, the psychic then cleared the whole consciousness and brought back its own quiet and peace. I explain all that to you so that you may begin to understand how these things work within and what is meant by the psychic and its action and influence.

The vision you had of the other luminous and peaceful and beautiful world was a sort of symbolic image of the true physical consciousness and the world in which it lives, the physical consciousness as it is when it is directly under the control of the psychic, and the character of the world which it tends to create for itself.

The Psychic and the Relation with the Divine

The psychic knows that the Divine is and affirms its knowledge against all appearances.

*

The direct relation with the Divine can only grow from within — it is there in the soul and it has to come out by sadhana — that is indeed the reason for doing sadhana. The natural mind of man follows its own ideas, the vital clings to its own desires, the physical follows its own habits — these divide from the Divine.

It is only when the psychic being grows and comes forward and governs the mind and vital and physical and changes them that this veil of personal ideas, desires and habits can fall — then the direct relation and nearness grows in the being till the whole consciousness is united with the Divine. When you go deep into the psychic, then you begin to feel the Mother near — when the mind or vital is under the influence of the psychic this sense grows in them also. That is the way in which it must come.

*

The realisation of the psychic being, its awakening and the bringing of it in front depend mainly on the extent to which one can develop a personal relation with the Divine, a relation of bhakti, love, reliance, self-giving, rejection of the insistences of the separating and self-asserting mental, vital and physical ego.

*

It may be either way [*that the psychic comes to the front — before the realisation of the Divine or after it*]. There is a touch and the realisation comes and the psychic takes its proper place as the result; or the psychic may come to the front and prepare the nature for the realisation.

Means of Bringing Forward the Psychic

Aspiration constant and sincere and the will to turn to the Divine alone are the best means of bringing forward the psychic being.

*

There is no approved method of bringing forward the psychic being. It depends on the aspiration, the growth of faith and devotion, the diminution of the hold of the mental and vital ego and their movements — at a certain point in this development the screen between the psychic and the rest of the nature thins and begins to break, the psychic becomes more and more visible and active and finally takes over charge. Sometimes it may come suddenly, but there is no rule for that.

*

There is no process for it [*getting the psychic in front*]. It comes like the other things — you have to aspire for it and it can only happen when you are sufficiently advanced.

*

It [*the psychic*] comes forward of itself either through constant love and aspiration or when the mind and vital have been made ready by the descent from above and the working of the Force.

*

It [*the dynamic descent from above into the heart*] can help the psychic to come forward, but it does not always do so automatically — it at least creates better conditions for the psychic.

*

To bring the psychic forward, selfishness and demand (which is the base of the vital feelings) must be got rid of — or at least never accepted.

*

Nothing done in the past or present can prevent the psychic from coming forward if there is the true will to get rid of these things and live in the psychic and spiritual consciousness.

*

If there is the will to surrender in the central being, then the psychic can come forward.

*

There is absolutely no reason why you should return when you have come with the intention of staying here for a sufficient time and it is better to keep to your intention.

It is not necessary to make an effort to bring your psychic being to the front; all that is necessary is a steady and quiet aspiration; if that is there always, all that is necessary to prepare for the result will be done by degrees and the psychic being will come fully to the front when all is ready and it is time. It happens usually that much in the mental, vital and physical has to be prepared before it can happen. This preparation cannot fail to be hastened by your stay here.

Bhakti and love are part of the psychic movement, a large part of it; in aspiring for the psychic change, you are aspiring for bhakti and love. But it is not useful to restrict your aspiration by a single movement like that of the Vaishnava sadhana; for this Yoga is more ample and contains, but is not confined to, what is essential in the Vaishnava sadhana. Whether you visit the physical Brindavan or not does not matter; what is necessary is to find the inner union through love and bhakti.

As for weeping, there is nothing against the tears that come from the inner aspiration; it is only when it is vital, outward, too much on the surface that it becomes a movement of disturbance and emotional disorder. Intensity of prayer is not at all to be rejected; it is one of the most powerful means of the sadhana.

As for the obstacle to meditation or experience, it would usually be when some part of the being is dealt with which has still to be prepared and to open. Such periods always occur in sadhana and one has to meet these with a patient and persistent aspiration and a quiet vigilance of self-introspection that will bring about the necessary opening. It should not awaken depression or lead to any relaxation of will and the effort of sadhana. Open yourself more and more, that is all that is needed.

Obstacles to the Psychic's Emergence

You have been keeping the psychic in the background during a thousand lives and indulging the vital. That is why the psychic is not strong.

*

The mind and the vital have always been dominant and developed themselves and are accustomed to act for themselves. How do you expect an influence [*of the psychic*] coming forward for the first time to be stronger than they are?

*

Of course the ego and the vital with its claims and desires is always the main obstacle to the emergence of the psychic. For they make one live, act, do sadhana even for one's own sake and psychicisation means to live, act and do sadhana for the sake of the Divine.

*

The psychic being emerges slowly in most men, even after taking up sadhana. There is so much in the mind and vital that has to change and readjust itself before the psychic can be entirely free. One has to wait till the necessary process has gone far enough before it can burst its agelong veil and come in front to control the nature. It is true that nothing can give so much inner happiness and joy — though peace can come by the mental and vital liberation or through the growth of a strong samata in the being.

*

It is the action of the psychic being, not the being itself, that gets mixed with the mental, vital and physical distortions because it has to use them to express what little of the true psychic feeling gets through the veil. It is by the heart's aspiration to the Divine that the psychic being gets free from these disabilities.

*

Even when the psychic is in front, there may be and are likely to be mental and vital difficulties — only then, there is also the right psychic power and perception behind to deal with them.

*

It [*the flow of love and joy from the heart centre*] can be misused on a large scale only if there is a strong and vehement vital ego not accustomed to correction or else a vital full of the *kāmavāsanā*. On a small scale it can be misused by the small selfishnesses, vanities, ambitions, demands of the lower vital supporting themselves upon it. If you are on guard against these things then there is no danger of misuse. If the psychic puts forth psychic discernment along with the love, then there is no danger, for the light of psychic discernment at once refuses all mixture or misuse.

*

That is of course the difficulty, even when one sees what is to be done and wishes to do it. One forgets at the moment when the control is needed. The habit of remembering and applying one's knowledge at the right moment comes only by a great patience and perseverance which refuses to be discouraged by frequent failure. Only if the psychic being is in front, then it reminds the mind and the thing can be more quickly done. It was your physical ill-health combined with the difficulty of the physical consciousness (which is always a thing of habits and repeats and clings to the old habits even when the mind wants to get rid of them) that prevented the emergence of the psychic from completing itself. With the disappearance of ill-health the difficulty may be more successfully tackled and achieved. As for the long period of seven years without the spiritual success there is nothing unusual in that — the old Yogins used to say that one must be ready for 12 years of preparation before the old nature will be sufficiently modified to allow of the spiritual opening. That is of course not inevitable; it can be done more briefly; but still it takes usually a long time — it has done so with most in the Asram. But in your case the first opening did come, it is only temporarily and not altogether closed, awaiting a second opening which should free the nature for the external as well as the inner change.

*

It [*the psychic*] may and does retire from the front or gets clouded over, but once it has been in front it is never relegated back behind the veil altogether and it can always return to the front with comparative ease.

*

The Emergence or Coming Forward of the Psychic

The conversion which keeps the consciousness turned towards the light and makes the right attitude spontaneous and natural and abiding and rejection also spontaneous is the psychic conversion. That is to say, man usually lives in his vital and the body is its instrument and the mind its counsellor and minister (except for the few mental men who live mostly for the things of the mind, but even they are in subjection to the vital in their ordinary movements). The spiritual conversion begins when the soul begins to insist on a deeper life and is complete when the psychic becomes the basis or the leader of the consciousness and mind and vital and body are led by it and obey it. Of course if that once happens fully, doubt, depression and despair cannot come any longer, although there may be and are difficulties still. If it is not fully, but still fundamentally accomplished, even then these things either do not come or are brief passing clouds on the surface — for there is a rock of support and certitude at the base, which even if partially covered cannot disappear altogether.

Mostly however the *constant* recurrence of depression and despair or of doubt and revolt is due to a mental or vital formation which takes hold of the vital mind and makes it run round always in the same circle at the slightest provoking cause or even without cause. It is like an illness to which the body consents from habit and from belief in the illness even though it suffers from it, and once started the illness runs its habitual course unless it is cut short by some strong counteracting force. If once the body can withdraw its consent, the illness immediately or quickly ceases — that was the secret of the Coué system. So too if the vital mind withdraws its consent, refuses to be dominated by the habitual suggestions and the habitual movements, these recurrences of depression and despair can be made soon to cease. But it is not easy for this mind, once it has got into the habit of consent, even a quite passive and suffering and reluctant consent, to cancel the habit and get rid of the black circle. It can be done easily only when the mind refuses any longer to believe in the suggestions or accept the ideas or feelings that start the circle.

*

The facts or arguments you put forward to support your diffidence or depression cannot stand in the light of the Yoga experience of others — if they were enough to justify discouragement, how many would have had to turn back from the way who are now far on towards the goal? I cannot now deal with them in detail, but they do not, any of them, justify your inference [*of unfitness for Yoga*].

Also, your psychic being does not deserve the censure you have bestowed upon it. What prevents it from coming out in its full power is the crust of past habits, formations, active vibrations of the mind-stuff and vital stuff which come from a mind and life which have been more creative and outgoing and expansive than indrawn and introspective. In many who are like this — active men and intellectuals — the first stage of Yoga is long and difficult with slow development and sparse experiences, most of the work being done in the subliminal behind the veil — until things are ready.

When the time comes for the definite opening and removal of the purdah between the inner and the outer man, I think I can promise you that you will find your power of Yoga and Yogic experience at least as unexpectedly complete as you, and others, have found your power for poetry — though necessarily its working out will take time, because it is not a detail but the whole life and the whole nature in which there must be the divine victory.

Chapter Four

Experiences Associated with the Psychic

The Psychic Touch or Influence

The psychic influence in the ordinary life of man tries to bring the truth of the soul into human action, human thought and feelings. When it is spiritualised, it tries to turn the human towards the Divine.

*

These are movements of the vital under the psychic touch. If there is the firm psychic foundation underneath, it will be felt as an underlying quietude and confidence or a fixed spirit of surrender.

*

The demands were there already — when the psychic touches there is an intensification of love but the lower vital mixes up the love with all sorts of demands.

*

The soft feeling [*in the head and below*] must be that of the psychic being spreading itself through the higher centres. Faithfulness is one of the first characteristics of the psychic being.

The Psychic Condition

What you describe shows that things are going on very well within, it is the psychic condition that is being gradually prepared as a basis for the sadhana. The special experiences of the burning of the psychic fire, descent of peace etc. are always intermittent until this basis is ready, but they help it to grow.

*

It is this freedom from all ties and entire and sole turning to the Mother that is the deepest psychic condition. It is coming to you as touches of that condition from the psychic, therefore there is not yet the permanent state; but these touches prepare the future permanence.

The fire which you feel in the chest must surely be the psychic fire, for it is there that is the seat of the psychic and the fact that it burns strongly when you sit alone points to the same thing.

The Psychic Fire

The psychic fire is the fire of aspiration, purification and tapasya which comes from the psychic being. It is not the psychic being, but a power of the psychic being.

*

The psychic being is a Purusha, not a flame — the psychic fire is not the being, it is something proper to it.

*

It [*a flame in the heart as big as a man's thumb*] is the psychic fire kindled in the heart. The psychic being in the heart is described by the Upanishads as of the size of a thumb, *aṅguṣṭha-mātraḥ puruṣo'ntarātmā* — it may manifest first as this psychic flame.

*

The fire [*one feels within*] is always the fire of sacrifice and self-offering, the fire of aspiration or the fire of tapasya.

*

That the constant fire of aspiration has to be lit is true; but this fire is the psychic fire and it is lit or burns up and increases as the psychic grows within and for the psychic to grow quietude is needful. That is why we have been working for the psychic to grow in you and for the quietude also to grow and that is why we want you to wait on the Mother's working in full patience and confidence. To be always remembering the Mother and always with the equal unwavering fire within means itself a considerable progress in sadhana and it must be prepared by various means such as the experiences you have been having. Keep steadfast in confidence therefore and all that has to be done will be done.

*

The experience of the Fire is quite correct, — it is the great fire of purification and concentration (i.e. gathering up of the consciousness and turning it fixedly towards the Divine), the psychic fire which all must pass through so as to reach the Mother permanently and completely.

*

It is egoistic if the ego thinks that it is the psychic fire. If the consciousness feels identified with the psychic fire and becomes conscious that the fire can burn out all impurities, then it is a true experience.

*

The central fire is in the psychic being, but it can be lit in all the parts of the being.

The Psychic Fire and Some Inner Visions

The fire you saw was the fire of the psychic being, the fire of aspiration and tapasya, burning under the earth, that is to say, in the subconscient. It opens the earth, the physical consciousness to the Divine Light. Moonlight may symbolise the spiritual consciousness and the room your own personal being or individual physical consciousness. With these clues it will be easy for you to understand the significance of your experience.

*

The fire you saw was again the psychic fire of purification and tapasya and the garland was the offering it was preparing for the Mother, the psychic and divine consciousness (pearl and diamond) in the sadhak. The beautiful place was also probably a symbol of the psychic and the lotus indicated the opening of the psychic consciousness.

The twelve-petalled lotus and the twelve-rayed sun indicate the same thing, the complete Truth-consciousness of the Divine Mother. It was rising but only half risen. The red colour was the sign of Power.

*

All these things are signs, now often repeated, of the process that is going on. The heat is the result of the psychic fire burning away obstacles — the coolness and complete quietude come as a result. The tendency to sleep is really a tendency to go inside into the depths of the inner consciousness due to the pressure for the change.

The wideness of light you saw was the wideness of the true consciousness liberated from the narrow limits of the human mind, human vital, human body consciousness. It is true that the mind is narrow, not only yours, but all human minds even the most developed, — compared with the wideness of the true consciousness which has no limits. It is precisely this wideness which will come by the sadhana and which these processes are preparing. The rain of flowers means a plenty of the psychic qualities and movements and the white flower of mental victory indicates the step towards it which is now being led up to — the victory in the mind of the inner light over the outer ignorance.

*

The difficulty in giving up habits is common to the physical mind in all people; nothing is more difficult to it. The fire you feel must be what we call Agni, the fire of purification acting on this physical mind to change it.

The bridge you saw was the symbol of transition from the ordinary to the spiritual consciousness; the wide plain was a symbol of the large peace and silence which comes with the spiritual consciousness when one rests in the Divine.

The perfumes you felt were true perfumes but not of the physical world. This body of flesh and blood is not the whole of ourselves; there is unseen by the eyes a subtle body also and one becomes aware of it when the inner consciousness opens. It was from deep within there that the perfumes came, perfumes of purity, of love and surrender (rose) etc. It is there deep within that the psychic being dwells and it is there that you are trying to go when the inward-going impulse or pressure comes; it is why you felt more and more peaceful, because you were going deeper and deeper into the psychic from which these fragrances came.

*

The heat in the body is due simply to the working that is going on within; it is what is called the heat of tapas — there is nothing unhealthy in it as in the heat of fever. The beautiful scent that you get is a subtle or psychic fragrance, just as the vision of the lotus is a subtle or psychic sight.

The psychic being is often seen or felt within in the form of a child, — it is perhaps that that you are feeling within you; it is calling for a complete sincerity, but sincerity is used here in the sense of opening to nothing but the divine influences and impulses. It does not mean that you have committed any fault, but only that the psychic in you wants you to be completely under its sole government, so that all in you may be for the Divine only. The feeling of sorrow is probably a response of the vital in you to this demand — thinking that it must have erred; but such a feeling of sorrow is not necessary. The vital can quietly wait for the psychic working to do all that is needed in due time.

Agni

It is the Agni fire that you feel. Agni is at once a fire of aspiration, a fire of purification, a fire of tapasya, a fire of transformation.

*

Agni in the form of an aspiration full of concentrated calm and surrender is certainly the first thing to be lighted in the heart.

*

It [*a feeling of warmth in the heart*] comes sometimes from the approach of Agni fire, sometimes from that of love or Ananda, sometimes simply from a touch of the Force.

*

The fear of the fire you saw is misplaced, for it is the fire of the purifying Agni that you see burning and that does no harm; it only clears away what should not be there. That is why it is followed by a lightness or an emptiness. You have only to be quiet and let the fire do its work. The heat one feels at that time is not the heat of fever or any other morbid heat. Afterwards, as you felt, all becomes cool and light.

*

The burning is sometimes the heat of a difficulty and resistance, but then it disturbs. When it does not disturb, it is usually the purifying fire of Agni.

*

It may be pressure of the Agni fire that you feel [*around the head and shoulders*] as the heat — especially if there is something that has to be purified or a difficulty burned away. The cool spray on the other hand comes as an accompaniment of the sense of purification.

*

The Fire [*felt in the forehead and eyes*] is the power of the Yoga — Yogashakti.

*

That kind of pull [*towards the Divine*] is not the same thing as the lighting of Agni. Agni meets men who are not leading the religious life at all but who have Agni burning in them and are intent to keep the fire ablaze — scientists, artists etc. who have the intense will of perfecting what they do and all their central energies are thrown into this flame. The same intense fire should burn in the Yoga.

*

It is the Mother's Force that works in the Agni.

Agni and the Psychic Fire

If it is in the heart it may be psychic fire — it is possibly not the joy that created the fire, but the decision you had come to to believe in the Mother's action whether the mind understood or not. Such an attitude encourages the opening of the psychic and would therefore bring at once the psychic joy and the kindling of Agni in the psychic centre.

*

It is some association in the mind probably coupling Agni with the psychic. Of course the individual Agni fire has its starting-point in the psychic, but the mere burning of the fire does not show that the psychic is coming forward.

When it burns in the heart, it is the fire *in* the psychic. The psychic fire is individual and takes usually the form of a fire of aspiration or personal tapasya. This Fire is universal and it came from above.

*

The psychic fire may burn in the vital. It all depends on whether it is the fire of the general Force that comes from above or the fire of your soul's aspiration and tapasya.

*

All that [*fire in the heart and elsewhere*] is simply the burning of the Agni in various parts of the being. It prepares it for transformation. But the coming forward of the psychic is another matter and its signs are psychological.

*

Agni is the psychic fire — it is not the Divine Presence. If the psychic is active and open, the Presence may be felt — it is not necessary for that that it should be in the front. Also it may be in the front, but the Divine Presence in the heart may not be felt as yet, there may be only the aspiration, bhakti, self-giving. There is no fixed law about these things — it develops differently in different natures.

Psychic Joy

It [*a feeling of joy, intense but calm and pure*] is not mere vital excitement or heightened nerve sensation, it is an attempt of the psychic to emerge from behind the veil and what you feel is the psychic joy. (The psychic is seated behind the heart, behind the emotional centre.) But when this psychic joy comes, it communicates itself to the mind, the vital and the body. You have then to be careful that no mixture comes in from the vital and the physical — such as the sex impulse. The mind, the vital, the physical must receive the psychic Ananda and make it their own, but not bring in their own deviations or any degraded mixture into it.

*

There is a dynamic joy as well as the self-existent joy in the soul itself.

Psychic Sorrow

There is a psychic sorrow which usually comes when the soul feels how strong is the resistance in the world and how much the Forces in it rage against the Mother.

*

It is the soul, the psychic being in you, behind the heart, that is awake and wants to concentrate the mind on the Divine. It is the nature of the mind to go out to other things, but now when it does that, there is the unease in the heart, the psychic sorrow because the heart feels at once that this is wrong and the head also aches because of the resistance to the Divine Force at work. This is a thing that often happens at an early stage, after the opening of the consciousness to the sadhana.

*

The vital took it up perhaps and gave it a more vehement and turbid expression — otherwise there is nothing disturbing in a psychic sorrow.

*

The psychic sadness is of a purifying and not a depressing kind.

*

There are many things that are spiritual that are not the essence of the higher consciousness. All that tends towards the transformation and helps to prepare it is spiritual. Psychic sorrow is a spiritual movement, but sorrow is not part of the essential character of the higher consciousness. Resignation, the ego's submission to the divine will, is a spiritual movement, but the higher consciousness has no need of resignation and a submitted ego is not a part of its essence, for it has no ego.

Psychic Tears or Weeping

Yes, there is a psychic sorrow of that kind [*tears of longing for the Mother*] — but psychic tears need not be sorrowful, there are also tears of emotion and joy.

*

The tears probably come from the inner psychic being (behind the heart) which is touched in this state of quietness and peace. It is the sign of an aspiration and devotion in the soul which is trying to come to the surface. If the psychic being can come to the surface and a harmony be established in the nature, all of it being turned towards the Divine, this kind of expression will cease.

*

The weeping that comes to you comes from the psychic being — it is the tears of psychic yearning and aspiration. At a particular stage it so comes to many and is a very good sign. The other feelings and tendencies are also from the same source. They show that the psychic is exercising a strong influence and preparing, as we say, to come in front. Accept the movement and let it fulfil itself.

*

A weeping that comes with the feeling you speak of is the sign of a psychic sorrow — for it translates as an aspiration of the psychic being. But depression and hopelessness ought not to come. You should rather cling to the faith that since there is a true aspiration in you — and of that there can be no doubt — it is sure to be fulfilled, whatever the difficulties of the external nature. You must recover in that faith the inner peace and quietude while at the same time keeping the clear insight into what has to be done and the steady aspiration for the inner and outer change.

*

It is quite correct that [*ordinary*] weeping brings in the forces that should be kept outside — for the weeping is a giving way of the inner control and an expression of vital reaction and ego. It is only the psychic weeping that does not open the door to these forces — but that weeping is without affliction, tears of bhakti, spiritual emotion or Ananda.

Your experience was a very beautiful one — the inner being realises by such experiences that which must be established in the waking state as the foundation of the spiritual consciousness and spiritual life.

Psychic Yearning

The yearning of the heart may be there but it should not disturb the peace.

*

I think it is better to stop it [*the yearning of the heart*] for the present. It is very possible that the vital is taking advantage of it to create dissatisfaction with the progress of the sadhana. The psychic yearning brings no reaction of impatience, dissatisfaction or disturbance.

*

Your new attitude towards food and outward things is the true attitude, the psychic attitude and shows that the psychic is already controlling the vital physical as well as the other parts of the vital nature.

As for the heart, the movement of longing for the Divine, weeping, sorrowing, yearning is not essential in this Yoga. A strong aspiration there must be, an intense longing there may very well be, an ardent love and will for union; but there need be no sorrow or disturbance. The quiet and silence you feel in your heart is the result of the pressure of the higher consciousness to come down. That always brings a quietude in mind and heart and as it descends a great peace and silence. In the silent heart and mind, there must be the true attitude and thus you have the feeling that you are the Mother's child, the faith and the will to be united with her. Along with that there may be an aspiration or silent expectation of what is to come. That also you seem to have. All therefore is well.

Psychic Intensity

I have read your letter of explanation of the "strange" ideas. I still maintain that your views on the lack of all intensity in the psychic things or in the spiritual or their inferiority to vital pleasure *are* strange, because they contradict all psychic and spiritual experience except that of the mere vairagis and make the choice of the spiritual life itself (Nirvana seekers excepted) quite inexplicable. Your arguments are not convincing. What have Ramakrishna's excesses or the fluctuations of Vivekananda's vital receptivity between exaltation and depression or Chaitanya's *viraha* to do with the question in issue? These are difficulties of the body and the vital. The question was of the intensity of *psychic* and *pure spiritual* experience — psychic devotion and love, peace, Ananda. You cannot base a general denial on your own particular experience, because you have only the initial experiences of calm etc. and have *not* got to the intensities as I have done and others before me have done. It is only when one lives centrally in the psychic with the mental, vital and physical as provinces held under its rule that one knows what psychic intensity is. It is only when the higher consciousness comes down in its floods that one can know what can be the intensities or ecstasies of spiritual peace, light, love, bliss. You can say, "I have not yet had these intensities", but you cannot say in a sweeping way, "They do not exist and I shall never have them", or "They are only tepid quiet little things, soothing and more capable of lasting, but not intense and glorious like the vital joys and pleasures." Do not cling to these notions born of the past limitations, but keep yourself open and plastic to greater possibilities in the future.

My own experience is *not* limited to a radiant peace; I know very well what ecstasy and Ananda are from the Brahmananda down to the *śārīra ānanda*, and can experience them at any time. But of these things I prefer to speak only when my work is done — for it is in a transformed consciousness here and not only above where the Ananda always exists that I seek their base of permanence.

The Psychic and Uneasiness

The psychic is not uneasy, it makes you uneasy when you do the wrong thing.

*

The uneasiness created by the psychic is not depression — it is in the nature of a rejection of the wrong movement.

If the uneasiness causes depression or vital dissatisfaction, it is not psychic.

*

The uneasiness is simply a reminder to you to be more vigilant in future.

*

The unhappiness is not necessary or inevitable in the sadhana, but it comes because your inner nature feels the touch of the Divine Presence indispensable to it and uneasy when it does not feel it. To feel it always a certain constant detachment within allowing you to remain within and do everything from within is necessary. This can more easily be done in quiet occupations and quiet contacts. For it is quietness and inwardness that enable one to feel the Presence.

Chapter Five

The Psychic and Spiritual Transformations

Psychisation and Spiritualisation

Psychisation means the change of the lower nature, bringing right vision into the mind, right impulse and feeling into the vital, right movement and habit into the physical — all turned towards the Divine, all based on love, adoration, bhakti — finally, the vision and sense of the Mother everywhere in all as well as in the heart, her Force working in the being etc., faith, consecration, surrender.

The spiritual change is the established descent of the peace, light, knowledge, power, bliss from above, the awareness of the self and the Divine and of a higher cosmic consciousness and the change of the whole consciousness to that.

*

Between psychisation and spiritualisation there is a difference. The spiritual is the change that descends from above, the psychic is the change that comes from within by the psychic dominating mind, vital and physical.

*

The psychic is the first of two transformations necessary — if you have the psychic transformation it facilitates immensely the other, i.e., the transformation of the ordinary human into the higher spiritual consciousness — otherwise one is likely to have either a slow and dull or exciting but perilous journey.

*

I never said anything about a "transformation of the psychic"; I have always written about a "psychic transformation" of the nature which is a very different matter. I have sometimes written of it as a psychisation of the nature. The psychic is in the evolution, part of the human being, its divine part — so a psychisation will not carry one beyond the present evolution but will make the being ready to respond to all that comes from the Divine or Higher Nature and unwilling to respond to the Asura, Rakshasa, Pishacha or Animal in the being or to any insistence of the lower nature which stands in the way of the divine change.

*

It is not the psychic but the mind that gets raised and transformed and its action intensified by the intuitivising of the consciousness. The psychic is always the same essence and adapts its action without need of transformation to any change of consciousness.

*

I have read your account of your sadhana. There is nothing to say, I think, — for it is all right — except that the most important thing for you is to develop the psychic fire in the heart and the aspiration for the psychic being to come forward as the leader of the sadhana. When the psychic does so, it will show you the "undetected ego-knots" of which you speak and loosen them or burn them in the psychic fire. This psychic development and the psychic change of mind, vital and physical consciousness is of the utmost importance because it makes safe and easy the descent of the higher consciousness and the spiritual transformation without which the supramental must always remain far distant. Powers etc. have their place, but a very minor one so long as this is not done.

The Psychic and the Higher Consciousness

What you see above is of course the true or higher consciousness — the Mother's — in which one sees all the world as one, a vast free consciousness full of freedom, peace and light — it is that that we speak of as the higher or divine consciousness. Even if it comes and goes, yet its effect on the heart shows that a connection has been established through the psychic — for the psychic is behind the heart. It is there above the head that the consciousness has to ascend and remain, while it also descends into the head and heart and lower vital and physical and brings there its wideness, light, peace and freedom.

*

It is the union of the consciousness above with the awakened psychic being that makes the true connection between what is above and the universe.

*

There is something in you that has become aware of the higher consciousness and gone up there — above the head where the ordinary consciousness and the higher planes meet. That has to be developed till the whole source of the consciousness is there and all the rest directed from there — with, at the same time, a liberation of the psychic so that it may support the action from above in the mind, the vital and the physical parts.

*

If the development of a higher consciousness did not bring things that were not before heard of by the mind, it would not be good for much. The unification of the psychic and the higher consciousness forces and activities is indispensable for the sadhana at one time or another.

*

Complete psychisation brings entire openness of the being to the Divine and to the Higher Consciousness and an entire inability to accept anything untrue and undivine.

*

The psychic when it acts as the main power, acts through a certain feeling and inherent psychic sense which repels the falsehood. But the ranges of mind above mind do not act in that way — there it is discrimination and will that act and their action is

The Psychic and Spiritual Transformations

wider but less sure and less automatic so to speak.

*

When the concentration is at the top of the head, it means that the mental being is joining the higher consciousness there and there is not much resistance or none. The other place indicates the joining is of the psychic being to the higher consciousness, hence the greater silence, as the psychic is more central than the mental being; but also there is the attempt to join through the psychic the rest of the lower consciousness to the higher and there there is a resistance. The mental joining does not affect the vital and physical, so they remain quiet or can do so for the present — the psychic joining puts on them a pressure to which the first reaction is the sense of fatigue and the last might be a turmoil. But the psychic joining if effectual is much more powerful for the change of the whole being.

The Psychic and Spiritual Movements

The two feelings are both of them right — they indicate the two necessities of the sadhana. One is to go inward and open fully the connection between the psychic being and the outer nature. The other is to open upward to the Divine Peace, Force, Light, Ananda above, to rise up into it and bring it down into the nature and the body. Neither of these two movements, the psychic and the spiritual, is complete without the other. If the spiritual ascent and descent are not made, the spiritual transformation of the nature cannot happen; if the full psychic opening and connection is not made, the transformation cannot be complete.

There is no incompatibility between the two movements; some begin the psychic first, others the spiritual first, some carry on both together. The best way is to aspire for both and let the Mother's Force work it out according to the need and turn of the nature.

*

The experiences you describe are coherent with each other and very clearly explicable. The first shows that some part of your mind was open and this aided by an opening in the psychic enabled you to ascend into the regions above, the ranges of the liberated spiritual mind with the infinite path of the spirit leading to the highest realisation. But the rest of the nature was not ready. The straining to recover the experience was not the right thing to do then; what should have been done was the aspiration for the purification and preparation of the nature, the permanent psychic opening and the increase of the higher spiritual opening above till there could be a total release of the being. The vehemence of the action of the forces was due to the resistance and the breaking of the knots in the head and different parts of the nature was their working for the release. The "electricity" passing through the spinal column was the passage of the Force making its way down through the centres. Obviously it is the dark resisting force of the vital, the desire nature, that rises up and clouds all up to the heart. On the other hand the flow from above and the silence it creates is a sign of the opening above being still there; for the silence, the quietude of the nature is a touch from above and very necessary for purification and release. What is lacking is the full opening of the psychic being behind the heart — for that could liberate the heart from the dark force and make possible a cleaning of the rest by a quiet and steady rather than a vehement working attended by chaotic action and struggle. When there is an opening in the spiritual mind but not a sufficient psychic change, there is or can be this kind of vehement force-action and resistance; when the psychic opens, then it acts on the whole nature, mind, vital, physical, governing them from within, to transform themselves and become ready for the complete spiritual opening and spiritual consciousness. Devotion and a more and more complete inner consecration are the best way to open the psychic.

*

It is very good. The ideas and feelings that came up from within you were those of the newborn psychic nature.

The feeling you had in the afternoon of the cessation of thought and the sensation of something within you going up above the head is part of the movement of the sadhana. There is a higher consciousness above you, not in the body, so above the head, which we call the higher, spiritual or divine consciousness, or the Mother's consciousness. When the being opens then all in you, the mind (head), emotional being (heart), vital, even something in the physical consciousness begin to ascend in order to join themselves to this greater higher consciousness. One has when one sits with eyes closed in meditation the sensation of going up which you describe. It is called the ascension of the lower consciousness. Afterwards things begin to descend from above, peace, joy, light, strength, knowledge etc. and a great change begins in the nature. This is what we call the descent of the higher (the Mother's) consciousness.

The unease you felt was because of the unaccustomed nature of the movement. It is of no importance and quickly goes away.

The Psychic Consciousness and the Descent from Above

As I have written often, there are two transformations in this Yoga. The first is when the psychic being comes forward and controls and changes the nature. This is what has happened in you with great rapidity; it must complete itself, but that it will do naturally. The second is the descent of the Mother's consciousness from above the head and its transformation of the whole being and nature. This also is now preparing in you. It is the reason of the pressure, the silence in the heart etc. What you experienced this time when you went above was the wideness of the higher being in that higher consciousness above with the Light coming down through it. That wideness and that light will afterwards come down into you and your consciousness will be changed into the light and wideness and all that is in them.

*

It is evident from what you write that the true consciousness is growing in you and that when it is there all is right — for what you describe in this morning's letter is the true psychic consciousness come up in some fullness. This fullness was not there before, so that is a very encouraging progress. But its remaining seems to depend on the concentration on the Mother. When there is the concentration on the Mother, then the progress can be smooth and continuous; when there is a failure of the concentration, you come into the outward physical mind and at once there is a conflict between the growing quietude and the inner psychic fire and the physical consciousness. The quietude seeks to hold and control the physical consciousness and the fire to burn out the wrong activities and imperfections, but the consciousness finds the pressure hard to bear; it feels dull and troubled by the heat. For when the fire has won, all is cool; when it has to burn the resistances, then there is heat, it becomes a fire of tapasya. This seems to be the explanation of these alternating conditions. It is important therefore to keep the concentration and remain fixed in the Mother; nothing else for the time has any importance comparatively with that.

As for the experience at the Pranam it was the other thing, the descent of the higher consciousness (the Mother's consciousness) from above, with its light, peace and wideness. When the individual consciousness is enveloped in that, rests in it, then you feel that you are lying in the Mother's lap. As the psychic consciousness grows from within, it becomes more and more possible for this to descend from above.

*

The concentration in the heart which is intended to bring out the psychic being and the calling down of the descent from above are two sides of the same thing and are complementary and can go naturally together.

*

Certainly the concentration in the heart is very necessary for the full transformation. When peace is established in the heart, it is possible for the psychic being to come forward and rule the mind, life and body. The descent from above prepares the being, but unless the psychic acts fully it cannot change by itself the outer being, though one can have a settled inner peace, freedom, light, not disturbed by the outer movements, but the outer movements will remain. It is only the combined action of the psychic and the spiritual power that can change it.

*

It is by meditation, by concentration, by the constant turning or call [*that aspiration and openness may be cultivated*] — secondly, by the keeping of the mind and vital still for the descent of the Presence, peace, light, Ananda and for the psychic being to emerge. When the psychic being is in front, the descent constant, then the constant feeling of the Divine in you and of yourself in the Divine becomes more easy to have.

*

One can receive [*forces from above*] always through the psychic part of the being, even before the veil is broken.

The Psychic and the Supermind

You were quite right in what you wrote about the supermind — people here do indeed use the "big word" much too freely as if it were something quite within everybody's grasp. The first thing to be done is the psychic change and until that has progressed sufficiently, supermind is a far-off thing and people need not think of it at all. You have certainly progressed, but the change of the outer nature is always a slow movement, so that need not distress you.

*

To merge the consciousness in the Divine and to keep the psychic being controlling and changing all the nature and keeping it turned to the Divine till the whole being can live in the Divine is the transformation we seek. There is farther the supramentalisation, but this only carries the transformation to its own highest and largest possibilities — it does not alter its essential nature.

*

The psychic when sufficiently developed can be strong enough to make the preliminary clearance [*of the lower vital*].

It is the supramental alone that can transform the material being, but the physical mind and physical vital can be very much changed by the action of the psychic and of the overmind. The entire change however is made only when there is the supramental influence. But for the present the psychic is the force that may be relied on for the preliminary purification of the lower nature.

Section Three

Spiritual Experiences and Realisations

Chapter One

Experiences of the Self, the One and the Infinite

Peace, Calm, Silence and the Self

That [*state of vast peace and calm*] is the basic experience of the higher consciousness — it is what is called the realisation of the Atman (the Self).

*

It is the Atman, the spiritual being above the mind — the first experience of it is a silence and calm (which one perceives afterwards to be infinite and eternal) untouched by the movements of mind and life and body. The higher consciousness lives always in touch with the Self — the lower is separated from it by the activities of the Ignorance.

*

When one becomes aware of the Self calm, silent, wide, universal, it is no longer covered over by the ignorance; when one identifies with the Self and not with the mind, life and body and their movements or with the small ego, that is the release of the Self.

*

And how is the outer nature to rise into the higher Prakriti before you realise the Self? The higher nature is that of the higher consciousness of which the first basis is the peace and wideness and realisation of the Self, the One that is all.

*

The gaining of peace makes it easier to get the experience of the pure and free Self.

*

If not aspiration, at least keep the idea of what is necessary —
(1) that the silence and peace shall become a wideness which you can realise as the Self, (2) the extension of the silent consciousness upwards as well so that you may feel its source above you, (3) the presence of peace etc. all the time. These things need not all come at once, but by realising what has to be in your mind, any falling towards a condition of inertia can be avoided.

*

What one feels first [*in the silence*] is the pure existence of the self, without any idea, characteristic or movement — existence pure and simple, Sat Brahman — or else one feels that and a vast peace and wideness. Afterwards other things are felt such as Ananda, but always with this as the basis.

*

A great wave (or sea) of calm and the constant consciousness of a vast and luminous Reality — this is precisely the character of the fundamental realisation of the Supreme Truth in its first touch on the mind and the soul. One could not ask for a better beginning or foundation — it is like a rock on which the rest can be built. It means certainly not only a Presence, but *the* Presence — and it would be a great mistake to weaken the experience by any non-acceptance or doubt of its character.

It is not necessary to define it and one ought not even to try to turn it into an image; for this Presence is in its nature infinite. Whatever it has to manifest of itself or out of itself, it will do inevitably by its own power, if there is a sustained acceptance.

It is quite true that it is a grace sent and the only return needed for such a grace is acceptance, gratitude and to allow the Power that has touched the consciousness to develop what has to be developed in the being — by keeping oneself open to it. The total transformation of the nature cannot be done in a moment; it must take long and proceed through stages; what is now experienced is only an initiation, a foundation for the new consciousness in which that transformation will become possible. The automatic spontaneity of the experience ought by itself to show that it is nothing constructed by the mind, will or emotions; it comes from a Truth that is beyond them.

*

The vastness, the overwhelming calm and silence in which you feel merged is what is called the Atman or the silent Brahman. It is the whole aim of many Yogas to get this realisation of Atman or silent Brahman and live in it. In our Yoga it is only the first stage of the realisation of the Divine and of that growing of the being into the higher or divine Consciousness which we call transformation.

*

A sadhak of integral Yoga who stops short at the Impersonal is no longer a sadhak of integral Yoga. Impersonal realisation is the realisation of the silent Self, of the pure Existence, Consciousness and Bliss in itself without any perception of an Existent, Conscient, Blissful. It leads therefore to Nirvana. In the integral knowledge the realisation of the Self and of the impersonal Sachchidananda is only a step, though a very important step, or part of the integral knowledge. It is a beginning, not an end of the highest realisation.

The True Self Within

The experience described in your letter is a glimpse of the realisation of the true Self which is independent of the body. When this settles itself there is the liberation (*mukti*). Not only the body, but the vital and mind are felt to be only instruments and one's self is felt to be calm, self-existent and free and wide or infinite. It is then possible for the psychic being to effect in that freedom the full transformation of the nature. All your former experiences were preparing for this, but the physical consciousness came across. Now that you have had the glimpse of the self separate from the body, this physical difficulty may soon be overcome.

*

The experience you have is the experience of the true self. Untouched by grief and joy, desire, anxiety or trouble, vast and calm and full of peace, it observes the agitations of the outer being as one might the play of children. It is indeed the divine element in you. The more you can live in that, the firmer will be the foundation of the sadhana. In this self will come all the higher experiences, oneness with the Divine, light, knowledge, strength, Ananda, the play of the Mother's higher forces. It does not always become stable from the first, though for some it does; but the experience comes more and more frequently and lasts till it is no longer covered by the ordinary nature.

The Self and the Sense of Individuality

Yes, the sense of individuality can disappear altogether when all is peace and wideness. One feels that the peace and wideness are oneself, but not in an individual sense — for it is the "Atman" of everybody else also. Afterwards there can come an experience of another kind of I, but it is a universalised I which contains everybody else and is in unison with everybody else and is itself contained in the Divine. This is what Yogins sometimes call the "large" as opposed to the small Aham. I have written of it as the true Person.

*

The Self is essentially universal; the individualised self is only the universal experienced from an individual centre. If what you have realised is not felt to be one in all, then it is not the "Atman"; possibly it is the central being not yet revealing its universal aspect as Atman.

*

The Self is felt as either universal, one in all, or a universalised individual the same in essence as others, extended everywhere from each being but centred here. Of course centre is a way of speaking, because no physical centre is usually felt — only all the action takes place around the individual.

*

All is in the self; when identified with the universal self, all is in you.

Also, the microcosm reproduces the macrocosm — so all is present in each, though all is not expressed (and cannot be) in the surface consciousness.

*

There is the experience of the microcosm (the universe in oneself) in which all that is in the macrocosm (the larger universe) is present. All these things are for experience, for knowledge and must be taken as such. No merely personal turn should be given to them.

The Disappearance of the "I" Sense

The essential "I" sense disappears when there is the stable realisation of the one universal Self in all and that remains at all moments in all conditions under any circumstances. Usually this comes first in the Purusha consciousness and the extension to the Prakriti movements is not immediate. But even if there are "I" movements in the Prakriti reactions, the Purusha within observes them as the continued running of an old mechanism and does not feel them as his own. Most Vedantists stop there, because they think that those reactions will fall away from one at death and all will disappear into the One. But for a change of the nature it is necessary that the experience and seeing of the Purusha should spread to all the parts, mind, vital, physical, subconscient. Then the ego movements of Prakriti can also disappear gradually from one field after another till none is left. For this a perfect samata even in the cells of the body and in every vibration of the being is necessary — *samaṁ hi brahma*. One is then quite free from it in works also. The individual remains but that is not the small separative ego, but a form and power of the Universal which feels itself one with all beings, an acting centre and instrument of the Universal Transcendent, full of the Ananda of the presence and the action but not thinking or moving independently or acting for its own sake. That cannot be called egoism. The Divine can be called an ego only if he is a separate Person limited as in the Christian idea of God by his separateness (though even there esoteric Christianity abolishes the limitation). An I which is not separate in that way is no I at all.

The Self and the Cosmic Consciousness

One has first to become aware of the Self and its wide silence and eternal peace and acquire the cosmic consciousness in which one is aware of the whole universe as one with oneself and to live in that. One has at the same time to be aware — it becomes possible when one lives in the cosmic consciousness, cosmic Self and cosmic Nature, — of the different beings in oneself, psychic, mental, vital, physical, and then there appears also the central being which stands above all of them and is the source of all the surface personalities. It is only then that one can know the aspect or bhava one is intended to manifest.

*

The Cosmic Spirit or Self contains everything in the cosmos — it upholds cosmic Mind, universal Life, universal Matter as well as the Overmind. The Self is more than all these things which are its formulations in Nature.

A Vision of the Universal Self

What you saw in the vision was the wide and luminous infinite of what is called the universal Self or spirit. It is that which is one of the fundamental things into which one enters when one reaches the higher consciousness and goes above. The personal being naturally feels itself as something very small and insignificant in that Infinite. But in that Infinite there are higher and higher levels and it is to these levels that the Mother was leading you when she took you by the hand. This often happens in meditation or trance when one has once gone upward into the spiritual infinity. The reason why you did not see the Mother's form was not that the Mother hid herself or anything in you came between, but that you were both moving in the formless Infinite as spiritual beings and so it was easier to feel the presence than to see any physical form. Not that the form cannot be there, but it is less insistent and therefore not so soon seen as on the physical plane.

The silence in the head and heart and the emptiness are both necessary and desirable. When they are there, the consciousness finds them natural and they give it the sense of lightness and release; that is why the thoughts or speech of the old kind are foreign to it and when they come give fatigue. This silence and emptiness must grow, so that the higher consciousness with its knowledge, light, Ananda, peace can come down in it and progressively replace the old things. They must indeed occupy not only head and heart but the whole body.

The Self Experienced on Various Planes

It is probably the true Cosmic Self or spirit with its cosmic consciousness and power that you feel on a plane above the ordinary mind or vital or physical — what plane is not as yet clear — for what you describe is common to this Self on whatever plane it manifests; it is felt like that as soon as the being or any part of the being detaches itself from the surface Ignorance.

*

The Self is met first on the level of the Higher Mind, but it is not limited to one station — it is usually felt as something outspread in wideness, but one may also feel a centralising consciousness in the Sahasrara or above it.

*

A complete silence makes realisation of the Self more possible — but that can be had on the Higher Mind level far below Overmind.

The Self and Time

In the self or pure existence there is no time or space — except spiritual space or wideness.

*

Yes — in the silence of the self there is no time — it is *akāla*.

*

Yes, that is correct. In the first realisation of silence in the higher consciousness there is no Time — there is only the sense of pure existence, consciousness, peace or a strong featureless Ananda. If anything else comes in it is a minor movement on the surface of this timeless self-existence. This and the sense of liberation that comes with it is the result of the mind's quiescence. At a higher level this peace and liberation remain, but can be united with a greater and freer dynamic movement.

The Self and Life

It is always possible to have realisations of a kind on the mental-spiritual plane even if the vital is still impure. There is a sort of separation of the mental Purusha and Prakriti which results in a knowledge that has no transforming effect on the life. But the theory of these Yogis is that one has to know the Self; life and what one does in life do not matter. Have you not read of the Yogi who came with his concubine and Ramakrishna asked him, "Why do you live like that?" He answered, "All is Maya, so it does not matter what I do so long as I know the Brahman." It is true Ramakrishna replied, "I spit on your Vedanta", but logically the Yogi had a case. For if all life and action are Maya and only the silent Brahman is real — well!

Experiences of Infinity, Oneness, Unity

What you felt as a strong subtle air was the concrete expression of consciousness or conscious existence in itself independent of the body. As yet the experience is still limited by the body, but when it is felt without that limit then it is a sense of a wide ether filling all space, Akash Brahman. As this grows, the body sense disappears and when the mind also is quite inactive, one feels oneself to be that spreading out to all Infinity.

*

The feeling you have of all being one and not this a tree or that such and such an object, seems to be a first touch of the realisation of all being One. For it is so that one sees things then, — all seems to be One and not something separate like a tree or a house. The tree or house is only a form in the One; the tree is really that One.

*

It is only by feeling all things as one spiritual substance that one can arrive at unity [*of matter, energy and mind*] — unity is in the spiritual consciousness. The material point is only one point among millions of millions — so that is not the base of unity. But once you get the unity in consciousness, you can feel through that the unity of mind substance, mind force, etc., the unity of life substance (mobile) and life force, the unity of material substance and energies. Being — consciousness of being — energy of consciousness — form of consciousness, all things are really that.

*

The spiritual consciousness [*mentioned in the preceding letter*] is that which is in contact with Sachchidananda, that is, with the pure existence, consciousness and bliss of the Divine. Any contact with Sachchidananda must bring either peace or bliss.

Living in the Divine

There can be no mental rule or definition [*of the kind of life possible after union with the Purushottama*]. One has first to live in the Divine and attain to the Truth — the will and awareness of the Truth will organise the life.

*

To be always merged in the Divine is not so easy. It can be done only by an absorption in one's own inner self or by a consciousness that sees all in the Divine and the Divine in all and is *always* in that condition. There is none [*here*] who has attained to that yet.

Chapter Two
Experiences on the Higher Planes

The Higher or Spiritual Consciousness

It [*the consciousness above the head*] is what we call the higher or spiritual consciousness — it contains or supports all the higher planes, the higher worlds. When one begins to feel this always above, it is a great step forward in the sadhana; then the consciousness can go up there and from there see, discern and control all that is in the mind, vital and body. It is the meeting-place of the ascending and descending forces, as you see.

Breaking into the Spiritual Consciousness

Of course, Krishnaprem's view about the canalisation of Niagara is my standpoint also.[1] But for the human mind it is difficult to get across the border between mind and spirit without making a forceful rush or push along one line only and that must be some line of pure experience in which, especially if it is the bhakta way, one gets easily swallowed up in the rapids (did not Chaitanya at last disappear in the waters?) and goes no farther. The first thing is to break into the spiritual consciousness, any part of it, anyhow and anywhere, afterwards one can explore the country, to which exploration there can hardly be a limit, one is always going higher and higher, getting wider and wider; but there is a certain intense ecstasy about the first complete plunge which is extraordinarily seizing. It is not only the bhakta's rapture, but the jnani's plunge into Brahma-Nirvana or Brahmananda or release into the still eternity of the Self that is of that seizing and

---

[1] *In a letter to the correspondent, Krishnaprem said that there are two stages of bhakti. In the first stage of rapturous adoration, the light and bliss of Krishna rush down into the bhakta just as water rushes over Niagara Falls. In the second stage the water flows through great pipes into mighty turbines which supply a continent with power.* — Ed.

absorbing character — it does not look at first as if one could or would care or need to get beyond into anything else. One cannot find fault with the Sannyasi lost in his laya or the bhakta lost in his ecstasy; they remain there probably because they are constituted for that and it is the limit of their leap. But all the same it has always appeared to me that it is a stage and not the end; I subscribe fully to the canalisation of Niagara.

Wideness and the Higher Consciousness

The first experience there [*on the higher plane*] is peace and calm and wideness. It is not till these are settled that other experiences of that plane can come.

*

The experience you had of the wideness with many roads opening was an image of the higher consciousness in which all the movements of the being are open, true and happy — the ignorance and incapacity of the lower nature disappear. It is that that the light from above is bringing.

*

Wideness is necessary for the working of the higher consciousness — if the being is shut up in itself, there can be intense experiences and some opening to touches from the heights, but not the full stable basis for the transformation.

*

Wideness is a sign of the extension of the consciousness out of the ordinary limits — whiteness of the wideness means that it is the pure consciousness one is feeling, unless it is white light or luminous white which indicates the Mother's consciousness there or some influence of it. The subtle barrier you felt must have been the same thing that prevents your ascent from the heart and from it going beyond into the regions above. There is always a sort of lid there and it is only when that is opened or disappears that one can go freely above. One can be aware of the "unseen wideness" but one is not oneself there until that is done.

*

If the workings are really those of the higher consciousness or if these predominate the ego fades out — but there is also often a wideness of opening to the universal mental, vital, physical existence and, if the sadhak responds more to these than to the higher consciousness, then he does not get free. Sometimes even the ego gets aggrandised. But if the psychic is awake, then there is not this danger; one finds one's true being in place of the ego.

*

She has had experiences but on the mental and vital plane. It is only a real descent of the higher consciousness from above that can give a peaceful and beautiful merging of the atoms (?)[2] into the wideness of the Divine — that is to say one feels the very cells sharing in that peace and wideness. This is possible even if the material body is ill. In most cases it is the subtle body that feels like that, but as the subtle penetrates everywhere the gross physical, the physical body also feels like that. But then it does not feel disturbed by the pains or motions of the illness — they do not affect its peace or Ananda.

Degrees in the Higher Consciousness

The plane makes a considerable difference in the power and luminosity and completeness etc. of the experience. A mental realisation is very different from an overmental or supramental although the Truth realised may be the same. So also to know Matter as the Brahman has a very different result from knowing Life, Mind, Supermind or Ananda as the Brahman. If realising the Divine through the Mind was just the same as realising him on higher planes, there would be no meaning in this Yoga at all

---

[2] *The question mark is Sri Aurobindo's. The sadhika had written, "Every atom of the body is merging peacefully and beautifully into the wideness." — Ed.*

— there would be no need of ascending to Supermind or bringing Supermind down.

*

The consciousness which he calls supramental, is no doubt above the human mind, but it should be called the higher consciousness. In this higher consciousness there are many degrees, of which the supramental is the summit or the source. It is not possible to reach that summit or source all at once; first, all the lower consciousness has to be purified and made ready. That is the meaning of the Light he saw, whose inner body or substance is too dense and powerful to be penetrated at present.

*

The higher consciousness is that above the ordinary mind and different from it in its workings; it ranges from higher mind through illumined mind, intuition and overmind up to the border line of the supramental.

*

The Self governs the diversity of its creation by its unity on all the planes from the Higher Mind upwards, for there some realisation or vision of the One Truth or the Universal is the natural frame and basis of the whole consciousness. But the higher one rises upward, the more the spiritual view changes, the power of consciousness changes, the Light becomes ever more intense and potent. The essential static realisation of Infinity and Eternity and the Timeless One remains the same, but the vision of the workings of the One becomes ever wider and is attended with a greater instrumentality of Force and a more comprehensive grasp of what has to be known and done. All possible forms and constructions of things become more and more visible, more perfectly put in their proper place, more luminously utilisable. A clear spacious thought-knowledge in the Higher Mind becomes a mass of illuminations in the Illumined Mind and heightens into direct intimate vision on the Intuition level. But the Intuition sees in flashes and combines through a constant play of light

— through a chain or coordinated harmony of revelations, inspirations, intuitions, swift discriminations. The Overmind sees calmly, steadily, in great masses and deep and large extensions of space and time and relation, globally, in wholes; it has the universal touch not only in spirit but in its manner. It creates and acts in the same way — for the Overmind is the world of the great Gods, the divine Creators. But each Godhead creates in his own way; he sees all but that all is seen from his own divine viewpoint. There is not the absolute supramental harmony and certitude. These are some of the differences. I speak of these planes in themselves — for when they act in the human consciousness, they are necessarily much diminished in their working, for they have to work with and depend on the human instrumentation or man's smaller seeking mental intelligence, his passionate turbid vital and mental, his cabined and narrow physical intellect — their workings get badly mixed up with these inferior modes of consciousness and their diluted light of ignorance. Only when these lower impotencies are quieted can those higher powers get a fuller force and reveal more of their original luminous character.

The Higher Planes and the Supermind

The Ignorance can act from above the head — but not as part of the higher planes — it comes from outside. The higher planes just above the head are not however the absolute Truth; that you only get in the supermind.

*

Absolute certitude about all things can only come from the supermind. Meanwhile one has to go on with what knowledge the other planes give.

*

The Truth manifesting on all the planes is one thing, the Supramental is another, although it is the source of all Truth.

*

To go into the supermind is impossible for the human mind. One has to rise into the higher planes of consciousness above human mind and transform the human mind into that; only afterwards can we hope to touch the supermind.

*

One has to go by stages, and to reach and be conscious on the higher planes between mind and Overmind is already sufficiently difficult without insisting on Supermind as the immediate goal.

*

One has to know about Overmind and Supermind but there should be no ambition to reach them — it should be regarded as a natural end of the sadhana which will come of itself. The concentration should be all on the immediate step — whatever is being done at the time. So have the working of the Power and let it work all out step by step.

Levels of the Higher Mind

What you see is perfectly correct. These three are three levels of the higher Mind — on the lowest the consciousness is in connection with the Divine not directly but through the touch of the Light, Peace, Power and Knowledge, on the second it is in the Light etc. and already sees the Divine, on the third it is in union with the Divine and surrendered. These are three well known conditions of the higher consciousness in its approach to the Divine.

An Illumined Mind Experience

You probably went up into the illumined Mind which has a pale blue light and were receiving there lights from the higher planes and occasionally seeing the flash of the full orb of the Divine Truth.

It is always a mistake for the mind to become active and wanting to know while the experience is going on — it usually stops the experience or disturbs or alters it in some way. The mind must remain passive till the experience is over.

Overmind Experiences

Overmind experience comes when one rises to the overmind plane and sees things as they are on that plane or as they look to the consciousness which sees the other planes from the overmind view. When one is in the mind, life or physical plane, then it is the overmind Influence that comes down and modifies the mind, life or physical workings in greater or less degree according to the possibilities or the thing to be done at the moment. It is not the sole power as it is in its own plane but works under mental, vital or physical conditions. Its power is more subjective than objective — it is easy for it to change our view and experience of the object and our knowledge about it, but not so easy for it to change the object or its nature or circumstances or the outward state of things in that plane.

*

It is perfectly simple, it is the attraction towards the Divine Oneness represented in concrete experience. Is it the concreteness of the experiences that puzzles you? All experience there [*in the Overmind*] tends to be concrete, there are no "abstract" truths as in the mind, — even thought in the Overmind is a concrete force and a palpable substance.

*

Yes — it is one aspect of the Truth: for in the Overmind there are many aspects of Truth, separate or combined together or arranged one above the other.

*

Both [*visions*] are true on different levels of the Overmind plane or in different cosmic formulations that come from the Overmind. All aspects are there in the Overmind, even those which the intellect considers contradictory to each other — in the Overmind they are not contradictions, but complementary to each other.

*

It is perfectly natural. In these experiences you become aware of the consciousness proper to other planes. Thus you get the experience of being a form of the Divine Consciousness, the Mother, and while the experience lasts you feel her power — when the experience ceases, you come back to your normal state, the power withdraws. These experiences impregnate the consciousness with the Overmind knowledge and they prepare it for transformation.

*

The overmind experience does not necessarily deliver from the lower vital and physical movements — it changes them only to a certain extent and prepares them for a greater Truth.

Overmind Experiences and the Supermind

People talk very lightly of the overmind and the supermind as if it were quite easy to enter into them and mistake inferior movements for the overmental or supramental, thereby confusing the Truth and delaying the progress of the sadhana.

*

Certainly, it [*the overmind descent*] is necessary for those who want the supramental change. Unless the overmind opens, there can be no direct supramental opening of the consciousness. If one remains in mind, even illumined mind or the intuition, one can have indirect messages or an influence from the supramental, but not a direct supramental control of the consciousness or the supramental change.

*

It is only the supermind that has an absolute freedom from error. The Overmind presents truths in all sorts of arrangements all of which taken together presents something like the whole truth — but these again are reflected in you in the terrestrial consciousness or conveyed to your terrestrial consciousness by the descent from the higher planes; but in receiving it the terrestrial consciousness can make mistakes in interpretation, in understanding, in application, in arrangement.

*

It is not very clear [*in the correspondent's letter*] what is meant by this Knowledge-Will. It is usually a description of the Supramental where there is no division between Knowledge and Will, each acting on each other or rather fixed together in oneness and therefore infallible. You say it has taken form in mind, vital and body; if that were so, it would mean the final and decisive transformation; so it cannot be the Supramental. It must be some overmind truth plane.

*

There are certain things in these three letters that are not correct, notably:

(1) He seems to say that beyond the overmind there is a plane of "higher luminous Intelligence". This is impossible. Beyond the overmind there is the Supermind — the overmind is the highest of all the planes below the supramental, and he is not yet in touch with the supramental. What he calls here the overmind cannot be the true overmind. His experiences are those of the mind opening to the higher mental planes and trying to bring down something from them and their powers into the mind, life and body.

(2) E.g. his classification of four worlds (Parvati-Shankar etc.) is an attempt of the mind to interpret something he had seen, but it has not got it at all right. If Mahasaraswati stopped him at this moment, it must have been because his mind was making a wrong formation and it was no use carrying it any farther.

At this stage of his Yoga he must observe what is going on, but not attach a definitive or final importance to any such classifications or mental arrangements. The mind at this stage sometimes gets these things correctly, sometimes makes formations of them which are not correct and have to be discarded or set right when a higher knowledge comes.

*

Your experience means manifestly the uniting of the Ishwara-Shakti sides of the manifestation — as in the Hara-Gauri figure — with the result of a universalisation of the individual consciousness indicated by the shooting out towards infinite distances. The currents are of course the currents of the double force working to make this liberation. The blue and gold must be the blue of Krishna and the gold of the Mother (Durga-Mahakali).

All this is not a supramental experience, but comes from the Overmind. But the overmind experiences must come first and liberate the consciousness. It is only after the overmind liberation that the true experience of the supermind can come.

*

You must realise that the supramentalisation of the overmind is one of the most difficult things possible and proceed with great care so as to avoid haste and error.

Reflected Experience of the Higher Planes

One can get the experiences of a higher plane by reflection or some partial descent in the lower.

*

It is the experience of the transcendent planes as reflected on the higher planes of consciousness (Overmind, etc.), in relation to them; just as one can have an experience of Sachchidananda and these planes as reflected in the mind or vital or physical consciousness, so one can have it there — but on each plane it appears in a different way.

Trance and the Higher Planes

The higher planes are not planes on which man is naturally conscious and he is even not open to their direct influence — only to some indirect influence from those nearest to the human mind. He can reach them only in a deep inner condition or trance and the higher he goes the less easy is it for him to be conscious of them even in trance. If you are not conscious of your inner being, then it is more difficult to be conscious in trance.

Living in a Higher Plane

To live in a higher plane and see the action on the physical from it as something separate is a definite stage in the movement towards transformation.

Section Four

The Spiritual Transformation

Chapter One

Ascent and Descent

The Meaning of Spiritual Transformation

What I mean by the spiritual transformation is something dynamic (not merely liberation of the self, or realisation of the One which can very well be attained without any descent). It is a putting on of the spiritual consciousness dynamic as well as static in every part of the being down to the subconscient. That cannot be done by the influence of the Self leaving the consciousness fundamentally as it is with only purification, enlightenment of the mind and heart and quiescence of the vital. It means a bringing down of Divine Consciousness static and dynamic into all these parts and the entire replacement of the present consciousness by that. This we find unveiled and unmixed above mind, life and body and not in mind, life and body. It is a matter of the undeniable experience of many that this can descend and it is my experience that nothing short of its *full* descent can thoroughly remove the veil and mixture and effect the full spiritual transformation.

*

The power of concentration above the head is to bring peace, silence, liberation from the body sense, the identification with mind and life and open the way for the lower (mental-vital-physical) consciousness to rise up to meet the higher Consciousness above and for the powers of the higher (spiritual or divine) Consciousness to descend into mind, life and body. This is what is called in this Yoga the spiritual transformation.

A Double Movement in the Sadhana

There is a double movement in the sadhana — the Divine Consciousness, Power, Light, Peace descending into all the body, the consciousness from all parts of the body rising upwards to meet the Divine Consciousness above — the descent and the ascent.

*

The sadhana is based on the fact that a descent of Forces from the higher planes and an ascent of the lower consciousness to the higher planes is the means of transformation of the lower nature — although naturally it takes time and the complete transformation can only come by the supramental descent. Your experiences here are forms of the widening experiences of this process.

*

The practice of this Yoga is double — one side is of an ascent of the consciousness to the higher planes, the other is of a descent of the power of the higher planes into the earth consciousness so as to drive out the Power of darkness and ignorance and transform the nature.

*

All the consciousness in the human being who is the mental embodied in living matter has to rise so as to meet the higher consciousness; the higher consciousness has also to descend into mind, into life, into matter. In that way the barriers will be removed and the higher consciousness will be able to take up the whole lower nature and transform it by the power of the supermind.

The earth is a material field of evolution. Mind and life, supermind, Sachchidananda are in principle involved there in the earth consciousness, but only matter is at first organised; then life descends from the life plane and gives shape and organisation and activity to the life principle in matter, creates the plant and animal; then mind descends from the mind plane, creating man. Now supermind is to descend so as to create a supramental race.

*

There are two movements — one an ascension of the lower consciousness to meet the higher, the other the descent of the higher consciousness into the lower. What you first experienced was an uprush of the lower consciousness from all parts so strong as to break the lid of the inner mind — that was the splitting of the skull — and to enable the joining of the two consciousnesses above to be complete. The result was a descent. Usually the first thing that descends from the higher consciousness is its deep and entire peace — the second is the Light, here the white light of the Mother. When the higher consciousness descends or is intensely felt, there is very usually an opening of the limited personal being into the cosmic consciousness — one feels a wide and infinite being which alone exists, the identification with the body and even the sense of the body disappears, the limited personal consciousness is lost in the Cosmic Existence. You had all this first in the impersonal way, but after the burning up of the psychic fire, you felt the Personal wideness, the cosmic consciousness of the Divine Mother and received her blessing.

*

If your consciousness rises above the head, that means that it goes beyond the ordinary mind to the centre above which receives the higher consciousness or else towards the ascending levels of the higher consciousness itself. The first result is the silence and peace of the Self which is the basis of the higher consciousness; this may afterwards descend into the lower levels, into the very body. Light also can descend and Force. The navel and the centres below it are those of the vital and the physical; something of the higher Force may have descended there.

Both Ascent and Descent Necessary

The lower consciousness ascends towards the higher to join it — the higher descends into the lower to transform it. It is the rule of the consciousness in this sadhana.

*

A going up and up higher, though a part of the total necessary movement, does not by itself have any effect on the outer being. It only divides the consciousness into two and its only logical outcome is Nirvana. I have always written that the descent is necessary to change the nature; ascent is useful to open the higher planes and exalt the level of the consciousness, but it does not change the lower being except superficially by opening to it certain possibilities it had not before. But the descent must first take place in the inner being. When the higher consciousness is settled in the inner being, then it can change the outer. But necessarily the descent must be dynamic, not merely that of a static peace; the inner peace must itself become dynamic.

The descent whether of peace or force or light or knowledge or Ananda must occupy the whole inner being down to the inner physical. Without that how is the outer to be transformed at all? It is an amazing idea to suppose that the outer can be changed while the inner is left to itself. What you had in the inner being was a static stillness which did not even entirely occupy the inner physical except at times — that was why the dynamic descent was necessary, but in the inner being or if possible the whole being, the inner outflowing into the outer, not in the outer being to the exclusion of the inner.

*

In the physical consciousness the descent is the most important. Something of the subtle physical can always go up — but the external physical consciousness can only do it when the force from above comes down and fills it. There is then a sort of unification made when the higher consciousness and the physical are one undivided consciousness and there is an ascent of forces from below and descent from above, simultaneous and mutually interpenetrating.

*

I am not speaking of mere rising above [*as the means of changing the external nature*]. The rising above has to be followed by the descent of the higher consciousness into the different parts of the being. That aided by the psychic development and aiding it changes the external nature.

*

It was an experience (by ascension) of the spiritual plane of being above in which there is absolute peace and light and Ananda. It is this that has to descend into the mind, vital and body and be the constant condition and the basis for the final transformation of the consciousness and nature.

*

There are two movements that are necessary — one is the ascent through the increasing of peace and silence to its source above the mind, — that is indicated by the tendency of the consciousness to rise out of the body to the top of the head and above where it is easy to realise the Self in all its stillness and liberation and wideness and to open to the other powers of the Higher Consciousness. The other is the descent of the peace, silence, the spiritual freedom and wideness and the powers of the higher consciousness as they develop into the lower down to the most physical and even the subconscient. To both of these movements there can be a block — a block above due to the mind and lower nature being unhabituated (it is that really and not incapacity) and a block below due to the physical consciousness and its natural slowness to change. Everybody has these blocks but by persistent will, aspiration or *abhyāsa* they can be overcome.

The Order of Ascent and Descent

There is no fixed rule in such things. With many the descent comes first and the ascension afterwards, with others it is the other way; with some the two processes go on together. If one can fix oneself above so much the better.

*

I think the descent is more usual than the ascent. Some sadhaks finish the ascent first or ascents and descents but more often the descents come first and the ascent (above the head) takes place only when there has been much working of peace, force, Ananda etc. in the body.

*

The movement of ascension cannot finish so long as the movement of descent is not ready to finish.

Ascent and Descent of the Kundalini Shakti

The spine is the main channel of the descent and ascent of the Force, by which it connects the lower and the higher consciousness together.

*

The sensation in the spine and on both sides of it is a sign of the awakening of the Kundalini power. More precisely, it is felt as a descending or an ascending current or currents, or both at the same time. There are two main nerve channels for the currents, one on each side of the central channel in the spine. The descending current is the Energy from above coming down to touch the sleeping Power in the lowest nerve centre at the bottom of the spine; the ascending current is the release of energy going up from the awakened Kundalini. This movement as it proceeds opens up the six centres of the subtle nervous system and by the opening one escapes from the limitations of the surface consciousness bound to the gross body, and great ranges of experience proper to the larger subliminal self, mental, vital, subtle-physical, are shown to the sadhaka. When the Kundalini meets the higher consciousness, as it ascends through the summit of the head, there is an opening to the higher superconscient reaches above the normal mind. It is by ascending through these in our consciousness and receiving a descent of their energies that it is possible ultimately to reach the supermind. This is the psycho-physical method which is elaborately systematised in the Tantra. In our Yoga it is not necessary to go through the systematised method, — for this psycho-physical process is only a part of the movement of the Yoga and it takes place spontaneously according to need by the force of the aspiration and the call for the workings of the Divine Power. As soon as there is an opening, the Divine Power descends and conducts the necessary working, does what is needed, each thing in its time, and the Yogic consciousness begins to be born in the sadhaka.

*

The force which you felt must evidently have been a rising of the Kundalini ascending to join the Force above and bring down the energy needed to ease the depression and then again rising to enforce the connection between the Above and the lower centres. The seeming expansion of the head is due to the joining of the mind with the consciousness of the Self or Divine above. That consciousness is wide and illimitable and when one rises into it the individual consciousness also breaks its limits and feels wide and illimitable. At such times one often feels as if there were no head and no body but all were a wide self and its consciousness, or else the head or the body is only a circumstance in that. The body or the physical mind is sometimes startled or alarmed at these experiences because they are abnormal to it; but there is no ground for alarm, — these are usual experiences in the Yoga.

*

There is a Yoga Shakti lying coiled or asleep in the inner body, not active. When one does Yoga, this force uncoils itself and rises upward to meet the Divine Consciousness and Force that are waiting above us. When this happens, when the awakened Yoga Shakti arises, it is often felt like a snake uncoiling and standing up straight and lifting itself more and more upwards. When it meets the Divine Consciousness above, then the force of the Divine Consciousness can more easily descend into the body and be felt working there to change the nature.

The feeling of your body and eyes being drawn upwards is part of the same movement. It is the inner consciousness in the body and the inner subtle sight in the body that are looking and moving upward and trying to meet the divine consciousness and divine seeing above.

*

Yoga means union with the Divine — a union either transcendental (above the universe) or cosmic (universal) or individual or, as in our Yoga, all three together. Or it means getting into a consciousness in which one is no longer limited by the small ego, personal mind, personal vital and body but is in union with the supreme Self or with the universal (cosmic) consciousness or with some deeper consciousness within in which one is aware of one's own soul, one's own inner being and of the real truth of existence. In the Yogic consciousness one is not only aware of things, but of forces, not only of forces but of the conscious being behind the forces. One is aware of all this not only in oneself but in the universe.

There is a force which accompanies the growth of the new consciousness and at once grows with it and helps it to come about and to perfect itself. This force is the Yoga shakti. It is here asleep and coiled up in all the centres of our inner being (chakras) and is at the base what is called in the Tantras the Kundalini shakti. But it is also above us, above our head as the Divine Force — not there coiled up, involved, asleep, but awake, scient, potent, extended and wide; it is there waiting for manifestation and to this Force we have to open ourselves — to the power of the Mother. In the mind it manifests itself as a divine mind-force or a universal mind-force and it can do everything that the personal mind cannot do; it is then the Yogic mind-force. When it manifests and works in the vital or physical in the same way, it is then apparent as a Yogic life-force or a Yogic body-force. It can awake in all these forms, bursting outwards and upwards, extending itself into wideness from below; or it can descend and become there a definite power for things; it can pour downwards into the body, working, establishing its reign, extending into wideness from above, link the lowest in us with the highest above us, release the individual into a cosmic universality or into absoluteness and transcendence.

Ascent and Descent and Problems of the Lower Nature

If one can remain always in the higher consciousness, so much the better. But why does not one remain always there? Because the lower is still part of the nature and it pulls you down towards itself. If on the other hand the lower is transformed, it becomes of one kind with the higher and there is nothing lower to pull downwards.

Transformation means that the higher consciousness or nature is brought down into the mind, vital and body and takes the place of the lower. There is a higher consciousness of the true self which is spiritual, but it is above; if one rises above into it, then one is free as long as one remains there, but if one comes down into or uses mind, vital or body — and if one keeps any connection with life, one has to do so, either to come down and act from the ordinary consciousness or else to be in the self but use mind, life and body — then the imperfections of these instruments have to be faced and mended; they can only be mended by transformation.

You say you rise a little above into this higher consciousness, but where do you rise? Into the quieted mind and above the vital or above the mind itself into something always calm and pure and free?

*

No. I did not intend any sarcasm by my question [*at the end of the preceding letter*]. You had written that by rising a little above the ordinary consciousness one was free from difficulties and that this was what one felt — I thought you meant that this was your own experience. So I put the question, as the experience of the quiet mind is one that can easily be broken by the invasions of the vital or the inertia of the physical being. The experience of the deeper freedom and calm which belongs to the self remains, but it can be covered up by the lower consciousness.

*

That [*thoughts about others*] can be only a temporary result of past activities. The endeavour should now be to make the ascent above into the silence of the Self in the higher universal consciousness above, for that was evidently what was trying to come when the disturbance broke in. That would probably bring also the descent of the permanent spiritual peace into all the being as a basis for the higher activities.

*

That you should be able to keep your consciousness uplifted is already something. As for the opening its coming and apparent closing is a normal experience — it needs several openings before the thing is settled by a permanent poise of the consciousness above and an increasing descent into the head and below. It is the pull from below that should get no indulgence — for that, though most do indulge in it, is a wrong crabby way of doing it. One must be safely stationed above before one can descend without a tumble. Not that the tumble if it comes precludes a going up again — it does not; but that is no reason for letting it happen.

*

Even if the permanent opening does not come at once, you have only to wait and it is bound to come. It is certainly a pity that the restlessness of the vital should kick so much against vacancy of the consciousness; for if you could stand it this emptiness, now neutral, and therefore not interesting to the vital, would become positive and be the peaceful recipient of the pouring from above. The difficulty is that the vital has always been accustomed either to doing something or to something doing and when it is doing nothing or nothing is doing (or it seems like that on the surface), it gets bored and begins to feel and talk or to do nonsense. However even with this obstacle, the Descent can come down — it need not wait for the Supramental.

*

Yes. To ascend is easier than to bring down; the higher consciousness gets entangled and impeded in the physical and the mind and vital.

*

Rising higher and higher and bringing down is the method of

the Yoga; but it is not possible to do it with full effect until one has so prepared oneself that one can rise above the head to the Self in the higher mind. It was the point you had reached but could not confirm before the difficulties came in from the physical consciousness.

Experiences of Ascent and Descent

The ascent of the consciousness in the lower centres into the higher and the descent of the higher powers and the white light indicates a farther preparation of the vital and physical being and its forces by spiritualisation of the centres.

*

All these are different actions of the Force on the adhar with the one intention of opening it up from above and below and horizontally also. The action from above opens it to the descent of forces from above the Mind and the ascent of consciousness above the lid of the ordinary human mind. The horizontal action opens it to the cosmic consciousness on all its levels. The action from below helps to connect the superconscient with the subconscient. Finally the consciousness instead of being limited in the body becomes infinite, rises infinitely above, plunges infinitely below, widens infinitely on every side. There is besides the opening of all the centres to the Light and Power and Ananda that has to descend from above. At present only the mind centres seem to receive fully the descent of Force, while the upper vital centres are being prepared with a minor action on other parts of the body. It is a matter of time and perseverance for the way to be entirely open.

*

The experience you feel is that of the Atman, the cosmic Self supporting the cosmic consciousness — not yet clear but in its first impression. When the consciousness goes down from that condition, it brings something of it into the vital and physical consciousness and the result is either that these parts or at least the vital open and get into touch with what has been brought down. The inert *tāmasikatā* or the unease in the legs comes because the physical is not able to receive or assimilate. This will disappear when that part opens and receives and is able to assimilate.

It was there the occasional descent of the Force to establish a connection — here the descent is taking another form intended to establish the fundamental experiences of the Realisation.

*

It is the beginning of a very decisive experience and realisation — first, the Ascent above the mind (head) into the spiritual plane. It is here that one releases and is released into the vastness, fullness, solace, freedom, peace and joy of the Infinite and becomes aware of the universal Self and the Divine. Its realisation is the foundation (when it is fixed and when one rises constantly above the body in the wideness of the infinite Being) of the spiritual state and the beginning of the spiritual transformation of the nature. What you have been having up to now is the psychic change; when the psychic and spiritual join together, then the transformation can be complete. For this the Descent is necessary and that is the second thing you are feeling, — the descent of the higher, spiritual or divine consciousness and energy into the whole system down to the bottom of the spine where is the Muladhara or centre of the physical consciousness. The Energy descends through all the levels and centres, mind centres, vital centres, physical centre and fills the whole body with the higher existence and consciousness. The ascent is the liberation (mukti) and when once this ascends, one is liberated from the body consciousness, one no longer feels the body as a form, no longer feels contained in the body, but widens out into the formless Vastness of the Divine. Or sometimes the body is felt as something very small in this vastness. In the Descent the body is felt but not as a confining form so much as an instrument and receptacle for this larger consciousness. Your description of the experience is unmistakable. All the elements are there. What has to happen is to get fixed in the wideness, freedom, stillness, peace of the consciousness above and for the Descent to continue till it has fixed the higher power of being everywhere below — in the body and in the subconscience below it and also all round the body so that one lives enveloped in this new consciousness and being.

*

The experiences you relate mark a great progress — the passage from the perception of the ascending Force to that of the descending Shakti. For the spiral coils of Light you saw and whose effects you felt — the merging in silence and peace, the peace of the Atman or the Brahman consciousness — are usually a first effect, they are visual forms of the dynamic descent of the Divine Force from above; also the passage from the realisation of the static Brahman with the sense of the unreality of the world-existence to the realisation of the status of the dynamic one. This is a considerable step in the integral Yoga.

The Brahman consciousness is sometimes described as a static one, but it has two aspects, static and dynamic, and it is when both are united that it becomes integral. This is the greater consciousness I speak of in the sentence quoted by you, greater than either that which perceives the Brahmic silence and immobility alone or that which perceives the cosmic existence and action alone.

Chapter Two
Ascent to the Higher Planes

Contact with the Above

These are the ordinary normal experiences of the sadhana when there is an opening from above — the contact with the peace of the Brahman, Self or Divine and the contact with the higher Power, the Power of the Mother. He does not know what they are, quite naturally, but feels very correctly and his description is quite accurate. "How beautiful, calm and still all seems — as if in water there were not even a wave. But it is not Nothingness. I feel a Presence steeped in life but absolutely silent and quiet in meditation", — there could hardly be a better description of this experience, — the experience of the peace and silence of the Divine or of the Divine itself in its own essential peace and silence. Also what he feels about the Force is quite correct, "something from above the manifested creation (mind-matter), a Force behind that is distinct from that which gives rise to emotions, anger, lust which are all purified and transformed gradually", in other words, the Divine or Spiritual Force, other than the cosmic vital which supports the ordinary embodied consciousness; that is also very clear. I suppose it is only a contact yet, but a very true and vivid contact if it gives rise to so vivid and true a feeling. It looks as if he were going to make a very good beginning.

*

One may get influences from above, but so long as the mind is not full of the higher calm, peace, silence, one cannot be in direct contact. These influences get diminished, mentalised, vitalised and are not the powers of the higher planes in their native character. Nor is this sufficient to get control of the hidden forces of all the planes of consciousness, which is perhaps what he means by occultism.

*

Indirect connection [*with the Divine*] is when one lives in the ordinary consciousness without being able to go up above it and receives influences from above without knowing where they come from or feeling their source.

*

Sometimes one feels an ascension above the head. I think he has had that, but that is the mind going up (when it is not simply a going out of the body) into the higher mental planes. To be above the mind one must first realise the self above the mind and live there.

*

Do you realise it [*the higher being*] as wide and infinite? When you are there do you feel it spread through infinity? Do you feel all the universe within you, yourself one with the self of all beings? Do you feel the one cosmic Force acting everywhere? Do you feel your mind one with the cosmic mind? your life one with the cosmic life? your matter one with the cosmic Matter? separative ego unreal? the body no longer a limitation? What is the use of merely saying that the higher being is wide and infinite? Do these realisations come when you are in the higher being and if not, why not? The inner being easily opens to all these realisations, the outer does not. So unless your inner being becomes conscious of itself, the mere ascent gives only height or some vague sense of other planes, not these concrete realisations.

Ascension or Rising above the Head

This is a fundamental experience of the Yoga. It is the free ascent of the consciousness to join the Divine. When, liberated from its ordinary identification with the body, it rises upward to have experiences of the higher planes, to link itself with the psychic or the true being or to join the Divine Consciousness, then there is this experience of ascension and of speeding or expanding through space. The joy you feel is a sign of this last movement, — rising to join the Divine; the passivity and expectancy of a descent are signs of the openness to the Divine that is its result; there is also the sense of this openness, an emptiness of the ordinary contents of the consciousness, a wideness not limited by the narrow prison of the physical personality. There is too, usually or very often, a massive immobility of the body which corresponds to the silence that comes on the mind when it is released from itself — the Silence that is the foundation of spiritual experience. What you have felt (the former experiences were probably preparatory touches) is indeed the beginning of this foundation — a consciousness free, wide, empty at will, able to rise into the supraphysical planes, open to the descent of whatever the Mother will pour into it.

*

Nothing needs to be done to bring the ascension — aspiration is sufficient. The object of the ascension is for the lower nature to join the higher consciousness so that (1) the limit or lid between the higher and the lower may be broken and disappear, (2) the consciousness may have free access to higher and higher planes, (3) a free way may be made for the descent of the higher Consciousness into the lower planes.

*

The lower consciousness rises to meet the higher consciousness — when it joins there is the sense of unity and the feeling of the one cosmic Self with Ananda and Peace or both as the result. This is called the ascent of the lower consciousness — it cannot remain all the time but it can become more and more frequent until the descent of the higher consciousness is ready.

*

That [*rising above the head*] is very good. Such risings help to break down the lid between the higher and lower planes in the consciousness and prepare the consciousness.

*

The rising of the energies of the consciousness to the crown of the head and beyond is a recognised movement of the sadhana. It is the forces of the lower Prakriti rising to connect themselves with the higher spiritual consciousness above. The hearing of bells is usually a sign of an opening of the consciousness; it is mentioned in the Upanishads as one of such significant sounds and is well known to Yogis.

*

(1) Freedom from cares, lightness of mind and body are very good results. They do not usually become permanent at once — it is sufficient if they are frequently or ordinarily there.

(2) Chest and head rising higher are sensations of the subtle body — it means that the mind and heart consciousness (thinking mental and emotional) are rising to meet the spiritual consciousness plane above the head.

(3) The sound is a sign of the opening of the consciousness and of the working of the inner Force. Such subtle sounds are very frequently heard by those who practise Yoga.

*

Everything in the adhar in the sadhana has at one time the tendency to rise and join its source above.

*

The upward movement and the silence are indispensable for the Truth to manifest.

Ascent and Return to the Ordinary Consciousness

I may say that the opening upwards, the ascent into the Light and the subsequent descent into the ordinary consciousness and normal human life is very common as the first decisive experience in the practice of Yoga and may very well happen even without the practice of Yoga in those who are destined for the spiritual change, especially if there is a dissatisfaction somewhere with the ordinary life and a seeking for something more, greater or better. It comes often exactly in the way that she describes and the cessation of the experience and the descent also come in the same way. This first experience may be followed by a very long time during which there is no repetition of it or any subsequent experience. If there is a constant practice of Yoga, the interval need not be so long; but even so it is often long enough. The descent is inevitable because it is not the whole being that has risen up but only something within and all the rest of the nature is unprepared, absorbed in or attached to ordinary life and governed by movements that are not in consonance with the Light. Still the something within is something central in the being and therefore the experience is in a way definitive and decisive. For it comes as a decisive intimation of the spiritual destiny and an indication of what must be reached some time in the life. Once it has been there, something is bound to happen which will open the way, determine the right knowledge and the right attitude enabling one to proceed on the way and bring a helping influence. After that the work of clearing away the obstacles that prevent the return to the Light and the ascension of the whole being and, what is equally important, the descent of the Light into the whole being can be begun and progress towards completion. It may take long or be rapid, that depends on the inner push and also on outer circumstances but the inner aspiration and endeavour count more than the circumstances which can accommodate themselves to the inner need if that is very strong. The moment has come for her and the necessary aspiration and knowledge and the influence that can help her.

Ascent and Dissolution

Once the being or its different parts begin to ascend to the planes above, any part of the being may do it, frontal or other. The sanskara that one cannot come back must be got rid of. One can have the experience of Nirvana at the summit of the mind or anywhere in those planes that are now superconscient to the mind; the mind spiritualised by the ascent into Self has the sense of *laya*, dissolution of itself, its thoughts, movements, sanskaras into a superconscient Silence and Infinity which it is unable to grasp, — the Unknowable. But this would bring or lead to some form of Nirvana only if one makes Nirvana the goal, if one is tied to the mind and accepts its dissolution into the Infinite as one's own dissolution or if one has not the capacity to reorganise experience on a higher than the mental plane. But otherwise what was superconscient becomes conscient, one begins to possess or else be the instrument of the dynamis of the higher planes and there is a movement, not of liberation into Nirvana, but of liberation + transformation. However high one goes, one can always return, unless one has the will not to do so.

Ascent and the Psychic Being

Any part of the being can go upward and meet its source there. The central being is always above; the psychic is its counterpart below. If the psychic goes up it may be also to join its source in the central being.

*

The psychic being and other parts can go up to join the higher consciousness there. It is part of the movement of ascent. Naturally the psychic wants a deeper union than can be had so long as it is veiled by the old ignorant nature; it wants the higher consciousness to come down and occupy and transform it so that complete union may be possible.

The Shakti going up from the Muladhara must be the Shakti of the physical nature. It wants transformation also, I suppose, but it has not the quiet and luminous but ardent aspiration of the psychic being — its aspiration is more troubled and tinged with unease.

*

In your experience the ascent was into the regions of the calm and silent Self above; when you came down you went into the depths of the psychic being and found there the same calm and wideness. This experience is of great importance for it means that the way to both these is now open to you — and these two are the fundamental experiences of our Yoga — the unveiling of the psychic and the self-realisation. Pursue your meditations in the same poise.

Ascent and the Body

The ordinary movement of sadhana is that of the inner being (mind, psychic, higher vital) rising towards the Divine Consciousness, — leaving the external being behind — but for this Yoga that is not enough, the physical and external being must also be able to rise into the Divine Consciousness.

*

What you have written is quite correct. The body is not connected ordinarily with the higher consciousness, it only receives what it can from the mind. It is being prepared for the direct connection by the ascent of the inner or subtle body into that plane and the descent from it of the higher Light.

*

No, the body itself cannot go up — how could it? The body is meant for keeping the consciousness linked to the physical world.

*

If all went up, there would be no more existence in the body. There is always some consciousness and therefore some self supporting the body.

*

When the consciousness is centred above, it can be said to be located above. That does not mean that there is no consciousness left in the lower parts.

Ascent and Going out of the Body

There are two different things. One is the consciousness actually going out of the body — but that brings a deep sleep or trance.

Ascent to the Higher Planes

The other is the consciousness lifting itself out of the body and taking its stand outside it — above and spread round in wideness. That can be a condition of the Yogin in the waking state — he does not feel himself to be in the body but he feels the body to be in his wide free self, he is delivered from limitation in the body consciousness.

*

There are two different experiences which from your account would seem to have happened together.

(1) An exteriorisation of the consciousness out of the body. Part of the consciousness, mental, vital or subtle physical or all together rises out of the body, leaving it in a strongly internalised condition, sleep or trance and can move about above on other planes or in the room and outside on the earth plane. In such cases the body can be seen as lying below or in the room, seen clearly as one sees a separate object with the physical eyes. A fear such as you had can come in these exteriorisations and bring the consciousness back with a rush to the body.

(2) An ascension of the consciousness to a position which is no longer in the body but above it. The consciousness can thus ascend and rise higher and higher with the awareness of entering regions above the ordinary mind; usually it does not go very far at first but acquires the capacity to go always higher in repetitions of this experience. At the close of the experience it returns to the body. But also there comes a definitive rise by which the consciousness permanently takes its station above. It is no longer in the body or limited by it; it feels itself not only above it but extended in space; the body is below its high station and enveloped in its extended consciousness. Sometimes indeed the extension is felt only above on the higher level and the enveloping extension below comes only afterwards as a later experience. But the nature of it is to be definitive, it is not merely an experience but a realisation, a permanent change. This brings a liberation from identification with the body which becomes only a circumstance in the largeness of the being, an instrumental part of it; or it is felt as something very small or

even non-existent, nothing seems to be left but a wide practically infinite consciousness which is oneself — or, if not at once infinite, yet what is now called a boundless finite.

This new consciousness is open to all knowledge from above, but it does not think with the brain as does the ordinary mind — it has other and larger means of awareness than thought. No methodical opening of the centres is necessary — the centres are in fact open, otherwise there could not be this ascent. In this Yoga their opening comes automatically — what we call opening is not that, but an ability of the consciousness itself on the various levels to receive the descent of the Higher Consciousness above. By the ascent one can indeed bring down knowledge from above. But the larger movement is to receive it from above and let it flow through into the lower mental and other levels. I may add that on all these levels, in mind, heart and below there comes a liberation from the physical limitation, a wideness which no longer allows an identification with the body.

In this experience there is not usually the fear you had, unless it is in the body consciousness, as it were, which is alarmed by the unfamiliarity of the movement and fears to be abandoned or cast off. But this occurs rarely and does not usually repeat itself. It is therefore likely that there was an exteriorisation at the same time. You speak of being able to leave and enter the body at will; but this capacity is needed only for the phenomenon of exteriorisation — in the ascension of consciousness the ascent and coming down become easy and ordinary actions and in the definitive realisation of a higher station above there is really no more coming down except with a part of the consciousness which may descend to work in the body or on the lower levels while the permanently high-stationed being above presides over all that is experienced and done.

*

It [*walking around as if in a dream*] is a very usual experience. It means that for a moment you were no longer in your body, but somehow either above or outside the body consciousness.

This sometimes happens by the vital being rising up above the head or, more rarely, by its projecting itself into its own sheath (part of the subtle body) out of the physical attachment. But it also comes by a sudden even if momentary liberation from the identification with the body consciousness, and this liberation may become frequent and prolonged or permanent. The body is felt as something separate or some small circumstance in the consciousness or as something one carries about with one etc. etc.; the exact experience varies. Many sadhaks here have had it. When one is accustomed, the strangeness of it (dreamland etc.) disappears.

Fixing the Consciousness Above

It is the aim of the sadhana that the consciousness should rise out of the body and take its station above, — spreading in wideness everywhere, not limited to the body. Thus liberated one opens to all that is above this station, above the ordinary mind, receives there all that descends from the heights, observes from there all that is below. Thus it is possible to witness in all freedom and to control all that is below and to be a recipient or a channel for all that comes down and presses into the body, which it will prepare to be an instrument of a higher manifestation, remoulded into a higher consciousness and nature.

What is happening in you is that the consciousness is trying to fix itself in this liberation. When one is there in that higher station, one finds the freedom of the Self and the vast silence and immutable calm — but this calm has to be brought down also into the body, into all the lower planes and fix itself there as something standing behind and containing all the movements.

*

It [*a feeling of rising above the head in meditation*] is not merely a sensation; it is an actual happening and a most important one. The consciousness is usually imprisoned in the body, centralised in the brain and heart and navel centres (mental, emotional, sensational); when you feel it or something of it go up and take its station above the head, that is the liberation of the imprisoned consciousness from the body-formula. It is the mental in you that goes up there, gets into touch with something higher than the ordinary mind and from there puts the higher mental will on the rest for transformation. The trembling and the heat come from a resistance, an absence of habituation in the body and the vital to this demand and to this liberation. When the mental consciousness can take its stand permanently or at will above like this, then this first liberation becomes accomplished (*siddha*). From there the mental being can open freely to higher planes or to the cosmic existence and its forces and can also act with greater liberty and power on the lower nature.

*

What you felt was not imagination at all, but the usual experience one has when the consciousness is lifted out of the body and takes its stand above the head. One is no longer bound then by the physical consciousness or the sense of the body — the body becomes only an instrument, a small part of the consciousness which has to be perfected. One enters into a larger free spiritual consciousness in place of the present bound and limited physical consciousness. If this lifting up above the body can be repeated always until it can be maintained, it will be a great landmark in your progress. It is the confinement in the physical consciousness that makes you (and everybody) narrow and selfish and miserable. Hitherto the higher consciousness with its peace etc. has been descending into you with great difficulty and fighting out the vital and physical resistance. If this release upward into the higher consciousness can be maintained, then there will be no longer the same difficulty. Much will still remain to be done, but the foundation will have been made.

*

There are various states of experience in which the expression "taken up out of the body" would be applicable. There is one in which one goes up from the centres in the body to a centre of consciousness extending above the physical head and takes up a position there in which one is liberated from subjection to the body sense and its heavy hold and this is certainly accompanied by a general sense of lightening. One can then be in direct connection with the higher consciousness and its power and action. It is not altogether clear from the description whether this is what happened. Again, there are phenomena of the breathing which accompany states of release or of ascension. But the breath here perhaps stands, generally, for the Life Principle.

Ascent and Change of the Lower Nature

One can remain in the higher consciousness and yet associate oneself with the change of the lower nature. No doubt, it is the Mother's Force that will do what is necessary, but the consent of the sadhak, the association of his will with her action or at least of his witness vision is necessary also.

*

Your tendency was to go up and to leave the higher consciousness to deal with the lower nature without any personal effort for that. That could have worked all right on two conditions: (1) that the peace and force would come down and occupy all down to the physical, (2) that you succeeded in keeping the inner being unmoved by the outer nature. The physical failed to absorb the peace, inertia arose instead; force could not come down; the suggestions from the outer nature proved too strong for you and between their suggestions and the inertia they interrupted the sadhana.

*

I have not said [*in the preceding letter*] that you made a mistake. I have simply said what happened and the causes. If you had been able to remain above and let the Force come down and act while you were detached from the outer nature, it would have been all right. You were able to go up because the Peace descended. You were not able to remain above because the Peace could not occupy sufficiently the physical and the Force did not descend sufficiently. Meanwhile the inertia arose, you got troubled more and more because of the vital suggestions in the outer nature and the rush of inertia, so you were unable to keep detached and let the Force descend more and more or call it down more and more. Hence the coming down into the physical consciousness.

*

It is simply that when you go high, or within, you enter into a higher consciousness than the ordinary one. Also then one feels the presence of the Divine, for the Divine is always there within and above in every human being. But to divinise the human consciousness entirely needs a long time — for the whole nature from top to bottom must be transformed.

Chapter Three

The Descent of the Higher Consciousness and Force

The Purpose of the Descent

The descent is that of the powers of the higher consciousness which is above the head. It usually descends from centre to centre till it has occupied the whole being. But at the beginning the action is very variable. It is only when the Peace from above has not only descended but established itself in the whole system that there is a continuous action. The descent comes in order to transform the consciousness but the transformation takes time. It is not done all in a moment.

*

The Force descends for two things:
(1) To transform the nature.
(2) To carry on the work through the instrument.
At first one is not conscious of either working, afterwards one becomes conscious of the Force working but not of how it works. Finally one becomes conscious entirely and in detail.

*

Naturally, when any of the higher consciousness descends it works to change the lower consciousness into a part of itself.

Calling in the Higher Consciousness

All limitations [*in one's nature*] can be surmounted, but if they are ingrained in the formation of the present being, it can only be done by calling in a higher power and consciousness than that of the personal mind and will. The higher consciousness can by what it brings correct or rebuild what is defective in the personal nature.

*

The consciousness is always there above you. It is when one opens oneself and calls it that it descends and works — whether in meditation or in work.

*

What comes from above can come when one is in a clear mind or when the vital is disturbed, when one is meditating or when one is moving about, when one is working or when one is doing nothing. Most often it comes when one is in a clear concentrated state, but it may not, — there is no absolute rule. Moreover the pull or call may produce no immediate effect and yet there may be an effect when one is no longer actually pulling or calling. All these mental reasons alleged for its coming or going are too rigid — sometimes they apply, very often they don't apply. One has to have faith, confidence, aspiration but one cannot bind down the Force as to when, how and why it will act.

*

It [*the higher consciousness*] descends in the atmosphere, but for it to be effective the individual must receive and respond. It descends also in the individual independently of the atmosphere.

Preparatory Experiences and Descent

The illumination above the head as usually seen in this Yoga is the Light of the Divine Truth. It is above the head that there is perpetually the Divine Peace, Force, Light, Knowledge, Ananda. These begin to descend into the body when the personal consciousness is prepared sufficiently. The preparation is usually full of vicissitudes such as these [*illness, sleeplessness, an inability to concentrate*] but one has to persist patiently, opening oneself more and more till that is ready.

*

The Descent of the Higher Consciousness and Force

Why should it [*a sense of purity in the being*] be an imagination? When the higher consciousness touches it creates so long as it is there an essential purity in which all parts of the being can share. Or, even if the exterior being does not share actively in it, it may fall quiescent so that there is nothing to interfere with the whole inner being realising the truth of a certain experience. The state does not last because it is only a preparatory touch, not the full or permanent descent; but while it is there it is real. The sex-sensation is of course the thing in the external being, the perversion or false representation in nature, that is the chief obstacle to the experience becoming frequent and then normal. It usually happens that such an opposite tries to assert itself after an experience.

*

The experiences you have had from above are spiritual experiences. The experience has come, but not yet taken possession of the centres — it is touching them so as to prepare. The Truth consciousness is the consciousness which lives in the Truth or in constant touch with it and not, as the ordinary mind does, in the Ignorance.

*

The experiences you have are a good starting-point for realisation. They have to develop into the light of a deeper state in which there will be the descent of a higher Consciousness into you. Your present consciousness in which you feel these things is only a preparatory one — in which the Mother works in you through the cosmic power according to your state of consciousness and your karma and in that working both success and failure can come — one has to remain equal-minded to both while trying always for success. A surer guidance can come even in this preparatory consciousness if you are entirely turned towards her alone in such a way that you can feel her direct guidance and follow it without any other influence or force intervening to act upon you, but that condition is not easy to get or keep — it needs a great one-pointedness and constant single-minded dedication. When the higher consciousness will descend, then a closer union, a more intimate consciousness of the Presence and a more illumined intuition will become possible.

*

It is good. The more you keep that dominant sense of the force and the calmness and increase it, the more the other feeling [*of inadequacy and restlessness*] will diminish and fade. It always happens that at first the Power and Peace only press, touch, invade at places, until a time comes when a part of the being always feels in that condition however much disturbance may assail the surface. Afterwards the disturbance is more and more pushed out till it is felt only outside the being, not in it. When that too goes, there is the complete peace and the full foundation.

*

Your letter of today makes it very clear what is happening. The Force that you felt had come down at first, came to open the way for the descent of the higher consciousness into the mind and body. That was why it descended with such force and the difficulty of holding or assimilating it was simply because the body was unaccustomed. But as often happens the Force is preparing its own reception and habituating the body to the descent. Having done that sufficiently it is coming down as a massive peace. The higher consciousness in its descent takes several fundamental forms — peace, power and strength, light, knowledge, Ananda. Usually it is the peace that descends first. This is not a mental, vital or physical peace of the ordinary kind, but something from above (spiritual), very firm, solid and concrete. It is its concreteness that makes you feel like a still massive block — a mass of the higher consciousness in place of the more tenuous substance of the ordinary nature. As for its being worth having, you can see that it is — it is indeed the beginning of the real transformation — all the rest hitherto has been mainly preparation and clearing of difficulties and impediments through all these years. This serene peace and massive stillness has to stabilise itself, fill the whole nature, widen itself until all existence internal and external seems full of it. This may take time, but the beginning once there it is sure to take place, if one is steady and constant. It becomes besides the sure base on which all the rest, — power and strength, light and knowledge, Ananda and divine love, can come in and securely fill the consciousness.

The usual mental means to widen the consciousness is to think of and feel oneself as spreading out into space beyond the body — as a corrective to the thought and feeling of oneself as identified with the body and shut up in it. After a time this leads to a substantial experience of wide consciousness beyond the body. The means to quieten the physical consciousness is to detach oneself from all restless vibrations, not by any struggle or effort but by a simple easy will of quietude. However now that the higher Force is bringing quietude, these mental means may not be necessary — for the peace from above usually brings the wideness of the self — though for some it brings it at once, for others it takes time.

Anyhow, the spiritual opening has been clearly made in you; the rest is a matter of development and time.

The Order of Descent into the Being

It [*the higher consciousness*] enters usually first into the mind, then into the vital and then into the body, because it is these that have to be changed and that is the natural order.

*

Whatever comes from above the head, whether it is Presence, Peace, Ananda, or anything else, normally descends into the head first, then after occupying all the mental centres it comes down into the heart and from there goes down into the vital centres and occupies the whole body. If there is a resistance, it is felt as a weight and a pressure — when the way is open, the pressure disappears and there is only the thing itself. It enters each centre as soon as the way to it is open.

*

The Force usually comes down through the head and afterwards descends lower in the body to the heart, afterwards through the navel downwards.

The sadhak becomes restless under the Force only if he resists it — otherwise it brings peace and calm and happiness and strength.

It is probably some other part of the mind — the vital mind or physical mind — it is these usually that resist.

*

Usually the descent in the head helps to quiet the mind.

*

If you mean the descent of the higher consciousness, that is felt in the heart region, not only in the centre, just as it is felt in the head. The touching of the head is only a first pressure. Afterwards there is a feeling of a mass of peace, force, light, Ananda or consciousness coming down in the head directly and descending further to the chest and so to the navel and through the body. For some it takes weeks or months, in others it descends rapidly.

*

Yes, it was the same experience [*as an earlier one*]. You went inside under the pressure of the Force — which is often though not always the first result — went into a few seconds' samadhi according to the ordinary language. The Force when it descends tries to open the body and pass through the centres. It has to come in (ordinarily) through the crown of the head (Brahmarandhra) and pass through the inner mind centre which is in the middle of the forehead between the eyebrows. That is why it presses first on the head. The opening of the eyes brings one back to the ordinary consciousness of the outer world, that is why the intensity is relieved by opening the eyes.

*

When things come in this order the head opens up first and the heart afterwards — finally all the centres. So what is there to be concerned about?[1] If you are satisfied only with peace, knowledge and mukti, then perhaps the heart centre may open to that only. But if you want the love, then the descending Power and Light will work for that also. So cheer up and don't get into a state of pother with imaginary difficulties.

*

The descent into the body first in the head, then down to the neck and in the chest is the ordinary rule. For many there is a big stop before it gets below the navel owing to some vital resistance. Once it passes that barricade it does not usually take long to come down farther. But there is no rule as to the time taken. In some it comes down like a flood, in others it goes through with a methodical and deliberate increase. I don't think the peace descent is in the habit of waiting for companions — more often it likes at first to be all by itself and then call down its friends with the message, "Come along, I have made the place all ready for you."

*

It is possible that there may have been too much haste in this attempt to open the navel and the lower centre. In this Yoga the movement is downward — first the two head centres, then the heart, then the navel and then the two others. If the higher experience is first fully established with its higher consciousness, knowledge and will in the three upper centres, then it is easier to open the three lower ones without too much disturbance.

The Effect of Descent into the Lower Planes

When a higher force comes down into a lower plane, it is diminished and modified by the inferior substance, lesser power and more mixed movements of that lower plane. Thus, if the Overmind Power works through the illumined mind, only part

---

[1] *The correspondent was concerned that he might receive knowledge but not love since his head centre seemed to be opening before his heart centre. — Ed.*

of its truth and force can manifest and be effective — so much only as can get through this less receptive consciousness. And even what gets through is less true, mixed with other matter, less overmental, more easily modified into something that is part truth, part error. When this diminished indirect Force descends farther down into the mind and vital, it has still something of the Overmind creative Truth in it, but gets very badly mixed with mental and vital formations that disfigure it and make it half effective only, sometimes ineffective.

*

(1) Part of it [*the descending higher consciousness*] is stored up in the frontal consciousness and remains there.

(2) Part of it goes behind and remains as a support to the active part of the being.

(3) Part flows out into the universal Nature.

(4) Part is absorbed by the Inconscient and lost to the individual conscious action.

Chapter Four
The Descent of the Higher Powers

The Descent of Peace, Force, Light, Ananda

The descent of Peace, the descent of Force or Power, the descent of Light, the descent of Ananda, these are the four things that transform the nature.

*

Light, Peace, Force, Ananda constitute the spiritual consciousness; if they are not among the major experiences, what are?

*

Presence, Peace, Force, Light, Ananda, these are five things that most commonly come down.

*

The being is not supposed to remain always empty. When the calm and peace of the pure existence is established, Force also has to descend as well as Light, Ananda and other things.

*

Wideness is only the first step — there must be the descent of light, knowledge, peace, force or power and the settling of these things and their constant development.

*

There is no rule, but the most normal course is for a certain Peace and Force and Light which is above the mind to descend and as the result of its workings the cosmic consciousness opens and in it higher and higher levels above mind. Many people get an opening into the cosmic consciousness first but without the basis of the higher Peace and Light it brings only a mass of unorganised experiences.

*

It is not really the plane that descends, it is the Power and Truth of it that descends into the material and then the veil between the material and it no longer exists.

Peace, Calm, Quiet as a Basis for the Descent

Peace and movement on the basis of peace are the first aspects of the One to establish themselves. Bliss and light do not fix so easily or so early — they have to grow.

*

The Peace, Purity and Calm of the Self must be fixed — otherwise the active Descent may find the forces it awakes seized on by lower Powers and a confusion created. That has happened with many.

*

It is not a matter of any particular act or feeling, but a sort of excited vibration with which the vital and physical consciousness meets the vital disturbance — it is evident in the tone and language of what you write when there is the stress of vital suggestion — but it used also to rise when you got the experiences in an excited vibration and bubbling of joy which would easily lapse into some rajasic movement or be replaced by the opposite excitement of suffering and disturbance. Quiet, quiet and more quiet, calm strength, calm gladness are what are needed in mind and nerves and body as a basis for the siddhi — precisely because the Force, the Light, the Ananda that come down are extremely intense and need a great stillness in the being to bear and support them.

*

It is the right fundamental consciousness that you have now got. The tamas and other movements of the lower universal Nature are bound to try to come in, but if one has the calm of the inner being which makes them felt as something external to the being, and the light of the psychic which instantly exposes and rejects them, then that is to have the true consciousness which keeps one safe while the more positive transformation is preparing or taking place.

That transformation comes by the descent of the Force, Light, Knowledge, Ananda etc. from above. So you are right in your feeling that you should open with a quiet *śānta samāhita* aspiration or invocation for the descent of the Light from above. Only it must be an aspiration in this calm and wideness, not disturbing it in the least — and you must be prepared for the result being not immediate — it may be rapid, but also it may take some time.

*

Yes, when things begin to descend, they must come down on a solid basis. That is why it is necessary to have peace as the first descent and that it should become as strong and solid as possible. But in any case to contain is the first necessity — then more and more can come and settle itself. Once these two things are settled — peace and strength, one can bear any amount of everything else, Ananda, Knowledge, or whatever it may be.

*

The experience of this "solid block" feeling indicates the descent of a solid strength and peace into the external being, — but into the vital physical most. It is this always that is the foundation, the sure basis into which all else (Ananda, light, knowledge, bhakti) can descend in the future and stand on it or play safely. The numbness was there in the other experience because the movement was inward; but here the Yogashakti is coming *outward* into the fully awake external nature, — as a first step towards the establishment of the Yoga and its experiences there. So the numbness, which was a sign of the consciousness tending to draw back from the external parts, is not there.

*

It is good — the strength is the next thing that has to come down after the peace and join with it. Eventually the two become one.

The Descent of Peace

When one has gone so far that peace from above can descend, that is a considerable progress.

*

Yes, surely the peace can come into the outer consciousness also; it is meant to do so. It is perfectly possible for the body to bear the peace and stillness. It is more difficult for it to bear the full play of the Force; but if the peace is first established in it, then there is no difficulty of that kind.

*

It [*peace*] has to be brought down to the heart and navel first. That gives it a certain kind of inner stability — though not absolute. There is no method other than aspiration, a strong quiet will and a rejection of all that is not turned towards the Divine in those parts into which you call the peace — here the emotional and higher vital.

*

They [*the mind and vital*] are always more open to the universal forces than the material. But they can be more restless than the material so long as they are not subjected to the peace from above.

*

The movement of universality by itself cannot prevent the vital from disturbing — it is the complete surrender and the complete descent of peace into all the being down to the most material that can do it.

*

Nobody said that you should not take the higher being as a first station. The question was about enforcing the peace of the higher being in the lower parts down to the physical so as to (1) create that separateness which would prevent the inner being from being affected by the superficial disturbance and resistance, (2) make it easier for the force and other powers of the higher being to descend.

*

Peace can be brought down into the physical to its very cells. It is the active transformation of the physical that cannot be *completely* done without the supramental descent.

*

The peace that descends from above can stop the lower action, if it settles in all the being. But that is not sufficient if one wants to develop the dynamic side of the being also on the lines of Yoga.

*

After the body is accustomed to the peace, the peace itself can become dynamic.

The Descent of Silence

What is trying to come down in you is the silence and peace of the Self — when that comes fully, then there is no ego-perception, it is drowned in the wideness of the silence and peace of the Self. But this realisation is at first in the static condition of the Self only — in the dynamic movements the ego may still be there owing to past habits — but each time an ego-movement is abandoned, the sense of the loss of ego becomes deeper and more complete. It is perhaps some impression of what is trying to come that has touched you.

*

It must have been the descent of the higher silence, the silence of the Self or Atman. In this silence one perceives, but the mind is not active, — things are sensed, but without any responsive connection or vibration. The silent Self is there as a separate reality, not bound or involved in the activity of Nature, aloof, detached and self-existent. Even if thoughts come across this silence, they do not disturb it; the Self is separate from the thinking mind also. In this connection the feeling "I think" is a survival from the old consciousness; in the full silence what one feels is "thought occurs in me" — the identification with thoughts as well as with the perception of objects ceases.

*

To still the mind *absolutely* is not so easy. It can be done usually only by the descent of the Silence from above and even then it is not complete until the whole system has been occupied by the higher silence and peace.

*

It is the silence and calm of the higher consciousness pressing down into the body. When it comes down fully then there is the "still statue" feeling at first. Afterwards the calm or silence becomes free and normal.

*

It is the wideness and silence of the being which makes transformation possible, because the lower movements disappear and in the emptiness the Truth from above can descend.

*

Who told you that whenever there was silence or genuine silence knowledge would come down? The silence is a fit vessel for anything from above, but it does not follow that when there is silence, everything is bound to come down automatically.

*

In what may be called the first silence, it is like that — silence alone with no emotion or other inner activity. When it deepens one can feel the Nirvana of the Buddhists or the Atmabodha of the Vedantins. Both force and bliss or either can descend into the silence, filling it with calm Tapas or silent Ananda.

The Descent of Force or Power

The experiences you have had are very clear evidence that you have the capacity for Yoga. The first decisive experiences in this Yoga are a calm and peace that is felt, first somewhere in the being and in the end in all the being, and the descent of a Power and Force into the body which will take up the whole adhar and work in it to transform mind, life and body into the instrumentation of the Divine Consciousness. The two experiences of which you wrote in your letter are the beginning of this calm and the descent of this Force. Much has to be done before they can be established or persistently effective, but that they should come at this stage is a clear proof of capacity to receive. It must be remembered however that the Yoga is not easy and cannot be done without the rising of many obstacles and much lapse of time — so if you take it up it must be with a firm resolve to carry it through to the end with a whole-hearted sincerity, faith, patience and courage.

*

It is the Mother's force that descended to work in the system. There are two things that have to be established in order to make a foundation for the workings of the sadhana in the waking consciousness, 1st a descent of Peace from above, 2nd a descent of the Force. If one has these two things permanently established in the consciousness, then one has the basis.

*

By Force I mean not mental or vital energy but the Divine Force from above — as peace comes from above and wideness also, so does this Force (Shakti). Nothing, not even thinking or meditating can be done without some action of Force. The Force I speak of is a Force for illumination, transformation, purification, all that has to be done in the Yoga, for removal of the hostile forces and the wrong movements — it is also of course for external work, whether great or small in appearance does not matter — if that is part of the Divine Will. I do not mean any personal force egoistic or rajasic.

*

Yes, it [*the Force*] is quite concrete. Usually at first it descends of itself from time to time — and also one calls it in face of a difficulty. But eventually it is always there supporting or determining all the action of the being.

*

The Force comes down as soon as it finds an opening and acts in the Adhara whenever it is ready. What determines the descent cannot always be mentally fixed. Aspiration, call, will, prayer, etc. create a favourable precondition in the head or heart or anywhere else and are sometimes the determining cause.

*

What you feel in the head is probably the first conscious descent into the body of the divine Force from above. Up to now it must have been working unfelt by you from behind the heart. If the concentration takes place naturally in the head you must allow it to do so, but the possibility of this has been prepared by the previous concentration in the heart, so that also need not be discontinued unless the force working in you insists on the upper concentration only. Aspiration can be continued in the same way until the conduct of the sadhana by the Mother's power is clearly felt and becomes to you the normal thing.

*

The experience you had was simply the descent of the Divine Force into the body. By your attitude and aspiration you called for it to work in you, so it came. Such a descent brings naturally a deep inward condition and a silence of the mind, and it may bring much more — peace, a sense of liberation, happiness, Ananda. It is very often attended as in this experience by a light or luminosity. It was felt enveloping the upper part of the body down to the cardiac centre, because it is these centres, the head and heart centres that are first invaded and occupied by whatever descends from above, Consciousness, Force, Light or Ananda. Usually, there is at first a pressure from above on the head, then one feels something entering the higher part of the head and then the whole head is occupied, as you feel now with the *fourmillement* at the time of concentration. Once the head with its mental centres is open and occupied, the Force descends rapidly to the heart centre, unless there is some obstacle or a resistance in the higher vital parts. From there it sends its stream into the whole body and begins to occupy the vital and physical centres — from the navel to the Muladhara. The coming of this experience, occupation of the body by the Force from above, is a great step forward in the sadhana.

The fear of a syncope was due only to the sanskara in the mind; it must be dismissed. The Force can very well come down in the full waking consciousness; if it brings a kind of samadhi, it is usually a conscious inner condition — the consciousness taken away from outward things, but in full power within. Even if a trance came, it would be a trance and not a swoon.

*

The good condition of openness with the Force descending and the constant remembrance — or whatever other form the condition takes — is the beginning of the true consciousness and its duration is always short at the beginning, because the ordinary consciousness is not accustomed to it, but to something else. But it always increases in duration and power until it is able to maintain itself even when the outer consciousness is occupied with other things. At first it remains there as something behind which emerges as soon as the outer preoccupation ends; afterwards it remains behind, but as something just felt, and in a later stage it is always there, so that there are two consciousnesses, the inner consciousness always connected with the Mother and full of her working or her presence or both and the surface consciousness occupied with outer things. Finally, even the surface consciousness begins to feel the direct connection in action itself. One need not mind if there are intervals when the true condition is not there. It does not prove that you are unfit; it is only a period in which what is not yet changed comes up to be worked upon and prepared for change. When the inner consciousness is well established, then these periods take place only in the surface consciousness and are no longer troublesome as before.

P. S. Probably the difficulty you feel is in the externalising mind the centre of which is in the throat. When there is no resistance there, the Force comes down to the heart level and below.

*

As for the dynamic descent, you say that the Force has descended to your forehead (inner mind) centre. It seems to be very slow in coming through. It has to come down to the heart centre and below before it can begin to be fully effective. Probably there must be something either in the physical mental (throat) or the emotional vital that obstructs the descent. That may be the reason of the union of the upper Agni and the psychic fire and the push on the psychic centre — something is trying to remove the difficulty.

*

The Power above the head is of course the Mother's — it is the power of the Higher Consciousness which is preparing its way of descent. This Higher Consciousness carrying in it a sense of wide and boundless existence, light, power, peace, Ananda etc. is always there above the head and when something of the spiritual Force comes down to work upon the nature, it is from there that it comes. But nothing like the full descent of the peace, bliss etc. can come so long as the being is not ready. Very usually the first preparation is to work on the mind and vital and physical nature in such a way that the soul, the psychic being can have a chance of manifesting itself and influencing the rest of the nature; for that purpose all the main darknesses in the mind and vital have to be combated and thrown out and the physical also prepared in an initial way so that the descent may be possible. This is what has been done so long in you. It has to be made stronger and more complete; but sufficient has been done for it to be possible to prepare the descent of the higher consciousness. There are two things that take place; an ascent of one's consciousness to the higher levels in and above the head, and a descent of the higher consciousness which is above into one's mind, vital and body. How it is done or by what stages or how long it will take varies with each person. But this new consciousness is very different from the ordinary one and many things happen in its coming which would not happen to the mind and might seem strange to it — e.g. the dissolution of the ego and the opening into a wider self or spirit not limited by the body, to which the body is only a small instrument and nothing more. One must therefore dismiss all fear of new things and accept with calm and confidence each field of new experience, relying on the Divine Mother-Force for guidance and support and protection throughout the change.

*

The sadhana is a difficult one and time should not be grudged; it is only in the last stages that a very great and constant rapidity of progress can be confidently expected. As for Shakti, the descent of Shakti before the vital is pure and surrendered, has its dangers. It is better for him to pray for purification, knowledge, intensity of the heart's aspiration and as much working of the Power as he can bear and assimilate.

*

Power can be everywhere, on any plane. What descends from above is power of the higher Consciousness — but there is a Power of the vital, mental, physical planes also. Power is not a special characteristic of the psychic or of the spiritual plane.

The Descent of Fire

The fire is the divine fire of aspiration and inner tapasya. When the fire descends again and again with increasing force and magnitude into the darkness of human ignorance, it at first seems swallowed up and absorbed in the darkness, but more and more of the descent changes the darkness into light, the ignorance and unconsciousness of the human mind into spiritual consciousness.

The Descent of Light

The descent of the Light producing a concrete illumination of the consciousness is always one of the decisive experiences of the sadhana.

*

You can tell her that Light like peace is one of the things that come down from the higher consciousness. It is the light of the Truth that is there — it is sometimes golden, sometimes white, sometimes blue of various shades, sometimes sunlight.

*

It is a true experience and the Light that you felt is the Light of the Truth from above. These things indicate that there is already an opening, but it takes time to become constant and complete. That always happens at first — there are periods in which the consciousness or something in it opens, there are others in which the opening is clouded until something more opens. This goes on until the whole consciousness has been sufficiently worked upon for the full opening and lasting experience to be there.

*

These are special forces of the Light and there is a play of them according to need, but the Light in itself can be lived in as much as one can live in Peace or Ananda.[1] As Peace and Ananda can pour through the whole system and fully stabilise themselves so that they are in the body and the body and the whole being are in them — one might almost say, are that, are the Peace and Ananda — so it can be with Light. It can pour into the body, make every cell luminous, fix itself and surround on all sides in one constant mass of Light.

*

---

[1] *The correspondent asked how one can "live in" the different forces of the Light such as the white light of the Mother, the pale blue light of Sri Aurobindo, the golden light of the Truth and the pink light of the psychic. — Ed.*

It depends upon the colour of the Light. In any case it is the light of a Force from above. All lights are indications of a Force or Power. It is the work of the Lights and the Forces they represent to act in their descent on the lower nature and change it.

The Descent of Knowledge

The knowledge comes from above like the light and peace and everything else. As the consciousness progresses, it comes from a higher and higher level. First it is the higher or illumined mind that predominates, then the intuition, next the overmind, lastly the supermind; but the whole consciousness has to be sufficiently transformed before the supramental knowledge can begin to come.

The Descent of Wideness

Like everything else, peace, Light, Power, so wideness descends.

*

Ananda comes afterwards — even if it comes at the beginning it is not usually constant. Wideness does not come because the consciousness is not yet free from the body. Probably when what is felt above the head comes down, it will be liberated into the wideness.

The Descent of Ananda

It is quite possible that if a too intense Ananda is allowed before the purity and peace are in the nature, it may disturb the system — though I don't know whether there is any instance of madness as a consequence. At any rate it is a fact that normally Ananda comes (in the natural course, I mean, if not pulled down) only occasionally so long as the peace and purity are not there as a base. It is probably right that it should be so.

*

You are dealing in the right way with the sex feeling. As to why it rose when you were using the name there are two reasons. One is that when you use the name, it is the Mother's power that you call there and the first result often is that the difficulty rises like a snake whose head is touched to resist the pressure or — if you look at it from another point of view — it rises to be dealt with. The other is that when what is to be brought down is the Ananda — of the force, light etc., but especially of the love — then the vital-physical passion rises up to try and mix with and get hold of the Ananda hoping to turn it to a sort of sublimated vital pleasure. It is well known that this happens to Vaishnavas very often when they do the Sankirtan. In your case it is probably the first reason, because the love-Ananda or any other is not yet coming, so that explanation is improbable. As for the Force descending into the head, it has two sides to it — one is peace and when that is prominent, there is the sense of coolness; when there is a strong dynamic action instead, the feeling may be of heat, Agni-power. Most people feel these two things; they are not imagination.

*

I did not say it [*a descent of Ananda*] was vital and mental, but that it was Ananda manifesting itself in the mental and vital — a quite different thing — for the one Ananda (the true thing) can manifest in any part of the being.

The Flow of Amrita

It [*a flow of sweet liquid in the mouth*] is a form of the flow of Ananda from above — when it takes a quite physical form the Yogins call it Amrita.

*

Sudhā is nectar or Amrita, the food or drink of the gods. It is applied in Yoga to something that flows down from the Brahmarandhra into the palate when there is strong concentration. But this is psychological, so it must be the psychic sweetness flowing into the system.

Chapter Five

Descent and Other Kinds of Experience

Descent and Experiences of the Inner Being

It is good that you felt the peace within and the movement in the heart. That shows the force is working not only from above but inside you, and this promises a farther progress. The full opening will come in time — the important thing is that you are on the right way and advancing more quickly than you realise.

*

Your experiences seem to be sound. The first is that of the higher (Yogic or spiritual) consciousness coming down into the body from above the head. It is felt often like a current flowing through the head into the whole body and the first thing it brings is a descent of peace. One result of this descent is that one feels an inner being in oneself which is detached from the outer action, supports it from behind, but is not involved in it — that is the second experience. The third about the sleep is also felt when one has confidence in the Mother and goes to sleep under her protection, as if in her lap, surrounded by her presence. As for the dream the legs indicate the physical consciousness which is still under a double pull, one upward to the higher consciousness so that the physical consciousness may unite itself with the spiritual, the other downward towards the lower consciousness. The looking towards me indicates the choice of the being for the upward movement.

*

The Power and Peace that come down come down from the higher consciousness above your head, from a greater self of which your mind, the human mind generally, is unaware. They are the power and peace of the Divine. When they envelop you from outside the body (therefore you feel them external), it is as a protection and an atmosphere. But also they descend into the body, into the head (mind), heart and navel (vital) and through the whole body working in you and doing what is necessary to change the consciousness. When you do not feel it there, when you feel it only as external, it is because you are very much in the external physical consciousness — but in reality it is there in your inner being working in you. When you recover the inner consciousness, you feel it again within and it wakes in you your own true consciousness, the psychic — and it is only the psychic that gives faith and devotion. It is however a great progress if, even when in the external physical consciousness, you feel the Peace enveloping you.

Descent and Psychic Experiences

The infinite calm you felt coming down was the calm of the Divine Consciousness — the higher or spiritual consciousness above the head, which descends as the higher parts of the being open to it. The experience of faith, love or aspiration come from the psychic being. It is when the psychic being is in front and governs all the nature and the Higher Consciousness descends through an open mind, vital and physical that the transformation of the nature begins to take place. The opposite experience of dryness, despair etc. comes from the resistance of the ordinary lower nature (lower vital, physical consciousness, especially). This resistance is to be got rid of — and one condition of that is never to indulge the desires of the lower vital and the body. You must turn them on the contrary wholly to the Divine.

*

The descent of the Silence is not usually associated with sadness, though it does bring a feeling of calm detachment, unconcern and wide emptiness, but in this emptiness there is a sense of ease, freedom, peace. The absorption as if something were drawing deep from within is evidently the pull of the inmost being, the psychic. There is a psychic sadness often when this inmost soul opens and feels how far the nature and the world are from what they should be, but this is a sweet and quiet sorrow, not distressing. It must be something in the mind and vital which is not yet awake to what has happened within you and gives this colour of dissatisfied and distressed seeking.

*

It is only by peace and light coming down there [*into the subconscious*] and by the rule of the psychic being over the physical that the subconscious parts of the being can be changed entirely. Before that only a certain control can be established.

*

Your description of the solid cool block of peace pressing on the body and making it immobile makes it certain that it is what we call in this Yoga the descent of the higher consciousness. A deep, intense or massive substance of peace and stillness is very commonly the first of its powers that descends and many experience it in that way. At first it comes and stays only during meditation or, without the sense of physical inertness or immobility, a little while longer and afterwards is lost; but if the sadhana follows its normal course, it comes more and more, lasting longer, and in the end an enduring deep peace and inner stillness and release becomes a normal character of the consciousness, the foundation indeed of a new consciousness, calm and liberated.

Your idea of the psychic is certainly a mental construction which should be avoided. The psychic has indeed the quality of peace — but that is not its main character as it is of the Self or Atman. The psychic is the Divine element in the individual being and its characteristic power is to turn everything towards the Divine, to bring a fire of purification, aspiration, devotion, true light of discernment, feeling, will, action which transforms by degrees the whole nature. Quietude, peace and silence in the heart and therefore in the vital part of the being are necessary to reach the psychic, to plunge in it, for the perturbations of the vital nature, desire, emotion turned ego-wards or world-wards are the main part of the screen that hides the soul from the nature. It is better therefore to be free from the mental constructions when you take the plunge and have only the sense of aspiration, of devotion, of self-giving to the Divine.

*

Yes, it is a very encouraging progress. If you keep the wideness and calm as you are keeping it and also the love for the Mother in the heart, then all is safe — for it means the double foundation of the Yoga — the descent of the higher consciousness with its peace, freedom and security from above and the openness of the psychic which keeps all the effort or all the spontaneous movement turned towards the true goal.

Descent and Other Experiences

The more important of the experiences you enumerate are those below.

(1) The feeling of calm and comparative absence of disturbing thoughts. This means the growth of quietude of mind which is necessary for a fully effective meditation.

(2) The pressure on the head and the movements within it. The pressure is that of the Force of the higher consciousness above the mind pressing on the mind (the mind centres are in the head and throat) and penetrating into it. Once it enters there it prepares the mind for opening to it more fully and the movements within the head are due to this working. Once the head centres and spaces are open one feels it descending freely as a current or otherwise. Afterwards it opens similarly the centres below in the body. The physical movement of the head must be due to the body not being accustomed to the pressure and penetration of the Force. When it is able to receive and assimilate, these movements no longer take place.

(3) The effect of the meditation in the heart extending itself to the head and creating movements there is normal — in whatever centre the concentration takes place the Yoga force

generated extends to the others and produces concentration or workings there.

(4) The sudden cessation of thought and all movements — this is very important, as it means the beginning of the capacity for the inner silence. It lasts only for a short while at the beginning of its manifestation but increases afterwards its hold and duration.

The direction of the sadhana is the right one and you have only to continue upon it.

We cannot say anything definitively about the outside affairs — I suppose in the circumstances you have to think about these things, but the sadhana has the greater importance.

We do not include Hathayoga practices in this sadhana. If you use only for health purposes, it must be as something separate from sadhana — on your own choice.

*

The last experience carries its own meaning. The first is a dream-experience in which the figures of the dream are probably symbols, — unless the Tibetan priest is an impression from a past life. The experience itself is that of concentration in a flame of aspiration with the result of an ascension into the higher planes of consciousness where the separative self disappears into the universal. The second is an experience of the descent of the higher consciousness through the spinal cord from the mental to the vital centres with the result of a momentary experience of that higher consciousness in its wide universality. The experience once had repeated itself but always with the same momentariness. It is the permanence of this experience that is in this Yoga the foundation of the spiritual consciousness and the spiritual transformation — as distinguished from the psychic which proceeds from the inner heart.

*

They are elementary experiences in the practice of Yoga and there is not much to be said about them, — still I will say this much, if it can help him.

(1) What does he mean by concentrating in the heart? I suppose not the physical heart? When we speak of concentrating in the heart in Yoga, we are speaking of the emotional centre and that like all the others is in the middle of the body in a line corresponding to the spinal cord. The places he speaks of are four centres — (1) crown of head = higher mental centre, (2) between the eyebrows = centre of will and vision, (3) throat = centre of externalising mind, (4) heart = (mental-vital) emotional centre with the psychic behind it (the soul, Purusha in the heart).

(2) The lights he sees indicate not some mere "physiological" phenomenon, but the first opening of an inner subtle vision which sees things that are not physical. At a later stage a descent of Light is one of the capital phenomena of the opening of the greater Yogic experience and of the working of the Divine Power on the adhar.

(3) What does he mean by chitta when he speaks of the force? Chitta as opposed to Chit or Vijnana etc. is only the basic mind-life consciousness out of which rises the stuff of (ordinary) thought, feelings, sensations etc. The Force which he feels is something quite different; it is the larger force exceeding the individual and when one feels it in its fullness, it is experienced as the cosmic force or something out of the cosmic force or else the Divine Force from above, according to its nature. His mind is not yet ready for the action of a greater Force, because it is full of mental notions and activities and it is for this reason that heat is generated in the friction between the two; when the other force withdraws and no longer tries to lay hold of the brain then the personal mind-action feels released (that is the reason for the sense of coolness) and goes about its ordinary motions. It is only in a silent (quiet — not necessarily empty) mind that the greater force can be received and work upon the system without too much reaction and resistance.

Chapter Six
Feelings and Sensations in the Process of Descent

Sensations in the Inner Centres

It [*a pressure felt in meditation*] is what we call the pressure of the Force (the Force of the higher spiritual or divine consciousness, the Mother's Force); it comes in various forms, vibrations, currents, waves, a wide flow, a shower like rain etc. It passes to each centre in turn, the crown of the head, the forehead centre, throat, heart, navel centres down to the Muladhara and spreads too throughout the body.

The rotatory movement is the movement of the Force when it is working and forming something in the being.

*

Pressure, throbbing, electrical vibrations are all signs of the working of the Force. The places indicate the field of action — the top of the head is the summit of the thinking mind where it communicates with the higher consciousness; the neck or throat is the seat of the physical, externalising or expressive mind; the ear is the place of communication with the inner mind centre by which thoughts etc. enter into the personal being from the general Nature. The sternum at the point indicated[1] holds the psychic and emotional centre, with its apex on the spinal column behind.

Pressure

When the Force comes down one at first feels a pressure. Afterwards it begins to enter the body, when once the way is open

---

[1] *The correspondent wrote that she felt electrical vibrations in the backbone at a point in the chest parallel to the bottom of the sternum.* — Ed.

for it. After entering the body it goes on working each time it descends, for the transformation of the nature.

*

This pressure on the head always comes at the beginning; it is the pressure of the Force on the adhar preparing to make its way into it. The feeling lasts so long as there is a resistance in the adhar to the entrance and working of the Force. If the mind opens to the Power, it will cease and you will feel the Power working in you or within you.

*

Tell him that the pressure on the head is a sign of the descent and working of the Force from above and of a certain resistance in the adhar which almost all sadhaks have at first. The calm is the result of the working. When the resistance disappears, the pressure is no longer felt but one becomes conscious of the working and of the calm descending into the body from centre to centre.

*

The pressure is that of the Divine Force which he calls by his prayer descending to do its work in the Adhar, its passage being marked by the current which he feels. The pain was due to some resistance in the Adhar; it disappears as soon as the system is accustomed to the descent and grows wide enough to admit it. The first result of the descent is the calm which he experiences; for it is only in a calm mind and vital (*manaḥ-prāṇa*) that the Divine Shakti can do her work rightly.

*

When there is a pressure of the Force on the Adhar to work on it or enter, this [*feeling of heaviness in the head*] is often felt, especially if there is a working of the Force in the head. This heaviness disappears if the system receives and assimilates the Force and there is a free flow in the body — till then the pressure or some kind of heaviness is often felt at one centre or another where the Force is working.

*

If it is only a weight or pressure on the head, it may be only the pressure of the Mother's Force. It comes like that to most people. Once the consciousness is open and the Force enters, there is no longer this feeling.

*

It is the pressure of the higher consciousness (planes of blue light beyond the ordinary mind) that has come down and is pressing upon the resistances down to the body and below. At the same time the weight of the subconscient Matter is being lifted up for release. That is the sense of these experiences.

*

A heaviness which gives strength is likely to be the indication of a descent. Sensations like a biting or pricking in the head often accompany it. It is usually a sign of some force from above trying to make its way through or to work in the physical stuff so as to prepare it for receiving.

*

That is some obstacle in the mind breaking under the pressure of Force, and each time there is a flash and a movement of the Force.

*

All that you note in your letter is very encouraging; it shows that the force is working in you and in the right way. There are two things that are necessary — the full connection of your mind and vital with your psychic being and the opening of the consciousness to Mother's consciousness above. Both of these are beginning. The voice that spoke was that of your soul, your psychic being; the impulse to go deep within was the movement to plunge into the depths of the psychic. The consciousness that rejected and threw away the anger and old movements was also that of the psychic.

The pressure you felt on the head comes always when there is the pressure from above of the Higher Consciousness, the Mother's consciousness, to come in and the coolness etc. you felt are also often felt at that time. The first result was the detachment from personal connections, the freedom, lightness, openness of heart, fearlessness, and also the sense of the Mother's presence. These things are signs of the true consciousness and part of the spiritual nature. They come first as experiences, afterwards they become more frequent, endure longer, settle into the nature.

*

It is the pressure of the Divine Power which you are feeling and it is that which gives you the sense of joy and living fullness. If you keep it and allow it to work in you, it will give you the positive experience and progress in sadhana which you need.

*

The pressure is usually felt only when the Force is acting on the consciousness in order to create an opening somewhere or for some other purpose. As soon as that is done, the pressure is not felt but instead a changed condition or else the working of the Force within but without any sense of pressure. When the condition of lightness, quietude, etc. comes, it means that something has opened to the psychic consciousness and become full of it. Emptiness is of several kinds, one when the consciousness is empty and free, which is a very good condition, another when it is empty and neutral, i. e. simply quiet without any positive power or psychic happiness, but not troubled or disturbed by anything, without any good or bad movement, and, finally, tamasic or inert emptiness. The first two conditions can be brought about by an action of the Force, and the first is a very good basis for spiritual experience and progress; the second also is not unfavourable and is often a needed stage, the consciousness becoming empty in order that it may be filled from within or from above with the true things. The third comes usually when the vital is quiescent and there is a complete inertia.

It is one of the two first that must be coming in you as a result of the action of the Force.

*

If the pressure is too great, the remedy is to widen the consciousness. With the peace and silence there should come a wideness that can receive any amount of Force without any reactions, whether heaviness or compulsion to remain withdrawn or the difficulty of the eyes etc.

*

The action of the Force does not always create a pressure. When it does not need to press, it acts quietly.

*

There is no necessity of feeling pressure. One feels force when something is being done or the force is flowing in or if it is there manifest in the body — but not when what is manifesting is peace and silence.

Perforation

If it is a feeling of a covering being perforated, then that is a sensation one often has when the Force is opening a way for itself through some resistance — here it must be in some part of the physical mind.
Keep full reliance on the Mother. When one does that, the victory even if delayed, is sure.

Vibration

An entire silence and inactivity of the mind cannot come at first — what is possible is a quietude of the mind, that is to say, a cessation of its absorption in its restless miscellaneous activity of ill-connected or unconnected thoughts and a concentration on the object of the sadhana. The imagination which the Mother recommended to you was a means of such concentration. A mental idea of the omnipresence such as comes to you is a good help for that also, especially if it brings the strong faith and reliance. The feeling of the vibration of the Mother's Force around the head is more than a mental idea or even a mental realisation, it is an experience. This vibration is indeed the action of the Mother's Force which is first felt above the head or around it, then afterwards within the head. The pressure means that it is working to open the mind and its centres so that it may enter. The mind centres are in the head, one at the top and above it, another between the eyes, a third in the throat. That is why you feel the vibration around the head and sometimes up to the neck, but not below. It is so usually, for it is only after enveloping and entering the mind that it goes below to the emotional and vital parts (heart, navel etc.) — though sometimes it is more enveloping before it enters the body. To see the light in the heart one has to go deep, but one can see light elsewhere without going in deep there. Light is often seen between the eyebrows first or in front at that level, for there is the centre of inner vision and a slight opening of it is sufficient for that — so also light is often seen round the head or above it, outside.

*

If it was a Light, you would see the Light. Vibrations are either of a Force or a Presence.

Electricity

Electricity shock always indicates a passage of dynamic Force.

*

It [*the sensation of an electric current in the spine*] is the flowing of the force through the spine. In the Tantric system the spine is considered as the natural passage of the Force, because it is in the spine that all the six centres rest.

Waves

Whatever comes from above can come like that in waves — whether it is Light or Force or Peace or Ananda. In your case it was the Force working on the mind in waves. It is true also that when it was like that, not in currents or as a rain or as a quiet flood, it is Mahakali's Force that is working. The first necessity when it is so, is not to fear.

Flow or Stream

The descent of the Consciousness from above is often felt as a flow of water. Also the image of the drilling open of the head to receive it is frequent (it symbolises the opening of the mind to the higher consciousness).

*

The stream which you feel coming down on the head and pouring into you is indeed a current of the Mother's Force; it is so that it is often felt; it flows into the body in currents and works there to liberate and change the consciousness. As the consciousness changes and develops, you will begin yourself to understand the meaning and working of these things.

*

The quiet flow is necessary for permeating the lower parts. The big descents open the way and bring constant reinforcement and the culminating force at the end — but the quiet flow is also needed.

Drizzle or Shower

I am glad to hear that these experiences are coming — they are a sign of rapid progress coming. The descent as of a drizzling rain is a very characteristic and well-known way of descent of the higher Consciousness; it brings peace but it also brings all other possibilities of the higher Consciousness too and, as you felt, the seeds of transformation of the physical consciousness — by the coming in it of the seeds of the powers and qualities of the higher Nature.

*

I am very glad that the experience we have been working to bring to you has come with such force and is increasing. It is the concrete descent of the higher consciousness, which once it settles marks always a definite turning-point in the sadhana. Even if it does not settle with a full stability at once, yet when it has once come with so much strength, there cannot be the least doubt that it will come more and more till it has done its work and is your permanent consciousness. The shower and drizzle, the hold[2] above the head and in the heart, the envelopment, the flaming of Agni within, the sense of firmness and solidity, the Peace and security and devotion, the sense of the Mother's hold are all signs of the descent — eventually it will penetrate everywhere and become something solid and stable occupying the whole consciousness and body.

Coolness

The coolness is always a quieting force making for peace.

*

This coolness [*felt in a passage rising from the heart to the head and then above it*] very often comes with the peace from above. If the passage is felt going up above the head, it means that there is now a direct communication with the higher Consciousness, the necessary opening having been made.

*

The coolness comes when the Force descends with peace and harmony into the vital and the body.

*

---

[2] *The correspondent felt "as if held in a hand of the Power". — Ed.*

A sensation of coolness indicates usually some touch or descent of peace. It is felt as very cold by the human vital because the latter is always in a fever of restlessness.

*

Pleasant coolness or coldness usually indicates a pacifying force bringing down calm or release. Knee to toe = the field of physical material consciousness.

*

If the coolness passed into dullness, it may well have been only physical. But perhaps there was an inflow, only afterwards came a reaction of the lower inertia which is the physical Nature's characteristic retort to peace and quietude. When the inertia comes up the old movements which the subconscient is prepared to supply always can mechanically come up with it. In a certain sense this inertia and the peace are the bright and dark counterparts of each other, tamas and *śama* — the higher Nature finding repose in peace, the lower seeking it in a relaxation of energy and a return towards the subconscient, tamas.

*

The coolness is a very common experience, but the cool smell is unusual. Sometimes people get a fragrance but without this close connection — perhaps they do not observe closely.

Stoniness

The feeling of stoniness is very usually a first impression in the body of the stillness in the cells which comes with the downflow of the Peace.

Sound

A sound[3] does sometimes come with a particular descent of the

---

[3] *In this case the correspondent heard the faint sound of dhum ... dhum ... dhum.* — Ed.

consciousness or force from above.

*

Your experience while going to the lawyers was an opening to the Force from above which, if sudden, is often attended by this kind of loud sound and the sensation of the opening of the head — it is in the subtle body that this opening of the head takes place though the sensation is felt as if physical. The Force came down and went up presided over by the Mother's forms of Mahalakshmi and Mahasaraswati and made the movement of ascent and descent (here in the spinal column which is the main channel of the Yogic force passing through the centres) which helps to join the higher with the lower consciousness. As a result came the feeling of identity with myself in your body. The cough shows probably some difficulty against concentration in the physical mind. The best is not to force concentration, but to remain quiet and call and let things work themselves out through the force of the Mother.

Chapter Seven
Difficulties Experienced in the Process of Descent

Alternations in the Intensity of the Force

Sometimes the descent comes with great force in order to open something, afterwards it becomes more quiet and normal until the consciousness is ready for a more sustained descent.

*

There are always alternations in the intensity of the Force at its work. It comes with great power and effects something that had to be done; then it is either concealed or retires a little or is felt but from behind a screen as you say, while something comes up that has to be prepared for illumination and then it comes in front again and does what has to be done there. But formerly while the support, help, even the deeper consciousness was always there, as you now rightly feel, yet when a veil fell, then it was all forgotten and you felt as if there was nothing but darkness and confusion. This happens to most sadhaks in the earlier stages. It is a great progress, a decisive advance if, at the time when the Force is working from behind the screen, you feel that it is there, that the help and support, the more enlightened consciousness is there still; this is a second stage in the sadhana. The third is when there is no screen and the Force and all else are always felt whether actively working or pausing during a transition.

The Need of Assimilation

When a new consciousness comes down, it is not possible at first to keep it all the time — the former consciousness has to get accustomed and receive and assimilate it, and that takes time.

*

It [*the need to rest*] may be simply the need of assimilation in the body. To remain quiet for a time after a descent of Force is the best way of assimilating it.

*

If the peace once becomes stable, there is no farther assimilation needed for that, as that means the whole system is sufficiently prepared to receive and absorb continuously. There may be periods of assimilation necessary for other things, but these periods need not interrupt the inner status. For instance if Force or Ananda or Knowledge begin to descend from above, there might be interruptions and probably would be, the system not being able to absorb a continuous flow, but the peace would remain in the inner being. Or there might even be something like periods of struggle on the surface, but the inner being would remain calm and still, watching and undisturbed and, if there is knowledge established within, understanding the action. Only for that the whole being vital, physical, material must have become open and receptive to the peace. Peace would then go on perhaps deepening and becoming wider and wider, but periods of interruption and assimilation would not be needed.

*

This feeling of being able to break a stone with the hand or for that matter break the world without anything at all except the force itself, is one that comes especially when the mind and vital have not assimilated the Power. It is the feeling of something extraordinary to them and omnipotent; the idea of breaking or crushing is suggested by the rajas in the vital. Afterwards when quietly assimilated this sensation disappears and only the feeling of calm strength and immovable firmness remains.

Pulling Down the Force

I mean [*by writing "let the Force come in"*] that you need not pull it down, but you should aid its entry by your full aspiration and assent.

*

This sort of giddiness and weakness and disturbance ought not to take place. When it comes it shows that more Force is being pulled down than is assimilated by the body. At such times you ought to rest till the disturbance has passed and there is a proper balance.

*

It is certainly a mistake to bring down the light by force — to pull it down. The supramental cannot be taken by storm. When the time is ready it will open of itself — but first there is a great deal to be done and that must be done patiently and without haste.

Shaking or Swaying of the Body

That [*shaking of the body*] sometimes happens when the Force is coming down. It must be allowed to pass off as the body becomes more quiet and assimilative.

*

The swaying motion takes place when the body is not accustomed to the descent; it tries by the movement to assimilate what is coming down.

*

The swaying is due probably to the body not being habituated to receive the Force — it should cease as soon as the body is accustomed.

*

Some have this swaying of the body when the peace or the Force begins to descend upon it, as it facilitates for it the reception. The swaying ceases usually when the body is accustomed to assimilate the descent.

The peace comes fully at the meditation time because the Mother's concentration at that time brings down the power of the higher consciousness and one can receive it if one is able to do so. Once it begins to come, it usually increases its force along with the receptivity of the sadhak until it can come at all times and under all conditions and stay longer and longer till it is stable. The sadhak on his side has to keep his consciousness as quiet and still as possible to receive it. The Peace, Power, Light, Ananda of the higher spiritual consciousness are there in all veiled above. A certain opening upwards is needed for it to descend — the quietude of the mind and a certain wide concentrated passivity to the descending Influence are the best conditions for the descent.

Headaches Due to Resistance

What you saw was indeed a sun, — the sun of blue light which is the light of a higher mind than the ordinary human mind. The sun is the symbol of Light and Truth. This higher spiritual Mind is trying to wake in you, but at the beginning there is always a difficulty because the consciousness is not habituated to receive, so there is the sense of pressure deepening sometimes into a feeling of headache or this feeling of the head preparing to split. It is nothing but a sensation in the physical created by the inner mind (this part of the head is the seat of the inner mind) trying to open under the touch from above.

*

Headaches "produced by a pressure from above", as you put it, are not due to the pressure or produced by it, but produced by a resistance. X's headaches have nothing to do with Yoga or sadhana.

*

The pressure [*from above*] does not "bring" a resistance. "If there were no resistance there would be no headache" is the proper knowledge, not the reverse. So long as you think that it is the pressure that brings the resistance, the very idea will create the resistance. X's case is not an example either of headache due to resistance or of headache due to pressure — it is due to ordinary physical and psychological causes.

*

Difficulties Experienced in the Process of Descent

To make people ill in order to improve or perfect them is not Mother's method. But sometimes things like headache come because the brain either tries too much or does not want to receive or makes difficulties. But these Yogic headaches are of a special kind and after the brain has found out the way to receive or respond, they don't come at all.

*

Headache is not a sign of the force descending, it is only a result sometimes of some difficulty in receiving it. If there is no difficulty in receiving, there is no headache. The signs of the force coming are the pressure to be quiet, the sense of peace coming or wanting to come and many others, such as a feeling in the head or body of something coming in like a stream or a current or shower etc.

*

Pain in the head and physical strain are due to resistance, but pressure and throbbing and electric sensation are only signs of the Force working, not of resistance. The sensation of coolness is a very good sign.

Talking Loudly

The sensations you describe in the crown of the head and the upper part of the forehead are such as one often gets when the higher consciousness or Force is trying to make an open passage through the mind for itself. So it is possibly that that is happening. As for the uneasiness or feebleness there when you talk loudly etc., that also happens at such times. It is because the concentration of energy which is necessary for the inner work is broken and the energies thrown out, exhausting the parts by two inconsistent pullings. It is better when any working is going on inside to be very quiet in speech and as sparing as possible. At other times it does not so much matter.

Fear of the Descending Force

The first condition of progress in sadhana is not to fear, to have trust and keep quiet during an experience. What happened was simply that the Force came down and tried to quiet the mind and hold the body still so that it might work. If you had not feared, that would have happened. But your terror made the mind and body resist and get the impression that they were being tortured or in danger. The feeling of the tough body and great force like a hand upon it is quite usual in this kind of experience and does not terrify the sadhak, but brings a great joy and release. In future you must try to be quiet and not have any fear or imagination of danger. Naturally when you thought that you could not bear it, the Force withdrew as you are not ready to receive.

Desires and Descent

The descent of Light etc. is always impermanent at first. First the Peace and Force and Light have to be settled in the mind, then in the vital (heart, navel and below) and the physical. The desires etc. will then have been pushed out into a kind of environmental consciousness from which they try to return and must be driven out from there also. This will create a firm basis for the rest of the sadhana.

*

He is to be congratulated on the victory in the matter of sex — it is very important to have that when the intense definitive experiences are beginning. For if once the actual penetrative descent is felt, the less the higher consciousness is met by the sex force the better, for then a dangerous mixture may take place or else a struggle which is better avoided.

The description of the Power he feels — which is obviously the true thing — is very accurate — it is so, like rain or a fall of snow, that it often comes at first. I take it from his use of the word "around", that it is an enveloping power that he feels. It does not begin for all in the same way — some only feel it above their heads occasionally descending on them and entering.

Tiredness, Inertia and Sleep

It [*feeling tired and heavy*] is probably a passing symptom of the attempt of peace to come down. I have heard from several in the first stages that the body was disinclined or felt unable to move about. It is of course an unnecessary reaction — the body wants to translate the pressure for inner immobility into an outward immobility.

*

There is no connection between the descent of Peace and depression. Inertia there may be if the physical being feels the pressure for quietude but turns it into mere inactivity — but that cannot be called exactly a descent — at least not a complete one, since the physical does not share in it.

*

By the descent the inertia changes its character. It ceases to be a resistance of the physical and becomes only a physical condition to be transformed into the true basic immobility and rest.

*

You need not worry about that [*the body's tendency to sleep*]. When there is a strong inward tendency, the body not being yet conscious enough to share the experience in a waking state tries to assimilate the descending forces through sleep. This is a common experience. When it has assimilated enough, it will be more ready.

Mixing with the World

That [*problem of "mixture"*][1] might apply to a sending out

---

[1] *The correspondent wrote that a person seeking transformation is different from others, like a red wave in the midst of the ordinary blue waves of the sea. Would such a wave, he asked, be dissolved and mixed with the ordinary waves or would it remain separate and transform them? — Ed.*

of the new waves upon the old sea, i.e. an attempt to transform the world. But the problem here is of self-transformation. Mixture comes by the old waves pressing in again; one has to prevent or get rid of the mixture. But the decisive movement is the descent of the things from above — when that becomes complete, then the being depends on the Above not on the Around. If the waves from the Around try to get in, it is they who are transformed (or rejected automatically), the roles are reversed.

Chapter Eight
Descent and the Lower Nature

The Resistance of the Lower Nature

If the habit of the ordinary nature is not any obstacle to the descent, then what is the need of sadhana? What prevents the whole higher consciousness from coming down and changing you into a superman in one second? It is because the things of the lower nature offer an obstinate resistance that long sadhana is necessary.

*

An uneasiness of that kind is always due to a resistance somewhere — something that remains closed and does not open when it is touched by the Force. It is due probably not so much to yourself as to other conflicting influences that are acting upon you.

*

If one brings down more force or light than some part of the being is ready for and that part resists — or if there is a struggle between descending and adverse forces in the body, then these things [*a burning sensation etc.*] can take place.

*

The feeling of resistance [*to the descent of the Force*] may be the result of the effort at response. When there is the free flow there is neither effort nor resistance.

*

The experience of the action in the three centres is perfectly all right (the opening to the higher consciousness and its characteristic action and results already beginning there) except for the pains which mean a resistance. These experiences are quite sound and according to the divine schedule. But the pain at the bottom of the neck indicates that in trying to pass from mind to higher vital towards the heart, the Consciousness encountered an obstruction. However that too is in the day's work. It will be overcome in due time. So nothing to grumble — there at least.

The concentration is all right — since it is proceeding so well, the concentration in the higher centres should continue, but as the consciousness comes down or to help its coming down to the vital centres, more concentration in the heart may be necessary hereafter.

*

What usually comes is a descent of the Divine Power to work upon the nature and prepare it for the Divine Presence in the heart. There is much in human nature that has to be changed before it can hold what descends — incapacity and limitation of the mind, insufficient purity in the heart and elsewhere, restlessness etc. To contain the descent a quiet mind and pure heart are needed. That is why there is the restlessness and sense of incapacity in her. That is a quite common experience. If she wants to go farther, she must aspire for calm, peace, purity, etc. in the mental and emotional being and allow what is descending to establish it in her.

*

It must be the vital-physical that is in action. It is under the pressure of the Force that the resistance recedes lower and lower down and manifests so as to have the pressure brought there also specifically for its expulsion.

*

The Power that is above your head has not only to be in connection with you, but to occupy the consciousness with its influence. The restlessness is due to a resistance of the lower consciousness which is not accustomed to the process by which this is done and probably feels uneasy — as you say you feel everything unsure. The body becoming unreal and all of one seeming to disappear are very usual results of the higher consciousness taking hold of the mind and they are very good signs — so too the sensation spreading from the head to the body is probably only the Power coming in. There should be no apprehension, for these things are quite normal in the transforming process. Probably the sense of unsureness is due to the part of the nature which founds itself on the body consciousness and feels nothing sure or solid except the body. In the new consciousness on the contrary what will be felt as sure and solid is the wide spiritual consciousness not limited by the body, in which the body is only a small circumstance hardly felt, an instrument only. The losing all consciousness must also be due to the consciousness going entirely inside as soon as the restlessness is forgotten or is no longer active.

*

That is good progress. As for the resisting part, there is for a long time a resistance from some layer of the physical — one layer opens, another beneath remains obscure. But if the pressure from above is continuous, the resistance gets exhausted at last.

The stillness of which you speak in the meditation is a very good sign. It comes usually in that pervading way when there has been sufficient purification to make it possible. On the other side, it is itself the beginning of the laying of the foundations of the higher spiritual consciousness.

*

You speak of a struggle (*yuddha*) beginning when the Force comes down, but such a result is not inevitable — it is not necessary that the progress should be through a struggle. That rather takes place before the Force is there in the being, while one is still making efforts to open oneself to it or when it is still pressing from above or has taken up something of the nature but not the whole. When the Force is there at work, the imperfections and weaknesses of the nature will necessarily arise for change, but one need not fight with them; one can look on them quietly as a surface instrumentation that has to be changed. It is not with "indifference" that one has to look at them, for that might mean inertia, a want of will or push or necessity to change; it is rather with detachment. Detachment means that one stands back from them, does not identify oneself with them or get upset or troubled because they are there, but rather looks on them as something foreign to one's true consciousness and true self, rejects them and calls in the Mother's Force into these movements to eliminate them and bring the true consciousness and its movements there. The firm will of rejection must be there, the pressure to get rid of them, but not any wrestling or struggle.

When you felt the Force, the concentration, the peace, it meant evidently the true consciousness coming; that could not produce the restlessness at night. If the restlessness were the result of the Force coming, it would follow that the more the Force comes down, the more the restlessness must increase. But that would be absurd and is not the case. What happened was simply that with the Force came a beginning of the inner or spiritual peace; in the nerves the old restlessness which was lying dormant rose up as a resistance, trying as all these habitual things of the nature do to prolong itself. As the peace enters the vital and the nervous being, these things naturally diminish and are eliminated. One has only to remain quiet and detached and let the Force in its working bring in the peace there also. If the difficulty persists, you will let us know so that we may see to it.

Descent into the Mind and Vital

The danger of the mental forces is that when the higher consciousness descends they tend (unless there is a deep silence) to become active in the consciousness for forming ideas of a mental type which can always be misapplied. First, there should be a basis of entire calm, peace and silence — if there is activity, it should be that of a knowledge coming down and the mind silent receiving it accurately. This you can easily have, provided the mind is quiet.

The danger of the vital is that of taking hold of love, Ananda, the sense of Beauty and using it for its own purposes, for vital human relations or interchange or else some kind of mere enjoyment of its own.

*

The wideness is that of the higher consciousness, golden being the colour of the light of Truth, and the Cow is the symbol of the Light of the higher consciousness descending, turning all into the Truth light.

The state of wideness and of quietude unaffected by anything that happens is the natural result of the descent which you saw in this figure. The impartial condition towards work or not work is also a result of this descent. Usually it is the vital that pushes to work and without this vital push one can do very little. When the higher consciousness descends into the mind and vital, this push becomes silent, but the faculty of work remains, — afterwards when the new consciousness is settled it takes up the work and carries it on with another force which replaces the push of the vital and is much greater.

*

In the first condition you are receiving through the mind and it is drawn back upon itself to receive the Presence and grow in the Light and Power from above. The body or external consciousness is probably not sharing in its outward-going parts, there is no effectuating energy for any work other than what the external consciousness is habituated to do.

In the second the vital is receiving directly and transforming immediately into kinetic energy; for it is the direct reception by the vital or else the active participation of the vital in the Light, Power or Ananda that makes externalisation, effectuation, all kinds of work and action possible and easy.

*

The opening of the vital mind (or any part) does not mean that the vital mind is absolutely open or wholly converted so that there shall never again be any darkness or ignorance or error or resistance or anything else but the higher consciousness there. It only means that the higher consciousness is able to come down there and work and establish something of itself there — as has been done in the thinking mind. Each plane, one after the other, has to open initially in that way down to the physical. So long as this initial opening is not made in all the parts, there can be no complete and final descent of the higher consciousness anywhere. If the nervous being and other physical parts are not open, even the thinking mind cannot be finally open, for it can be affected by resistance, darkness etc. from below. If the vital mind is open, that does not mean that it is open so wholly that it is already divine and is not feeling pride or other wrong movements.

As for the nervous being, it is part of the physical consciousness, below the physical mind and not above it — the nerves are part of the body.

*

The attitude which he describes, if he keeps it correctly, is the right one. It brought him at first the beginning of a true experience, the Light (white and golden) and the Force pouring down from the Sahasradala and filling the system; but when it touched the vital parts it must have awakened the prana energies in the vital centres (navel and below) and as these were not pure, all the impurities arose (anger, sex, fear, doubt etc.) and the mind became clouded by the uprush of impure vital forces. He says that all this is now subsiding, the mind is becoming calm and in the vital the impulses come but do not remain. Not only the mind but the vital must become calm; these impulses must lose their force of recurrence by rejection and purification. Entire purity and peace must be established in the whole *ādhāra*; it is only then that he will have a safe and sure basis for further progress.

The reason why the force flows out of him must be because he allows himself to become too inertly passive and open to everything. One must be passive only to the Divine Force, but vigilant not to put oneself at the mercy of all forces. If he becomes passive when he tries to see God in another person, he is likely to put himself at the disposal of any force that is working through that person and his own forces may be drained away towards the other. It is better for him not to try in this way; let him aspire for the Peace and Strength that come from above and for entire purity and open himself to that Force only. Such experiences as the feeling of the Divine everywhere (not in this or that person only) will then come of themselves.

*

It is when the true contact and the Light and Force can be steadily brought down *into the whole being* (including the lower vital and body) that the basis and organisation [*of the being*] can be founded and settled.

Descent into the Physical Consciousness and Body

This is a very great progress — to be able to receive the higher consciousness while doing external things with the physical mind and body — it shows that the physical consciousness is fast opening. What you feel is indeed the Grace coming down and bringing the higher divine or spiritual consciousness with it with all that is there. All that (peace, power, Ananda) will develop afterwards more clearly.

*

It [*the descent of the higher consciousness into the most physical*] brings light, consciousness, force, Ananda into the cells and all the physical movements. The body becomes conscious and vigilant and performs the right movements, obeying the higher will or else automatically by force of the consciousness that has come into it. It becomes more possible to control the functionings of the body and set right anything that is wrong, to deal with illness and pain etc. A greater control comes over the actions of the body and even over happenings to it from outside, e.g. minimising of accidents and small mishaps. The body becomes a more effective instrument for work. It becomes possible to minimise fatigue. Peace, happiness, strength, lightness in the whole physical system. These are the more obvious and normal results which grow as the consciousness grows, but there are many others that are possible. There is also the unity with the earth-consciousness, the constant sense of the Divine in the physical, etc.

It is, of course, not easy to make the physical entirely conscious in this way — for it is the seat of unconsciousness and obscurity and inertia — but a partial and sufficiently effective introduction of the higher consciousness can be established as a basis and the rest of the ground conquered as its force increases in the body.

*

Your recent experiences are of considerable importance: the triple condition of the being, the sense of the Divine everywhere, that of the Divine Child in the universe. The last two are self-evident in their significance. As to the triple condition it indicates the proper direction of the realisation of the sadhana in three parts of the being. The mind has to merge in the one infinite consciousness of the silent self which will then envelop the whole being; the heart has by adoration and love and surrender to live in the dynamic Divine and be its dwelling place; the vital and physical (below the navel) have to be the instruments of the Divine Will, instruments pure, surrendered, expressing nothing but that Will.

The Blue Light coming below the level of the Muladhara means that it has entered into the physical (physical mental, physical vital, material) consciousness. The two main obstacles here are the mechanical mind with its memories and desires of the past and the most outward sex movements; these have to be overcome (especially the mechanical mind, for the other may be easily overcome if not supported by the vital proper) for the Light to possess all the physical consciousness. It is probably why it rose so strongly when the Light came to these parts.

*

That is to say, [*when there is sometimes stillness and sometimes mechanical thoughts*] the Power is still working on the physical consciousness (the mechanical mind and the subconscient) to bring stillness there. Sometimes the stillness comes but not complete, sometimes the mechanical mind reasserts itself. This oscillation usually takes place in a movement of the kind. Even if there is a sudden or rapid transforming shock or downrush,

Descent and the Lower Nature

there has to be some working out of this kind afterwards — that at least has always been my experience. For most, however, there comes, first, this slow preparatory process.

*

It is not a question only of the force working — but of the force descending into the body. The force descends in order to establish quietude, peace, light or whatever else comes from the higher consciousness. When the force comes only to do some work it comes and goes after doing its work. But this is a question of establishing something in the mind, vital and body.

*

It [*how the body receives the higher dynamism*] depends on the condition of the body or rather of the physical and the most material consciousness. In one condition it is tamasic, inert, unopen and cannot bear or cannot receive or cannot contain the force; in another rajas predominates and tries to seize on the dynamism, but wastes and spills and loses it; in another there is receptivity, harmony, balance and the result is a harmonious action without strain or effort.

*

Probably the accumulated Force became more than the physical being could receive. When that happens, the right thing to do is to widen oneself (one can learn to do it by a little practice). If the consciousness is in a state of wideness, then it can receive any amount of Force without inconvenience.

*

It was the descent of the higher consciousness not only into the mind but the whole body and the whole being. That is what you must get fixed in you, having it not only as a descent but as your normal consciousness. Of course that does not happen in a day (except in rare cases). The descent repeats itself until it is strong enough to hold the whole body.

*

What will happen when the supramental consciousness takes hold of the body fully, can be decided only by the descent itself — there must be no premature attempt to do it or decide it with the Mind, before the Descent is an accomplished reality — for that would only retard the Descent and perhaps spoil the body.

Experiences in the Subtle Body and the Physical Body

It [*the higher consciousness*] can come into the physical consciousness direct in the sense that the rest can remain passive, but it must pass through the subtle to reach the material.

*

All experiences that penetrate the centres are recorded in the body and seem to be the body's experiences,[1] but one has to distinguish between the reflection of the experiences there and the experiences that belong to the physical body consciousness itself. It is a matter of consciousness and fine discernment. There is no absolute law about the time.

*

It can be a rushing of Force into the subtle body which the physical records and feels the effect. When Force descends into the head it means that it has come down into the mind, when it is felt in the heart it means it has entered into the emotional vital, when it is in the Muladhara and below it means it is acting on the physical consciousness. The centres are all in the subtle body although there are corresponding parts in the gross physical.

*

I spoke [*in the preceding letter*] only of the fact that what one feels recorded in the physical body may be actually taking place only in the subtle body. Whether in a particular case it is that or a direct experience in the physical body also, is a matter to be

---

[1] *The correspondent wrote that he sometimes felt peace or silence or force as "tangibly present" in his body. — Ed.*

seen in each case. One must distinguish for oneself which it is.

*

Any reflection or outflowing [*of the Force*] from the subtle body into the physical would also be felt as tangible.

*

Why "mere" record? If you think the experiences in the subtle body are feeble vague things, you are mistaken — they can be quite as intense, swift, palpable, massive as those of the body.

Descent into the Subconscient and Inconscient

It [*the correspondent's experience*] is the approach of the higher consciousness to the subconscient through the psychic and vital which are the connecting links. Without the vital the action would not be complete, without the psychic it would not be possible.

*

I do not see what is your difficulty. That there is a divine force asleep or veiled by Inconscience in Matter and that the Higher Force has to descend and awaken it with the Light and Truth is a thing that is well known; it is at the very base of this Yoga.

Note on the Texts

Note on the Texts

LETTERS ON YOGA — III, the third of four volumes, contains letters in which Sri Aurobindo speaks about the experiences and realisations that may take place in the practice of his system of Yoga. The letters have been arranged in four parts dealing with these broad subject areas:

1. The Place of Experiences in the Practice of Yoga
2. The Opening of the Inner Senses
3. Experiences of the Inner Consciousness and the Cosmic Consciousness
4. The Fundamental Realisations of the Integral Yoga

The letters in this volume have been selected from the extensive correspondence Sri Aurobindo carried on with his disciples and others between 1927 and 1950. Letters from this corpus appear in seven volumes of THE COMPLETE WORKS OF SRI AUROBINDO: *Letters on Poetry and Art* (Volume 27), *Letters on Yoga* (Volumes 28 – 31), *The Mother with Letters on the Mother* (Volume 32), and *Letters on Himself and the Ashram* (Volume 35). The titles of these works specify the nature of the letters included in the volumes, but there is some overlap. For example, a number of letters in the present volume are also published in *Letters on Himself and the Ashram*. Another volume, *Autobiographical Notes and Other Writings of Historical Interest* (Volume 36), contains letters written by Sri Aurobindo before 1927, as well as some written after that date, mainly to persons living outside the Ashram.

The Writing of the Letters

Between 1927 and 1950, Sri Aurobindo replied to hundreds of correspondents in tens of thousands of letters, some of them many pages in length, others only a few words long. Most of his replies, however, were sent to just a few dozen disciples, almost all of them resident members of his Ashram; of these disciples, about a dozen received more than half the replies. Sri Aurobindo wrote most of these letters between 1931 and 1937, the prime period of his correspondence. Letters before and after this period were written on a more restricted scale and confined to a few persons for special reasons.

Disciples in the Ashram wrote to Sri Aurobindo on loose sheets or sent him the notebooks in which they kept diaries as a record of their spiritual endeavour and a means of communicating with him. These notebooks and loose sheets reached Sri Aurobindo via an internal "post" once or twice a day. Letters from outside which his secretary thought he might like to see were sent at the same time. Correspondents wrote in English if they knew the language well enough, but a good number wrote in Bengali, Gujarati, Hindi or French, all of which Sri Aurobindo read fluently, or in other languages that were translated into English for him. The disciples usually addressed their letters to the Mother, since Sri Aurobindo had asked them to do so, but most assumed that he would answer them. He generally replied in the notebook or on the sheets sent by the correspondent, writing beneath the correspondent's remarks or in the margin or between the lines; sometimes, however, he wrote his reply on a separate sheet of paper. In some cases he had his secretary prepare a typed copy of his letter, which he revised before it was sent. For correspondents living outside the Ashram, Sri Aurobindo sometimes addressed his reply not to the correspondent but to his secretary, who quoted, paraphrased or translated the reply and signed the letter himself. In these indirect replies, Sri Aurobindo often referred to himself in the third person.

While going through Sri Aurobindo's letters, the reader should keep in mind that each letter was written to a specific person at a specific time, in specific circumstances and for a specific purpose. The subjects taken up arose in regard to the needs of the person. Sri Aurobindo varied the style and tone of his replies according to his relationship with the correspondent; to those with whom he was close, he sometimes employed humour, irony and even sarcasm.

Although written to specific recipients, these letters contain much of general interest, which justifies their inclusion in a volume destined for the general public. For the reasons mentioned above, however, the advice in them does not always apply equally to everyone. Aware of this, Sri Aurobindo himself made some cautionary remarks about the proper use of his letters:

> I should like to say, in passing, that it is not always safe to apply practically to oneself what has been written for another. Each sadhak is a case by himself and one cannot always or often take a mental rule and apply it rigidly to all who are practising the Yoga.
>
> The tendency to take what I lay down for one and apply it without discrimination to another is responsible for much misunderstanding. A general statement, too, true in itself, cannot be applied to everyone alike or applied now and immediately without consideration of condition or circumstance or person or time.
>
> It is not a fact that all I write is meant equally for everybody. That assumes that everybody is alike and there is no difference between sadhak and sadhak. If it were so everybody would advance alike and have the same experiences and take the same time to progress by the same steps and stages. It is not so at all.[1]

The Typing and Revision of the Letters

Most of the shorter items in this volume, and many of the longer ones, were not typed or revised during Sri Aurobindo's lifetime and are reproduced here directly from his handwritten manuscripts. A good number of the letters, however, as mentioned above, were typed for Sri Aurobindo and revised by him before sending. Other letters were typed by the recipients for their own use or for circulation within the Ashram. At first, circulation of the letters was restricted to members of the Ashram and others whom Sri Aurobindo had accepted as disciples.

---

[1] First and third passages: *Letters on Himself and the Ashram*, volume 35 of THE COMPLETE WORKS OF SRI AUROBINDO, pp. 473 and 475. Second passage: *The Mother with Letters on the Mother*, volume 32, p. 349.

When these letters were circulated, personal references were removed. Persons mentioned by Sri Aurobindo were indicated by their initials or by the letters X, Y, Z, etc. Copies of these typed letters were kept by Sri Aurobindo's secretary and sometimes presented to Sri Aurobindo for revision before publication. These typed copies sometimes contained errors, most of which were corrected by him while revising.

Sri Aurobindo's revision sometimes amounted merely to making minor changes here and there, sometimes to a complete rewriting of the letter. He generally removed personal references if this had not already been done by the typist. When necessary, he also rewrote the openings or other parts of the replies in order to free them from dependence on the correspondent's question. As a result, some of these letters have an impersonal tone and read more like brief essays than personal communications.

The Publication of the Letters

Around 1933, Sri Aurobindo's secretary Nolini Kanta Gupta began to compile selections from the growing body of letters in order to publish them. During Sri Aurobindo's lifetime, four small books of letters were published: *The Riddle of This World* (1933), *Lights on Yoga* (1935), *Bases of Yoga* (1936) and *More Lights on Yoga* (1948). Sri Aurobindo revised the typescripts of most of the letters in these books. During this revision, he continued the process of removing personal references. A letter he wrote in August 1937 alludes to his approach to the revision:

> I had no idea of the book being published as a collection of personal letters — if that were done, they would have to be published whole as such without a word of alteration. I understood the book was meant like the others [*i.e., like Bases of Yoga, etc.*] where only what was helpful for an understanding of things Yogic was kept with necessary alterations and modifications.... With that idea I have been not only omitting but recasting and adding freely. Otherwise as a book it would be too scrappy and random for public interest. In the other books things too personal were omitted — it seems

to me the same rule must hold here — except very sparingly where unavoidable.

A number of letters not included in the four books mentioned above were published in the mid and late 1940s in several journals associated with the Ashram: *Sri Aurobindo Circle*, *Sri Aurobindo Mandir Annual*, *The Advent* and *Mother India*. Many letters in these journals were revised by Sri Aurobindo before publication.

By the mid-1940s a significant body of letters had been collected, typed and revised. In 1945 plans were made, with Sri Aurobindo's approval, to publish a collection of his letters. The work of compiling and editing these letters was done under his guidance. At that time, many typed or printed copies of letters, some revised, some not, were presented to Sri Aurobindo for approval or revision. The resulting material was arranged and published in a four-volume series entitled *Letters of Sri Aurobindo*. Series One appeared in 1947, Series Two and Three in 1949 and Series Four in 1951. The first, second and fourth series contained letters on Yoga, the third letters on poetry and literature. In 1958, most of these letters on Yoga, along with many additional ones, were published under the titles *On Yoga II: Tome One* and *On Yoga II: Tome Two*, as Volumes VI and VII of the Sri Aurobindo International University Centre collection. The first tome, with further additions, was reissued in 1969. In 1970 a new edition of the letters was published under the title *Letters on Yoga*; this edition contained many new letters not included in *On Yoga II*. The three volumes of the enlarged edition constituted volumes 22, 23 and 24 of the Sri Aurobindo Birth Centenary Library.

The present edition, also titled *Letters on Yoga*, incorporates most of the Centenary Library letters, but also contains a large number of letters that have come to light in the four decades between the two editions. One source of new letters is the correspondences of several disciples which were published in books after the Centenary Library edition had been issued. Govindbhai Patel's correspondence was published in 1974 in a book entitled *My Pilgrimage to the Spirit*; an enlarged edition appeared in 1977. Nagin Doshi's correspondence, *Guidance from Sri Aurobindo: Letters to a Young Disciple*, was brought out in three volumes in 1974, 1976 and 1987. *Nirodbaran's Correspondence with*

Sri Aurobindo came out in two volumes in 1983 and 1984. Sahana Devi's correspondence came out in 1985 in a book entitled *At the Feet of Sri Aurobindo and the Mother*. Prithwi Singh's correspondence came out in 1988 as *Sri Aurobindo and the Mother to Prithwi Singh*. Dilip Kumar Roy's correspondence was issued in four volumes in 2003, 2005, 2007 and 2011 under the title *Sri Aurobindo to Dilip*. A second source of new material is individual letters and small collections of letters published in Ashram journals and elsewhere after the Centenary Library had been issued. A third source is letters transcribed from manuscripts or from early typed copies. Many unpublished letters were discovered while reviewing correspondences long held by the Ashram; some of these had never been assessed to find letters for publication; others had been assessed, but relatively few letters were selected at the time. Additional letters were received by the Ashram upon the passing away of disciples. From the three sources mentioned above, many letters have been found that are worthy of publication. The present edition contains about one-third more letters than appear in the Centenary Library.

The Selection, Arrangement and Editing of the Letters

In compiling the present edition, all known manuscripts, typed copies or photographic copies of manuscripts and printed texts of letters were checked. From these sources, letters that seemed to be of general interest were selected. Electronic texts of the letters were then made and carefully checked at least twice against the handwritten, typed, photocopied, and printed versions of the texts.

The selected letters have been arranged according to subject and placed in the four volumes of the present edition. Each volume is divided and subdivided into parts, sections, chapters and groups with descriptive headings; each group, the lowest unit of division, contains one or more letters devoted to the specific subject of the group.

The present volume consists of 1164 separate items, an "item" being defined as what is published between one heading or asterisk and another heading or asterisk. Many items correspond exactly to individual letters; a good number, however, contain only part of the individual letters; a small number consist of two or more letters (or parts of them) that were joined together by early typists or editors and then revised in that form by Sri Aurobindo.

Whenever possible, the letters are reproduced to their full extent. In some cases, however, portions of the letters have been omitted because they are not of general interest. A number of letters, for example, begin with personal remarks by Sri Aurobindo unrelated to the more substantial remarks which follow; these personal openings have often been removed. In some letters, Sri Aurobindo marked the transition from one part of a letter to another with a phrase such as "As to"; these transitional phrases have often been retained and stand at the beginning of abbreviated letters — that is, letters in which the first part of the letter has been omitted or placed elsewhere.

A number of letters, or portions of them, have been published in more than one volume of THE COMPLETE WORKS OF SRI AUROBINDO. Most of this doubling of letters occurs between *Letters on Yoga* and *Letters on Himself and the Ashram*. The form of these letters is not always the same in both places. In *Letters on Himself and the Ashram*, the manuscript version of a given letter has often been used because it contains Sri Aurobindo's remarks on himself or the Mother or members of the Ashram. These personal remarks, as noted above, were usually removed by Sri Aurobindo when he revised the letter for publication as a letter on Yoga. This revised form of the letter has generally been reproduced in *Letters on Yoga*. Thus, a number of letters are available both in their original form and their revised form.

As in previous collections of Sri Aurobindo's letters, the names of Ashram members and others have often been replaced by the letters X, Y, Z, etc. In any given letter, X stands for the first name replaced, Y for the second, Z for the third, A for the fourth, and so on. An X in a given letter has no necessary relation to an X in another letter. Names of Ashram members to whom Sri Aurobindo referred not as sadhaks but as holders of a certain position — notably Nolini Kanta Gupta in his position as Sri Aurobindo's secretary — are given in full. Sometimes the names of people who played a role in the history of the period are also given.

In his letters Sri Aurobindo sometimes wrote Sanskrit words in the devanagari script; these words have been transliterated into roman script in this edition. Words in Bengali script have likewise been transliterated. This policy is in accord with the practice followed in Sri Aurobindo's lifetime.

The reader may note that Sri Aurobindo almost always spelled the word "Asram" without an "h" in his manuscripts. Around 1945, due to failing eyesight, he began dictating most of his writings to his amanuensis Nirodbaran; Nirodbaran sometimes spelled the word without an "h", sometimes with one. In the present edition, the word is always spelled as it occurs in the manuscripts, both those of Sri Aurobindo and of Nirodbaran. In headings and other editorial matter, the spelling "Ashram" has been used, since this is now the official spelling of the Sri Aurobindo Ashram.